Western Man
An Interdisciplinary Introduction to the History of Western Civilization

THE JUDEO-CHRISTIAN HERITAGE

Edited by

William J. Courtenay
University of Wisconsin

HOLT, RINEHART AND WINSTON, INC.
New York   Chicago   San Francisco   Atlanta   Dallas   Montreal   Toronto

Cover illustration: A mosaic from the Beth Alpha synagogue in the Valley of Jezreel, Israel (6th century A.D.). Such mosaic floors were common in Palestine in the Christian era before the Islamic conquest. The syncretistic tendency of some Jewish communities in this period is revealed here by the use of signs of the zodiac, the seasons, and the central image of the sun-god in his chariot. The traditional Roman signs of the constellations have been altered to conform to the Jewish festivals. Similarly, two of the animals appear with cloven hooves (Lev. xi). Regardless of the pagan origin of the symbols, the mosaic reflects the Jewish belief in the orderliness of God's universe. (Israel Information Service)

The Scripture quotations in this publication are from the Revised Standard Version of the Bible, copyrighted 1946 and 1952 by the Division of Christian Education of the National Council of Churches of Christ in the U.S.A., and used by permission.

The maps appearing on pages 9, 16, and 73 are based on maps in L. H. Grollenberg, *Atlas of the Bible* (New York: Thomas Nelson and Sons, 1956), pp. 9, 44, 65.

Art research editor: Enid Klass

Copyright © 1970 by Holt, Rinehart and Winston, Inc.
All Rights Reserved
Library of Congress Catalog Card Number: 70-113826
SBN: 03-082829-5
Printed in the United States of America
0123 17 987654321

Preface

"What is history for?" [History is] "for" human self-knowledge, . . . [and knowing] yourself means knowing, first, what it is to be a man; secondly, knowing what it is to be the kind of man you are; and thirdly, knowing what it is to be the man *you* are and nobody else is. Knowing yourself means knowing what you can do; and since nobody knows what he can do until he tries, the only clue to what man can do is what man has done. The value of history, then, is that it teaches us what man has done and thus what man is.

R. G. Collingwood, The Idea of History *(New York: Oxford University Press, 1957), p. 10*

For more than a decade there has been a great deal of discussion about the relation between history and the social sciences. Many historians have wanted to make use of those disciplines which are chiefly concerned with man's psychological makeup and with his physical and social environments. To date, however, there has been a wide gap between this wish and visible accomplishments, especially in the content of university and college courses. The series "Western Man" is the product of several years of experimentation with a number of ways of organizing such an interdisciplinary course in the history of Western civilization. We had tried various combinations of texts, books of readings, paperbacks, and offprints in an attempt to reach this goal, but each combination created as many pedagogical problems as it solved. What we seemed to need in order to present exciting material in manageable and teachable form was a carefully edited integration of primary historical materials, interpretative works, and the analytical tools of sociologists, anthropologists, psychologists, and other social scientists. The result—after several years of selecting, editing, and trial in the classroom—is this series of volumes.

We have constructed these volumes in the belief that the study of one's personal and cultural history is an indispensable means by which experience is organized. We considered it desirable, therefore, that students know something about the historical development of the concept of the psyche, soul, personality, or self so that they might understand the relationship between the accomplishments made by Western man and the view of the self at a given moment in history. Likewise it is important to understand the unique historical circumstances which were the source of, and gave a particular stamp to, the institutions which comprise Western society and the values which in large part structure our individual and collective behavior. The goal of this series, then, is to give the student some insight into the concept of self, social institutions, and values as they have developed in the West from ancient to modern times.

This particular purpose has made it necessary to treat the various stages in the history of Western civilization selectively. In *The Contribution of Ancient Greece*, for example, the focus is on the emergence of self-awareness and the concomitant development of natural philosophy, abstract mathematics, rhetoric, moral philosophy, epistemology, metaphysics, political theory, formal logic, and the concept of natural law. In *The Judeo-Christian Heritage*, on the other hand, emphasis is placed primarily on the development of the religious concepts and moral values of Western society. *The Imprint of Roman Institutions* provides the student with an understanding of the early stages in the evolution of Western political and legal institutions, and the transformation of classical culture in that institutional matrix. Each period in Western history emerges as one in which a lasting dimension was given to the concept of self, social institutions, or values or to any combination of these three.

We have attempted to create a series of volumes which, with the addition of a few readily available paperbacks, can be used as the full reading assignment in a course in the history of Western civilization. Individual volumes can of course be used separately and in upper level courses. It is hoped that instructors and students will find that conceptual materials introduced in each volume will be useful in considering other historical problems.

We would like to express our deep appreciation to the students, friends, editors, and spouses who gave either support or active assistance while we were at work on this project. We would also like to thank those colleagues in the Western civilization program at Stanford University who tested our materials in the classroom and gave us both criticism and suggestions.

Donald Buck
Cupertino, Calif.

William J. Courtenay
Madison, Wis.

David W. Savage
Worcester, Mass.

Jacqueline Strain
Rohnert Park, Calif.

Fall 1970

Contents

Preface   v

Introduction   xi

1 / The Religious Conceptions of Early Hebrew Society: The Exodus Event   1

   J. Milton Yinger / A Definition of Religion   1
   John E. Smith / The Individual, the Religious Community, and the Symbol   5
   The Exodus from Egypt   11
   Harold Knight / The Hebraic Understanding of Man   19
   The Creation Story   23
   Aubrey R. Johnson / The One and the Many in the Israelite Conception of God   26

2 / The Origins of Hebrew Morality: The Covenant at Mount Sinai   33

   J. Milton Yinger / The Relationship of Religion and Morality   34
   Law and Covenant at Mount Sinai   37
   S. A. Queen and R. W. Habenstein / The Hebrew Family   48
   The Fall of Mankind   54
   Johannes Pedersen / Mercy in Hebrew Law   55
   Gerhard von Rad / The Old Testament Concept of Righteousness   57

3 / The Conquest and Settlement of Palestine: Acculturation and Charisma 63

Acculturation 66
Bernhard W. Anderson / The Temptations of Canaanite Culture 81
Johannes Pedersen / The Song of Deborah and Holy War 86
Max Weber / The General Character of Charisma 93
The Story of Gideon 95

4 / Political Disintegration and Prophetic Renewal: The Deepening of the Ethical Conscience 103

J. Lindblom / The Nature of Prophecy 107
Amos: The Call for Social Justice 111
Hosea: The Call for Covenant Fidelity 114
Jeremiah, Ezekiel: Yahweh's Covenant with the Individual 126
H. Wheeler Robinson / The Emergence of the Individual Through the Prophetic Consciousness 128
Mircea Eliade / The Prophetic Understanding of History 130

5 / Legalism, Separatism, and Eschatological Withdrawal: Post-Exilic Judaism 137

David F. Aberle / Relative Deprivation and Eschatological Movements 139
Howard Clark Kee, Franklin W. Young, and Karlfried Froehlich / Post-Exilic Judaism 144
The Apocalypse of Daniel 157
Anthony Wallace / Revitalization Movements 159
The Dead Sea Scrolls 164

6 / From Corporate Righteousness to Individual Salvation: Eschatology and Ethics in the Teaching of Jesus 175

The Gospel According to Matthew 184
A. N. Wilder / Eschatology and Ethics in the Teaching of Jesus 200
F. C. Grant / The Agrarian Focus of New Testament Ethics 204

7 / The Institutionalization of Charisma and the Transformation of the Judeo-Christian Ethic: Paul and the Early Church   211

   Thomas F. O'Dea / The Institutionalization of Religion   214
   K. S. Latourette / The Spread of Christianity into the Non-Jewish World   217
   Paul's Concept of the Church   220
   Paul's Letter to the Romans   229

Suggestions for Further Reading   249

Maps

The Fertile Crescent   9

The Route of the Exodus from Egypt:
The Nile Delta and the Sinai Peninsula   16

The Campaigns of Joshua and the Judges   73

Introduction

This volume appears in a series that approaches the history of European culture with the perspectives gained from disciplines that have not traditionally been part of the historian's craft. Its purpose is to examine one portion of the cultural heritage of the ancient world that had important implications for the formation of contemporary Western civilization. It seeks to do this by providing materials for discussion drawn from primary sources, historical narrative, and analyses of underlying issues and problems by contemporary scholars in the social sciences. Although the materials in this volume form a self-contained unit—and thus can be used apart from the series—some knowledge of Greek history and of the conceptual tools utilized in *The Contribution of Ancient Greece* is helpful.

The historical development to be examined in this book is the Judeo-Christian tradition. Among those nations that occupied the lands beyond the eastern edge of the Mediterranean—an area whose river valleys nourished successive empires well into the first millennium B.C.—the West is most heavily indebted to the cultural heritage of a small and politically insignificant buffer zone, Palestine, and the Hebrew peoples who adopted it as their homeland. That heritage influenced specific areas of Western culture, principally the religious and ethical concepts that have been of primary importance in creating the value system as well as the mental apparatus by which Western man often relates to the world of the unknown. In particular, Western civilization has received from the Hebrew tradition and its stepchild, Christianity, the concept of a personal God, a linear and purposive view of history, and a particular ethical system. These concepts were not the individual creation of a Moses, an Isaiah, or a Jesus but developed across many centuries out of the response of a socioreligious community to specific events in its history.

The most durable of these aspects of the Judeo-Christian heritage has been the ethical system. As one historian has recently noted, "in spite of a decline of belief in the existence of God, in the direct intervention of the Almighty in human affairs, and in knowledge obtained by Divine Revelation, Christianity continues to affect fundamentally our behavior toward ourselves and others. . . . The Christian doctrine of the Golden Rule is at the center of our rules regarding ideal behavior among men. The Christian principle of love for the human individual, as exemplified in the life of Christ and as expressed in the injunction to 'love thy neighbor as thyself' (Lev. 19:18 and Matt. 19:19) finds expression in our laws and customs. The Ten Commandments are specific exhortations regarding what to do and what not to do, which in general have approval in our culture today."[1]

[1] Shepard B. Clough, *Basic Values of Western Civilization* (New York: Columbia University Press, 1960), pp. 76–77.

The value structure of a society is one of the most essential aspects of its worldview, that is, the way in which the society perceives and explains itself and the world around it. Such a value structure not only explains the meaning and destiny of the individual and tribe but also internalizes a code of behavior that has proven effective in preserving the social body. Few things in a society are untouched by the value system. As one social scientist has observed, "for any individual organism or organization, there are no such things as 'facts.' There are only messages filtered through a changeable value system."[2] In order to understand a particular worldview, therefore, it is necessary to study the interaction between ethics and social structure, a relationship that seldom remains static for any society, especially one that comes into frequent contact with other cultures. In the following chapters, that relationship between ethics and society, the way in which each informs and conditions the other, will be examined in the context of the historical development of Hebrew society and psychology.

Some initial words of caution concerning the sources are perhaps appropriate. In approaching Hebrew society one is faced with source material of a different type from that relating to Greek civilization. Rather than drawing upon epic, poetic, and philosophical literature, the historian of Hebrew culture must rely primarily upon a religious-historical document, the Bible, which is broader in scope and content than any one Greek source and yet is far more limited than the combined Greek documents. Furthermore, unlike the writings of Homer, Hesiod, Thucydides, and Plato, each of which can be placed at a particular point in Greek history, the Bible was a continually changing literary collection, shaped by the needs and experiences of the Hebrew people and infinitely more important to their psychology, religion, and legal system than any single document in Greek culture. While the Bible is unique in preserving the earliest tribal and family traditions of any cultural group, the older elements never remained unchanged but were usually understood and rewritten on the basis of later experience. Much of what we know of Hebrew society, therefore, must be carefully extracted from a document shaped by religious conceptions that emerged and changed in the course of Hebrew history.

Because of the complex nature of the composition of the Bible, which tended to fuse traditions of various periods, it is difficult if not impossible to describe Hebrew society in any extensive way before the period from 1200 to 1000 B.C. At that time the Hebrews were an agricultural, noncommercial society, preserving in oral form the traditions of tribe and family dating back almost a millennium. These traditions, filled with the imagery and perspectives of a nomadic desert origin, centered around the Exodus from Egypt, the key religious event through which the Hebrews understood almost all aspects of their culture. The interpretation the Hebrews placed upon the event of the Exodus, in turn, was conditioned in no small measure by the social structure and psychology of these people at that time. The religious and moral conceptions of early Hebrew society, which developed out of the interaction between the historical events that brought them into Palestine and their mental and social structure, will be examined in the first two chapters. In succeeding chapters the development of the Hebrew ethic and its relation to the concept of purposive history will be traced down to the early Christian community. The focus of all chapters, therefore, will be upon the ethical or moral rather than upon the doctrinal or theological implications and consequences of the Judeo-Christian faith.

---

[2] Kenneth E. Boulding, *The Image* (East Lansing, Mich.: Michigan State University Press, 1956), p. 14.

CHAPTER 1

THE RELIGIOUS CONCEPTIONS OF EARLY HEBREW SOCIETY:
The Exodus Event

The mutual involvement of God and nature is . . . a common characteristic of most primitive or ancient world views. Sky and god, rain and deity are somehow together, aspects of the same thing. The radical achievement of the Hebrews in putting God entirely outside of the physical universe and attaching all value to God is recognized as an immense and unique achievement.

Robert Redfield, The Primitive World and Its Transformations *(Ithaca, N.Y.: Cornell University Press, 1953), p. 102.*

The Exodus . . . is the central moment in Israel's history. Here was her true beginning, the time of her creation as a people. Here began the purposive movement of events that made it possible later to see all history and nature embraced within the divine design. So deeply was the Exodus etched upon Israel's memory that her maturing faith was essentially a reliving and reinterpretation of this historic event.

Bernhard W. Anderson, Understanding the Old Testament, *2nd ed., © 1966, p. 11. Reprinted by permission of Prentice-Hall, Inc., Englewood Cliffs, New Jersey.*

Although the major achievements of the Greeks and Hebrews were made in two different areas of human endeavor (those of philosophy and religion, respectively), these achievements are complementary in the sense that both represent an attempt by man to answer what he considers to be ultimate questions. Because such a view implies a somewhat unorthodox approach to the study of religion, it will be necessary to begin by considering a definition of religion.

A DEFINITION OF RELIGION
J. Milton Yinger[1]

Paul Tillich [a twentieth-century theologian] has said that religion is that which concerns us ultimately. This can be a good

[1] Reprinted with permission of The Macmillan Company from *Religion, Society and the Individual* by J. Milton Yinger. © by The Macmillan Company 1957, pp. 9-10, 12-13, 15-16.

starting point for a functional definition. While there are important disagreements concerning the "ultimate" problems for man, a great many would accept the following as among the fundamental concerns of human societies and individuals: How shall we respond to the fact of death? Does life have some central meaning despite the suffering, the succession of frustrations and tragedies? How can we deal with the forces that press in on us, endangering our livelihood, our health, the survival and smooth operation of the groups in which we live—forces that our empirical knowledge is inadequate to handle? How can we bring our capacity for hostility and our egocentricity sufficiently under control that the groups within which we live, without which, indeed, life would be impossible, can be kept together?

Put in this way, these questions appear to be self-conscious and rational. They are more appropriately seen as deep-seated emotional needs, springing from the very nature of man as an individual and as a member of society. The questions appear first of all because they are felt—the death of a loved one wrenches our emotions, the failure to achieve that for which we yearn saddens and bewilders us; the hostility between ourselves and those around us infuses our social contacts with tension and prevents the achievement of mutual values. Religion may develop an intellectual system to interpret and deal with these questions, but they express first of all an underlying emotional need, not a group of rationally conceived problems.

Religion, then, can be defined as a system of beliefs and practices by means of which a group of people struggles with these ultimate problems of human life. It is the refusal to capitulate to death, to give up in the face of frustration, to allow hostility to tear apart one's human associations.

All men experience these wrenching difficulties to some degree. For some persons, however, they stand out as the most significant experiences of life. These individuals are impelled to try to discover some meaning in what seems to be senseless suffering, some road to salvation through the obstacles of human life. The beliefs and rites that make up a religion are the expressions of those who have felt the problems most intensively, who have been most acutely sensitive to the tragedies of death, the burdens of frustration, the sense of failure, the disruptive effects of hostility. Powered by the strength of their feelings, such religious innovators have created "solutions" appropriate to the enormity of the problems—solutions that frequently have burst the bonds of man's senses and of nature, but have brought their adherents some relief. Thus religions are built to carry the "peak load" of human emotional need.

Defined in this way, religion is—and seems likely to remain—an inevitable part of human life. Although the ways of struggling with these ultimate problems are enormously diverse, and seem destined for continuous change, the problems themselves are universal. A society that did not furnish its members with beliefs and practices that sought to deal with these ultimate problems would struggle along with an enormous burden of tragedy unallayed and hostility unrestrained—if indeed it could survive at all. This is only to say that some effort to deal with these questions is essential to human life as we know it, and not to say that any given religious system adequately answers these questions.

Religion, of course, is not alone in attempting to deal with the ultimate problems of human life. Rational efforts are important in all societies. Moreover, there

A statuette of the Bird Deity. This Egyptian sculpture (*ca.* 4000 B.C.), depicting the female form with uplifted arms and the head of a bird, is among the earliest representations of man's attempt to comprehend and surmount the tragedy of death. (Courtesy of The Brooklyn Museum)

are many individual emotional responses to insecurity and the problem of evil in addition to religion. Even in the healthiest and wealthiest and most rational of societies, however, secular responses cannot eliminate the problems of suffering, evil, and hostility. Realizing the gap between their hopes and the realities of their existence, men everywhere seek *closure* by a leap of faith that says: this need not, this will not, be true. Some time, some place, some how, suffering and evil will be defeated. (The enormous variation in conceptions of time, place, and method measures the range of religious expressions.) . . .

A primary difficulty with a functional definition is that there is no obvious point at which one may draw a line and say: "Here religion ends and non-religion begins." In a religiously-heterogeneous and changing society, the question of "private" systems of belief and practice arises. Are they to be called religions? Are they not attempts to fulfill the same functions that shared and historically identified faiths seek to perform? In our view, one should answer this question in the negative. There is, to be sure, some truth in the statement that, "his work is his religion," or "he has dedicated himself to the discovery of a cure for cancer," with the implication that this is "his religion." There can be religious aspects of private systems of belief and action. A complete religion, however, is a social phenomenon; it is shared; it takes on many of its most significant aspects only in the interaction of the group. Both the feelings from which it springs and the "solutions" it offers are social, they arise from the fact that man is a group-living animal. The "ultimate questions" which we have identified as the center of the religious quest are ultimate primarily because of their impact on human association. Even death is not fundamentally an individual crisis, but a group crisis, threatening to tear the fabric of family and community.

Joachim Wach [a contemporary sociologist] holds that all religions, despite their wide variations, are characterized by three universal expressions: the theoretical, or a system of beliefs, the practical, a system of worship, and the sociological, a system of social relationships. Until all of these are found, one may have religious tendencies, religious elements, but not a full religion. . . . Although the first of these expressions—the system of belief—is the one that modern man is most likely to think of as the heart of religion, both ethnological and etymological evidence suggests that religion as worship and religion as a system of social relationships may be the more basic aspects, belief coming in as an attempt to give coherence and meaning to worship and associations that have developed out of deeply felt needs. The word religion may have derived from the Latin *religare*, to bind together, or from *religere*, to rehearse, to execute painstakingly, suggesting both group identity and ritual. The testimony of most anthropologists gives support to the proposition that it is the acts of religion, and the associations, more than the beliefs, that give it a vital place in the life of preliterate societies. This may be less true in a literate society where the practice of seeking out explanations is more fully established and where religious specialists seek to relate religion to a complex and changing society.

The growing importance of the "belief" aspects of religion, however, should not lead us to misinterpret the nature of a religious intellectual system. It is a group of "mighty hypotheses," of "over-beliefs," of deductions that leap beyond those admissible by a calm appraisal of the facts. Man is not calm in face of the needs from which religion springs. . . .

Perhaps our approach can be summed up in these words: The human individual, blessed (and sometimes cursed) with the power of language, capable, therefore, of anticipating the future, including a foreknowledge of his own death, able to verbalize ideal states, to create standards, is continually threatened with failure, with frustration, with his conception of justice unfulfilled. These problems tend to loom up as overwhelming or "absolute evils." Religion is man's attempt to "relativize" them by interpreting them as part of some larger good, some conception of the absolute that puts the individual's problems into new perspective, thus to remove or reduce their crushing impact. At the same time, man's social relations, his societies, are threatened by these same problems. Fear and frustration can lead to disrupting hostilities, unless they can be reinterpreted as part of a shared experience. In addition to that, there is the tendency of each individual to think only of himself, to make his joys, his desires into "absolute goods," threatening the patterns of mutual adjustment that social life requires. Religion is the attempt to "relativize" the individual's desires, as well as his fears, by subordinating them to a conception of absolute good more in harmony with the shared and often mutually contradictory needs and desires of human groups.

The need to answer the ultimate questions, therefore, forms a common motive linking the Greek and Hebrew achievements in philosophy and religion. This motive may be traced to man's unique biological and psychological make-up, which not only creates the need to order experience but also provides the means by which this may be done: the ability to manipulate symbols. We have already noted that there is a difference between philosophy and religion. This difference can be expressed in terms of symbolic behavior. Whereas Greek philosophy involved what has been called discursive reasoning, Hebrew religion employed another method of ordering experience: the nondiscursive or symbolic.

The Individual, the Religious Community, and the Symbol
John E. Smith[2]

Much has been written, both past and present, about symbolism and the symbolic character of religion. It is a subject that is likely to be attended by misunderstanding and confusion because it is elusive and has been interpreted in diverse ways. The first point to be noticed is that it will not do to call religion "symbolic" if all that is intended is a fairly loose and perhaps even arbitrary characterization of religious faith and its object as "poetical" or "figurative." It is not in this loose and usually derogatory sense that the term, "symbolic," is to be understood. Religious faith is symbolic as is its systematic articulation in theology, because both have to do with a type of meaning which, though related in a determinate way to the visible world, points beyond that world to an ultimate meaning and purpose which is both its ground and its goal. But although, in Biblical faith, God transcends the world, He is, nevertheless, thought to manifest Himself through various aspects of it and

[2] Pp. 160–64, 167, "The Individual, the Religious Community and the Symbol" by John E. Smith in *Symbols and Values: An Initial Study,* edited by Lyman Bryson, *et al.* Copyright 1954 by The Conference on Science, Philosophy and Religion in Their Relation to the Democratic Way of Life, Inc. Reprinted by permission of Harper & Row, Publishers.

certain events in it. Thus, there are various media—persons, places, natural objects, times, events—which may be called the bearers of the divine.

These media are regarded as symbols and signs of God and as they *are not* God but *mean* God, they must be interpreted or read by those to whom is given the power to understand. Therefore, when it is said that the inspired man of God, the prophet, has the task of "discerning the signs of the times," this is a statement which may be taken as, in a sense, literally true. The prophet experiences God via the medium of such symbols and, at least for Biblical faith, if God is not grasped in this way, He is not grasped at all.

Those original communications between God and man upon which Biblical religion is based are analogous in themselves to the situation where two individual persons seek to communicate with each other. When I intend or mean something and want to express that meaning to another, I can do so only through the use of a medium symbolic in nature. The mind of my neighbor is not open to direct inspection nor can it be known simply by conceiving of him in his general characteristics. As an individual person distinct from myself, but, as I believe, similarly seeking for meaning and purpose in life, he is an active intelligence who can only express himself to me through a medium or language which I must be able to read if I am to enter into his consciousness and understand who he is and what he intends. This medium may be varied in character and may be in the form of words, gestures, deeds, etc., but whatever its form, it is essential and cannot be done away with if the chasm which exists between two selves, in virtue of the fact that they are really two selves, is to be bridged. This can be done only through a dialectical process lasting through time in which each self attempts to understand the meanings and intentions of others by reading their symbolic expressions. It is not any illegitimate narrowing of the gulf between God and man to think of God's manifesting of Himself as analogous to this process of communication. The Bible, seen from this vantage point, is a vast structure of symbols and sign-events which are expressive of the nature and purpose of God; it represents, as well, a record of man's attempt to grasp and to express the divine nature and purpose as it appears in the constitution of nature and the turning points of human history. God and man are engaged in a cosmic dialogue and in it man is attempting to understand the divine intentions through the symbols which are expressive of Him. It is not simply the literal or physical description of these symbols that is of importance, but the *meaning* which is being expressed through them.... "Whatever literal character may be ascribed to these 'events' in time, they are ... revelatory of that which is before all time and before all worlds."[3] These events can be revelatory only when taken as symbols or sign-events of a meaning which is expressed through them. This ultimate meaning which is before all time is, at least in part, what is meant by God....

Gradually it has come to be understood that man is the "meaning seeking" animal and that, in the process of seeking what all things mean, he discovers his capacity to express what he has learned about himself and his world in a form which is relatively permanent and able to be communicated from self to self. It is thus that man comes to be called the sign reading or symbolic

[3] Wilber M. Urban, *Humanity and Deity* (London: George Allen & Unwin, Ltd., 1951), p. 245.

animal. It has become customary to distinguish between sign and symbol in order to show that man alone is capable of having a symbolic response and of grasping and expressing symbolic meaning as distinct from the sign or signal response. There can be no doubt that this distinction, or one like it, must be made and kept. There is, however, a problem of usage, which though verbal, is liable to cause confusion and should be cleared up. The term, "sign," is often used in at least two senses, a broad and a narrow one. In the broad sense, "sign" means literally *anything* (words, sounds, events, etc.) which "stands for" or conveys a meaning or needs to be read. On this usage, sign is a class name embracing many different types of signs like icons, symbols, etc. These types are all said to share the general characteristics of signs, but may be distinguished by reference to the precise way in which they mean and the type of meaning which is involved. When sign is used in this broad sense all symbols are called signs. There is, however, a narrow sense of the term, "sign," according to which it means either "signal" like a bell in a stimulus-response situation, or a conventional, arbitrary mark to be assigned meaning for some technical purpose and having no intrinsic or internal relation to what it stands for. It is mainly with symbols that we are concerned in religion and not with signs in the narrow sense (except in the case of Biblical "signs" which are, as Paul Tillich has pointed out, more properly called *sign events*). For symbols are expressive of what they mean in their own nature and are thus neither arbitrary nor accidental, whereas an algebraic sign, for example, is arbitrary in the sense that there is no necessary connection between the sign and the meaning assigned to it.

Religious faith in seeking to lay hold on God is necessarily symbolic in its expression. It seeks what is beyond all literal seeing, and to achieve its goal it must avail itself of symbolic media. On this account religion is not bound up with symbolic meaning by accident or by human choice or preference; it is symbolic by its very nature. Many attempts have been made, through the disciplines of theology and metaphysics, to "break through" religious symbolism and translate the language of religion with its image and its myth into conceptual language. An appraisal of the final success or failure of such ventures falls beyond our purpose, but it is doubtful whether the affirmations of religion can ever be cast in a wholly non-symbolic form such as a rationalistic theology proposes to do. At any rate, the point to be stressed is that the conditions surrounding the self-manifestation of God require that every grasp and articulation of God's nature and purpose be effected via the symbolic medium.

Religion is symbolic not only because God is beyond the confines of our sense experience but because its grasp of God must be articulated in order to be preserved through time. The only way in which the revelatory experience of an Amos, an Isaiah, a Peter, or a Paul can be preserved is via a symbolic medium. Apart from this it would vanish as soon as it was born. The medium of such preservation is the sacred literature, customs, institutions, etc., of the community together with the body of commentary and interpretation which grows up around it. This literature is itself a body of symbols and signs which need to be interpreted both by the members for the community and by the community for the members. Thus the Bible is not only a record of the attempt on the part of the "men of God" to read and understand through their own experience the symbols of the divine plan, but it is itself set forth in symbolic form and thus requires further interpretation. This accounts for the perennial difficulties over interpretation; actually man is always, in a sense, at a second remove from the mystery which is God; first, the symbols and sign events themselves, and secondly, the normative attempt to read and record them found in the sacred literature which, in turn, needs to be read and interpreted and so on to the end of time....

The original experiences, sign events, crucial occurrences out of which Biblical religion emerged, were, to be sure, individual experiences, experiences of the great men of faith, but they did not and could not remain merely individual. The selves for whom these experiences were first real had to recognize them as symbols and signs of God and to interpret them for themselves through that inner reflective dialogue which is of the very nature of self-conscious life. Furthermore, not only did these individuals seek to interpret their own experiences for themselves and in so doing express them in symbolic form, but their experience, in becoming the basis for a community, came to be interpreted by others who in turn sought to interpret it for still others and so on without end. In this process there was a continual grasping of symbols and signs and a continual attempt to read or interpret them through further symbols and signs. It is this long process of interpretation, as preserved in the sacred literature of the tradition together with commentary upon it, which forms the *common basis* of the community.

As Smith points out, "the Bible, when seen from this vantage point, is a vast structure of symbols and sign events which are expressive of the nature and purpose of God." The key sign event in the Jewish religion was the Exodus from Egypt and the resulting covenant between the Hebrew people and their God which made them into a religious community. Until recently the Exodus and the history of the Hebrew people that preceded it were known only through the Biblical account, which, as we have said, tended to fuse events and the emotional response to those events. However, because of advances in the archeological and linguistic study of the ancient Near East, we now possess a rather accurate picture of the course of Hebrew history leading up to the Exodus from Egypt and the migration into Palestine.

The Hebrews were originally a seminomadic people related in language and culture to other Semitic-speaking[4] people who periodically swept out of the grasslands of northern Arabia into the more civilized environment of the Fertile Crescent[5] during the third and second millenniums B.C. These people wandered with their flocks on the fringes of more developed cultures. The inhabitants of Mesopotamia around 2000 B.C. often referred to these seminomadic wanderers in general as 'Apiru or Habiru,[6] the term from which the Biblical word Hebrew was derived. The Habiru appeared to the Mesopotamians as rootless wanderers plying many trades. They were shepherds, artisans, musicians, mercenaries, and sometimes outright plunderers. During the second millennium B.C. the Habiru were absorbed by the various settled communities in which they found themselves and acquired national or tribal names.

Early in the second millennium another Semitic seminomadic people, the Amorites, came out of the Arabian desert and took control of Mesopotamia. By 1750 B.C. the Amorites had ex-

[4] Semitic, like Indo-European, is one of the major linguistic families. Semitic-speaking peoples include Arabs, Babylonians, Assyrians, Phoenicians, Carthaginians, and Hebrews.

[5] A phrase coined by J. H. Breasted to describe the rich, cultivated areas of the ancient Near East that formed an arc, curving north of the Arabian desert and joining the river valley of the Nile in the west with the valleys of the Tigris and Euphrates in the east.

[6] Hä bĭ rū—accent on the second syllable.

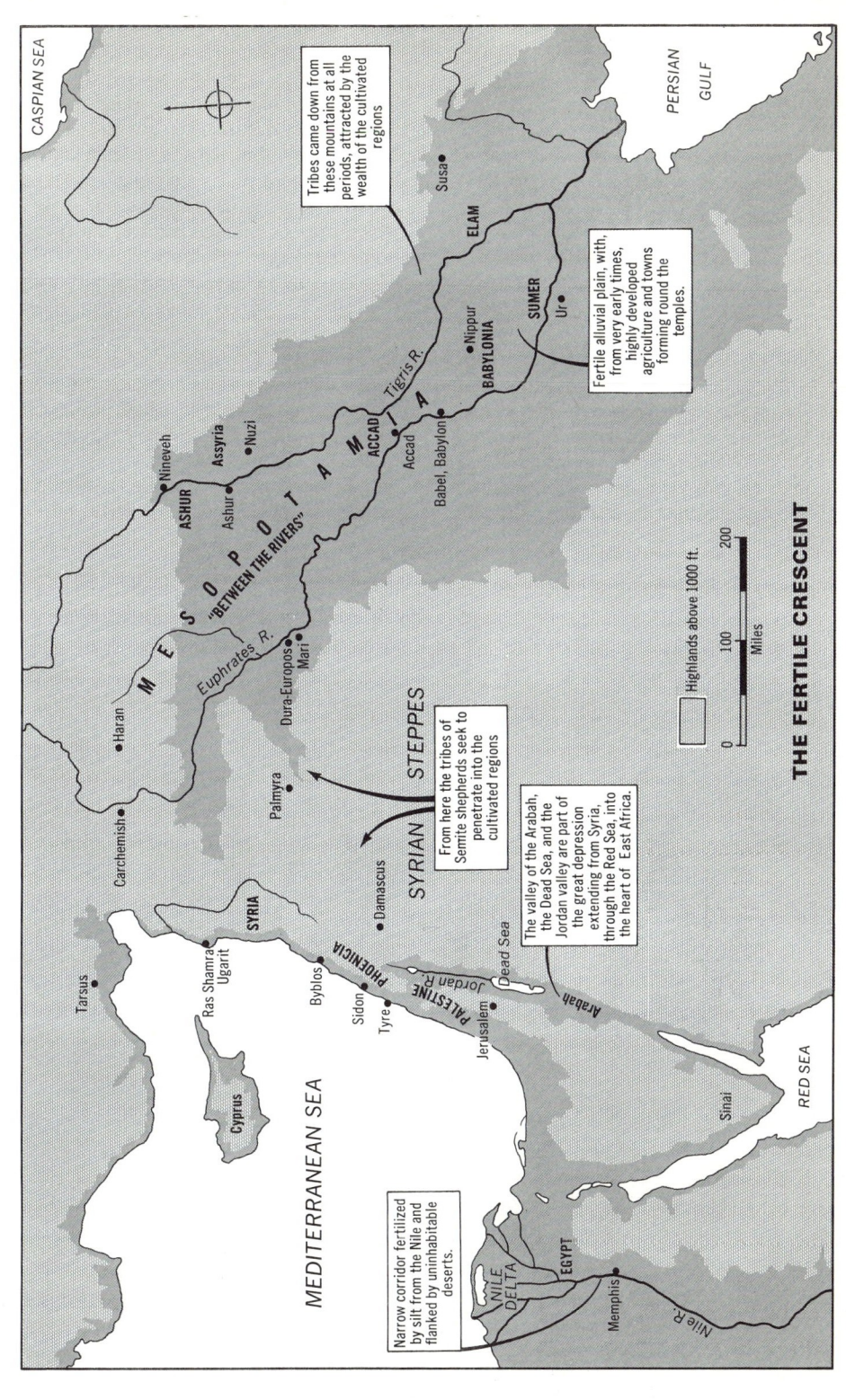

10   The Religious Conceptions of Early Hebrew Society

tended their influence into the area of Canaan, or Palestine. This Amorite hegemony, known as the First Babylonian Dynasty, reached its apex in the reign of Hammurabi (ca. 1728–1686 B.C.) and disintegrated shortly after his death. It appears likely that the Hebrews, that is, that particular tribe of Semitic Habiru whose tradition identified them with the patriarch Abraham, were Amorites or closely related to them. According to tradition Abraham led his pastoral people from the Amorite city of Ur in Mesopotamia to the sparsely settled hill country of Palestine during the eighteenth century B.C.

At the beginning of the seventeenth century B.C. some of the Hebrew tribes migrated out of Palestine into Egypt to escape drought and famine. Tradition identifies their leader as Jacob, grandson of Abraham. This migration coincided with or followed upon the invasion and conquest of Egypt by the Hyksos, who ruled in Lower Egypt for more than a century. The Hyksos were a mixture of many peoples, primarily Semitic, which may be one reason for the favored position accorded the Hebrews during the first part of their stay in Egypt. Around 1550 B.C., however, the Egyptians drove out the Hyksos, and the foreign element residing in Egypt, including the Hebrews, came into disfavor. For over two centuries the Hebrews and other Semitic groups made up a suppressed class, which often provided slave labor for the building projects of the Pharaohs. About 1290 B.C. a group of Hebrews and other enslaved peoples united under the leadership of Moses and fled from Egyptian

A wall painting from an Egyptian tomb of the Eighteenth Dynasty showing slaves making bricks. (The Metropolitan Museum of Art, Egyptian Expedition, Rogers Fund, 1930)

The Religious Conceptions of Early Hebrew Society

bondage. Escaping eastward into the Sinai Peninsula these people roamed its scorched wilderness for a generation and finally reentered Palestine during the last half of the thirteenth century B.C. The entire journey from Egypt to Palestine was termed by the Hebrews the Exodus. Before the Exodus the Hebrews had been merely a mixture of seminomadic people indistinguishable from hundreds of other tribes, but those who fled Egypt were welded together by Moses into a self-conscious community of Israelites.[7] The following selection from the Book of Exodus narrates God's call of Moses and the flight of the Hebrews from Egypt under his leadership.

THE EXODUS FROM EGYPT[8]

3 Now Moses was keeping the flock of his father-in-law, Jethro, the priest of Mid'ian; and he led his flock to the west side of the wilderness, and came to Horeb, the mountain of God. ²And the angel of the LORD appeared to him in a flame of fire out of the midst of a bush; and he looked, and lo, the bush was burning, yet it was not consumed. ³And Moses said, "I will turn aside and see this great sight, why the bush is not burnt." ⁴ When the LORD saw that he turned aside to see, God called to him out of the bush, "Moses, Moses!" And he said, "Here am I." ⁵ Then he said, "Do not come near; put off your shoes from your feet, for the place on which you are standing is holy ground." ⁶And he said, "I am the God of your father, the God of Abraham, the God of Isaac, and the God of Jacob." And Moses hid his face, for he was afraid to look at God.

⁷ Then the LORD said, "I have seen the affliction of my people who are in Egypt, and have heard their cry because of their taskmasters; I know their sufferings, ⁸ and I have come down to deliver them out of the hand of the Egyptians, and to bring them up out of that land to a good and broad land, a land flowing with milk and honey, to the place of the Canaanites, the Hittites, the Amorites, the Per'izzites, the Hivites, and the Jeb'usites. ⁹And now, behold, the cry of the people of Israel has come to me, and I have seen the oppression with which the Egyptians oppress them. ¹⁰ Come, I will send you to Pharaoh that you may bring forth my people, the sons of Israel, out of Egypt." ¹¹ But Moses said to God, "Who am I that I should go to Pharaoh, and bring the sons of Israel out of Egypt?" ¹² He said, "But I will be with you; and this shall be the sign for you, that I have sent you; when you have brought forth the people out of Egypt, you shall serve God upon this mountain."

¹³ Then Moses said to God, "If I come to the people of Israel and say to them, 'The God of your fathers has sent me to you,' and they ask me, 'What is his name?' what shall I say to them?" ¹⁴ God said to Moses, "I AM WHO I AM." And he said, "Say this to the people of Israel, 'I AM has sent me to you.'" ¹⁵ God also said to Moses, "Say this to the people of Israel, 'The LORD, the God of your fathers, the God of Abraham, the God of Isaac, and the God of Jacob, has sent me to you': this is my name for ever, and thus I am to be remembered throughout all generations. ¹⁶ Go and gather the elders of Israel to-

---

[7] The terms Israel and Israelite have a special meaning. "Israel" was a second name given to Jacob, whose descendants became known as the children of Israel, or the Israelites. The term Israelite applied not only to those who traced their ancestry from Abraham but also to those who worshiped the God of Abraham, Isaac, and Jacob. After the entry into Palestine it became more of a religious than an ethnic term, and it replaced the term Hebrew as a descriptive noun for those who had formed a covenant with God at Mount Sinai.

[8] The Bible, Exod. 3:1–22; 13:17—14:31.

gether, and say to them, 'The LORD, the God of your fathers, the God of Abraham, of Isaac, and of Jacob, has appeared to me, saying, "I have observed you and what has been done to you in Egypt; 17 and I promise that I will bring you up out of the affliction of Egypt, to the land of the Canaanites, the Hittites, and Amorites, the Per'izzites, the Hivites, and the Jeb'usites, a land flowing with milk and honey."' 18And they will hearken to your voice; and you and the elders of Israel shall go to the king of Egypt and say to him, 'The LORD, the God of the Hebrews, has met with us; and now, we pray you, let us go a three days' journey into the wilderness, that we may sacrifice to the LORD our God.' 19 I know that the king of Egypt will not let you go unless compelled by a mighty hand. 20 So I will stretch out my hand and smite Egypt with all the wonders which I will do in it; after that he will let you go. 21And I will give this people favor in the sight of the Egyptians; and when you go, you shall not go empty, 22 but each woman shall ask of her neighbor, and of her who sojourns in her house, jewelry of silver and of gold, and clothing, and you shall put them on your sons and on your daughters; thus you shall despoil the Egyptians." . . .

13 . . . 17 When Pharaoh let the people go, God did not lead them by way of the land of the Philistines, although that was near; for God said, "Lest the people repent when they see war, and return to Egypt." 18 But God led the people round by the way of the wilderness toward the Red Sea. And the people of Israel went up out of the land of Egypt equipped for battle. 19And Moses took the bones of Joseph with him; for Joseph had solemnly sworn the people of Israel, saying, "God will visit you; then you must carry my bones with you from here." 20And they moved on from Succoth, and encamped at Etham, on the edge of the wilderness. 21And the LORD went before them by day in a pillar of cloud to lead them along the way, and by night in a pillar of fire to give them light, that they might travel by day and by night; 22 the pillar of cloud by day and the pillar of fire by night did not depart from before the people.

14 Then the LORD said to Moses, 2 "Tell the people of Israel to turn back and encamp in front of Pi-ha-hi'roth, between Migdol and the sea, in front of Ba'al-zephon; you shall encamp over against it, by the sea. 3 For Pharaoh will say of the people of Israel, 'They are entangled in the land; the wilderness has shut them in.' 4And I will harden Pharaoh's heart, and he will pursue them and I will get glory over Pharaoh and all his host; and the Egyptians shall know that I am the LORD." And they did so.

5 When the king of Egypt was told that the people had fled, the mind of Pharaoh and his servants was changed toward the people, and they said, "What is this we have done, that we have let Israel go from serving us?" 6 So he made ready his chariot and took his army with him, 7 and took six hundred picked chariots and all the other chariots of Egypt with officers over all of them. 8And the LORD hardened the heart of Pharaoh king of Egypt and he pursued the people of Israel as they went forth defiantly. 9 The Egyptians pursued them, all Pharaoh's horses and chariots and his horsemen and his army, and overtook them encamped at the sea, by Pi-ha-hi'roth, in front of Ba'al-zephon.

10 When Pharaoh drew near, the people of Israel lifted up their eyes, and behold,

The Religious Conceptions of Early Hebrew Society 13

the Egyptians were marching after them; and they were in great fear. And the people of Israel cried out to the LORD; [11] and they said to Moses, "Is it because there are no graves in Egypt that you have taken us away to die in the wilderness? What have

A statue of Rameses II (1290–1224 B.C.) from the temple of Luxor. Rameses II was probably the pharaoh at the time of the Exodus. (Archives Photographiques, Paris)

you done to us, in bringing us out of Egypt? 12 Is not this what we said to you in Egypt, 'Let us alone and let us serve the Egyptians'? For it would have been better for us to serve the Egyptians than to die in the wilderness." 13And Moses said to the people, "Fear not, stand firm, and see the salvation of the LORD, which he will work for you today; for the Egyptians whom you see today, you shall never see again. 14 The LORD will fight for you, and you have only to be still." 15 The LORD said to Moses, "Why do you cry to me? Tell the people of Israel to go forward. 16 Lift up your rod, and stretch out your hand over the sea and divide it, that the people of Israel may go on dry ground through the sea. 17And I will harden the hearts of the Egyptians so that they shall go in after them, and I will get glory over Pharaoh and all his host, his chariots, and his horsemen. 18 And the Egyptians shall know that I am the LORD, when I have gotten glory over Pharaoh, his chariots, and his horsemen."

19 Then the angel of God who went before the host of Israel moved and went behind them; and the pillar of cloud moved from before them and stood behind them, 20 coming, between the host of Egypt and the host of Israel. And there was the cloud and the darkness; and the night passed without one coming near the other all night.

21 Then Moses stretched out his hand over the sea; and the LORD drove the sea back by a strong east wind all night, and made the sea dry land, and the waters were divided. 22And the people of Israel went into the midst of the sea on dry ground, the waters being a wall to them on their right hand and on their left. 23 The Egyptians pursued, and went in after them into the midst of the sea, all Pharaoh's horses, his chariots, and his horsemen. 24And in the morning watch the LORD in the pillar

A relief of the Eighteenth Dynasty showing Egyptian chariots with horses and charioteers awaiting the pharaoh. (The Metropolitan Museum of Art, Gift of Egypt Exploration Society, 1927)

of fire and of cloud looked down upon the host of the Egyptians, and discomfited the host of the Egyptians, 25 clogging their chariot wheels so that they drove heavily; and the Egyptians said, "Let us flee from before Israel; for the LORD fights for them against the Egyptians."

26 Then the LORD said to Moses, "Stretch out your hand over the sea, that the water may come back upon the Egyptians, upon their chariots, and upon their horsemen." 27 So Moses stretched forth his hand over the sea, and the sea returned to its wonted flow when the morning appeared; and the Egyptians fled into it, and the LORD routed the Egyptians in the midst of the sea. 28 The waters returned and covered the chariots and the horsemen and all the host of Pharaoh that had followed them into the sea; not so much as one of them remained. 29 But the people of Israel walked on dry ground through the sea, the waters being a wall to them on their right hand and on their left.

30 Thus the LORD saved Israel that day from the hand of the Egyptians; and Israel saw the Egyptians dead upon the seashore. 31And Israel saw the great work which the LORD did against the Egyptians, and the people feared the LORD; and they believed in the LORD and in his servant Moses.

Much of the Biblical account of the Israelite Exodus from Egypt seems strange and unconvincing to the modern reader whose worldview has little place for the supernatural. The understandable skepticism that prevents a sympathetic reading of the Exodus account, the sense of disbelief or at least dislocation experienced in trying to bridge the gap between the modern and Hebraic worldviews, can be eased somewhat through a consideration of two factors that have shaped the account as we have it today.

The first factor is a confusion in the text over the term "Red Sea." The Hebrews did not cross what we know today as the Red Sea nor is such a claim made in the Hebrew text. The interpretation that they did cross it was based on a misreading that occurred in the Greek translation of the Old Testament upon which some of our present English translations are still based. The preferred reading is "Sea of Reeds" or "Lake of Reeds," which could apply to the northwestern arm of the Red Sea, known today as the Gulf of Suez, but more probably applies to one of the flat shallow marshy areas east of the Nile delta in the region of Lake Timsah or the Bitter Lakes. Almost annually high winds from the east intermittently dry or flood this and similar marshy regions near the Red Sea and the Persian Gulf. The Biblical account, which specifically describes such an east wind, suggests also that the Israelites avoided the fortified border north of the lake region and chose, instead, to cross the marshes (Pi-ha-hi'roth) further south, either those on the southern edge of Lake Timsah or those between the Bitter Lakes and the Gulf of Suez. It is probable that the Israelite "crossing" coincided with such a natural phenomenon. A partially dried marsh could easily have allowed the passage of the Israelites on foot and trapped the wheels of the heavy Egyptian chariots. Given the fortunate timing of the appearance and disappearance of the wind, which permitted the Israelites to cross the marsh and submerged the Egyptians trapped in the mud, it would have been surprising if the Israelites had not seen in such a dramatic reversal of their fortunes the action of their God. The miracle, therefore, for the one who wishes to view the event as an action of God, lies not in the suspension of the laws of nature (a concept foreign to the early Hebrews) but in the timing of the occurrence.

It is not difficult to understand how the same event can appear as accidental fortunate timing to some people and as a miraculous divine action to others. Almost everyone has at one time experienced a fortunate turn of events that seemed at the time more than accidental chance. Such an occurrence appears to the participant as a "miracle" in spite of the fact that the nonparticipant would not view it in that way. The continuing importance of the occurrence, the continuing affirmation of its miraculous quality,

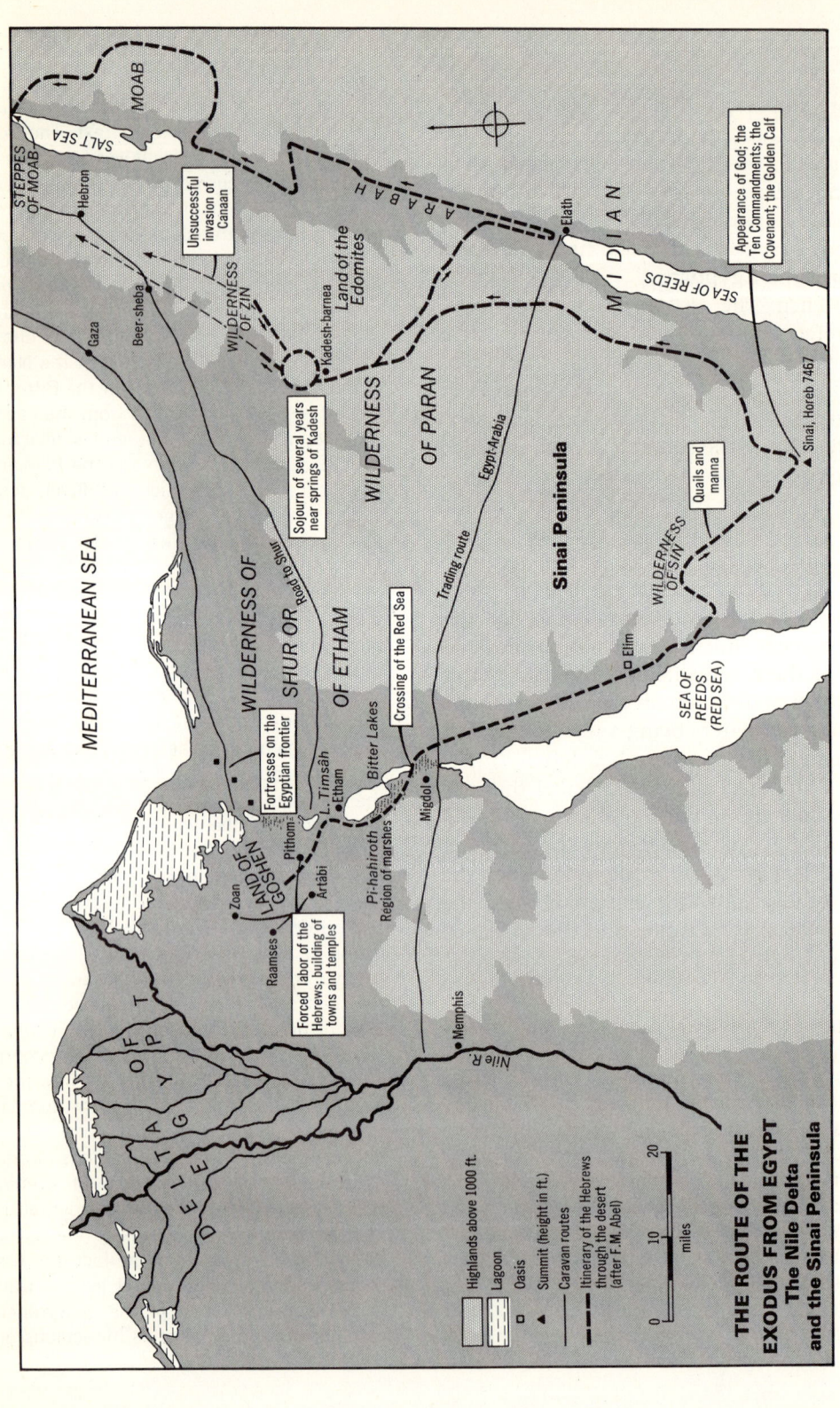

depends usually on the degree to which such an occurrence alters the worldview or behavior pattern of the participant.

The defeat of the Egyptians in the marshes of the lake region had great importance for the Israelites. They believed they saw in it a sign of God's special care, although for the Egyptians the event had no such significance. However, the Israelites' faith was not based upon a miraculous event which "proved" that what they believed was factually and rationally true. Rather, their faith was an affirmation that what to others might appear as a perfectly normal historical event was for them charged with religious significance—it was a sign event.

> The crossing was an event which lay wholly within the nexus of nature and history as these are scientifically understood. But for Israel this was God's "time" and became a revelatory event which compelled those who saw it to reinterpret the meaning of both nature and history. It was the redemptive event which became the foundation of Israel's existence as the people of God. It was for Israel not simply a source of objective meaning, but also of abiding wonder. The event is for the Old Testament what Jesus as Christ is for the New Testament—the normative redeeming and revealing act of God. . . .
>
> In terms of the relativities of historical process, even the utter destruction of Pharaoh's forces was an event of very minor import. It did not alter the fortunes of the empire of Egypt. The writers and editors of this account may have been under no illusions about this, for Egypt was frequently a threat to Israel's political security. Yet this insignificant event was in Israel the key that transformed the meaning of all history. Egypt was the same Egypt. But for the community of faith that sprang from this event, it no longer bore the same meaning as heretofore. They had seen "the great hand" of God.[9]

[9] By J. Coert Rylaarsdam, "Exegesis of the Book of Exodus," in G. A. Buttrick (ed.), *The Interpreter's Bible,* Vol. I, pp. 935, 939. Copyright 1952 by Pierce and Smith. Used by permission of Abingdon Press.

The second factor that has shaped the Biblical account of the Exodus is its means of preservation: oral tradition. The Exodus, along with the symbolic religious meaning it held for the descendants of Moses' followers, was preserved in the memory of the community in oral form, handed down from one generation to another until it received written form during the reigns of David and Solomon in the tenth century B.C. As with the other traditions in the Hebrew past that came to be preserved in the Pentateuch (the first five books of the Old Testament), the oral tradition of the Exodus was not everywhere identical; it differed somewhat among the tribal regions in Palestine and among various interest groups, such as the royal household or the priesthood. Scholars have identified four major literary strands within the Pentateuch which reflect four differing approaches to or interpretations of the history of the Hebrew people before the settlement in Palestine. These four strands not only reflect separate oral traditions but were strongly conditioned by the political events immediately preceding their written form as well as the religious viewpoint of the group that preserved them.

The fact that multiple accounts of the Exodus were preserved within Israel goes far to explain the repetition and conflicting approaches present within the final account. In addition, oral tradition tends to poeticize, dramatize, or—more accurately—to fuse event and interpretation in such a way that what the group sees in and feels about the event colors and shapes its remembrance. Thus one can see in the present account of the Exodus both a repetition and a heightening of the drama of God's action.

> By means of a process of communal embellishment the account was gradually altered and the event lifted out of its setting in the context of natural process. This process of providing the account with a "supernatural" dress continued after the Old Testament canon [the authoritative number and version of the Old Testament books] was closed, but we can see it taking place in the development of the contents of the canon also. In this brief pas-

sage we detect three stages. The first is entirely natural: God uses an east wind to drive back the water, enabling the Israelites to cross over safely ([chapter 14] vss. 15, 19a, 21b, 22a). The second account (vss. 16, 19b, 20, 21a) attributes the disappearance of the water to Moses' use of the magic rod and hints that the cloud was a "supernatural" phenomenon. In the third account (vss. 17-18, 22b) the waters are so separated by the rod as to stand like walls.[10]

Such "communal embellishment" alters only certain aspects of an event passed down in oral form. Oral tradition among nonliterate societies is a surprisingly reliable means of factual transmission, as is reflected in the Exodus account by the fact that enough of the place names and of the sequence of events has remained across a thousand years of oral transmission so that the historical event can be satisfactorily reconstructed. Such transmission, however, is subject to the creative role of communal memory, which, first, preserves only what is important for the community, second, tends to fuse event and interpretation, and, third, reinterprets the event on the basis of later experience. Such a process underlines the symbolic nature of the Exodus for the Hebrew community.

> The significance and value of this total complex is symbolic rather than historical. The mosaic as a whole attests Israel's faith, resting on the historic experience of its escape from slavery; it aims at showing that not Pharaoh or the gods of Egypt but the living God of Israel makes nature serve man—or rather, makes nature serve his purposes for man's fulfillment.[11]

The tendency to clothe and express a religious experience in symbols, while common to men of all periods, is especially characteristic of the myth-making activity of primitive man, a category that is generally appropriate for the Hebrews of the second millennium B.C. The experience of deliverance from slavery and the victory over the Egyptians in the marshes of the lake region did not happen to a Hebrew society without structure and psychology. The particular view of God, man, and nature present within the Exodus account and throughout the Bible was conditioned not only by the experience itself but also by the early Hebrew social structure and worldview.

One of the primary sociological factors conditioning the Hebrew conception of God was the patriarchal structure of the Hebrew family.

> Throughout historic times the ancient Hebrew family may be legitimately described as patriarchal and polygynous. By the term patriarchal we mean that great power was vested in the male head of each household. This was especially marked during the period of nomadic pastoral life, and under the circumstances then obtaining was probably quite necessary to survival.[12]

A second, environmental, factor was that the early Hebrews were a nomadic pastoral people whose dominating and conditioning religious experience took place in a desert wilderness. Yahweh,[13] the Israelite name for God, may have been adopted by Moses from the mountain, desert God of the Kenites, among whom Moses had settled before the Exodus and into one of whose priestly families he had married. Regard-

---

[10] *Ibid.*, p. 936.
[11] By J. Coert Rylaarsdam, "Introduction to the Book of Exodus," in G. A. Buttrick (ed.), *The Interpreter's Bible*, Vol. I, p. 839. Copyright 1952 by Pierce and Smith. Used by permission of Abingdon Press.
[12] S. A. Queen and R. W. Habenstein, *The Family in Various Cultures* (3rd ed.; Philadelphia: J. B. Lippincott Company, 1967), p. 141. By permission of the publishers.
[13] The name YHWH is the third person singular of the verb "to be" or "to happen," and was probably derived from God's answer to Moses: "I am who I am" or "I cause to be what will be." Although the pronunciation of the name is difficult to ascertain, since ancient Hebrew was written without vowels, most scholars prefer Yahweh. Because of the sacred character of the name, it was withdrawn from usage after the Exile, and orthodox Jews today still prefer to refer to God as Adonai, or Lord. The term Jehovah resulted from adding the vowels of Adonai to the consonants YHWH.

less of the origin of the name, the nature and attributes of the Israelite God were ascertained in the course of the wanderings on the Sinai Peninsula. It is this factor that probably explains the marked differences between Yahweh and the gods of settled, agricultural regions.

A third, psychological, factor was the Hebrew conception of man, which, although heavily dependent upon the Israelite conception of God, represents a primitive view in which the body and soul are not distinguished, nor is the concept of self particularly developed.

THE HEBRAIC UNDERSTANDING OF MAN
Harold Knight[14]

For the Hebrew, man is not a being composed of two distinct and separate entities—body and soul—but an un-analysed complex psycho-physical unity. This follows from the naïveté of the Hebrew consciousness in which thought is subsumed beneath life, action and sense-impression. The Hebrew conception of the personality of man is that of an unbroken integrated unity which is identified with the animated body. It is highly significant that the Hebrew language has no special term either for body or soul, for Hebrew thought does not work in these categories which presuppose the metaphysical analysis of human life.

The Hebrew seeks to interpret the mystery of life by means of the two terms—*nephesh* (breath) and *ruach* (wind). The former is the breath-principle viewed as the center and source of life in a human being.... It is the bearer both of the animal life of physical appetite and desire, and of the higher psychical consciousness. It is referred back to the breath of Yahweh as its ultimate source, but it is conceived as constituting the unique individuality of its human possessor. It is the fundamental soul-substance which is manifested in all that the individual person is and does. *Ruach*, on the other hand, is an impersonal term which emphasizes man's absolute dependence upon God. Whereas it is usual to say my *nephesh*, in the sense of "I myself," it would be quite impossible to speak of my *ruach*. *Ruach*, properly denoting "wind," is thought of as the universal life-stream which flows from God and expresses the activity of God in the world which He has created. In its manifestations, *ruach* suggests the irresistible might of the wind which sweeps across vast desert spaces and in the track of which all things are driven helplessly hither and thither. In its essence it signifies mysterious, supernatural power which lies beyond man's control. It is the instrument of the effects wrought by Yahweh in the life of the world and of man, but it does not impart divinity, or bring about union with the divine. In the Hebrew consciousness, the immanent working of God seems to be specially connected with the elemental force of the wind. God walks or flies upon the wings of the wind; the winds are His messengers. The wind is the breath of God's mouth; by which the heavens were created; and the waters of the Red Sea piled up. With the Hebrew incapacity to distinguish the physical from the psychical, this conception of the wind as a force emanating from God soon gave birth to the conception of the Spirit of God, which, operating as an invisible wind-like influence, produced supernormal effects in human life. The operation of the *ruach* came to be the accepted explanation of all that was striking or unusual in human conduct.

... [*Ruach*] expresses the fact that the deepest springs of life in man flow from

[14] Harold Knight, *The Hebrew Prophetic Consciousness* (London: Lutterworth Press, 1947), pp. 7–11.

Bedouin couple crossing the Negev Desert. Such wilderness stretches, where the individual is dominated by the expanse of arid, empty desert, are a major geographical feature of the Middle East. (Leonard Freed from Magnum)

the infinite and all-pervasive life of God which is poured out upon mankind from above. *Ruach* is conceived as something which enters into a man from outside. When he dies, God withdraws this vitalizing breath, but it could not be said that his *ruach* expires. *Nephesh,* on the other hand, is man's inalienable possession. It is his in virtue of the fact that he is a living being. Hence, it can be said that his *nephesh* dies. *Ruach* denotes the central zone of man's consciousness which is most readily accessible to the control of the invasive Spirit of God. But this subtle differentiation in the usage of the two terms in no way implies the break-up of the primitive Hebrew conception of man as a unity. The cardinal postulate of Hebrew psychology—that man is a physical organism animated by a breath-soul—remains unaffected.

It follows from this understanding of human nature that the Hebrew, unlike the Greek, recognizes no antithesis between flesh and soul. The true antithesis for the Hebrew is that between man and God, or between the human flesh-soul and the divine *ruach*. So far from being contrasted, flesh and soul might almost be said to be fused, in Hebrew anthropology. The soul is a bundle of psychic energies, stamped with a certain character, and manifesting itself through the flesh. The life of the soul is indissolubly linked to that of the flesh; the idea of a discarnate soul is utterly foreign to the Hebrew mentality. The departed in Sheol are not souls freed from their bodies, but faint shadows of the former man, whose unified psycho-physical life is thus feebly prolonged. Yahweh's breathing into the clay does not mean that the dead body was animated by the infusion of a soul, but that it was changed into something living by becoming endowed with the life-giving breath.

This organic relation of body and soul results in the fact that, for the Hebrew, the spiritual consciousness of man is dispersed throughout the body and inheres in its various parts. The soul is identified with the various bodily organs through which it acts and manifests itself. Soul and body are fused with a completeness which it is difficult for us to understand. Physical sustenance reacts upon the soul, fortifying it; fasting afflicts the soul. The soul life pulsates throughout the body. . . . We may say that, in the consciousness of the Hebrew, the soul is felt to stamp ineffaceably every movement of the body.

As a result of this psychology, the desert environment, the structure of Hebrew family life, and, most important, the Exodus experience itself, the Israelites conceived God in a way that distinguished them completely from their contemporaries in the second millennium B.C. The Israelites made a radical and unique distinction between God and man and between God and nature. God was not in nature as its moving or motivating force; rather he was above nature, transcendent. God was creator and sustainer of the universe, and although he acted in historical events in the realm of nature, he was never identified with nature.

God is conceived in the Judaic-Christian tradition as the infinite, self-existent Creator of everything that exists, other than himself.

In this doctrine, creation means far more than fashioning new forms from an already given material (as a builder makes a house, or a sculptor a statue); it means creation out of nothing—*creatio ex nihilo*—the summoning of a universe into existence when otherwise there was only God. There are two important corollaries of this idea.

First, it entails an absolute distinction between God and his creation, such that it is logically impossible for a creature to become the Creator. That which has been created will forever remain the created. To all eternity the Creator is the Creator and the creature is creature. Any thought of man becoming God is thus ruled out as meaningless by the Judaic-Christian conception of creation.

A second corollary is that the created realm is absolutely dependent upon God as its Maker and as the source of its continued existence. Hence we find that this radical notion of creation *ex nihilo* expresses itself in prayer and liturgy as a sense of dependence upon God for man's being from moment to moment. We have a part in the universe not by some natural right, but by the grace of God; and each day is a gift to be received in thankfulness and responsibility toward the divine Giver.[15]

When we read in Psalm XIX that "the heavens declare the glory of God; and the firmament sheweth his handiwork," we hear a voice which mocks the beliefs of Egyptians and Babylonians. The heavens, which were to the psalmist but a witness of God's greatness, were to the Mesopotamians the very majesty of godhead, the highest ruler, Anu . . . . In Egypt and Mesopotamia the divine was comprehended as immanent: the gods were in nature . . . . But to the psalmist the sun was God's devoted servant who "is as a bridegroom coming out of his chamber, and rejoiceth as a strong man to run a race." The God of the psalmists and the prophets was not in nature. He transcended nature—and transcended, likewise, the realm of mythopoeic thought. It would seem that the Hebrews, no less than the Greeks, broke with the mode of speculation which had prevailed up to their time.[16]

The Hebrew God, however, was not only transcendent; he was active in nature and human affairs.

Basic to Israel's faith is the conviction that God is not aloof from the world of daily affairs, or bound by an iron chain of cause-and-effect sequences. The Israelites had a sense of the immediacy of God's presence. They believed that any event—ordinary or extraordinary—could be a sign of his will and activity.[17]

Lacking the conception of a natural order which operates according to specific laws, the Hebrews considered the whole of creation to be dependent upon the will of God. "Natural" events, such as the rising of the sun or the birth of a child, and "unusual" events, such as the crossing of the "Red Sea," were alike signs of Yahweh's loving concern for his people. The only order the Hebrews saw in the world around them was attributable to the consistency of Yahweh's action.

The Hebrew vocabulary includes no word equivalent to our term "Nature." This is not surprising, if by "Nature" we mean "The creative and regulative physical power which is conceived of as operating in the physical world and as the immediate cause of all its phenomena." The only way to render this idea into Hebrew would be to say simply "God." We should have to describe a particular physical activity through anthropomorphic phrases, such as the "voice" of God, heard in the thunder; the "hand" of God, felt in the pestilence; and "breath" of God, animating the body of man; the "wisdom" of God, ultimately conceived as His agent in creation. In fact, we may say that such unity as "Nature" possessed in Hebrew eyes came to it through its absolute dependence on God, its Creator and Upholder. It has been said that "Greek philosophy began, as it ended, with the search for what was abiding in the flux of things."[18] The Hebrew found that in God.[19]

[17] Bernhard W. Anderson, *Understanding the Old Testament*, 2d ed., © 1966, p. 49. Reprinted by permission of Prentice-Hall, Inc., Englewood Cliffs, New Jersey.

[18] John Burnet, *Early Greek Philosophy* (2d ed.; London, 1908), p. 15.

[19] H. Wheeler Robinson, *Inspiration and Revelation in the Old Testament* (New York: Oxford University Press, 1946), p. 1.

[15] John Hick, *Philosophy of Religion* (Englewood Cliffs, N.J.: Prentice-Hall, Inc., 1963), p. 8.

[16] H. Frankfort, *Before Philosophy* (Baltimore, Md.: Penguin Books, Inc., 1949), p. 237.

A further characteristic of the Hebrew conception of God that separated it from contemporary views lay in the belief that it was *one* God, Yahweh, who led the Israelites out of bondage. From this time on the Hebrews were committed not only to the worship of this one God (monolatry) but also to the belief that only Yahweh possessed real divinity, that all other gods either were fictions or were weaker, smaller gods under the control of Yahweh (monotheism).[20] Yahweh stood alone without any family connections, any consorts or children. Nor was he specifically identified with any geographical location or natural phenomenon. While Yahweh had anthropomorphic features, he could not be represented in any visual or tangible form. He was beyond the limits of human perception.

This "otherness" of Yahweh was expressed as holiness. His holiness extended to any thing or any place that came into close relationship with him. This could apply to such things as the ground around the burning bush where Moses encountered Yahweh or to the Ark of the Covenant, where Yahweh's presence was supposed to dwell. It could also apply to a people. Israel, for example, was called a holy nation because it had a covenant with Yahweh. Yahweh's holiness made it necessary that his people approach him through the practices and rituals of a cult administered by holy persons or priests.

> In the cult the holy and profane enter into relationships with one another. In his sense of "the holy" the worshiper is made aware of the presence of the "otherness" of the divine. This otherness is a present reality, but it is also incomprehensible, imponderable, and "beyond." The deity cannot be approached cavalierly or without fear. He is unapproachable, full of zeal and uncanny power. The presence of the divine means the presence of holiness. It is with holiness that the worshiper has to do, but he must know what is holy and what is not. Woe betide him who does not regard the distinction! It is because God is holy that the cult is necessary.[21]

The concept of God as transcendent creator, above and yet active in nature, is most clearly illustrated in the Biblical version of the creation story. In the following selection from the Book of Genesis, the repetitions and breaks in continuity reflect once again the fusion of multiple versions.

THE CREATION STORY[22]

1 In the beginning God created the heavens and the earth. ²The earth was without form and void, and darkness was upon the face of the deep; and the Spirit of God was moving over the face of the waters.

³And God said, "Let there be light"; and there was light. ⁴And God saw that the light was good; and God separated the light from the darkness. ⁵ God called the light Day, and the darkness he called Night. And there was evening and there was morning, one day.

⁶And God said, "Let there be a firmament in the midst of the waters, and let it separate the waters from the waters." ⁷And God made the firmament and separated the waters which were under the firmament from the waters which were above the firmament. And it was so. ⁸And God

---

[20] There was a time when Biblical scholars believed that Hebraic religious thought had evolved from the polytheism of the patriarchal period (*ca.* 2000 B.C.), through the belief in one tribal god among many of the Mosaic period (*ca.* 1300 B.C.), to the implicit monotheism of the earlier prophets (*ca.* 750 B.C.), finally culminating in the explicit monotheism of Second Isaiah (*ca.* 540 B.C.). Neat as this evolutionary theory may be, it has been challenged by recent scholarship. According to this view Israel's understanding of her one God, while undergoing maturing changes from the time of Moses, was basically monotheistic from the time of the Exodus.

[21] By James Muilenberg, "The History of the Religion of Israel," in G. A. Buttrick (ed.), *The Interpreter's Bible*, Vol. I, p. 341. Copyright 1952 by Pierce and Smith. Used by permission of Abingdon Press.

[22] The Bible, Gen. 1:1–2:9; 2:18–25.

called the firmament Heaven. And there was evening and there was morning, a second day.

⁹And God said, "Let the waters under the heavens be gathered together into one place, and let the dry land appear." And it was so. ¹⁰ God called the dry land Earth, and the waters that were gathered together he called Seas. And God saw that it was good. ¹¹And God said, "Let the earth put forth vegetation, plants yielding seed, and fruit trees bearing fruit in which is their seed, each according to its kind, upon the earth." And it was so. ¹² The earth brought forth vegetation, plants yielding seed according to their own kinds, and trees bearing fruit in which is their seed, each according to its kind. And God saw that it was good. ¹³And there was evening and there was morning, a third day.

¹⁴And God said, "Let there be lights in the firmament of the heavens to separate the day from the night; and let them be for signs and for seasons and for days and years, ¹⁵ and let them be lights in the firmament of the heavens to give light upon the earth." And it was so. ¹⁶And God made the two great lights, the greater light to rule the day, and the lesser light to rule the night; he made the stars also. ¹⁷And God set them in the firmament of the heavens to give light upon the earth, ¹⁸ to rule over the day and over the night, and to separate the light from the darkness. And God saw that it was good. ¹⁹And there was evening and there was morning, a fourth day.

²⁰And God said, "Let the waters bring forth swarms of living creatures, and let birds fly above the earth across the firmament of the heavens." ²¹ So God created the great sea monsters and every living creature that moves, with which the waters swarm, according to their kinds, and every winged bird according to its kind. And God saw that it was good. ²²And God blessed them, saying, "Be fruitful and multiply and fill the waters in the seas, and let birds multiply on the earth." ²³And there was evening and there was morning, a fifth day.

²⁴And God said, "Let the earth bring forth living creatures according to their kinds: cattle and creeping things and beasts of the earth according to their kinds." And it was so. ²⁵And God made the beasts of the earth according to their kinds and the cattle according to their kinds, and everything that creeps upon the ground according to its kind. And God saw that it was good.

²⁶ Then God said, "Let us make man in our image, after our likeness; and let them have dominion over the fish of the sea, and over the birds of the air, and over the cattle, and over all the earth, and over every creeping thing that creeps upon the earth." ²⁷ So God created man in his own image, in the image of God he created him; male and female he created them. ²⁸And God blessed them, and God said to them, "Be fruitful and multiply, and fill the earth and subdue it; and have dominion over the fish of the sea and over the birds of the air and over every living thing that moves upon the earth." ²⁹And God said, "Behold, I have given you every plant yielding seed which is upon the face of all the earth, and every tree with seed in its fruit; you shall have them for food. ³⁰And to every beast of the earth, and to every bird of the air, and to everything that creeps on the earth, everything that has the breath of life, I have given every green plant for food." And it was so. ³¹And God saw everything that he had made, and behold, it was very good. And there was evening and there was morning, a sixth day.

2 Thus the heavens and the earth were

finished, and all the host of them. 2 And on the seventh day God finished his work which he had done, and he rested on the seventh day from all his work which he had done. 3 So God blessed the seventh day and hallowed it, because on it God rested from all his work which he had done in creation.

4 These are the generations of the heavens and the earth when they were created.

In the day that the LORD God made the earth and the heavens, 5 when no plant of the field was yet in the earth and no herb of the field had yet sprung up—for the LORD God had not caused it to rain upon the earth, and there was no man to till the ground; 6 but a mist went up from the earth and watered the whole face of the ground—7 then the LORD God formed man of dust from the ground, and breathed into his nostrils the breath of life; and man became a living being. 8 And the LORD God planted a garden in Eden, in the east; and there he put the man whom he had formed. 9 And out of the ground the LORD God made to grow every tree that is pleasant to the sight and good for food, the tree of life also in the midst of the garden, and the tree of the knowledge of good and evil. . . .

18 Then the LORD God said, "It is not good that the man should be alone; I will make him a helper fit for him." 19 So out of the ground the LORD God formed every beast of the field and every bird of the air, and brought them to the man to see what he would call them; and whatever the man called every living creature, that was its name. 20 The man gave names to all cattle, and to the birds of the air, and to every beast of the field; but for the man there was not found a helper fit for him. 21 So the LORD God caused a deep sleep to fall upon the man, and while he slept took one of his ribs and closed up its place with flesh; 22 and the rib which the LORD God had taken from the man he made into a woman and brought her to the man. 23 Then the man said,

"This at last is bone of my bones and
flesh of my flesh;
she shall be called Woman,
because she was taken out of Man."

24 Therefore a man leaves his father and his mother and cleaves to his wife, and they become one flesh. 25 And the man and his wife were both naked, and were not ashamed.

The early Hebrew, as the creation story suggests, saw the solitary individual as an incomplete person living in an abnormal situation. "It is not good that man should be alone" expresses a general maxim of Hebrew society which has a far wider significance than simply the institution of marriage. Man, in the proper sense of the term, was part of a family, a community, and a tribe. In fact, the distinction between man as individual and man as part of a community or representative of it was relatively unimportant, as was the distinction between body and soul.

> When we look at the soul, we always see a community rising behind it. What it is, it is by virtue of others. It has sprung up from a family which has filled it with its contents, and from which it can never grow away. The family forms the narrowest community in which it lives. But wherever it works, it must live in community, because it is its nature to communicate itself to others, to share blessing with them.[23]

Consequently, the individual and the community are seldom differentiated, a feature common to primitive societies. This tendency in

---

[23] Johannes Pedersen, *Israel: Its Life and Culture* (London: Oxford University Press, 1964), Vols. I–II, p. 263.

Hebrew thought to pass indiscriminately from the one to the many, to consider the individual as a group and the community as one, has been termed "corporate personality." The following selection indicates the importance of this concept and its relation to the Hebraic conceptions of God and man.

THE ONE AND THE MANY IN THE ISRAELITE CONCEPTION OF GOD
Aubrey R. Johnson[24]

One may say that man is thought to possess an indefinable "extension" of the personality which enables him to exercise a subtle influence for good or ill within the community. In its positive or beneficent aspect this power is known as "blessing," while in its negative or maleficent aspect the extended personality makes its influence felt as a "curse."

In this way the spoken word may be regarded as an effective "extension" of the personality. The obvious example is that of Isaac who, having once bestowed blessing upon Jacob, is unable to retract his words and nullify their effect in favour of the rightful recipient; once uttered they act creatively in quasi-material fashion.[25] Of course, as one learns from the same story, words vary in their range, so that it is not every word which may be regarded as a potent "extension" of the personality; everything depends upon the occasion, the degree of vital power possessed by the speaker, and the extent to which, as the English idiom has it, he puts his "soul" into what he says. Hence Isaac, having put his "soul" into bestowing blessing upon Jacob, can only express what is practically a curse over Esau.

The value ascribed to the word as a potent "extension" of the personality has a close parallel in the similar importance attached to the name; and here we meet one of the most widespread, as it has been one of the most lasting, conceptions of this kind. Thus to the Israelite, when the time comes for that dissolution of the personality which is known as death, it is in this particular "extension" that he may continue to live most powerfully. Hence the extermination of the name is regarded as the greatest disaster which can befall a man, and various measures are adopted to preserve his memory. The need of male offspring for this particular purpose finds typical expression in the legislation providing for the so-called levirate marriage, which lays down that, if a man should die childless, his wife

> shall not marry without unto a stranger: her husband's brother shall go in unto her and take her to him for a wife and enter into a levirate marriage with her; and the first male child she beareth shall maintain the name of his dead brother, so that his name may not be wiped out of Israel [Deut. 25: 5–6].

For the same reason Absalom set up a pillar in the neighbourhood of Jerusalem, it being expressly said that he adopted this method because he had no (surviving?) son to perpetuate his name. The same point of view is revealed by Bildad when he thus describes the ultimate fate of the wicked [Job 18: 17–18]:

> His memory doth perish from the earth;
> He hath no name abroad.

---

[24] Aubrey R. Johnson, *The One and the Many in the Israelite Conception of God* (2d ed.; Cardiff: University of Wales Press, 1961), pp. 2–17, 21–22, 27, 37. Quoted by permission of Professor Aubrey R. Johnson and the University of Wales Press Board.

[25] Genesis 27, where Jacob, disguised as his brother Esau, receives from his blind father Isaac the blessing reserved for the eldest son.

> He is driven from light into darkness;
>   He is chased out of the world.
> He hath neither offspring nor progeny among
>   his people;
> There is no survivor where he dwelt.

The last point serves to introduce an aspect of the Israelite conception of man which is of the first importance for the present study. It recalls the fact that (in a way wholly in line with the grasping of a totality) a man's personality is thought of as extending throughout his "house" or "household." The father, of course, is the head; and next in order of importance are alternatively the wife (or wives) and the sons, then the sons' wives and the daughters. . . . however, the strong solidarity felt to exist within such a social unit is also thought to extend to the whole of the property, so that the household in its entirety is regarded as a psychical whole—the extended personality of the man at its head.

One consequence of the importance attached in this way to members of one's household as "extensions" of the personality may be seen in that feature of Hebrew style which points to what may be called an oscillation as between the conception of the "lord" or "master" of the household, and that of a servant who (as such an "extension" of his master's personality) acts as his agent, notably as a "messenger." A case in point is to be found in the story of Joseph's dealings with his brethren in Egypt [Gen. 44: 4-9]:

> When they were gone out of the city, and were not yet far off, Joseph said unto his steward, Up, follow after the men; and when thou dost overtake them, say unto them, Wherefore have ye rewarded evil for good? Is not this it in which my lord drinketh, and whereby he indeed divineth? Ye have done evil in so doing. And he overtook them, and he spake unto them these words. And they said unto him, Wherefore speaketh my lord such words as these? Far be it from thy servants to do such a thing. Behold, the money, which we found in our sacks' mouth, we brought again unto thee out of the land of Canaan: how then should we steal out of thy lord's house silver or gold? With whomsoever of thy servants it be found, let him die, and we also will be *my lord's servants*.

The last reference, as one would expect and as the sequel shows, must virtually be to Joseph, although the words are addressed to his steward; but the steward himself, as the "extension" of his lord's personality, is able to say (in the name of Joseph, so to speak) [Gen. 44: 10]:

> Now also let it be according unto your words: he with whom it is found shall be *my* servant; and ye shall be blameless.

Through the agency of his steward Joseph is regarded as being present—"in person." In short, the "messenger," as an "extension" of his master's personality, not merely represents but *is* virtually the "lord."

In the same way any part of a man's property is thought to form an "extension" of the personality. Hence, when Elisha sent his servant Gehazi ahead with his staff, which was to be the particular instrument for restoring the Shunammite's son to life, he warned him against bestowing blessing upon anyone whom he might meet. In carrying the staff Gehazi would be bearing some of Elisha's forceful personality; and accordingly he was to preserve this power intact and not run the risk of weakening it, or even losing it altogether, by bestowing it rashly upon those for whom it was not intended. This instance, no doubt, is somewhat exceptional; but that is because Elisha was an exceptionally powerful person. In varying degree the same principle holds good of any individual, so that the bestowal of a gift is nothing less than a sharing of one's personality. Thus a gift is sometimes called a "blessing"—and inevitably so, for it involves a transference of one's vital power quite as much as, and perhaps more than, the spoken word. . . .

Accordingly, in Israelite thought the individual, as a centre of power capable of indefinite extension, is never a mere isolated unit; he lives in constant reaction toward others. Moreover, the latter fall into two classes, those with whom he is close-knit within the sphere of the social unit as his extended or larger "self" and those who are outside this sphere: and here again one may see evidence of the grasping of totality, for from first to last in the work of those different schools of thought which did so much to mould the Hebrew Scriptures the conception of the social unit is dominated by that of kinship. . . .

The nucleus of the social unit or kin-group is the household, which (as already observed) is a psychical whole representing the extended personality of the man at its head. Nevertheless, kinship extends far beyond the borders of the household; and wherever it is recognized there is the recognition of a psychical whole. . . .

The social unit or kin-group, however widely conceived, is a single *nephesh* or "person"—albeit what H. Wheeler Robinson has designated a "corporate personality." Thus the dissatisfaction of the Israelites during the period of the Wandering is expressed by saying that the *nephesh* of this people grew impatient; and they are represented as voicing their impatience thus: "Our *nephesh* is sick of this cursed food!" Examples of this kind, which may be multiplied, serve to explain the fact that any association of individuals suggestive of homogeneity . . . may be treated as a kin-group forming a single *nephesh* or corporate personality.

In the light of such examples one can understand the attractiveness of the theory (so liable to over-emphasis) that "the narratives of Genesis present us, not with real, historical personages, but with personifications." So, too, it is little wonder that the attempt has been made to interpret the "I" of many of the Psalms in terms of such collective units.

Further, it may be noticed in passing that this point of view is not peculiar to the Hebrew records; it appears also in the Tell el-Amarna tablets in a letter sent by the city of Irkata to the Pharaoh, thus:

> This tablet is the tablet of Irkata. To the king, our lord, thus (saith) Irkata and the people of her . . . (?): At the feet of the king, our lord, seven times seven times do we fall. To our lord, the sun, thus (saith) Irkata: Let the heart of the king, the lord, know that we guard Irkata for h(i)m. . . .
>
> May the king, our lord, hearken to the words of his faithful servants, and give a present to his servant, while our enemies look on and eat dust!

The parallel with the foregoing passages from the Hebrew records is so close that this letter might not seem to require further comment. Nevertheless the tablet is of additional interest in that it introduces another aspect of the conception of the social unit which is of the first importance in the present connexion. This appears in the last sentence given above, i.e.:

> May the king, our lord, hearken to the words of his faithful *servants*, and give a present to his *servant*, while our enemies look on and eat dust!

Here there is obvious indication of an oscillation in the mind of the writer according as he thinks of the social unit in question as an association of individuals (and thus uses the plural "servants") or as a corporate personality (and thus uses the singular "servant"); and such oscillation with regard to the social unit may frequently be found in Israelite thought. This appears most clearly, perhaps, in the colourful account of the Israelites' attempt to pass through Edom on their way to the Promised Land. It runs thus [Num. 20: 14–21]:

> And Moses sent messengers from Kadesh to the king of Edom: Thus saith thy brother Israel. Thou knowest all the trouble that hath befallen us: how our fathers went down to Egypt, and we dwelt in Egypt many days, and the Egyptians maltreated us and our fathers; and when we cried unto Yahweh, He heard our voice, and sent a Messenger (*or* Angel), and brought us forth out of Egypt; and, behold, we are in Kadesh, a city on the border of thy territory. Prithee, let us pass through thy land. We will not pass through field or through vineyard; neither will we drink well-water. We will go along the king's way; we will not turn aside to the right hand nor to the left, until we pass through thy territory. And Edom said to him: Thou shalt not pass through me, lest I come out with the sword against thee. And the children of Israel said unto him: *We will go up by the highway; and, if we drink thy water, I and my cattle, then I will give the price thereof: only ('tis nothing!) let me pass through on my feet.* And he said: Thou shalt not pass through. And Edom came out to meet him with a weighty company and with a strong hand. Thus Edom refused to allow Israel to pass through his territory, and Israel turned away without troubling him further (*lit.* from upon him).

Here the oscillation in thought between the conception of the social unit as an association of individuals (with the resultant use of plural forms) and as a corporate personality (with the consequent use of the singular) is unmistakable. Of course, we sometimes betray a similar oscillation when we have occasion, for example, to think of a committee; but our thinking is not so dominated by this point of view as that of the Israelites seems to have been....

We may now apply something of what we know concerning the Israelite conception of man to an elucidation of the corresponding conception of God.

In the earliest portions of the Hebrew Scriptures, ... Yahweh is conceived in strongly anthropomorphic fashion; and this has its counterpart in those continued anthropopathic references, in which psychical functions of an emotional, volitional, or an intellectual kind are ascribed to Yahweh, as when He is said to be compassionate and merciful, to love and to hate, to be angry—and so on. We must notice at once, however, a distinction of the first importance between the conception of man and that of God: for we may not say of the latter (as was said of the former) that psychical functions have a physical basis; or, at least, we may not do this and, at the same time, give the term "physical" the same content in each case. Thus even in the earliest records Yahweh, though undoubtedly pictured in the form of a man, was nevertheless thought of as a Being of a different substance from the latter. In fact, it seems that He was normally conceived ... in terms of a light and rarefied substance best explained as "like fire." ... Yahweh, like the heavenly forces under His control, differs from mankind as being of a more rarefied substance "like fire"—in short, "Spirit," a term which is reserved in the case of man (at least in the early period) to describe the more vigorous manifestations of life on his part, especially such as might be attributed to the influence of the Godhead. This being the case (and provided that we are careful to define our terms), we must say that, so far as the conception of God was concerned, psychical functions had a "spiritual" rather than a physical basis.

However, this is not all; for here we may remind ourselves that in Israelite thought, while man was conceived, not in some analytical fashion as "soul" and "body," but synthetically as a psychical whole and a unit of vital power, this power was found to reach far beyond the contour of the body and to make itself felt through indefinable "extensions" of the personality. Now the same idea is quite clearly present in the conception of the Godhead....

We have already touched upon the fact that any manifestation of unusual vigour which marked a man out as an exceptionally powerful personality . . . might be attributed to the influence of the "Spirit" of Yahweh; but, clearly, such examples must be understood in terms of the "Spirit" as an "Extension" of Yahweh's Personality. Thus, even in such cases as those in which the "Spirit" of Yahweh is said to have "donned" Gideon (like a garment)[26] or to have "rushed" upon Samson or upon Saul, it may hardly be said to have been regarded as an impersonal force. This is important in view of the fact that . . . there is only one certain instance in the Hebrew Scriptures in which the "Spirit" is *clearly* personalized. The instance in question is that of the "spirit" who, in Micaiah's vision, proposed to be a lying or deceptive "spirit" in the mouth of all Ahab's prophets. In the light of the Israelite conception of man, however, it would seem that this "spirit," as a member of Yahweh's heavenly Court (or "Household!"), should be thought of as an individualization within

[26] For the story of Gideon see Chapter 3, pp. 95–100.

the corporate "Spirit" of Yahweh's extended Personality; in other words, that we must be prepared to recognize for the Godhead just such fluidity of reference from the One to the Many or from the Many to the One as we have already noticed in the case of man. . . .

God is thought of in terms similar to those of man as possessing an indefinable extension of the Personality which enables Him to exercise a mysterious influence upon mankind. In its creative aspect this appears as "blessing"; in its destructive aspect it makes itself felt as a "curse."

Thus it is that (again as in the case of man) the "Word" may be regarded as a potent "Extension" of Yahweh's Personality. Not to spend too much time upon this point, we may remind ourselves of the familiar passage [Isa. 55:10–11]:

> As the rain cometh down
> > And the snow from heaven,
> And returneth not thither,
> > But watereth the earth,
> And maketh it bring forth and bud,
> > That it may give seed to the sower and bread to the eater,
> So shall My "Word" be that goeth forth out of My Mouth;
> > It shall not return unto Me void,
> But it shall perform that which I please,
> > And succeed in that whereto I sent it.

These lines reflect that primitive and widespread conception of the power of the spoken word which lies behind so many magical practices; and there is good reason to believe that, so far as the prophets in general were concerned, this conception was often something more than mere poetical imagery. In fact, it is wholly in line with those magical ideas which have rightly been recognized as lying behind their so-called symbolism. The "Word" is one with the "thing" which is to be performed; it has objective reality, and thus forms a powerful "Extension" of the divine Personality.

In the same way the "Name" is an important "Extension" of Yahweh's Personality analogous to that which is observable in the case of man. Thus it is that a knowledge of the "Name" is a matter of ritual importance. . . .

In considering the Israelite conception of man . . . one seems driven to ask the question . . . as to whether we should not . . . be prepared to recognize possible traces [in the Godhead] of that very wide "Extension" of the Personality which would embrace the social unit—conceived either as an association of what we should call individuals or as a corporate personality.

There seems to be no gainsaying the fact that at one time in Israel . . . Yahweh was worshipped as a member, albeit the chief member, of a Pantheon. . . .[27]

When we find an oscillation as between the One and the Many in the Israelite conception of Yahweh, we should be prepared to interpret it in this light. . . .

This point may be concluded by simply referring to such passages as [Gen. 3:22; 11:5-7; Isa. 6:8]:

> And Yahweh God said, Behold, the man is become *as one of Us,* to know good and evil.
> And Yahweh came down to see the city and the tower, which the children of men built. And Yahweh said, Behold, they are one people, and they have all one language; and this is what they begin to do: and now nothing will be withholden from them, which they purpose to do. Go to, let *Us* go down, and let *Us* there confound their language.
> And I heard the voice of the Lord saying: Whom shall *I* send, and who will go for *Us*?

. . . We have here a point of view which needs to be borne in mind as an aid to the solution of, not only textual and literary problems, but even more those problems which are associated with the attempt to employ such terms as "polytheism" and "monotheism" in connexion with Israelite thought, and also those which are inherent in the question of the prophetic psychology or, again, that of revelation. It may also be argued that along this line we gain a new approach to the New Testament extension of Jewish Monotheism in the direction of the later Trinitarianism. This is apparent already in . . . the discussion of the "Spirit" . . . .

We can see how it was possible for a Jewish Christian to relate his Messiah so closely with the divine Being as to afford a basis for the later (and Greek) metaphysical formulation of the doctrine of the Trinity.

---

[27] [Whether this preceded the Exodus or was adopted from Canaanite culture after the settlement in Palestine is difficult to determine.]

The oscillation between the one and the many, whether it be expressed as an individual representing or embodying a group or as a group conceived of as one individual personality, is a basic presupposition not only for the religious concepts of ancient Israel but for the ethical concepts as well. It is this communal foundation for the Hebrew ethic that will be explored in the next chapter.

STUDY QUESTIONS

1. What is religion and how is it equipped to answer questions of ultimate concern? Does it perform a function in society that cannot be handled by philosophy or science?

2. How does the religious use of symbols differ from symbolic action in other areas of life?

3. What is the function of religious cult, or ritual?

4. In what ways did the religious conceptions of the early Hebrews effectively meet the ultimate questions facing them?

5. How can the same event be interpreted in a religious and in a nonreligious way? Is not the "miraculous" nature of the crossing of the "Red Sea," for example, *proof* that God was acting there, proof that should have convinced the Egyptians as much as it did the Israelites? If, on the other hand, one removes the miraculous element and makes the crossing only a natural event which was fortunately timed for the Israelites, does that not mean that they were mistaken in their belief that Yahweh had acted in that event?

6. Is religious belief based on the historicity of miracles (that is, the belief that supernatural events have indeed happened in the past), or do the elements of miracle follow from the affirmation of belief?

7. In what respects does early Hebrew society express a primitive worldview?

8. What areas of Hebrew thought and religion might be affected by the concept of "corporate personality"?

9. To what degree did the social structure and psychology of the early Hebrews affect their concept of God?

For those who have used The Contribution of Ancient Greece *edited by Jacqueline Strain:*

10. In what ways did the Hebraic understanding of the relationship between God and nature differ from that of the Greeks in the Homeric era, from that of the Ionian philosophers of the sixth century B.C., and from that of Plato and Aristotle? How does one account for these differences?

11. How does the Hebrew concept of the soul and death compare with that of prearchaic Greece?

CHAPTER 2

THE ORIGINS OF HEBREW MORALITY:
The Covenant at Mount Sinai

The origin of the prohibitions [contained in the Ten Commandments] is to be found in the Semitic clan-association, and . . . they were the authoritative commandments of the elders of the clan or the family, though they do not receive their authority so much from the individual power of these figures as from the sanctified order which they represent.

> M. E. Andrew in J. J. Stamm and M. E. Andrew, The Ten Commandments in Recent Research ("*Studies in Biblical Theology,*" *2d series, no. 2; London: SCM Press, 1967), p. 50.*

From the ancient Hebrews, we in twentieth-century North America have received a heritage transmitted largely through the Old Testament. With specific reference to the family this heritage includes the traditions of male dominance, respect for women of one's own group and class, the command to "honor thy father and thy mother," pride in a patrilineal family tree, a double standard of sex morals, and some definitions and rules pertaining to incest and sexual perversions. Of course these culture traits have not come down to us unchanged, nor can we attribute them exclusively to the ancient Hebrews. Nevertheless there is a continuity which cannot be ignored and which helps to account for some aspects of the family patterns of contemporary North America.

> *Stuart A. Queen and Robert W. Habenstein,* The Family in Various Cultures *(3rd ed., New York: J. B. Lippincott Company, 1967), pp. 138–139. By permission of the publishers.*

Since about the year 1500, society has increasingly come to conform to the pattern which . . . could . . . be described as atomistic or individualistic. The individual is regarded as the prime reality, society as merely a secondary phenomenon. But the basic conceptions of the Old Testament, or at any rate of the five Books of Moses, are rooted in, and the product of, the communal way of life under which, as Aristotle has classically expressed it, the whole is prior to the parts—under which, in other words, society is regarded as the prime reality, and the individual is merely a secondary phenomenon. The two social systems are so contrary to each other, and the forms of thought and feeling respectively belonging to them so antagonistic, that the discrepancy between the old doctrine and the new world and world-view was bound to be felt, and felt with increasing urgency. Indeed, it is not too much to say that under the changed conditions, the ethic of Genesis and Exodus was very widely experienced as downright unethical.

Werner Stark, "The Sociology of Knowledge and the Problem of Ethics," Transactions of the Fourth World Congress of Sociology, Milan, 1959 (Louvain, 1961), Vol. IV, p. 86.

The escape of the Israelites from Egyptian slavery, described in the last chapter, was only the first act of a three-part drama that Israel remembered as "the Exodus" and relived in an annual liturgical ceremony. The second act of the drama was the creation at Mount Sinai of the covenant between the Israelites and Yahweh that henceforth became the foundation for Hebrew law and morality. The third and final act—the conquest of Palestine—was simply the fulfillment of Yahweh's promise, implicit in the call of Moses and explicit in the prologue to the Ten Commandments.

Popular memory often focused on the victorious battle scenes of the first and last acts, on the great deeds of Yahweh on behalf of his people, as the following liturgical résumé from Deuteronomy suggests:

> . . . And the Egyptians treated us harshly, and afflicted us, and laid upon us hard bondage. Then we cried to the Lord God of our fathers, and the Lord heard our voice, and saw our affliction, our toil, and our oppression: and the Lord brought us out of Egypt with a mighty hand and an outstretched arm, with great terror, with signs and wonders; and he brought us into this place and gave us this land, a land flowing with milk and honey.[1]

However, it was the second act that was of crucial importance to Israel and that was expanded throughout the following centuries by priest and prophet. For it was in the wilderness of Sinai, before the "mountain of the Lord," that Israel became a nation and obligated herself to a particular religious belief and moral system. The laws and customs of the ancient Hebrews were assumed under and given moral force by the covenant at Sinai, thus receiving a religious justification. Since this interdependence of religion and morality is not common to all societies, it may be well to examine more closely the relationship of religion to ethics and morals. The following selection is a careful attempt by a contemporary sociologist to do this.

The Relationship of Religion and Morality
J. Milton Yinger[2]

Several generalizations emerge in the study of the relationship of religion and morality. It is possible and desirable to define them in independent terms and to separate them analytically. Their origins, their causes, their internal variations, and their relationships to society and culture can be studied separately. At the same

[1] The Bible, Deut. 26:6–9.

[2] Reprinted with permission of The Macmillan Company from *Religion, Society and the Individual* by J. Milton Yinger. © by The Macmillan Company 1957, pp. 28–31.

time, it is vastly clear that they are interdependent in most times and places. There are many types of relationship, with widely varying consequences. There is no clear-cut line between moral codes and religious prescriptions, for they may be identical, mutually reenforcing, entirely distinct, or antithetical. The religious idea of "sin" is not synonymous with the moral idea of "wrong," for the former implies a supra-social norm (as well, perhaps, as a social norm) while the latter implies only evil social results. Yet a given act may fall under both proscriptions.

One cannot clearly establish an evolutionary line from a religion without moral concern, to one where moral questions are found, although subsidiary, to a situation where morality is the central question of religion, to a supposed final situation where religion has vanished and only a moral system remains. This pattern overlooks their separate quality, stemming from distinctive needs and problems. In theological terms, religion is concerned with "is-ness," morality with "ought-ness." Morality seeks, for example, to control conditions that lead to death—to prohibit cruelty and murder, to reduce sources of illness and hunger. Religion seeks to help one to adjust to the fact of death. Morality is concerned with the relationship of man to man; religion is concerned with the relationship of man to some higher power or idea, sometimes, but not always, in addition to the moral concern. Even a purely naturalistic and humanistic religion is not to be equated with a moral code, although it doubtless will have fewer norms that are unrelated or antithetical to existing moral codes, for it is basically concerned with the development of a satisfying response to that which *is* in human existence.

These statements are largely, of course, matters of definition. It is the contention of the author that such analytic separation of religion and morals, however much they may be empirically related, is necessary to adequate study and particularly to the explanation of the wide variety of relationships. The distinction cannot be based on differences in prescribed rules of conduct, for religion, morality, and law may require the same acts; although some deeds may involve only one of the sanctions. The distinction is in terms of the authority and the sanctions that are attached to the codes.

Disagreements concerning the relationship of morality and religion have arisen from the failure to see that we need not choose between two opposite theories. It is not necessary to say, either that they are aspects of one system, or that they are entirely separate. The evolutionary theorists, in their belief that there was a progressive development toward ethical monotheism, tended to describe the religious and moral codes of primitive societies in separate terms. As knowledge of primitive religions grew, it became clear that there were many types of relationship with morals. In particular, the belief that they were sharply distinct, that only the "higher religions" had an ethical content, was shown to be inadequate. . . .

Malinowski and other functionalists have swung the pendulum to the other extreme from the conception that morality and religion are separate. . . . Seeking for conclusions concerning "the nature of religion in general," Malinowski declares:

> Myth, ritual, and ethics are definitely but three facets of the same essential fact. . . . Take away from the natives the belief in the reality of their sacred lore, destroy their sense of the spirit world as it exists and acts upon

them, and you will undermine their whole moral outlook.[3]

It is highly desirable to call attention to the functional interconnections of morals and religion, but the evidence does not support the proposition that one type of relationship is characteristic of "the nature of religion in general." In a broad sense, since they are aspects of a socio-cultural *system*, they can be thought of as "facets of the same essential fact." They cannot exist together in society without mutually influencing each other. The morals of a society are often reenforced by the claim that they are supported by divine sanctions; and the conceptions of the gods are frequently affected by associating them with the moral qualities most admired. This should not obscure, however, the separate needs, patterns, and functions that may be involved.

A glance at ancient Greece and Judaism reveals the possibilities of different patterns of relationship. The law of Moses, in early Hebraic religion, is a combination of rules of ritual, prescribed beliefs, and moral requirements. In this tradition, religion is a source and a sustainer of morality. "We see that even in its rudest form Religion was a moral force, the powers that men revered were on the side of social order and moral law; and the fear of the gods was a motive to enforce the laws of society, which were also the laws of morality."[4] This relationship became ever closer in the later development of Judaism. In the work of the eighth century prophets, and after, the dualism was reduced to a minimum.

[3] Bronislaw Malinowski, *The Foundations of Faith and Morals* (London: Oxford University Press, 1936), pp. 25–26.

[4] W. Robertson Smith, *Lectures on the Religion of the Semites* (3d ed.; London: A. & C. Black, Ltd., 1927), p. 53.

The religious life and the moral life became as nearly identical as in any major religion. This is, of course, the primary source of the Christian approach to this question. . . .

In Ancient Greece, there was a sharper separation of morality and religion. When Socrates, Plato, Aristotle, and most of the other philosophers sought to discover the nature of moral obligation, the source of the distinction between right and wrong, they did not relate their answer to a religious system [but to the political order]. The differences among them are less important in this connection than the common perspective that morality is to be discussed in human and social terms. Greek religion, on the other hand, was primarily concerned with the frightening aspects of individual life and death, not with moral obligation and community need. . . .

The moral code of the Hebrews, unlike that of the Greeks, was almost totally infused with religious conceptions. This is reflected in the fact that the laws governing the life of Israel, regardless of their date of origin, are placed in the Biblical account between the giving of the law at Sinai and the conquest of Palestine, many of them recorded as direct pronouncements spoken by Yahweh to Moses. The law, for the Israelites, was of divine origin; it consisted of obligations based on a covenant initiated by Yahweh and accepted by the Israelites in return for being "purchased" from slavery. Henceforth they were bound to Yahweh as "his people," redeemed slaves, who were consequently obligated to obey Yahweh's will, a will set forth in the commandments of the law.

The Israelites, therefore, saw the covenant as a product of Yahweh's initiative.

[Yahweh] was believed to have freely chosen this particular group for Himself and to require from it a fidelity doubtless crude and limited enough in detail, but moral in spirit. Yahweh was forever "the out-of-Egypt bringing God" (as a German might phrase it); Israel was the chosen people, linked to him by no quasi-physical tie such as that of a nature-God, but by a moral act. It was this relation which (under changing forms and details of expression) underlay the covenant of Yahweh with his people. The relation of moral obligation as well as of feeling has a special name (*chesed*) in Hebrew, which is inadequately translated as "loving-kindness." It means much the same as *agápē* in the New Testament. Observe that the covenant is with the nation, not with the individual Israelites except as members or representatives of the nation. Throughout the whole period of the Old Testament, this covenant with the "corporate personality" of Israel . . . remains the all-inclusive fact and factor, whatever the increase in the consciousness of individuality.[5]

The covenant and the moral laws included within it occupy the central section of the Book of Exodus. The following selection contains the giving of the law and the sealing of the covenant. Once again the multiple accounts are reflected in the breaks in continuity and the conflicting versions of how close the elders and Aaron (representing the priesthood) were permitted to approach Yahweh.

LAW AND COVENANT AT MOUNT SINAI[6]

19 On the third new moon after the people of Israel had gone forth out of the land of Egypt, on that day they came into the wilderness of Sinai. 2 And when they set out from Reph′idim and came into the wilderness of Sinai, they encamped in the wilderness; and there Israel encamped before the mountain. 3 And Moses went up to God, and the LORD called him out of the mountain, saying, "Thus you shall say to the house of Jacob, and tell the people of Israel: 4 You have seen what I did to the Egyptians, and how I bore you on eagles' wings and brought you to myself. 5 Now therefore, if you will obey my voice and keep my covenant, you shall be my own possession among all peoples; for all the earth is mine, 6 and you shall be to me a kingdom of priests and a holy nation. These are the words which you shall speak to the children of Israel."

7 So Moses came and called the elders of the people, and set before them all these words which the LORD had commanded him. 8 And all the people answered together and said, "All that the LORD has spoken we will do." And Moses reported the words of the people to the LORD. 9 And the LORD said to Moses, "Lo, I am coming to you in a thick cloud, that the people may hear when I speak with you, and may also believe you for ever."

Then Moses told the words of the people to the LORD. 10 And the LORD said to Moses, "Go to the people and consecrate them today and tomorrow, and let them wash their garments, 11 and be ready by the third day; for on the third day the LORD will come down upon Mount Sinai in the sight of all the people. 12 And you shall set bounds for the people round about, saying, 'Take heed that you do not go up into the mountain or touch the border of it; whoever touches the mountain shall be put to death; 13 no hand shall touch him, but he shall be stoned or shot; whether beast or man, he shall not live.' When the trumpet sounds a long blast, they shall come up to the mountain." 14 So Moses went down from the mountain to the people, and consecrated the people;

---

[5] H. Wheeler Robinson, *Corporate Personality in Ancient Israel* (Philadelphia: Fortress Press, 1964), p. 26.

[6] The Bible, Exod. 19:1–24:11.

This mountain of red granite near the tip of the Sinai Peninsula has been traditionally regarded as Mount Sinai or Mount Horeb. (The Matson Photo Service, Alhambra, California)

and they washed their garments. ¹⁵And he said to the people, "Be ready by the third day; do not go near a woman."

¹⁶ On the morning of the third day there were thunders and lightnings, and a thick cloud upon the mountain, and a very loud trumpet blast, so that all the people who were in the camp trembled. ¹⁷ Then Moses brought the people out of the camp to meet God; and they took their stand at the foot of the mountain. ¹⁸And Mount Sinai was wrapped in smoke, because the LORD descended upon it in fire; and the smoke of it went up like the smoke of a kiln, and the whole mountain quaked greatly. ¹⁹And as the sound of the trumpet grew louder and louder, Moses spoke, and God answered him in thunder. ²⁰And the LORD came down upon Mount Sinai, to the top of the mountain; and the LORD called Moses to the top of the mountain, and Moses went up. ²¹And the LORD said to Moses, "Go down and warn the people, lest they break through to the LORD to gaze and many of them perish. ²²And also let the priests who come near to the LORD consecrate themselves, lest the LORD break out upon them." ²³And Moses said to the LORD, "The people cannot come up to Mount Sinai; for thou thyself didst charge us, saying, 'Set bounds about the mountain, and consecrate it.'" ²⁴And the LORD said to him, "Go down, and come up bringing Aaron with you; but do not let the priests and the people break through to come up to the LORD, lest he break out against them." ²⁵ So Moses went down to the people and told them.

20 And God spoke all these words, saying,

² "I am the LORD your God, who brought you out of the land of Egypt, out of the house of bondage.

³ "You shall have no other gods before me.

⁴ "You shall not make yourself a graven image, or any likeness of anything that is in heaven above, or that is in the earth beneath, or that is in the water under the earth; ⁵ you shall not bow down to them or serve them; for I the LORD your God am a jealous God, visiting the iniquity of the fathers upon the children to the third and the fourth generation of those who hate me, ⁶ but showing steadfast love to thousands of those who love me and keep my commandments.

⁷ "You shall not take the name of the LORD your God in vain; for the LORD will not hold him guiltless who takes his name in vain.

⁸ "Remember the sabbath day, to keep it holy. ⁹Six days you shall labor, and do all your work; ¹⁰ but the seventh day is a sabbath to the LORD your God; in it you shall not do any work, you, or your son, or your daughter, your manservant, or your maidservant, or your cattle, or the sojourner who is within your gates; ¹¹ for in six days the LORD made heaven and earth, the sea, and all that is in them, and rested the seventh day; therefore the LORD blessed the sabbath day and hallowed it.

¹² "Honor your father and your mother, that your days may be long in the land which the LORD your God gives you.

¹³ "You shall not kill.

¹⁴ "You shall not commit adultery.

¹⁵ "You shall not steal.

¹⁶ "You shall not bear false witness against your neighbor.

¹⁷ "You shall not covet your neighbor's house; you shall not covet your neighbor's wife, or his manservant, or his maidservant, or his ox, or his ass, or anything that is your neighbor's."

18 Now when all the people perceived the thunderings and the lightnings and the sound of the trumpet and the mountain smoking, the people were afraid and trembled; and they stood afar off, 19 and said to Moses, "You speak to us, and we will hear; but let not God speak to us, lest we die." 20 And Moses said to the people, "Do not fear; for God has come to prove you, and that the fear of him may be before your eyes, that you may not sin."

21 And the people stood afar off, while Moses drew near to the thick cloud where God was. 22 And the LORD said to Moses, "Thus you shall say to the people of Israel: 'You have seen for yourselves that I have talked with you from heaven. 23 You shall not make gods of silver to be with me, nor shall you make for yourselves gods of gold. 24 An altar of earth you shall make for me and sacrifice on it your burnt offerings and your peace offerings, your sheep and your oxen; in every place where I cause my name to be remembered I will come to you and bless you. 25 And if you make me an altar of stone, you shall not build it of hewn stones; for if you wield your tool upon it you profane it. 26 And you shall not go up by steps to my altar, that your nakedness be not exposed on it.'

21 "Now these are the ordinances which you shall set before them. 2 When you buy a Hebrew slave, he shall serve six years, and in the seventh he shall go out free, for nothing. 3 If he comes in single, he shall go out single; if he comes in married, then his wife shall go out with him. 4 If his master gives him a wife and she bears him sons or daughters, the wife and her children shall be her master's and he shall go out alone. 5 But if the slave plainly says, 'I love my master, my wife, and my children; I will not go out free,' 6 then his master shall bring him to God, and he shall bring him to the door or the doorpost; and his master shall bore his ear through with an awl; and he shall serve him for life.

7 "When a man sells his daughter as a slave, she shall not go out as the male slaves do. 8 If she does not please her master, who has designated her for himself, then he shall let her be redeemed; he shall have no right to sell her to a foreign people, since he has dealt faithlessly with her. 9 If he designates her for his son, he shall deal with her as with a daughter. 10 If he takes another wife to himself, he shall not diminish her food, her clothing, or her marital rights. 11 And if he does not do these three things for her, she shall go out for nothing, without payment of money.

12 "Whoever strikes a man so that he dies shall be put to death. 13 But if he did not lie in wait for him, but God let him fall into his hand, then I will appoint for you a place to which he may flee. 14 But if a man willfully attacks another to kill him treacherously, you shall take him from my altar, that he may die.

15 "Whoever strikes his father or his mother shall be put to death.

16 "Whoever steals a man, whether he sells him or is found in possession of him, shall be put to death.

17 "Whoever curses his father or his mother shall be put to death.

18 "When men quarrel and one strikes the other with a stone or with his fist and the man does not die but keeps his bed, 19 then if the man rises again and walks abroad with his staff, he that struck him shall be clear; only he shall pay for the loss of his time, and shall have him thoroughly healed.

20 "When a man strikes his slave, male or female, with a rod and the slave dies under his hand, he shall be punished.

The Origins of Hebrew Morality

21 But if the slave survives a day or two, he is not to be punished; for the slave is his money.

22 "When men strive together, and hurt a woman with child, so that there is a miscarriage, and yet no harm follows, the one who hurt her shall be fined, according as the woman's husband shall lay upon him; and he shall pay as the judges determine. 23 If any harm follows, then you shall give life for life, 24 eye for eye, tooth for tooth, hand for hand, foot for foot, 25 burn for burn, wound for wound, stripe for stripe.

26 "When a man strikes the eye of his slave, male or female, and destroys it, he shall let the slave go free for the eye's sake. 27 If he knocks out the tooth of his slave, male or female, he shall let the slave go free for the tooth's sake.

28 "When an ox gores a man or a woman to death, the ox shall be stoned, and its flesh shall not be eaten; but the owner of the ox shall be clear. 29 But if the ox has been accustomed to gore in the past, and its owner has been warned but has not kept it in, and it kills a man or a woman, the ox shall be stoned, and its owner also shall be put to death. 30 If a ransom is laid on him, then he shall give for the redemption of his life whatever is laid upon him. 31 If it gores a man's son or daughter, he shall be dealt with according to this same rule. 32 If the ox gores a slave, male or female, the owner shall give to their master thirty shekels of silver, and the ox shall be stoned.

33 "When a man leaves a pit open, or when a man digs a pit and does not cover it, and an ox or an ass falls into it, 34 the owner of the pit shall make it good; he shall give money to its owner, and the dead beast shall be his.

35 "When one man's ox hurts another's, so that it dies, then they shall sell the live ox and divide the price of it; and the dead beast also they shall divide. 36 Or if it is known that the ox has been accustomed to gore in the past, and its owner has not kept it in, he shall pay ox for ox, and the dead beast shall be his.

22 "If a man steals an ox or a sheep, and kills it or sells it, he shall pay five oxen for an ox, and four sheep for a sheep. He shall make restitution; if he has nothing, then he shall be sold for his theft. 4 If the stolen beast is found alive in his possession, whether it is an ox or an ass or a sheep, he shall pay double.

2 "If a thief is found breaking in, and is struck so that he dies, there shall be no bloodguilt for him; 3 but if the sun has risen upon him, there shall be bloodguilt for him.

5 "When a man causes a field or vineyard to be grazed over, or lets his beast loose and it feeds in another man's field, he shall make restitution from the best in his own field and in his own vineyard.

6 "When fire breaks out and catches in thorns so that the stacked grain or the standing grain or the field is consumed, he that kindled the fire shall make full restitution.

7 "If a man delivers to his neighbor money or goods to keep, and it is stolen out of the man's house, then, if the thief is found, he shall pay double. 8 If the thief is not found, the owner of the house shall come near to God, to show whether or not he has put his hand to his neighbor's goods.

9 "For every breach of trust, whether it is for ox, for ass, for sheep, for clothing, or for any kind of lost thing, of which one says, 'This is it,' the case of both parties shall come before God; he whom God shall condemn shall pay double to his neighbor.

10 "If a man delivers to his neighbor an ass or an ox or a sheep or any beast to keep,

and it dies or is hurt or is driven away, without any one seeing it, 11 an oath by the Lord shall be between them both to see whether he has not put his hand to his neighbor's property; and the owner shall accept the oath, and he shall not make restitution. 12 But if it is stolen from him, he shall make restitution to its owner. 13 If it is torn by beasts, let him bring it as evidence; he shall not make restitution for what has been torn.

14 "If a man borrows anything of his neighbor, and it is hurt or dies, the owner not being with it, he shall make full restitution. 15 If the owner was with it, he shall not make restitution; if it was hired, it came for its hire.

16 "If a man seduces a virgin who is not betrothed, and lies with her, he shall give the marriage present for her, and make her his wife. 17 If her father utterly refuses to give her to him, he shall pay money equivalent to the marriage present for virgins.

18 "You shall not permit a sorceress to live.

19 "Whoever lies with a beast shall be put to death.

20 "Whoever sacrifices to any god, save to the Lord only, shall be utterly destroyed.

21 "You shall not wrong a stranger or oppress him, for you were strangers in the land of Egypt. 22 You shall not afflict any widow or orphan. 23 If you do afflict them, and they cry out to me, I will surely hear their cry; 24 and my wrath will burn, and I will kill you with the sword, and your wives shall become widows and your children fatherless.

25 "If you lend money to any of my people with you who is poor, you shall not be to him as a creditor, and you shall not exact interest from him. 26 If ever you take your neighbor's garment in pledge, you shall restore it to him before the sun goes down; 27 for that is his only covering, it is his mantle for his body; in what else shall he sleep? And if he cries to me, I will hear, for I am compassionate.

28 "You shall not revile God, nor curse a ruler of your people.

29 "You shall not delay to offer from the fulness of your harvest and from the outflow of your presses.

"The first-born of your sons you shall give to me. 30 You shall do likewise with your oxen and with your sheep: seven days it shall be with its dam; on the eighth day you shall give it to me.

31 "You shall be men consecrated to me; therefore you shall not eat any flesh that is torn by beasts in the field; you shall cast it to the dogs.

23 "You shall not utter a false report. You shall not join hands with a wicked man, to be a malicious witness. 2 You shall not follow a multitude to do evil; nor shall you bear witness in a suit, turning aside after a multitude, so as to pervert justice; 3 nor shall you be partial to a poor man in his suit.

4 "If you meet your enemy's ox or his ass going astray, you shall bring it back to him. 5 If you see the ass of one who hates you lying under its burden, you shall refrain from leaving him with it, you shall help him to lift it up.

6 "You shall not pervert the justice due to your poor in his suit. 7 Keep far from a false charge, and do not slay the innocent and righteous, for I will not acquit the wicked. 8 And you shall take no bribe, for a bribe blinds the officials, and subverts the cause of those who are in the right.

9 "You shall not oppress a stranger; you know the heart of a stranger, for you were strangers in the land of Egypt.

10 "For six years you shall sow your land

and gather in its yield; ¹¹ but the seventh year you shall let it rest and lie fallow, that the poor of your people may eat; and what they leave the wild beasts may eat. You shall do likewise with your vineyard, and with your olive orchard.

¹² "Six days you shall do your work, but on the seventh day you shall rest; that your ox and your ass may have rest, and the son of your bondmaid, and the alien, may be refreshed. ¹³ Take heed to all that I have said to you; and make no mention of the names of other gods, nor let such be heard out of your mouth.

¹⁴ "Three times in the year you shall keep a feast to me. ¹⁵ You shall keep the feast of unleavened bread; as I commanded you, you shall eat unleavened bread for seven days at the appointed time in the month of Abib, for in it you came out of Egypt. None shall appear before me emptyhanded. ¹⁶ You shall keep the feast of harvest, of the first fruits of your labor, of what you sow in the field. You shall keep the feast of ingathering at the end of the year, when you gather in from the field the fruit of your labor. ¹⁷ Three times in the year shall all your males appear before the Lord God.

¹⁸ "You shall not offer the blood of my sacrifice with leavened bread, or let the fat of my feast remain until the morning.

¹⁹ "The first of the first fruits of your ground you shall bring into the house of the Lord your God.

"You shall not boil a kid in its mother's milk.

²⁰ "Behold, I send an angel before you, to guard you on the way and to bring you to the place which I have prepared. ²¹ Give heed to him and hearken to his voice, do not rebel against him, for he will not pardon your transgression; for my name is in him.

²² "But if you hearken attentively to his voice and do all that I say, then I will be an enemy to your enemies and an adversary to your adversaries.

²³ "When my angel goes before you, and brings you in to the Amorites, and the Hittites, and the Per′izzites, and the Canaanites, the Hivites, and the Jeb′usites, and I blot them out, ²⁴ you shall not bow down to their gods, nor serve them, nor do according to their works, but you shall utterly overthrow them and break their pillars in pieces. ²⁵ You shall serve the Lord your God, and I will bless your bread and your water; and I will take sickness away from the midst of you. ²⁶ None shall cast her young or be barren in your land; I will fulfil the number of your days. ²⁷ I will send my terror before you, and will throw into confusion all the people against whom you shall come, and I will make all your enemies turn their backs to you. ²⁸ And I will send hornets before you, which shall drive out Hivite, Canaanite, and Hittite from before you. ²⁹ I will not drive them out from before you in one year, lest the land become desolate and the wild beasts multiply against you. ³⁰ Little by little I will drive them out from before you, until you are increased and possess the land. ³¹And I will set your bounds from the Red Sea to the sea of the Philistines, and from the wilderness to the Eu·phra′tes; for I will deliver the inhabitants of the land into your hand, and you shall drive them out before you. ³² You shall make no covenant with them or with their gods. ³³ They shall not dwell in your land, lest they make you sin against me; for if you serve their gods, it will surely be a snare to you."

24 And he said to Moses, "Come up to the Lord, you and Aaron, Nadab, and Abi′hu, and seventy of the elders of Israel, and worship afar off. ² Moses alone shall

come near to the LORD; but the others shall not come near, and the people shall not come up with him."

³ Moses came and told the people all the words of the LORD and all the ordinances; and all the people answered with one voice, and said, "All the words which the LORD has spoken we will do." ⁴ And Moses wrote all the words of the LORD. And he rose early in the morning, and built an altar at the foot of the mountain, and twelve pillars, according to the twelve tribes of Israel. ⁵And he sent young men of the people of Israel, who offered burnt offerings and sacrificed peace offerings of oxen to the LORD. ⁶And Moses took half of the blood and put it in basins, and half of the blood he threw against the altar. ⁷ Then he took the book of the covenant, and read it in the hearing of the people; and they said, "All that the LORD has spoken we will do, and we will be obedient." ⁸And Moses took the blood and threw it upon the people, and said, "Behold the blood of the covenant which the LORD has made with you in accordance with all these words."

⁹ Then Moses and Aaron, Nadab, and Abi'hu, and seventy of the elders of Israel went up, ¹⁰ and they saw the God of Israel; and there was under his feet as it were a pavement of sapphire stone, like the very heaven for clearness. ¹¹And he did not lay his hand on the chief men of the people of Israel; they beheld God, and ate and drank.

Within this account of the divine origin of the laws governing Hebrew society, two different groups of laws are recorded. The first collection, known as the Decalogue, or Ten Commandments (Exod. 20:3-17), is assumed to be the oldest, and although it is unlikely that its present form exactly recalls the obligations of the covenant at Sinai, its wording and form do suggest a nomadic setting and probably date from the Mosaic period. The second collection, known as the Covenant Code (Exod. 20:22-23:33), is considered later, because it reflects the agricultural concerns of a settled people, such as the Israelites became in Palestine.

The Decalogue differs greatly from the Covenant Code both in form and function. The Covenant Code . . . is an instrument for the concrete and comprehensive regulation of a society in its civil and religious dimensions. Its so-called profane laws are in the form of case law. They rest on concrete precedents. They can be applied and/or expanded to cover new situations. The cultic sections of the code are in the nature of regulative rubrics. They too are concerned with details and specific problems. The Decalogue is different. It is rather a statement of general principles in terms of which such laws as one finds in the Covenant Code are to be understood and administered. The "ten words" are not the outcome of or applicable to any concrete social or cultic situation. The Decalogue has something of the flavor of a "bill of rights" in which, in general terms, the prerogatives of all—God, parents, fellow Israelites—are recognized. The Decalogue cannot function in a society except indirectly, by means of an instrument such as the Covenant Code.[7]

Both the Decalogue and the Covenant Code, while reflecting respectively the nomadic and agricultural periods in the life of Israel before the rise of the monarchy, occur in Exodus as the obligations of a contractual relationship. Such a placement of Hebrew law within a religious covenant acted as a reminder to the Israelites that their communal life was to be an implementation of the Exodus revelation.

The covenant is central in the implementation of the faith which constituted Israel's response to the Exodus. It is the symbol that

[7] J. Coert Rylaarsdam, "Introduction to the Book of Exodus," in G. A. Buttrick (ed.), *The Interpreter's Bible,* Vol. I, p. 843. Copyright 1952 by Pierce and Smith. Used by permission of Abingdon Press.

The law code of Hammurabi (*ca.* 1728–1686 B.C.), inscribed on this stele, is the best-known example of conditional, or case, law in the ancient world. Case law declares the specific legal punishment resulting from specific crimes. The stele, standing almost 8 feet high, is crowned with a relief that depicts Hammurabi receiving the symbols of his royal office, the rod and ring, from the enthroned sun-god, Shamash. (Archives Photographiques, Paris)

describes the relationship in which Yahweh and his people stand to one another. In various parts of the Old Testament different aspects of this relationship are stressed. Sometimes the covenant is seen mainly in the historic actuality of revelation at the Exodus and in the founding of Israel as the people of God. Sometimes the abiding and even the unbreakable character of the relationship is stressed. At still other times the demands conceived by Israel to be incumbent upon it in this relationship—the laws, the statutes, and ordinances—are made virtually synonymous with the covenant (Deut. 4:13). In general the prophets, when they utilize the metaphor to describe the relation of God to Israel, stress the theocentric, dynamic, and personal aspects of the relationship. Legal and priestly movements, however, stress its institutional, statutory, and static aspects. . . .

The Hebrew word for covenant, *b*e*rith,* has the significance of bond or agreement. The etymology of the word is not certain. The meanings of "cutting," "binding," and "eating"—all associated with covenant making—show the variety of opinions as to the primitive meaning of the word. For the religious purpose it served in Israel the term was borrowed from social usage. In social practice covenants [or treaties] were of two general kinds. There were covenants between equals, in which the obligations and privileges under the agreement were equally shared. It seems that under the foreign influence of the nature mysticism . . . Israelites increasingly conceived of their covenant with Yahweh as such a covenant between equals, in which God was as dependent upon Israel as Israel was upon him. Thus in the covenant relationship Yahweh had in effect forfeited his own freedom. This was a growing assumption against which the prophets protested. But in social relationships there were also agreements, known as covenants, between partners not equal: for example, between a king and his subjects, or between a lord and his servants. In such a covenant the core of the agreement is really a promise or gift made by the stronger party. This is, however, normally conditioned upon certain demands or obligations to be met by the weaker party. In any case, the promise, central in such a covenant, does not destroy the freedom of him who gives it.[8]

[8] *Ibid.,* p. 841.

The covenant of Sinai belongs to this second kind of covenant, or treaty, namely an agreement between unequal partners. In return for the deliverance already given and the promise of land and prosperity in the future, the Israelites vowed obedience to the will of Yahweh as revealed in a particular moral code and sealed by a cultic ritual. While the form of the covenant as a whole is that of a treaty between unequal partners, the content of the covenant and the form of its specific stipulations represent rather the law of the family and tribe as dictated by the elders of the community. At the heart of the moral code lies the Decalogue: direct, apodictic, unconditional prohibitions of a general nature, stemming ultimately from the patriarchal authority of the head of the family. In addition, there are more specific laws, such as those in the Covenant Code, which were created to meet specific ethical and cultic situations. Both of these codes

> reflect the life of civil bodies, of society at large, or of particular groupings within that society . . . . The sexual taboos are designed to keep order within the family. Exod. 23 1-3, 6-9 specialize on safeguarding legal institutions.[9]

The covenant in which these laws are placed does not create the social order it seeks to protect. Rather,

> the commandments point to an order given to man, not created by contract. . . . The Decalogue and the Covenant Code . . . do not insist that their laws are novel. That Israel has a "torah" [law] in contradistinction to her neighbors is a late idea (Deut 4 8). To avoid the term "natural order," because it is fraught with philosophical preconceptions, we might say: The commandments presuppose a social order which antedates all historical beginnings and therefore is not made

[9] E. Gerstenberger, "Covenant and Commandment," *Journal of Biblical Literature,* LXXXIV (1965), 48. This material is thoroughly copyrighted by the *Journal of Biblical Literature,* which protection is not lessened by reproduction in this volume.

The action which gave a binding force to the Covenant was the ceremony of sealing. The sealing could be performed as a ritual or, where the agreement was written, could be appended in the form of a seal. Authenticating seals were widely used in the ancient world as official signatures or as marks of personal ownership. The most common type of seal in Mesopotamia was the small cylinder or spool that could be rolled over a soft material to make an impression. These seals could be quite artistic, having religious or mythological significance. The seal above shows the sun-god, seated, receiving two lesser gods and a worshiper. The seal below shows a lion-griffin attacking a bull, in conjunction with the worship of the sun-disk. (The Pierpont Morgan Library)

a subject of reflection. The family with its taboos, the legal institutions, the distinctions between social classes, age groups, friends and enemies, the established religious practices and social habits are all taken for granted. The commandments simply warn not to violate the given order, because disaster would strike the community in case of trespassing. The implicit understanding is that the divine power guards the organization of man. The Deity will step in to punish the evildoer. But the commandments need not spell out these consequences. They are self-evident. Neither is it necessary to add special oaths and curses to reinforce the commandments. Man is not a covenant partner who acknowledges an agreement. Rather he accepts the inherited rules for his society because he knows they are good and because he has no other choice. These rules are not temporary agreements; they are bound to particular persons, historical groups, or nations. They are universal and timeless.

[These commandments] have been preserved and transmitted within the society which they sought to protect. Not priests or prophets but fathers, tribal heads, wise men, and, secondarily, court officials . . . are the earliest guardians of the precepts. Basically it is the father, who addresses his son directly, counseling him for life. The father speaks from experience and with authority, and thus the peculiarly persuasive tone of the commandments, which does not need the threat of legal punishment, becomes explainable. The father even can instigate new commandments which are binding for his family or clan . . . . The son is to regard the social institutions and not to change their eternal order. Failing to listen and obey will result in unhappiness and catastrophe.[10]

Since the content of the Hebrew moral code was provided by the already existing social order of the family and the tribe, it is well to examine in closer detail the patriarchal structure of Hebrew society. The following selection on the Hebrew family describes the power of the male head of the household.

The Hebrew Family
S. A. Queen and R. W. Habenstein[11]

The basic unit of ancient Hebrew society was the household (*beth*). It often included several marriage groups, for which, interestingly, we find no Hebrew name. In the nomadic stage the household included the patriarch, his wives and concubines, their small children, grown sons with their wives and children, slaves, bond servants, and sometimes strangers who had placed themselves under the patriarch's protection. All these lived together in the same camp, occupying numerous tents. The patriarch exercised great authority over his household, but apparently this did not extend to matters of life and death over wives, except in case of adultery. It appears that there was such power over children in the earliest period, although this was later diminished. A man might sell his daughter to a fellow Hebrew, though not to a foreigner. Also a man's children might be claimed by his creditors. In this situation they were not only under their father's power, but were part of his assets. If a man "bought" a Hebrew servant he must release him after six years of servitude. He was forbidden to beat his servants to death. If he injured them very seriously he must let them go free. A child who struck or cursed his parents was to be stoned but evidently not by the father. At

---

[10] *Ibid.*, pp. 49-51.

[11] S. A. Queen and R. W. Habenstein, *The Family in Various Cultures* (3rd ed.; Philadelphia: J. B. Lippincott Company, 1967), pp. 143-147, 151-152, 155-157. By permission of the publishers.

The central importance of the family remained a constant feature of Hebrew history. (*Left*) The figurine of a mother and child, found at Beth-Yerah, dates from the Early Bronze Age. (*Below*) The gravestone relief of a Jewish family from Syria was carved in the second century A.D. (*Left*, by courtesy of the Israel Department of Antiquities and Museums; *below*, the Metropolitan Museum of Art Purchase, 1902)

least in the period of living in towns a disobedient son was to be stoned by the citizens after complaint by the father.

A number of related households constituted a clan (*mishpahah*). A number of related clans constituted a tribe (*shebet*); the twelve tribes constituted the nation (*am*). All of these were regarded as extensions of the family and the whole people was united by a sense of kinship.

We have observed that the conjugal family group was completely swallowed up in the household and had almost no independent existence, but this must not obscure the evidence of strong husband-wife and parent-child attachments. Households sometimes grew to very great size, but occasionally the numbers became too great, or the flocks were too large for the available pasturage, and such a household was divided. So we have the story of Abraham and Lot, who amicably agreed to travel in separate directions in order that there might be a sufficient living for both parts of the previously united group. A similar division was arranged by Jacob and Esau.

In sharp contrast to our system, marriage among the ancient Hebrews was not the culmination of "free choice" and romantic love on the part of a boy and girl. It was most frequently arranged by their fathers and in early times closely resembled wife purchase, if indeed it was not exactly that. . . .

As indicated above, the essential requirement for marriage was usually an agreement by fathers of the young man and young woman. It appears, however, that the wishes of the young folks themselves were not wholly ignored . . . . In a later period the consent of the two immediate parties to a marriage was required along with that of their parents. Eventually they did not have to have their parents' consent if they were of age, but respect for parents doubtless meant that marriages were seldom contracted against the latter's will . . . .

Betrothal was counted as the beginning of marriage even though the union might not be consummated until much later. Betrothal involved agreement between fathers of the young man and young woman, in later periods agreement between the young persons themselves . . . .

After betrothal the girl might be taken immediately to her husband's house for celebration of the nuptials. In early times this was usual. In later centuries it was frequently delayed. Likewise, in early times the wedding involved almost no ceremony at all, greatest importance being attached to the betrothal. As the two events were more and more separated, the betrothal declined in importance and the wedding gained. . . .

From what has already been said it is apparent that women were definitely subordinate. On the other hand they seem to have been generally respected and loved. In early times a woman was always in the power of some man—her father, her brother, her husband, or her father-in-law. But a widowed mother living with her son, or a divorcée, was relatively free. In one sense woman was treated as property, but she was valuable property and was as a rule well cared for. She was not isolated, as among the Mohammedans and the Athenians, but had considerable freedom and influence. . . .

As to division of labor, men's work usually included tending the flocks, tilling the soil, performing religious ceremonies, and carrying on political activities and war. Women did spinning, weaving, made clothing, prepared food in accordance with ritual law, organized and conducted the housework, and sometimes sold the products of household industry. . . .

As we have already seen, authority especially in the early nomadic period, was vested in the patriarch, usually the oldest living male in a household. But he was not entirely free to rule in an arbitrary manner. He was restrained by the customs and traditions of his people, especially by the unwritten laws which had the sanction of religion. "Thus saith the Lord" must have been a powerful restraining and guiding influence. Later there were various public officials from "elders of the city" to the king. These officials passed on questions relating to the virginity of a betrothed maiden, premarital sex relations in general, adultery, the levirate,[12] and inheritance. But so far as we can discover, the arrangement of marriage and divorce were primarily matters to be settled by the family itself and not by the community or state during the periods in which we are particularly interested.

As examples of the mores and laws which governed family life "from the outside," we shall refer to several rules pertaining to marriage, concubinage, the levirate, . . . and sexual behavior.

The Hebrews, like all other peoples, had laws prohibiting marriage between persons within certain degrees of kinship and affinity. In earliest times stress was laid on the mother's line. Thus a man might marry his half-sister if they had different mothers, but not if they had the same

[12] A Hebrew family custom requiring one of the brothers of a man who died without children to marry his widow and beget a son in the name of the dead brother, so that "his name may not be blotted out of Israel" (Deut. 25:6).

mother. In those early days the prohibition included mother's sister, mother, and daughter. Later regulations extended the ban to paternal half-sister, stepmother, mother-in-law, and daughter-in-law. The levitical code barred, in addition to the preceding, marriage of a man with any wife of his father, his father's sister, father's brother's wife, daughter's daughter, son's wife or daughter, brother's wife . . . and wife's sister (during the lifetime of the wife). This rather elaborate definition of relationships considered incestual is set forth in the eighteenth chapter of Leviticus and has been cited by modern lawmakers in support of their legislation. If the reader is surprised that all this has been stated in terms of action by the man, he must remember that in such matters the initiative belonged to the male sex. Hence it was quite natural that Hebrew law should impose these prohibitions directly on the man and only indirectly on the woman. . . .

In general the sexual code of the ancient Hebrews was stern and harsh. It enforced a double standard requiring fidelity of women but not of men, usually punishing women more severely than men. However, in case of adultery the death penalty was to be inflicted on both offenders if the woman were married. . . .

In case of sex relations with a betrothed girl, the death penalty was prescribed for a man, not because of his injury to the girl, but because he had violated another man's rights. If the affair had taken place "in the field" no penalty was imposed upon the girl because it was assumed that she could not have secured help. But if it happened in town she too was to be stoned to death . . . . If a husband accused his bride of not being a virgin, his parents were supposed to take "the tokens of her virginity" to the elders of the city. If they adjudged her innocent her husband could not divorce her at any time, but if they found her guilty she was to be stoned to death. If a betrothed girl who was a bond-maid had intercourse with some man, both were to be punished but neither was to be put to death. Presumably this was on the ground that she was not as important as a free woman. The man was required to bring a ram to the priest as a trespass offering. Nothing further is said about what should be done to the girl. In the case of sex relations between a man and a woman neither married nor betrothed, the man was required to make a payment to her father—fifty shekels is specified in one passage—and he must make the girl his wife if her father consented.

Prostitution was probably very rare in the early period and was mildly forbidden after the development of town life. Indeed, a harlot might live in a Hebrew community without any special condemnation. . . . However, if the prostitute were attached to some heathen cult, perhaps to a temple, then the prohibition was stern. . . .

Generalizing about the "external" controls of sex and family life we may say that the regulations were founded on these principles: (1) Sexual relations with foreigners represented disloyalty to the Hebrew nation and heresy against its religion. (2) Irregular sexual behavior by or with a woman was an invasion of the property rights of her father or husband. (3) Other sexual irregularity, such as intercourse during menstruation or soon after childbirth, sodomy, and sex relations with animals, was likely to bring on some supernatural penalty. Marriage, concubinage, and the levirate were in part means of perpetuating, not only a family line, but the Chosen People.

In conclusion let us remind ourselves, that the Hebrew family, for most purposes, was not the small conjugal group, but the household or even larger kinship group. Marriage was not unimportant, but the wedded couple was absorbed in the consanguine family of three generations and many collateral relatives.

The ancient Hebrew family in the sense of household had a most inclusive array of functions. Through it children were produced and reared "that a man's house might not die out of Israel." It was an almost self-sufficient economic unit. The head of the household was a religious functionary who conducted various ceremonies and supervised the ritual cleanliness and dietary laws. In early times he had charge of *teraphim,* or sacred images. The household was an educational institution wherein the elders were the teachers who gave practical and religious instruction to the youth. It was a protective agency, caring for handicapped members and taking in impoverished "brothers" as well as "sojourners." In a sense the household determined right and wrong, made laws, and administered justice. It would have been possible for life to go on almost without any other social group or institution.

As nomadic life gave way to living in towns, the nuclear family became more often a separate unit. As concubinage was reduced, procreation became more definitely a function of the conjugal group. Also child-rearing and economic provision or maintenance were more identified with the small nuclear family. On the other hand, religious ceremonies were to a large degree transferred to the synagogue and the temple. Hence we see that among the ancient Hebrews there was not a fixed array of functions permanently identified with either the nuclear or the extended family.

The meaning and implementation of Hebrew ethics are complicated not only by their origin in family customs and covenant obligations but also by the fact that they reflect, and for much of their history operate within, a primitive psychology. We have seen in Chapter 1 how some of the features of early Hebrew culture, such as the concepts of God and nature, are strikingly different from those of other Near Eastern peoples. We have also seen that the Hebrews conceived of man as a "psycho-physical unity" and in so doing reflect the absence of development toward a more complex understanding of human psychology. The conception of man as a psycho-physical unity is based not only on the absence in Hebrew of any clear distinction between body and soul but also on the relationship of thinking, willing, and acting. The distinction among these activities lies at the very heart of the Western ethical tradition. The structure of the Hebrew language, however, has suggested to some scholars that these three functions were not distinguished in Hebrew psychology. According to this view there was no theoretical, objective thinking that could be separated from willing and doing. Thinking and acting were simply aspects of one movement of the soul in response to an image that entered the heart or self. Supposedly thought led directly and immediately to action as part of one process. Therefore to "know" something always implied "doing" something.

This view of the relationship between Hebrew language and thought is based on the fact that many of the important words of the Hebrew language have several different meanings. For example, the verb *zkr* can mean both to think and to act; the noun *dabhar* can mean both word and event. This lexical overlapping may indicate that at an early period in Hebrew and other Semitic languages the primitive mind did not make these distinctions. While the Hebrew man of 1500 B.C. probably could make such distinctions, he continued to relate thinking and acting closely, and no great dichotomy had yet grown up. Therefore, while there is not necessarily a semantic identification between thinking and acting in Hebrew thought and culture, the two meanings of the verb *zkr* remain closely related. In fact, this close association of thought and action, common to the Semitic languages, seems to parallel the stage of development in the Greek language reached in the Homeric period.

> The heart is commonly connected with the process of thought [in Homeric Greek]. The *phrén* is the seat of the mental and emotional faculties, of perception and thought. The idiom differs slightly from that of Hebrew. It is not common to speak of objects or events rising on the heart or returning to the heart. Rather, the common expression is "to place it in the heart." Like Hebrew, one persuades or turns the heart toward an action.
> The Greek idiom in Homer denotes both the process of thought as well as the action which follows. To set an idea in the heart is also to fix the path of action. Phoenix is alarmed that Achilles wants to "set the homeward journey to his heart," because such will surely issue in action. The gods determine the acts of men by setting an idea in the heart of man which he in turn must execute. . . . We conclude, therefore, that no significant contrast can be made between Homeric Greek and the Semitic usage.[13]

Hebrew psychology throughout most of the Old Testament period remains, therefore, similar to that of Homeric Greece and does not follow the Greek line of development. Thought and action, while perhaps not identical, remain so closely related that "knowing" the will of God implies "doing" the will of God throughout the Old Testament period. Moreover, moral law recognized actions as much as, if not more than, intentions. In fact, given the close relationship

---

[13] Brevard S. Childs, *Memory and Tradition in Israel* ("Studies in Biblical Theology," no. 37; London: SCM Press, 1962), p. 26.

between thinking and doing, it is through the actions that one discovers the intentions, the inner life of the soul revealed in action.

In a society where the prohibitions of family and tribe were clearly stated and given divine sanction and where actions were assumed to bespeak intentions, it might seem easy to determine individual moral responsibility. However, this would overlook the lack in early Hebrew society of a clear distinction between the individual and the community. As the selection by Johnson in Chapter 1 indicated, the ancient Israelite did not maintain a clear distinction between the one and the many. Man is always part of a family or kinship group, just as the group can be thought of as one corporate personality. Consequently, the actions of an individual, for good or ill, involve those of the same blood, and the Hebrew saw nothing unusual in the commandment that visited "the iniquity of the fathers upon the children to the third and fourth generation." This teaching of inherited guilt is nowhere better depicted than in the Biblical account of the Fall of Adam and Eve, from which the Christian doctrine of original sin was drawn.

The Fall of Mankind[14]

2 . . . [15] The LORD God took the man and put him in the garden of Eden to till it and keep it. [16]And the LORD God commanded the man, saying, "You may freely eat of every tree of the garden; [17] but of the tree of the knowledge of good and evil you shall not eat, for in the day that you eat of it you shall die." . . .

3 Now the serpent was more subtle than any other wild creature that the LORD God had made. He said to the woman, "Did God say, 'You shall not eat of any tree of the garden'?" ²And the woman said to the serpent, "We may eat of the fruit of the trees of the garden; ³ but God said, 'You shall not eat of the fruit of the tree which is in the midst of the garden, neither shall you touch it, lest you die.' " ⁴ But the serpent said to the woman, "You will not die. ⁵ For God knows that when you eat of it your eyes will be opened, and you will be like God, knowing good and evil." ⁶ So when the woman saw that the tree was good for food, and that it was a delight to the eyes, and that the tree was to be desired to make one wise, she took of its fruit and ate; and she also gave some to her husband, and he ate. ⁷ Then the eyes of both were opened, and they knew that they were naked; and they sewed fig leaves together and made themselves aprons.

⁸And they heard the sound of the LORD God walking in the garden in the cool of the day, and the man and his wife hid themselves from the presence of the LORD God among the trees of the garden. ⁹ But the LORD God called to the man, and said to him, "Where are you?" ¹⁰And he said, "I heard the sound of thee in the garden, and I was afraid, because I was naked; and I hid myself." ¹¹ He said, "Who told you that you were naked? Have you eaten of the tree of which I commanded you not to eat?" ¹² The man said, "The woman whom thou gavest to be with me, she gave me fruit of the tree, and I ate." ¹³ Then the LORD God said to the woman, "What is this that you have done?" The woman said, "The serpent beguiled me, and I ate." ¹⁴ The LORD God said to the serpent,
"Because you have done this,
cursed are you above all cattle,
and above all wild animals;
upon your belly you shall go,
and dust you shall eat
all the days of your life.

[14] The Bible, Gen. 2:15-17; 3:1-24.

15 I will put enmity between you and
    the woman,
  and between your seed and her seed;
he shall bruise your head,
  and you shall bruise his heel."
16 To the woman he said,
"I will greatly multiply your pain in
    childbearing;
  in pain you shall bring forth children,
yet your desire shall be for your husband,
  and he shall rule over you."
17 And to Adam he said,
"Because you have listened to the voice
    of your wife,
  and have eaten of the tree
of which I commanded you,
  'You shall not eat of it,'
cursed is the ground because of you;
  in toil you shall eat of it all the days
    of your life;
18 thorns and thistles it shall bring forth
    to you;
  and you shall eat the plants of the
    field.
19 In the sweat of your face
  you shall eat bread
till you return to the ground,
  for out of it you were taken;
  you are dust, and to dust
  you shall return."
20 The man called his wife's name Eve, because she was the mother of all living. 21 And the LORD God made for Adam and for his wife garments of skins, and clothed them. 22 Then the LORD God said, "Behold, the man has become like one of us, knowing good and evil; and now, lest he put forth his hand and take also of the tree of life, and eat, and live for ever"— 23 therefore the LORD God sent him forth from the garden of Eden, to till the ground from which he was taken. 24 He drove out the man; and at the east of the garden of Eden he placed the cherubim, and a flaming sword which turned every way, to guard the way to the tree of life.

The sense of corporate responsibility, expressed in the story of the Fall, underlies the entire Hebrew moral code. Most of the laws, as we have already indicated, protect the family and the kinship group. This sense of corporate unity was extended to the weak and defenseless within Hebrew society and even to strangers who might temporarily sojourn among them.

MERCY IN HEBREW LAW
Johannes Pedersen[15]

The law of the Israelites strongly enforces *mercy* towards the weak. They also are included in the covenant; their rights are to be respected, and life is to be made tolerable for them. Job lays great stress on this when speaking of his former righteous conduct: If I saw one perishing for lack of clothing, and that he had no covering—if his loins have not blessed me, and if he were not warmed with the fleece of my sheep! (Job 31:19-20). It is an honorable obligation on the part of the great always to uphold the lesser, but it is more or less the duty of every Israelite. . . .

When an Israelite becomes poor and is obliged to borrow, interest must not be taken, and if his mantle is taken as a pledge, it shall be delivered to him in the evening, that he may cover himself with it for the night (Exod. 22:24-26). The

---

[15] Johannes Pedersen, *Israel: Its Life and Culture* (London: Oxford University Press, 1964), Vols. I-II, pp. 355-357, reprinted by permission of Banner og Korchs Forlag, Copenhagen. This edition is a photo reprint of the original English edition published in 1926.

"Law of Holiness" also enforces that one must not defraud nor rob one's neighbour, nor keep back the wages of the hired man. And when a man is impoverished, one must not let him go down nor take interest on loans. On this point all the codes are agreed. The Deuteronomy says that it is not permitted to lend upon interest to an Israelite; that one may do towards strangers. One must not take the nether or the upper millstone to pledge, one must not penetrate into his house in order to get a pledge, nor keep his raiment in the night.

The chief thing is everywhere to show mercy to those of the same covenant: One must not curse a deaf man, nor put a stumbling-block before the blind, and in particular there are three kinds of weak people who should be protected: widows, fatherless and *gērīm*, clients; in short, all of the Israelite community who are without a family to uphold them.

The cherubim were winged creatures with the body of a lion and a woman's head. This ivory carving of a cherub, or sphinx, comes from ninth-century Samaria in northern Palestine and reflects the presence of Phoenician art in Israel. (By courtesy of the Israel Department of Antiquities and Museums)

It is said in the Book of Covenant: Thou shalt neither vex a *gēr* nor oppress him; for ye were *gērīm* in the land of Egypt. Ye shall not afflict any widow or fatherless child. If thou afflict them in any wise, and they cry at all unto me, I will surely hear their cry; and my wrath shall wax hot, and I will kill you with the sword, and your wives shall be widows and your children fatherless (Exod. 22:20–23).

Another law ordains: And when ye reap the harvest of your land, thou shalt not wholly reap the corners of thy field, neither shalt thou gather the gleanings of thy harvest. And thou shalt not glean thy vineyard, neither shalt thou gather every grape of thy vineyard, thou shalt leave them for the poor and the *gēr*: I am Yahweh, your God.

We find both of these laws combined in the Deuteronomy [the fifth book of the Pentateuch], the same law which bids one not to shut one's hand against one's poor brother, but to help him willingly and give him all that he needs. The *gēr* is to be acknowledged as belonging to the community. The Book of Covenant mentions twice that he must not be oppressed (Exod. 22:20; 23:9). In the "Law of Holiness" [a section of Leviticus, the third book of the Pentateuch] it is even said: Thou shalt love him as thyself. The *gēr* is entitled to this, because he is nearly an Israelite. . . .

That which the law demands is in all cases the keeping of the covenant. The neighbour is to be maintained in his honour, the free development of his soul is respected, provided he does not disturb the growth of others. It must be extended to everyone who is included in the covenant of the people; he must have his share in the love of every Israelite: "Thou shalt not hate thy brother in thine heart, thou shalt do justice to thy kinsman and not bear sin for his sake. Thou shalt not avenge nor bear any grudge against the children of thy people, but thou shalt love thy neighbour as thyself. I am Yahweh." The covenant must be inspired by some of the instinctive feeling which connects the family.

It is, therefore, the preservation or damaging of the covenant that determined moral or immoral action, whether one has in mind the covenant that bound the family together or the covenant with Yahweh which included and reinforced all of these lesser covenants. In spite of the impression of absolute norms suggested by the Hebrew law, these laws functioned only in relationships: the relationship between man and God, the relationships within the family, the relationships within the community at large. Keeping the covenant meant to act righteously within a relationship. In the same way, to sin was to break covenant. Consequently, righteousness was the primary obligation Yahweh demanded of his people. This term, however, did not carry with it all of its modern connotations. The following selection makes its Old Testament meaning clear.[16]

THE OLD TESTAMENT CONCEPT OF RIGHTEOUSNESS
Gerhard von Rad[17]

There is absolutely no concept in the Old Testament with so central a significance for all the relationships of human

---

[16] In this selection the terms righteousness and righteous have been substituted for the Hebrew words. The Hebrew word for righteousness is sometimes translated as justice.

[17] Gerhard von Rad, *Old Testament Theology*, Vol. I (Edinburgh: Oliver and Boyd, 1962), pp. 370–375, 377–378, 380–382.

life as that of righteousness. It is the standard not only for man's relationship to God, but also for his relationships to his fellows, reaching right down to the most petty wranglings—indeed, it is even the standard for man's relationship to the animals and to his natural environment. Righteousness can be described without more ado as the highest value in life, that upon which all life rests when it is properly ordered. But what do we mean by it? Theology has for long now ingenuously explained the concept in the light of her own presuppositions, that is, the presuppositions of the West. Its content seemed to be given by the translation in the Vulgate [the chief Latin translation of the Bible] (*iustitia*), and by the German word *Gerechtigkeit,* namely, a man's proper conduct over against an absolute ethical norm, a legality which derives its norm from the absolute idea of justice. From this absolute norm, it was supposed, issued absolute demands and absolute claims. In social respects justice so understood watches with complete impartiality over these claims and takes care that each man gets his own (*iustitia distributiva*). Thus, the only remaining question was, what is the norm that the Old Testament presupposes? But, oddly enough, no matter how urgently it was sought, no satisfactory answer to this question of an absolute norm could be found in the Old Testament. The reason was that the question itself was a wrong one, and in consequence the statements in the Old Testament simply could not be brought into harmony with this way of thinking. . . . As we now see, the mistake lay in seeking and presupposing an absolute ideal ethical norm, since ancient Israel did not in fact measure a line of conduct or an act by an ideal norm, but by the specific relationship in which the partner had at the time to prove himself true. "Every relationship brings with it certain claims upon conduct, and the satisfaction of these claims, which issue from the relationship and in which alone the relationship can persist, is described by our term righteous." [18] The way in which it is used shows that "righteous is out and out a term denoting relationship, and that it does this in the sense of referring to a real relationship between two parties . . . and not to the relationship of an object under consideration to an idea." [19] To some extent, therefore, the specific relationship in which the agent finds himself is itself the norm: only, it must be borne in mind that people are constantly moving in very many relationships, each one of which carries its own particular law within it. A man belongs to the family, to a political association (clan, nation), he is involved in economic life, and, if circumstances so decree, he can also come into association with foreigners—every day may bring a new relationship. And over and above all these, there is the relationship which Jahweh had offered to Israel, and which was chiefly maintained in the cult. Here too the same holds true—the just man is the one who measures up to the particular claims which this relationship lays upon him. When Israel praises the justice of Jahweh, she thanks him that he stands on Israel's side and in his action avows himself to her. The Song of Deborah [which we shall study in the next assignment] already speaks of "Jahweh's righteous acts" and by this term means his saving acts in history. . . .

But in spite of all the variability in what is said about Jahweh's righteousness, expression is given to an idea which was

[18] H. Cremer, *Biblisch-theologisches Wörterbuch* (7th ed.; Gotha, 1893), pp. 273-275.

[19] *Ibid.*

constitutive for Israel—Jahweh's righteousness was not a norm, but acts, and it was these acts which bestow salvation. . . .

Men's common life was also judged wholly from the point of view of faithfulness to a relationship. . . .

Naturally, it was quite frequently the task of the local judge to investigate a man's conduct with reference to his loyalty to a relationship, and to declare him blameless or deserving of punishment. Nevertheless it cannot be held that this Old Testament concept of righteousness is specifically forensic [i.e., only judicial] for it embraces the whole of Israelite life, wherever men found themselves in mutual relationships. And in particular, conduct loyal to a relationship includes far more than mere correctness or legality, that is, righteousness in our sense of the word. Such dependence upon one another demanded the showing of kindness, faithfulness, and, as circumstances arose, helpful compassion to the poor or the suffering. . . . A very extreme piece of evidence for righteousness (in whose paradox the old storyteller himself certainly delighted) is handed on in the story of Tamar, the daughter-in-law of Judah. Dressed as a cult prostitute she seduced her father-in-law and conceived by him. As she was being led out to be put to death, the motive of her action became known. She wanted even by the most extreme of means to raise up descendants for her dead husband's family, and because she had shown loyalty to her relationship to this family, she was "more righteous" than her father-in-law, who had refused to give her his youngest son in marriage (Gen. XXXVIII .26). But what in the world has this to do with our concept of righteousness? Thus our German word *Gerechtigkeit* [or the English "justice"] is unfortunately not only a very inadequate rendering of the Hebrew righteousness, but is often virtually misleading.

These two areas of relationship, of men with one another and of men with God, seem to some extent independent, and certainly in practice they often enough were. So the impression could be given that there was both a secular concept of righteousness and a purely religious one, and that the latter was possibly only a product of later theological reflection—a secondary application, as it were, of the civil concept of righteousness to the sphere of religion, the relationship of men with God. But that would be an utterly false description of the facts of the case. For what we look upon as two areas of relationship divorced from one another were bound together, just in this early period, in a continuing "primitive pansacrality." Jahweh took his people's part and gave drastic evidences of his righteousness: but he also issued the orders of life which alone made men's life together possible. His commandments were not indeed any absolute "law," but a kindly gift rendering life orderly. "Jahweh is in their midst as righteousness, . . . every morning he gives his decision, like the light which does not fail" (Zeph. III.5). The prophet is thinking here of the manifold directions which Jahweh proclaimed in the cult, and also of those which he gave for the legal sphere, in which his will for order is renewed daily. Here too it is once more evident that Israel did not envisage herself as related to a world of ideal values, but to events coming from Jahweh. The righteousness of Jahweh was, too, a continuous event directed towards Israel and was consequently a subject of proclamation. It had always been Israel's conviction that her whole community life was sustained by a constantly forthcoming righteousness which flowed over upon her. . . .

We have therefore arrived at a comparatively unified picture: from the earliest times onwards Israel celebrated Jahweh as the one who bestowed on his people the all-embracing gift of his righteousness. And this righteousness bestowed on Israel is always a saving gift. It is inconceivable that it should ever menace Israel. No references to the concept of a punitive righteousness can be adduced. . . . But if we put the question the other way round and ask how Israel's righteousness and the righteousness of individuals were conceived in relationship to Jahweh, what we find is not so uniform. We encounter in fact very diverse statements and very varied reflexions. Actually, what here comes under discussion is nothing less than the cardinal question of how Israel and the individual conceived of themselves in their existence before Jahweh. Initially, we notice that the references which mention human righteousness in relationship to Jahweh are only infrequently found in the earlier literature, while appearing extensively in the exilic and post-exilic texts. There must certainly have been some decided change. But it would be very precipitate to conclude forthwith that older Israel simply did not know of the demand for a righteousness in relationship to Jahweh.

Our best starting-point is the so-called liturgies of the gate, which represent a curious ceremony that took place at the entry of a procession into the pre-exilic Temple, and some idea of which is given in Pss. XV and XXIV. The people coming in seek admission at the gate of the outer forecourt, and ask what the prerequisites of this are: "Who may ascend the mountain of God, who may stand in his holy place?" To this the cultic officials answer from within: "He whose hands are clean and whose heart is pure, who does not direct his thought towards evil, who does not swear deceitfully. . . ." This means that a selection of Jahweh's commandments was put before those who entered. Admittedly, we do not have to conclude from this that in ancient Israel the fulfilling of the commandments was in principle antecedent to the reception of salvation in the cult, since those seeking admission were certainly not coming before Jahweh for the first time—they had been members of the community of Jahweh from the beginning. But this much becomes clear: those who came to worship were asked for something like a declaration of loyalty to Jahweh's will for justice. These commandments were regarded as perfectly capable of being fulfilled, and indeed as easy to fulfill. The question whether those who sought entrance avowed themselves to be loyal to them now, and had been so in the past, was therefore nothing but the question of their righteousness. Hence "the gates of righteousness" are spoken of, through which only "righteous people" enter. Indeed, we can quite safely generalise and say that every proclamation of the commandments—not just that in the ceremonial of the liturgy of the gate—was always at the same time a question about Israel's righteousness, her readiness for her part to say yes to the relationship of community offered to her by Jahweh. . . . Of course, this righteousness which Jahweh attributes to a man can be lost—it can be forfeited through conduct or actions which run counter to community with Jahweh. When Jahweh is angry, then "all our righteousness becomes like a polluted garment." If that is so, in so far as the damage is not irreparable and Jahweh has not delivered the sinner up to death, the man must make confession of the offence before Jahweh and repent. If, however, we now ask what the essence of the righteous person is, what are the characteristics that go to make him up, first and foremost is that the righteous man keeps the commandments. In this respect there has been no change from the earlier period, in which, as we saw, man's faithfulness to the relationship had to prove itself in recognizing the commandments and keeping them. The ingenuousness with which the men at prayer constantly protest that they have kept the commandments and claim the title of "righteous" is astonishing. To understand these statements, we must in no circumstances bring to bear upon them the question whether men can render adequate obedience in the eyes of God. . . . We have seen, of course, that the fulfilling of the commandments was nowhere experienced as a burden, which men at best could only partially carry out, but was rather an act of avowal. In consequence, these men were ready to claim the title of righteous for themselves without further ado, since what was understood was something quite other than a moral self-evaluation. Century upon century they had been taught by the cult that Jahweh alone could bestow this title, and that he assigned it to those who clung to him. It is not in the least surprising, therefore, that the men designate themselves as *the* righteous ones, since anyone who participated vocally in the cult in any kind of way was righteous—the voice of those who were excommunicated, banned, etc., is of course not preserved. How little any presumptuous moral self-qualification was implied in this term becomes particularly clear from the fact that Israel stubbornly knew of two possibilities and two only—a man was either righteous in the eyes of Jahweh or he was not. All intermediate stages, all the shades between black and white, with which a moral evaluation has to reckon, are completely absent. If a man was righteous in the eyes of Jahweh, then he was so completely, and never in an approximate or an incipient way. This is the standpoint from which we have to try to understand the confidence, and indeed the eagerness, with which later Israel fashioned the picture of the righteous one *par excellence* and applied it to herself. The positive characteristics of the righteous one are, according to Ps. I, first a strong emotion, namely a *delectari* [delight] in the revelation of the will of Jahweh, and next, the continuity of the inner relation of his life with this revelation of Jahweh's will.

STUDY QUESTIONS

1. What have been the consequences for Western culture of the close interrelation of religion and morality in the Judeo-Christian tradition? Can and should one be separated from the other?

2. In what ways did the structure of Hebrew society determine Hebrew law and morality?

3. What import does the idea of inherited guilt and of corporate responsibility have for ethics in the Western tradition? What aspects of the Judeo-Christian tradition presuppose a sense of corporate unity?

4. In what ways did Hebrew psychology determine Hebrew law and moral-

ity? What impact did the Hebrew understanding of self, family, and community have for Hebrew ethics? What effect does the weak concept of the "will" have on the early Hebrew ethic?

5. Does language determine and/or reflect differing apprehensions of external reality?

6. To what degree does the Israelite's covenant with Yahweh depend upon the Exodus from Egypt? How did the Israelites interpret the covenant? What importance does the Exodus have for Hebrew ethics? What importance does the covenant have for Hebrew ethics?

7. What are the sanctions of the early Hebrew ethic? In what ways were Hebraic ethical norms enforced?

8. Is the Hebrew ethic an absolute ethic or a situational, contextual, ethic? If absolute ethical norms are not present within Hebrew law, how might they have entered the Judeo-Christian tradition? Can the Hebraic concept of law be described as legalism?

9. What is the effect of apodictic law, such as is contained in the Ten Commandments, on personal and social ethics?

For those who have used The Contribution of Ancient Greece *edited by Jacqueline Strain:*

10. What parallels could one draw between the early Hebrews and the pre-archaic Greeks? What differences do you find significant?

11. In what ways did the Hebrew and Greek understanding of law, values, and moral sanctions differ?

12. In what ways does early Hebrew society fit Redfield's model of a "folk society"?

13. To love one's neighbor as oneself, often considered the heart of the Christian ethic, is part of Hebrew law (Lev. 19:18). To what degree is this teaching based upon the primitive view, described by Redfield, that "a person is myself in another form." What meaning and function does this concept have in a nonprimitive society?

CHAPTER 3

THE CONQUEST AND SETTLEMENT OF PALESTINE:
Acculturation and Charisma

Joshua summoned all Israel, their elders and heads, their judges and officers, and said to them, ". . . be very steadfast to keep and do all that is written in the book of the law of Moses, turning aside from it neither to the right hand nor to the left, that you may not be mixed with these nations left here among you, or make mention of the names of their gods, or swear by them, or serve them, or bow down yourselves to them, but cleave to the Lord your God as you have done to this day. For the Lord has driven out before you great and strong nations; and as for you, no man has been able to withstand you to this day. One man of you puts flight to a thousand, since it is the Lord your God who fights for you, as he promised you. Take good heed to yourselves, therefore, to love the Lord your God. For if you turn back, and join the remnant of these nations left here among you, and make marriages with them, so that you marry their women and they yours, know assuredly that the Lord your God will not continue to drive out these nations before you; but they shall be a snare and a trap for you, a scourge on your sides, and thorns in your eyes, till you perish from off this good land which the Lord your God has given you."

Josh. 23:2, 6–13.

The more generalized values are, the more persistent they seem to be. What might be called the basic premises of a people regarding the nature of man and the universe can go unchanged despite considerable modification in technology and other aspects of culture. These inferred values of a culture appear to have a greater continuity in many, if not all cases, and for this reason have themselves been conceptualized as selectors, molders, and integrators. If they have a controlling position they may be said to screen the incoming material and to order its placement in the existing system.

Reproduced by permission of the American Anthropological Association from the American Anthropologist: *Vol. 56 (1954), pp. 973–1002.*

The Exodus from Egypt and the creation of the covenant at Sinai were the first two stages in the migration of the Israelites from the delta of Egypt to the hill country of Palestine. According to the Old Testament tradition (Gen. 12:1–7), Yahweh had promised Abraham and his descendants the land of Palestine (or Canaan), but the realization of the Israelite hope was delayed more than a

64 The Conquest and Settlement of Palestine

generation because of their lack of military strength and what they felt to be their lack of faith. Shortly after the death of Moses, however, the wandering "covenant community" under the leadership of Joshua invaded and conquered the Promised Land. The conquered peoples among whom the Israelites settled, most of whom were Canaanites, had an advanced culture based on agriculture and commerce which supported a stratified and partially urbanized society. The

Twelfth-century B.C. Canaanite captives from a relief in the temple of Rameses III in Egypt. The Israelites were similar to the Semitic Canaanites in their general appearance. (The Oriental Institute, University of Chicago)

The Conquest and Settlement of Palestine 65

process whereby the conquering nomads and the conquered farmers and merchants adjusted or reacted to one another is usually termed culture-contact or, more frequently, acculturation. Before dealing with the specific stages and results of the contact between the Israelites and Canaanites, it is best to understand some of the principles and mechanisms that anthropologists have discerned in the acculturation process, especially those affecting religion and morality.

Canaanite maiden, carved in ivory, from Megiddo. (The Oriental Institute, University of Chicago)

Acculturation[1]

Acculturation may be defined as culture change that is initiated by the conjunction of two or more autonomous cultural systems. Acculturative change may be the consequence of direct cultural transmission; it may be derived from noncultural causes, such as ecological or demographic modifications induced by an impinging culture; it may be delayed, as with internal adjustments following upon the acceptance of alien traits or patterns; or it may be a reactive adaptation of traditional modes of life. Its dynamics can be seen as the selective adaptation of value systems, the processes of integration and differentiation, the generation of developmental sequences, and the operation of role determinants and personality factors.

An autonomous cultural system is one which is self-sustaining—that is, it does not need to be maintained by a complementary, reciprocal, subordinate, or other indispensable connection with a second system. Such units are systems because they have their own mutually adjusted and interdependent parts, and they are autonomous because they do not require another system for their continued functioning. An autonomous cultural system is what is usually called "a culture" in the anthropological literature, but the more explicit denotation at once makes the concept more definitive and delimits the incidence of acculturation as defined. Thus, cultural changes induced by contacts between ethnic enclaves and their encompassing societies would be definable as acculturative, whereas those resulting from the interactions of factions, classes, occupational groups, or other specialized categories within a single society would not be so considered. Hence, socialization, urbanization, industrialization, and secularization are not acculturation processes unless they are cross-culturally introduced rather than intraculturally developed phenomena....

Boundary-maintaining Mechanisms

One order of difference among cultural systems which may be objectively verifiable, common, and therefore significant is variation in their boundary-maintaining mechanisms. These comprise the techniques and ideologies by means of which a system limits participation in the culture to a well-recognized in-group. Here the relatively "open" society of the United States, which has admitted diverse immigrants for many years, may be contrasted with the "closed" systems of the Southwestern Pueblos which admit few aliens and censure their own members who do not conform to the key values of the culture. Boundary-maintaining mechanisms appear to include the relative presence or absence of devices by which the knowledge of customs and values is restricted to in-group members and thus shielded from alien influence. In some systems the whole range of culture is open to inspection by members of other societies while in others key customs are carefully guarded from outside observers.

Some examples of specific boundary-maintaining mechanisms which may operate in a closed system are: ritual initiations into the in-group; cleansing ceremonies to reintroduce an in-group member to his society after an absence; secret activities

---

[1] The Social Science Research Council Summer Seminar on Acculturation, 1953, "Acculturation: An Exploratory Formulation," by Evon Z. Vogt and others. Reproduced by permission of the American Anthropological Association from the *American Anthropologist:* Vol. 56, 1954, pp. 973–1002.

for in-group members only; localizing ceremonies in the homeland; the cultivation of self-defining concepts, such as ethnocentrism, or racism; the posting of territory or the lowering of isolationist "curtains"; the designation of contact agents or alien "handlers"; high evaluation of the group's language or dialect; the erection of legal barriers.

All of these devices are widely practiced, but not to the same extent nor for the same purpose. However, their concentration or lack of it may be the mark of a closed or resistant system as opposed to an open or susceptible one under contact conditions. . . . Before validating an "open-closed" typology based upon boundary-maintaining mechanisms it would be necessary to examine more closely the data we have on precontact conditions. It is possible that some of the proliferation of boundary-maintaining mechanisms is a postcontact phenomenon and that closed systems are really a manifestation of reactive adaptations.

"Flexible" vs. "Rigid" Systems

Another important typological distinction might be based upon the relative "rigidity" or "flexibility" of the internal structure of a cultural system. A tight or rigid interrelatedness—or its opposite—may prevail either with respect to the total value structure of a society or with respect primarily or solely to its social structure. Inclusiveness, precision, articulation, and range of variation might be utilized as yardsticks of integration in social or in over-all value configurations: multiple or single avenues to prestige or other goals, ambiguous vs. clearly defined interpersonal relations, authoritarian vs. equalitarian social controls, ascribed vs. achieved statuses, prescribed vs. situationally defined activities, specified vs. alternative patterns of conduct, and so forth. The acme of tight integration, on the social side at least, is probably achieved in systems which sanction autocratic powers in one or a few elite roles, such as absolute monarchies, theocracies, and gerontocracies. . . .

In itself, degree of integration affords no basis for predicting contact reactions. If, however, the outlines of a social structure or an underlying value system are unequivocal and inflexible previous to contact, they are more likely to be so under challenge from outsiders. Furthermore, if they are of a positive and invariant nature they will probably be supported by strong rationalizations and emotional commitments. If, in addition, there are relatively few key or command values in its hierarchy, a system is likely to be rigid and self-consciously resistant to alteration on contact, since it is already organized defensively probably as a result of external or internal challenges in the past. But here again, as with boundary-maintaining mechanisms, it is important to ascertain whether we are in fact dealing with precontact phenomena.

Self-correcting Mechanisms

While boundary-maintaining mechanisms refer to the surface tension attributes of the cultural "organism," self-correcting mechanisms refer to the ability of the cultural "organism" to shift function and to adapt internally, irrespective of its outer protective devices. The analysis of the forces of equilibrium within social structures, focusing attention upon their dynamic qualities and potentialities for variation, is also useful for the study of acculturation. This conceptual dimension recognizes the overt and covert struggles for power and position, the divisive tendencies of factionalism, and the centrifugal tensions produced by individual rejection of group expectations. It is assumed that in most, if not all, systems there is some degree of real or latent conflict, contradiction, or opposition of interests between certain segments of a society; even in groups where there are no major conflicts there is never full assent or conformance with respect to ascribed and achieved status and role. All this is another way of saying that no way of life is completely satisfying to all members of a society; and that the existing reward system will be sufficiently frustrating to some who, by their challenging attitudes, may threaten the values of the society.

Set off against this assumption of disruptive tendencies is the complementary one which asserts that there must be counterforces at work sufficient at least to maintain the pattern of a particular social order. These adjustive devices are highly variable depending on the value definitions of the culture. They include measures of social control ranging from the arbitrary use of force to techniques for insuring the personalization of a social ethic. Some operate to provide an area of permissiveness in individual role performance. Others set aside, with varying degrees of approval, occasions and contexts for the relaxation of restrictive rules of personal conduct, as in tacitly sanctioned acts of aggression or periods of license. Double standards of performance or contradictory estimates of the same behavior are often resolved by the device of compartmentalization, that is, by segregating them and giving them situational validation. Almost always potential areas of conflict are reduced by a differential allocation of rewards that is supported by some rationalization and by a recognized means of recruiting and sustaining leadership. Whatever the adjustment devices might be, they too must be meshed in some systematic way and be as mutually adjustable as the social system that they regulate. . . .

The importance of our three typological distinctions may be pointed up by suggesting that "hard-shelled, vertebrate" cultural systems—that is, cultures with many boundary-maintaining mechanisms and with "rigid" internal structures—whose self-correcting mechanisms are functioning smoothly may be found to be least susceptible to change in acculturation. On the other hand, "soft-shelled, invertebrate" cultural systems—that is, cultures with few or no boundary-maintaining mechanisms and with "flexible" internal structures—which are off balance, or in a state of disequilibrium, are likely to be most susceptible to change in acculturation. These biological analogies are obviously meant only to be suggestive. Furthermore, it is clear that such an "outrageous hypothesis" would require modification in two directions: (1) under certain conditions of extreme acculturation pressure the "hard-shelled vertebrates" may suddenly crack up completely; and (2) under other conditions it seems possible for the "soft-shelled, invertebrate" cultures to "ingest" great quantities of alien cultural material and still preserve many of their basic patterns and values. But perhaps we have said enough to indicate the kinds of hypotheses that can be derived from this facet of our formulation. . . .

PROCESSES OF ACCULTURATION

Any autonomous cultural system is in a continuous process of change. The change that is induced by contact therefore does not represent a shift from a static to an active state but rather a shift from one sort of change to another.... It is assumed that change is an inherent property of cultural systems; it cannot be assumed that the analytic properties of internal and acculturative change are identical.... The processes which flow from the conjunction of two or more cultural systems are obviously numerous, varied, and complex, and it is evident that we need additional concepts to deal with these dynamic phenomena....

Intercultural Transmission

One of the obvious invariant processes of acculturation that takes place through the intercultural networks outlined above is the transmission of cultural materials (objects, traits, or ideas) between the two systems. It may be as little as the transmission of a steel ax in exchange for furs, or it may be as much as the transmission of a whole new religious theology, but it always takes place. The classic concept of "diffusion" applies directly to this transmission process. In the most general terms we can make two statements about intercultural transmission: (1) that the patterns and values of the receiving culture seem to function as selective screens in a manner that results in the enthusiastic acceptance of some elements, the firm rejection of other elements; and (2) that the elements which are transmitted undergo transformations in the receiving cultural systems, and may also undergo transformations within the intercultural network while in the process of being transmitted. At any rate, these transformations are also probably intimately related to the value systems of receptor cultures. These value systems may be conceptualized as operating with gyroscope-like qualities; that is, the cultural elaborations of the system are kept going in certain "directions" and the cultural materials ingested appear to fall into place within the pre-existing framework....

Cultural Creativity

Acculturation is, however, neither a passive nor a colorless absorption. It is a culture-producing as well as a culture-receiving process. Acculturation, particularly when not forced, is essentially creative. It is a productive process even though in consequence there may be a decrease in the number and variety of pre-existent elements. Abandonment or voluntary loss is compensated for in the same or some other area of culture; and to the extent that an introduced element may serve as an alternative to an indigenous one, there is an actual gain in number and variety....

Cultural Disintegration

Although the incorporation of new traits is essentially a creative process it may have destructive consequences for the borrowing culture as an autonomous system. This result is clearly a possibility if the incorporation is forced by the donor group. Under coercion the receptor group not only loses its political independence; more important from the standpoint of its cultural autonomy, it loses its freedom to modify creatively what it is forced to accept as given. This strait-jacketing of acceptance forbids the flexibility of reinterpretation and reassociation that is essential to the independent functioning of a cultural system. When it is accompanied, as it usually is with captive cultures, by the mandatory elimination of certain customs, it is easy to understand why systems so enthralled proceed to "disintegrate." They do so because they have lost the prerogative of integrating what they want and rejecting the rest. Their creative mechanisms have been blocked.

Even when force is absent the conjunction of two systems usually creates tendencies that are at least potentially disintegrative. These tendencies develop in a system to the extent that its borrowed traits set up differentiating alternatives which demand partisan commitments by the society's members. In this way factional struggles, such as those between what are usually called "progressives" and "conservatives," develop. Contests for status and prerogatives are also common when cross-cultural influences are pronounced enough to unsettle traditional controls. Cleavages may take place along age, sex, or other social borders. Intergenerational conflicts are commonplace features of acculturation wherever cultures meet; . . . In addition to divisions along pre-existing group or class lines there are many others which gerrymander an exposed population in accordance with individual preferences for or against introduced objects, procedures, and ideas.

Presumably, any autonomous system is capable of indefinite growth as long as it can maintain its internal controls. Since this is evident as far as internally stimulated change is concerned, there is no reason to suppose that a radically distinct situation is precipitated by the injection of an alien trait. There are probably variable tolerances for growth, assuming that other factors, such as rate and force of presentation of new ideas, can be held constant. Some culture types may be not only more rigid in adhering to their value orientations but also for the same reason less able to assimilate new elements under contact without creating intolerable tensions among their carriers. This may be the case with a closely integrated system; extensive undermining of a command value may dispose the entire system to collapse, although the door is open for subsequent reintegration. Also it is likely that at some periods in its history a system is more vulnerable than it is at others, as, for example, when it is in a crucial phase of adjusting its conflicts or of striving to restore its equilibrium. Still, provided the shock of contact is not too unsettling, it may be assumed that a system operating under its own controls is able to absorb alien materials just as it adjusts to internal changes under the force of its own adaptive mechanisms.

When its autonomy is threatened a system may respond belligerently; that is, it may resort to force to maintain its independence. This has happened repeatedly as expanding systems have sought to dominate others in the path of their exploitations. Failure to maintain cultural and political independence often results in a reaction of defeatism which may be manifested in the neglect of ceremonial observances, the establishment of a dependency relationship with the dominant group, and population decline.

Reactive Adaptation

Another response to threat when the pressure is less nearly overwhelming is to withdraw and to encyst native values. In this instance there is, so to speak, a reactive adaptation to threat: native forms are reaffirmed and re-enforced by a renewed commitment to them. . . . More familiar and more spectacular expressions of the same phenomenon have repeatedly occurred as nativistic reactions of one sort or another, including revivalistic cults, nationalistic movements, and isolationist programs.

Progressive Adjustment

If we assume that neither withdrawal from alien contact nor the complete annihilation of a group occurs, conjunctive relations at any time must fall under one of two headings: progressive adjustment or stabilized pluralism. Progressive adjustment can lead predominantly in the direction of fusion or that of assimilation. In fusion the approximation of the two autonomous systems is roughly mutual, though probably never perfectly so. "Bilateral" could be used in describing the ideal typical pole of fusion on the continuum, with "unilateral" characterizing the opposite theoretical absolute of assimilation. Obviously, the trend of adjustment in most contact situations is toward some point between the poles of a balanced blending and the total submersion of one culture by the other. It is nevertheless useful to gauge and attempt to account for differences of trend.

Cultural Fusion An intercultural network can develop into a genuine third sociocultural system through a process of fusion. If it does, it must exhibit the attributes of uniqueness and autonomy possessed by parent systems. It is probable that in almost every instance some modification of unilaterally extended roles will be necessary to adjust to the peculiarities of the system with which they must articulate. Some distinctiveness is also to be expected from the emergence of *ad hoc* roles, such as those of designated go-betweens, proxies, and buffering agents, which did not previously exist in either system. It is possible, too, for a cluster of intercultural roles to give rise to a new institution, such as a plantation system or an arbitration council, which is relatively autonomous. However, isolated complexes of this character do not necessarily constitute an intercultural role network that is either an integrated system or a distinctive sociocultural body. A real third system probably emerges only with the disappearance of the original two through fusion in a given territory. . . .

Assimilation The second type of progressive adjustment is the assimilation of one group by another. In some ways it is the dichotomous opposite of fusion. . . . Acculturation is a necessary but not sufficient condition of assimilation. . . .

Although it is never fully realized, assimilation implies an essentially unilateral approximation of one culture in the direction of the other, albeit a changing or ongoing other. Complete assimilation, like complete fusion, is much less frequent in fact than is indicated by the frequency with which the term is used in the literature. . . .

Stabilized Pluralism

In order to understand progressive adjustment, it is also necessary to explore cases of arrested fusion or incomplete assimilation. By this is meant stabilized pluralism, namely, the failure of two cultures in contact completely to lose their autonomy. . . . Theoretically, at least, stabilized pluralism implies only an extreme slackening of the rate of progressive adjustment. In any event, a common pattern of adjustment appears in the many cases of a relatively stabilized relationship between two contacting cultures, as happens in some caste systems, in the adaptations of enclaves and their dominant hosts, and in the symbiotic connection between some sedentary and nomadic groups in the Old World. In these instances an intercultural system has reached a point of institutionalized adjustment to serve the interests of both groups. Often parallel ethnic institutions develop in the two societies in continuous and stabilized contact. These institutions are significant in acculturative adaptation in at least three respects. They ameliorate the stresses of interethnic situations and provide contexts for validating acculturation under relatively permissive conditions. They also provide criteria of acculturation for members of the ethnic group and as such they may express selective emphases of dominant cultural forms, symbols, and valuations due to the socially differentiated position of the two groups. Further, they legitimatize the status system of the ethnic community in which one may expect to find transplanted important aspects of the stratification criteria of the dominant society. . . .

Differential Rates of Change

Change under contact conditions, like change under internal stimulation, seems to proceed at uneven rates in different areas of culture regardless of the nature of the intercultural system. It has often been remarked that in the conjunction between Western and non-Western cultures technology appears to alter more readily than do other aspects of a system. This may be due in part to the emphasis placed upon technology in the Western world as well as to its evident superiority over most local forms. Since material accomplishment represents values held by the invaders in such cases, the same considerations may help to explain why Westerners, when they are affected by contact, also adopt objects rather than behaviors and ideas.

In point of fact, the conventional categories of cultural description—technology, social organization, religion, etc.—do not readily lend themselves to an analysis of differential change. *All* cultural segments have their concrete aspects, and these more explicit behaviors and apparatus are as a rule more readily mastered than symbolic and valuational aspects. In religion, for example, objects and rituals may be assimilated as rapidly as new tools. They may be integrated as long as they enhance prevailing security and orientational functions. In the absence of coercion even more clearly efficient implements have been rejected or ignored when perceived to interfere with basic cultural understandings. . . . Furthermore, adoption of a foreign object can in most cases be an individual matter; at any rate it does not necessarily raise the social complications and the need for common consent that are inescapable with the transfer of an alien kinship system or marriage custom.

Intangibles also appear to show levels of differential change. Specific and isolated ideas and behaviors are thought to be more vulnerable than those integrated with a more inclusive set of values. The more generalized values are, the more persistent they seem to be. What might be called the basic premises of a people regarding the nature of man and the universe can go unchanged despite considerable modification in technology and other aspects of culture. These inferred values of a culture appear to have a greater continuity in many, if not in all cases, and for this reason have themselves been conceptualized as selectors, molders, and integrators. If they have a controlling position they may be said to screen the incoming material and to order its placement in the existing system.

It has been suggested that the greatest resistance to change and reorganization will occur in certain universal categories of cultural adaptation: maintenance systems, communication systems, and security systems. . . . By contrast, there are elements which are only weakly supported by moral judgments of right and wrong,

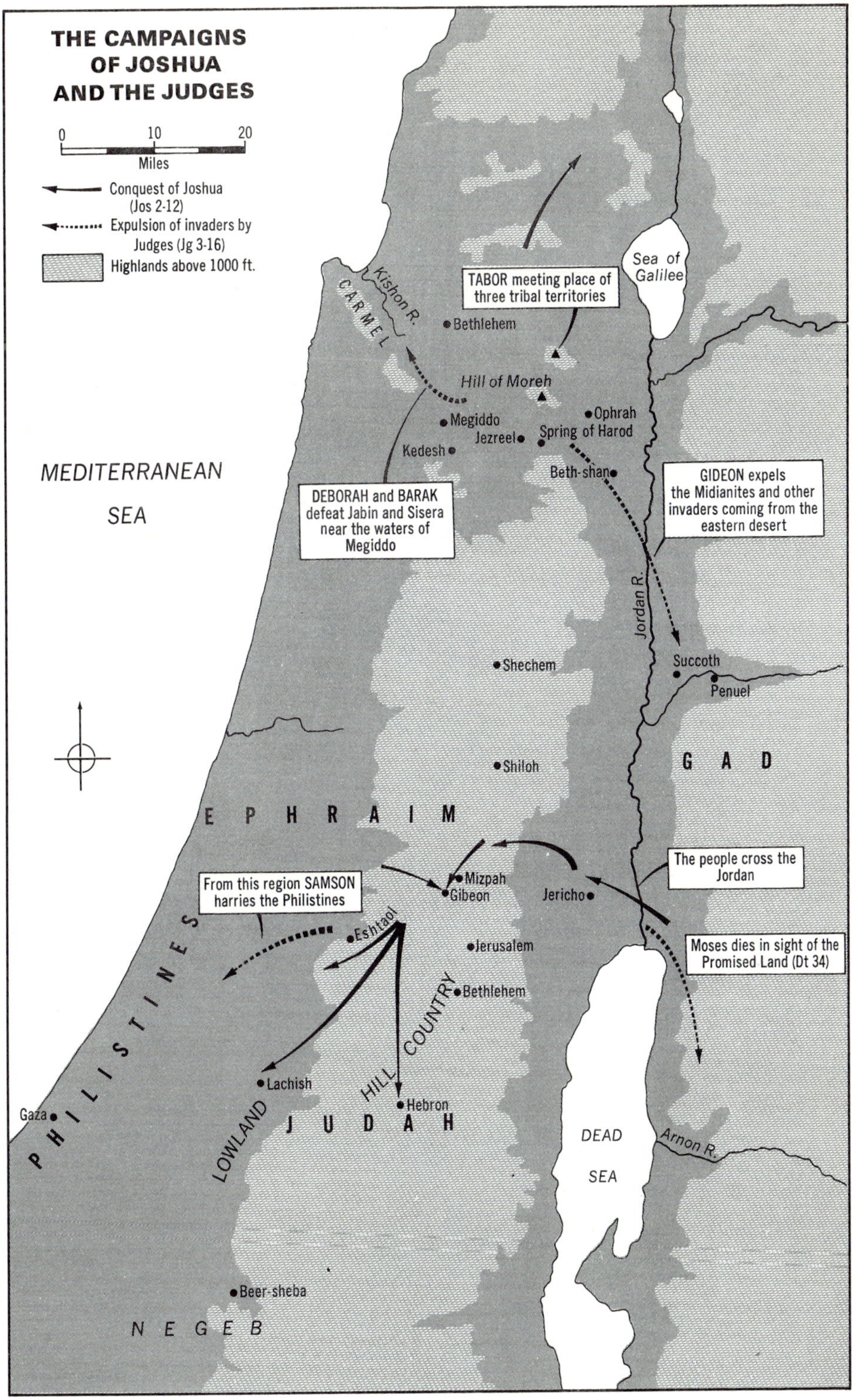
THE CAMPAIGNS OF JOSHUA AND THE JUDGES
0
10
20
Miles
Conquest of Joshua (Jos 2-12)
Expulsion of invaders by Judges (Jg 3-16)
Highlands above 1000 ft.
Sea of Galilee
TABOR meeting place of three tribal territories
Kishon R.
CARMEL
Bethlehem
Hill of Moreh
Megiddo
Ophrah
Jezreel
Spring of Harod
Kedesh
MEDITERRANEAN SEA
Beth-shan
GIDEON expels the Midianites and other invaders coming from the eastern desert
DEBORAH and BARAK defeat Jabin and Sisera near the waters of Megiddo
Jordan R.
Succoth
Penuel
Shechem
Shiloh
GAD
EPHRAIM
The people cross the Jordan
From this region SAMSON harries the Philistines
Mizpah
Gibeon
Jericho
Eshtaol
Jerusalem
Moses dies in sight of the Promised Land (Dt 34)
Bethlehem
HILL COUNTRY
PHILISTINES
Lachish
Hebron
Gaza
LOWLAND
JUDAH
DEAD SEA
Arnon R.
Beer-sheba
NEGEB

The valley of the Jordan River as it runs from the Sea of Galilee to the Dead Sea. Being below sea level, the vegetation is lush and semitropical. (Zionist Archives and Library)

propriety and inpropriety, desirability and undesirability, and hence more susceptible to change. In most cases these less resistant aspects would include what are rated as luxury products, such as ornamentation, art, and leisure activities, in so far as they are not symbolic of deeply held values.

The value structure of a culture almost invariably acts as the most important agent for the transformation and integration of alien beliefs and practices. However, when the values of one culture sharply contrast with those of another and when these same values are deeply involved in the social and economic structures of the respective societies, one may expect acculturation to include reactive adaptations resulting in ethnocentrism, militant rejection of alien groups, or a stabilized pluralism. In the course of the Israelite conquest and settlement of Palestine, many of these aspects of acculturation came into operation as a result of the need of the Israelites to adapt to a new environment and to a new people, whose culture was already integrated with that environment.

The Hebrews were to find Palestine a land of few resources and very difficult to unify. The area of Israel proper, west of the Jordan River, was only about six thousand square miles [approximately the size and shape of the state of New Hampshire] and much of that was rocky hill country, offering pasture but little good land for agriculture. The Jordan, flowing in a deep rift from the Anti-Lebanon Mountains to the Dead Sea splits Palestine in two. While the valley of the river is hot and desert-like with oases, beyond it to the east in Transjordania were fertile plains, reasonably well-watered and productive until they petered out into the desert. But Israel, the chosen land of the Hebrews, was the rugged hill country which lay between the Jordan and the coastal plain. It fell into three main subdivisions: Judah in the south, from Jerusalem to the desert, Israel in the center, and Galilee to the north near the Sea of Galilee. Because it was a land of mountain shrubbery, a land well suited to herding sheep and goats and to a small-scale cereal production, it was quite literally a land of milk and honey. Water was scarce and had to be stored in cisterns for use during the hot summer season. Although the coastal plain was productive, it was bordered by sand dunes and had no good harbors for sea trade. Yet Palestine, because it was situated between Egypt and Syria, was a vital link in the communications of the Fertile Crescent, and is usually described as a "land of passage." The road from Egypt ran through the coastal plain to Mt. Carmel on the north. From Megiddo, an important control point, it turned along the north side of Carmel into the large plain of Esdraelon, then crossed the Jordan River and bent northeast to Damascus. Except for this gap to the northeast, northern Palestine was closed by mountains. The hill country itself was isolated, and the Hebrews living there tended to maintain an ingrown and provincial life.[2]

In the Old Testament account the Israelites under the leadership of Joshua suddenly invaded and conquered Palestine. Archeological evidence and even some Biblical accounts seem to indicate that the conquest was accomplished by a gradual infiltration, first of the more remote and poorly defended hill country, eventually of the more populous and settled valley regions. Both the "sudden" and the "gradual" versions of the conquest probably contain elements of historical fact. About mid-thirteenth century B.C. the poorly armed Israelite invaders began to move out of the desert into the central hill country where they joined with their brethren who had settled there centuries before. Since the plains and crossroads of Palestine were dominated by fortified Canaanite towns blocking the Israelites' settlement of the fertile areas, the complete conquest of Palestine was a long drawn-out affair. A few of these towns fell to invading tribes, but for the most part the Israelites remained in the hill country until they gained enough strength to assault the better defended

[2] Carl Roebuck, *The World of Ancient Times* (New York: Charles Scribner's Sons, 1966), p. 127.

An oasis near Jericho reveals the sharp contrast between the Jordan valley and the rugged hills of the Judean desert beyond. (Israel Government Tourist Office)

Canaanite towns. In the twelfth century B.C. the stronger Israelite tribes managed to advance into the valley country to complete their conquest.

As a means of subjugating and controlling Palestine, the Israelites organized themselves into a loose twelve-tribe confederacy. The covenant with Yahweh bound the tribes together with a common religious tie, yet allowed a considerable degree of political autonomy for each of them. The tribes assembled as a confederacy at the main sanctuary of Shiloh to celebrate the great religious feasts centered around the Ark of the Covenant.

The Ark was, according to Biblical tradition, a wooden chest in which Moses had placed the two stone tablets on which the Ten Commandments were recorded. It appears that the Ark

An experimental trench dug into Tell Judeideh in northern Syria, showing the remains from different levels of human habitation in this one spot. Because of the tendency in the ancient Middle East to rebuild cities and villages on the same location, such mounds, or tells, often contain a record of several thousand years. (The Oriental Institute, University of Chicago and L. H. Grollenberg, O.P.)

Level I	A.D. 600–300 Remains of an early Christian church of the first centuries A.D.	Level VIII	1800–2000 B.C. Painted pottery similar to that of the Hyksos period
Level II	A.D. 300–64 B.C. Village of the time of St. Paul	Level IX	2000–2400 B.C. Use of bronze for weapons and axes
Level III	64–500 B.C. Colony of the time of the Persian Empire	Level X	2400–2600 B.C. Evidence of commercial relations with northern Mesopotamia
Level IV	500–1000 B.C. Layer dating from the period of the Syro-Hittite Empire	Level XI	2600–3100 B.C. Importation of cylinder seals from Ur, the city of Abraham
Level V	1000–1200 B.C. Traces of pottery of the "Peoples of the sea"	Level XII	3100–3400 B.C. Beginning of the widespread use of metal
Level VI	1200–1600 B.C. Period of the migration of peoples; pottery from many different regions, particularly Cyprus	Level XIII	3400–3800 B.C. Pottery shaped by hand, as beautiful in form as that of later periods
Level VII	1600–1800 B.C. Links with the East; clay statues of the Mother-Goddess type	Level XIV	3800–4500 B.C. Earliest traces of a Syrian village

also served as a portable throne upon which Yahweh was invisibly enthroned—invisibly because the second commandment prohibited the worship of images. In time of war the Israelites carried the Ark into battle; this signified that Yahweh personally led them.

The twelve-tribe confederacy protected Israelite political independence, but in the process of settling down in Palestine and adapting themselves to a new environment and way of life the Hebrews naturally came into contact with the Canaanite culture of the neighboring valleys. In contrast to Hebrew society, which was based on kinship institutions—the tribe, clan, and family—Canaanite social organization was adapted to an agrarian-urban environment. The Canaanite towns and the surrounding fields were ruled by local kings. Some of the towns were hill fortresses holding strategic passes; others lay at the crossing of caravan routes; and still others were seaports. As a consequence of the mixed nature of its economy and population, Canaanite society, unlike that of the Hebrew invaders, tended to be divided into socioeconomic classes —aristocratic landowners, priests, merchants, peasants, and slaves. The priests formed an

The excavations at Jericho, a city that dates back to 7000 B.C. Here a section of the wall tower can be seen. (Israel Information Services)

especially powerful upper class, which, through its control of the temples, had acquired large landholdings and many slaves. In some cases their great wealth had turned them into moneylenders. The commercial element of Canaanite society is attested to in the Old Testament where the term Canaanite often designates a merchant or trader. This mixed urban population was fed by produce from the cultivated lands surrounding the cities, and thus Canaanite life was never far removed from agriculture.

Soon after the Israelites gained a foothold in the richer valleys and plains adjacent to the hill country, many began to forsake the seminomadic life for farming on individual homesteads. While continuing to affirm the concept that all the land ultimately belonged to Yahweh and was given to the entire covenant community as a trust, a sense of private ownership, at least at the family level, began to emerge. Not only was much of the newly acquired land better suited to agriculture than to herding, it was obviously able to produce and sustain the more advanced and luxurious culture of the Canaanites. Tilling the soil, therefore, needed little justification, and it was natural that the Israelites, new to farming, should borrow their agricultural technology from their more experienced Canaanite neighbors.

One of the most important "tools" used by

A relief from the third century A.D. depicting the Ark of the Covenant. (The Matson Photo Service, Alhambra, California)

The Mother-Goddess, the personification of fertility, was the major figure of agricultural religions in the ancient Mediterranean world. In this ivory carving from the fourteenth century B.C., she stands between two goats and holds stalks of grain. (Archives Photographiques, Paris)

the Canaanites to insure the productivity of the soil was their religion, a nature religion based upon the changing seasons and the desire to guarantee fertility through imitative magic. For the Israelites, Yahweh had proven himself effective in protecting them during their wanderings and in granting them military success during their invasion of Palestine. But in the face of total ignorance over what powers their God might have to bring rain and nourishment to the soil, the Israelite farmers relied on the proven success of the Canaanite "method."

This solution resulted in a long and far-reaching examination of the nature and meaning of Israel's allegiance to Yahweh. Inasmuch as it called for a religious self-examination, born out of the transition from the desert of Sinai to the fields of Palestine, it affected every Israelite. But the transition was less dramatic for the shepherds of the hill country than it was for the farmers of the plains, and in time these economic differences resulted in a division that had important political repercussions.

This conflict, which occupied Israel throughout the rest of the Old Testament period, began through the confrontation with Canaanite religion. In order to appreciate the implications of this conflict for Israel's faith, some aspects of this particular nature religion should be examined.

THE TEMPTATIONS OF CANAANITE CULTURE
Bernhard W. Anderson[3]

To appreciate the nature of the struggle of the period of the judges,[4] we must know something about the religion of Canaan, which in the Old Testament is described

[3] Bernhard W. Anderson, *Understanding the Old Testament*, 2d ed., © 1966, pp. 102–108. Reprinted by permission of Prentice-Hall, Inc., Englewood Cliffs, New Jersey.

[4] That is, the entire period of the conquest and settlement of Palestine. The significance of the term judge will be treated shortly.

as the worship of the Baals and Ashtarts. . . . The title "Baal" means "lord" or "owner," and designates the male deity who owns the land and controls its fertility. His female partner is known as "Baalath," "lady," although in the cases cited above her personal name is Ashtart. It was believed that these fertility powers were connected with particular localities or towns, in which case one could speak of many Baals and Ashtarts, as numerous as the cities of the land . . . . But it was also possible to regard these local powers as manifestations of the great "lord" and "lady" who dwell in the heavens, in which case worshipers could address Baal and Ashtart in the singular as cosmic deities.

A modern farmer, despite his training in the science of agriculture, sometimes marvels at the strange powers of fertility that work in the soil (even yet called "mother Earth") to bring about a fruitful harvest. In those moments he is linked with his ancient predecessors—men of the soil who from time immemorial have marveled at the astonishing mystery of nature without which there could be no agriculture. In the Fertile Crescent, where the whole culture was dependent upon the fruitfulness of the soil, this mystery was viewed in a religious way. The ground, it was said, is the sphere of divine powers. The Baal of a region is the "lord" or "owner" of the ground; its fertility is dependent upon sexual relations between him and his consort. When the rains came and the earth and water mingled, the mysterious powers of fertility stirred again. New life was resurrected after the barrenness of winter. This astonishing revival of nature, men believed, was due to sexual intercourse between Baal and his partner, Baalath.

Furthermore, man was not a mere spectator of the sacred marriage. It was believed that by ritually enacting the drama of Baal it was possible to assist—through magical power—the fertility powers to reach their consummation, and thereby to insure the welfare and prosperity of the land. The cooperation with the powers of fertility involved the dramatization in the temples of the story of Baal's loves and wars. Besides the rehearsal of this mythology, a prominent feature of the Canaanite cult was sacred prostitution.... In the act of temple prostitution the man identified himself with Baal, the woman with Ashtart. It was believed that human pairs, by imitating the action of Baal and his partner, could bring the divine pair together in fertilizing union.

Enough has been said to indicate that Canaanite religion was highly erotic. But this eroticism was not just the expression of a desire for pleasure through sex (as it so often is in modern culture). Rather, it was believed that the whole natural sphere, to which the existence of the farmer was intimately bound, was governed by the vitalities of sex—the powers of the masculine and the feminine. Through sexual ceremonies farmers could swing into the rhythms of the agricultural world, and even keep those rhythms going through the techniques of religious magic. The kind of magic in question is often called sympathetic or imitative magic. It rests on the assumption that when men imitate the action of the gods, a power is released to bring that action about. (For example: the "rainmaker" who, by pouring water from a tree and thereby imitating rain, induces the gods to end a drought.)

The pattern of nature religion found in Canaan was of one piece with the myth and ritual which, in varying forms, was spread throughout the whole Fertile Crescent. In Babylonia, for example, the Tammuz cult dramatized the relations between the god Tammuz and the goddess Ishtar. In Egypt the Isis cult was based on the worship of the god Osiris (Horus) and his female counterpart Isis (Hathor). And, as we have seen, in Canaan the Baal cult dramatized the relations between the storm god Baal and his consort, known as Anath or Ashtart (the Canaanite equivalent of Ishtar). The basic similarity of these religions encouraged a great deal of borrowing back and forth, for they appealed to a common concern about man's relation to nature....

Here, then, was a practical religion for farmers. In Canaan, Baal was recognized as the lord of the earth: the owner of the land, the giver of rain, the source of the grain, wine, and oil. People believed that the agricultural harvest would not be plentiful unless the fertility powers were worshiped according to the ways of Canaan. To have ignored the Baal rites in those days would have seemed as impractical as for a modern farmer to ignore science in the cultivation of the land.

It is not surprising, then, that the Israelites, unaccustomed to the ways of agriculture, turned to the gods of the land. They did not mean to turn away from Yahweh, the God of the Exodus and the Sinai covenant. To Yahweh they would look in times of military crisis; and to Baal they would turn for success in agriculture. Thus they would serve Yahweh and Baal side by side.... Perhaps it was believed that one faith was the official public religion, and the other was a religion for home and farm life. In any case, it was not felt that the two religions were contradictory or mutually exclusive.

There was a strong tendency for the two faiths to coalesce in popular worship. As we know from archaeology, in the outlying regions of Israel people had in their possession figurines, small statuettes of the goddess of fertility, Ashtart. Elements of ritual and mythology were taken over from Canaanite religion and incorporated into the worship of Yahweh. Former Canaanite sanctuaries, like Bethel, Shechem, and perhaps Gilgal, were rededicated to Yahweh, and the Canaanite agricultural calendar was adopted for the timing of the pilgrimage festivals. . . . Parents began naming their children after Baal, apparently with no thought of abandoning Yahweh. One of the judges, Gideon, was also named Jerub-baal, which means "let Baal contend," or perhaps "may Baal multiply." Saul and David, both ardent devotees of Yahweh, gave Baal names to their children. As late as the eighth century B.C., Israelites—according to the prophet Hosea—actually addressed Yahweh as "Baal," and by worshiping him according to the rituals of Baal sought the blessings of fertility (Hos. 2). At the popular level this syncretism—that is, the fusion of different religious forms and views—went on to some degree from the time Israel first set foot on Canaanite soil.

As we have noticed, this syncretism was going on constantly in the commingling cultures of the Fertile Crescent, for the religions of the area had a great deal in common. But Israel's faith was based on the novel belief in a *jealous* God who would tolerate no rivals. According to the terms of the covenant, Israel was to have "no other gods before Yahweh." Yahweh's lordship over his people was absolute, extending into every sphere of life. Therefore, to believe that Yahweh was lord in one sphere (history) and Baal in another (fertilization of the soil) was a fundamental violation of the meaning of the covenant. . . .

According to Israel's faith . . . the power of the divine was disclosed in the sphere

Figurines of Ashtart (Astarte), which emphasize the aspects of reproduction, were often used by the Canaanites as amulets and charms. (By courtesy of the Israel Department of Antiquities and Museums)

of history—that is, in the wonder of a *non-recurring event* (the Exodus) which was at once the sign of God's deliverance of his people from servitude and the call to obey his will within a covenant community. Unlike Baal, Yahweh has no consort at his side. He is neither sexual in nature, nor is he to be worshiped by sexual rites.

To be sure, Israel's faith does not take a negative view toward sex, for sex belongs to the divine creation and as such is hallowed (see Gen. 1:27–28). But although Yahweh is Lord of fertility, he is not a fertility god subject to the death and resurrection of the natural world. He is "the Living God" who reveals himself in the

Phoenician-Canaanite idol representing Baal. (Archives Photographiques, Paris)

arena of men's history—where human life touches life, where injustices oppress and hopes for deliverance are felt, where men are called to make decisions that alter the course of the future. While Baal religion taught men to *control* the gods, Israel's faith stressed *serving* God in gratitude for his benevolence and in response to the task which he lays upon his people. Yahweh could not be coerced by magic. He could only be trusted or betrayed, obeyed or disobeyed, but in all things his will was sovereign.

With their desert background, Israel's more discerning leaders sensed the fundamental opposition between the stern demands of Yahweh and the erotic religion of Canaan. Was the meaning of man's life in Canaan disclosed in his relation to divine powers within nature, or in his relation to the Lord of history? This fundamental question was not answered overnight. In Canaanite religion, Israel's faith met the challenge of its opposite, but it took many generations for the true strength and uniqueness of the Mosaic faith to be seen. . . .

During the conquest and settlement of Palestine religious assimilation was periodically checked by the fear of internal and external enemies. When threatened militarily, Israel turned not to Baal, the god of fertility, but to Yahweh, the God of history. In all probability

The remains of the temple-fortress at Megiddo. The height of Megiddo can be seen in comparison to the plain in the distance. (The Oriental Institute, University of Chicago)

Israel might have succumbed to the Canaanite religion had it not been for the military crises that periodically threatened the political existence of the tribal confederacy. A time of crisis was also a time of covenant renewal—a reaffirmation of faith in, and loyalty to, Yahweh. War, then, helped to prevent the cultural assimilation of the Israelites. The following analysis of the Song of Deborah, one of the oldest passages in the Old Testament and generally regarded as a first-hand account of one of the last battles against the Canaanites (the Battle of Megiddo, ca. 1125 B.C.), illustrates the meaning the Israelites attached to war.

THE SONG OF DEBORAH AND HOLY WAR
Johannes Pedersen[5]

In early Israel war was a natural condition, because life, honour, and peace had to be constantly created and recaptured. Just as the individual and his kin must maintain their ground by unwearying fighting and reprisal, so also the larger family communities and the whole people had to make a place for themselves among other nations by struggle and strife. The fighting of a people, too, might be an act of "vengeance" to uphold the honour of the nation, and the Israelites entertained no doubt that the right won by the strong man measuring his strength against other men in war was a true right.

The leading part played by warfare in the life of the people is shown by the fact that the wanderings in the desert are described as a military expedition. The men are organised according to tribes in the camp around the sanctuary. Each unit gathers round its pennon or banner as its rallying point. . . . The sanctuary is carried in front of the people on the march, certain trumpet blasts are the signal for breaking camp, and it is expressly stated that the same trumpets are used both in war and in the cult assembly. The whole people is one great host of warriors.

This impression of the importance of war is confirmed by the old historical narratives, and we have a single poem which, more than any other, gives direct expression to the psychic condition engendered by war in the earliest times. This is the Song of Deborah [Judg. 5], which may be rendered thus:

2. For vehement action in Israel, for the noble deeds of warriors, bless ye Yahweh.
3. Hearken ye kings, give ear ye princes. Sing, sing will I unto Yahweh, I will chant unto Yahweh, the God of Israel.
4. Yahweh, when thou wentest out of Seir, when thou advancedst from the steppe of Edom, the earth quaked, yea, the heavens o'erflowed, yea, the clouds o'erflowed with water.
5. Mountains crumbled before Yahweh, before Yahweh, the God of Israel.
6. In the days of Samgar ben Anath, in the days of Jael, the high roads lay deserted, wayfarers stole along tortuous paths.
7. Hamlets (?) decayed, they decayed in Israel, until thou arosest Deborah, thou arosest, thou mother in Israel.
8. New gods are chosen, then is there fighting about the gates; but no shield or spear is seen among the forty thousand of Israel.
9. My heart is with the chiefs of Israel, those who proved noble among the people. Bless ye Yahweh.
10. Riding tawny she-asses, sitting on rugs, or wandering on the road. Chant!
11. . . . among the water troughs they sing the

---

[5] Johannes Pedersen, *Israel: Its Life and Culture* (London: Oxford University Press, 1964), Vols. III–IV, pp. 1–8, 12–15, 18–19, reprinted by permission of Banner og Korchs Forlag, Copenhagen. This edition is a photo reprint of the original English edition published in 1926. The extensive Biblical references in this selection have been minimized.

The Conquest and Settlement of Palestine

righteous acts of Yahweh, the righteous works of his . . . in Israel. Then the people of Yahweh went down to the gates.
12. Forward, forward, Deborah. Forward, forward, chant a lay. Rise up Barak, seize thy captives, Abinoam's son.
13. Then . . . descend unto the mighty, Yahweh's people descend for me among heroes.
14. From Ephraim is their root; "after thee, Benjamin, among the kinsmen."
Chiefs came down from Machir, from Zebulon those who wielded the sceptre.
15. Thy chieftains, Issachar, were with Deborah; . . . and Issachar are loyal to Barak; into the valley were they sent in his train.
Great were the heart-searchings in Reuben's divisions.
16. Why didst thou sit among the cattle-pens listening to the piping of the shepherds? For Reuben's divisions the heart-searchings were great.
17. Gilead lives beyond Jordan; why does Dan dwell like a sojourner near ships?
Asher sat by the seashore, remained by his creeks.
18. Zebulon is a people that endangers its life unto death, and Naphtali dwells on the high expanses.
19. Kings came and fought, then fought the kings of Canaan; at Taanach on the waters of Megiddo they gained no spoil of silver.
20. The stars fought from the heavens, from their courses they fought against Sisera.
21. The river of Kishon swept them away, the primeval river, the river of Kishon. My soul, go forth with strength.
22. Then thundered the horses' hoofs, in his stallions' fiery chase.
23. Cast off Meroz, says Yahweh's *mal'ākh,* cast off its citizens forever. For they did not come to Yahweh's assistance, to Yahweh's assistance among the heroes.
24. Blessed among women is Jael, the wife of Heber the Kenite, blessed among women in tents.
25. He asked water, she gave him milk, in a lordly bowl she gave him sour milk.
26. She put out her hand to the tent-peg, put out her right hand to the workmen's hammer; she smote Sisera, shattered his head, split and fractured his temple.
27. He swayed, sank, lay at her feet; he swayed, sank at her feet; where he swayed, he sank, slain.
28. Out of the window she peered, behind the lattice she wailed, Sisera's mother. Why is his chariot so long in coming, why delay the hoof-beats of his team?
29. The wise among her ladies made answer, nay, thus she made answer to herself:
30. No doubt they are taking and dividing the spoil: a woman, two women to each man. Spoil of dyed stuffs for Sisera, spoil of dyed embroidered stuff, doubly embroidered and dyed stuff for my neck.
31. Thus, O Yahweh, let all thine enemies perish; but those who love Him are like the sunrise in its might.

The vigorous stanzas of the poem present a series of pictures, the import and profundity of which partly elude us. Expressions are used which have since become obsolete in the language, allusions so slight that we do not understand them and in some cases the text is probably corrupt.

The opening lines indicate the theme, the magnificent feat performed by the people, but the glory for it is given to Yahweh. The poem begins and ends with the God of the people; it is His might which has been active throughout the great achievement. Hence His power is first described, and to begin with the narrative takes us back to the earliest history of the people. While Heaven and earth quake, Yahweh advances from the southward plains where the fathers of Israel wandered. In a few lines (vv. 6–8) the poet then draws a picture of the state of things before the battle. Uncertainty prevails everywhere, communications are being interrupted, men have to steal warily from place to place, Israel was decaying, for as yet no real leader had arisen. A change of culture is setting in. New gods are adopted and the people is faced by the struggle for the strongholds . . . and yet the Israelites, few in number though they are, are unprepared and unarmed.

But out of this confusion of disintegration, all at once there appears a people led by mightly chieftains, willing to abandon themselves to the passion of war, some riding their asses, others afoot, all with a single aim. Their objective is the "gates," the fortified cities; the confidence of the chiefs is due to the fact that the God is with them, it is by His strength and righteousness that they have hitherto maintained their position as a people (vv. 9–11).

The poet has now arrived at the point when the battle is about to begin. Without any transition a call is addressed to the leaders. Deborah, the woman who urged the people to fight, is requested to let her rousing war song be heard; Barak, the hero, is to open the battle. But just as it is about to begin, the poet reviews the tribes. Ephraim, Benjamin, Machir, Zebulon, Issachar form the core. The more distant tribes hesitate, or they have settled down and disregard the summons (vv. 12–18).

Suddenly there is a change in the spirit of the poem. The battle is described in short stanzas. The poet does not enlarge on what is happening, the exploits of the Israelite army are not even mentioned. Only the enemy is referred to, but the few and hastily sketched pictures convey a powerful impression of the defeat of the hostile army, and thus of the victory of Israel. The battlefield is at Taanach and Megiddo. Here came the Canaanite kings, sure of their prey, but they took no gain. They had no luck, even the stars fought against them. Two pictures suffice to call up all their misery. We see their corpses being whirled away by the river Kishon, and their horses dashing riderless across the plain (vv. 19–22).

Thus victory and defeat are completed. Now Israel is left victorious in all her power. But the poet has still a few words to add. An Israelite community, Meroz, has failed Yahweh, and yet—it must be taken for granted—it was near the battlefield. This conduct has placed it outside Israel, it cannot belong to the people any more (v. 23). Possibly its betrayal became apparent during the flight of the Canaanite chief, whose ignominious death is the next incident to be described in the poem.

The narrative centres round a eulogy of the woman Jael, only half Israelite, who caused his death. We merely learn his name, Sisera, in passing. Three stanzas describe the scene with his murder. He is standing in her tent asking for water; not content to comply with his request, she pours out milk for him in a lordly bowl, thus making him feel as safe as an honoured guest. But while he is drinking, and his face is hidden behind the bowl, she seizes the hammer and tent-peg and fractures his temple. All this is narrated in few and brief words, but the poet lingers over the description of how the smitten foe sways, sinks to the ground and lies at the feet of the woman.

This important incident does not, however, exhaust the sweetness of victory to the poet. The defeat of the foe is to be followed up to the last detail. He takes his hearers into the enemy's camp, and measures the greatness of his people's victory by the disappointed expectations of the women left at home. He does not mar his joy by words of mockery. With a clear and restrained objectivity he describes the expectation of the hostile chief's mother as she is sitting in her bower with her women.

Their talk, as repeated here seems sober enough. Why does he not come? The wisest of the women agree with her; the spoil is so enormous that the distribution takes time. No comment is made on the conversation, and no superfluous remark describes the mother's reception of the message of defeat when it comes at last. The picture of the expectation of the women is left clear and unobscured; therefore it reflects the victory of Israel in its whole extent. Immediately after this, the poet breaks into a song of triumph: Thus shall the enemies of Yahweh perish, but His people shall continually renew its power, like the rising sun. . . .

The Israel revealed to us in the Song of Deborah consisted of a number of tribes which had settled among the Canaanites, chiefly in the highlands of Canaan. The mixing with the Canaanites had not yet gathered headway, but it had begun. The people was becoming acquainted with new gods, and at the same time it lived in fear of the strong Canaanites ensconced in their cities and ruling by such means as civilisation gave them. Thus the nation was threatened by weakening and disintegration both from within and from without.

The poem shows that the tribes did not form an organised unity. Some stayed away, others were half-hearted, those who came, gathered to the assistance of Yahweh upon the summons of the leaders. . . . In early times the Israelites could only be induced to concerted action by their feeling of fellowship, and it exerted its influence as far as it went. No external framework kept the tribes together, those who hung back were threatened by the curse, by repudiation from the psychic fellowship. The upbearer of this fellowship was the ancient God of the people. This means that the unity was a unity of soul. It was due to a community of kind and a common history, which manifested itself in a uniform cult. But whether this inherited cult had found common forms after the immigration into Canaan is a question not easily answered.

The psychic unity which characterised early Israel was preserved more or less, and became especially conspicuous during war, because all the forces of the people were concentrated in it.

In the Song of Deborah we see how everything is intensified, how events loom larger than usual and attain cosmic dimensions. The first stanza, we may resume, sets forth the elation filling the souls of the warriors. A woman, herself carried away by her enthusiasm, urges them onward and sets the forces in motion. All depends on the chieftains, but most of all on the leader, in whom the will of all is bound up. The river that witnesses the flight is no ordinary stream, it is a primeval river. All space takes part in the battle, in the heavens the stars in their courses fight against the enemies of Israel.

The intense effort made by the people to gather all its strength is seen from the fact that it is Yahweh, the fountain-head and source of all Israelitish life, who directs the battle and brings it to an end. It is His strength and will which animate the chieftains and the people. He advances in all His might from His old home where the real history of the people began. The poem reaches its climax as it proclaims the death of His enemies and the eternal growth of His friends.

We hear nothing of the gods of the Canaanites; but it is a matter of course that they participate in the battle on the other side. The hostile armies meet in battle, each bringing its entire world with it. Each people appears in all its strength, with its history, and its God.

The picture of warfare in early Israel shown to us in the Song of Deborah corresponds entirely to what we learn from other traditions. All efforts are directed towards creating and maintaining that state of increased psychic strength which is requisite in war.

For the army to preserve its concentrated strength it is necessary that every man in it should possess absolute purity. We know that purity is consistent with the integrity of the soul; impurity destroys its integrity and therefore impairs the strength of the soul.

Some of the Israelite military laws exemplify the strictness with which purity had to be maintained. Among the things which cause impurity are the issues of the body, especially such as belong to sexual life. Hence one law lays down that a warrior who has had an issue of the body in the night shall keep outside the camp all day and only be admitted to the camp again at sunset after washing. Similarly the waste products voided from the body are to be kept outside the camp and carefully buried in the ground. . . .

The Israelites call the warrior's state *kōdesh*, the term which we render by the word "holiness." Holiness has its root in the soul, it is a common force impregnating all the warriors. Not merely they themselves, but everything that belongs to them is pervaded by the same force. The warriors are "the sanctified of Yahweh," but their weapons, too, are sacred as long as they themselves are in the war-like state. This property can be transferred to the weapons by annointing them. The entire camp constitutes a sacred sphere, from which all that is unclean must be kept away, as well as from the persons of the warriors. Thus the camp with the army forms a firm coherent organism. The unity is given through the common spirit of the people, but it is intensified in the same degree as the common strength is increased and all disrupting impurity kept away.

The army is the people in a condensed and intensified form. As the army assembles and prepares for war, the holiness is created which is the prerequisite of its power to act. To be carried through successfully a war must be "sanctified." . . . The relation to the source of power, the God of the people, must be in good order, that he may constantly take part in the battle. . . .

Strengthened by their sanctification and the surety of victory thus acquired the warriors can now go to war. They must preserve what they have acquired by avoiding an infringement of their holiness. If they succeed, God's strength and thus God Himself is with them throughout. "Yahweh, thy God, walks with thee in the midst of thy camp to save thee and deliver up thine enemies to thee; therefore thy camp shall be sacred, that He may not see anything abominable in thee and turn away from thee."

By carrying sacred objects with them in the camp, the army further sought to secure this divine presence. Taking into account the Israelite views in general it is a matter of course that their ensigns and banners were to them not merely practical signs, under which they assembled. They were "symbols" and thus an external expression of a special psychic power. But when much was at stake, the most sacred treasures of the people were exposed to the danger of war in the hope that they would secure victory. . . .

We know this best from the old stories about the Ark. . . . In the narratives describing the journey of the Israelite hosts through the wilderness, it is the Ark that leads the people. When it started Moses pronounced the characteristic words: Rise up Yahweh, let thine enemies be scattered. Let thy foes flee before you. And when it halted he said: Return, Yahweh! The myriads of Israel's tribes. Surely we have here the cries with which the Ark was greeted when it was at war. . . .

Thus we obtain full corroboration of what we learned from the Song of Deborah. Yahweh was with the Israelites in the battle. They fought "before the face of Yahweh," they were "Yahweh's hosts," the war was His war, the enemy His enemy.

Everything that the Israelites did on preparing for war meant a strengthening of the soul, and this strengthening showed itself in the perfect certainty of victory. They sought to confirm it in many ways. A chieftain might fortify himself and the compact with God by making a promise. The promise might be of an offering, preferably of special significance. . . . Or the promise may be to surrender completely what is captured. In all these cases the holy state of the warriors is intensified. . . .

Weapons were not the only means by which the Israelites fought their enemies. Both armies, the Israelite and the hostile host, were under the same law. When Israel increased its psychic strength through its god, the enemy fortified himself through his own god. The object of the contest was to weaken and paralyse the enemy, and the best thing was to hit in the centre of his soul. This could be done by means of the curse.

Among the Arabs the curse constituted a very essential part of the battle. In the Old Testament, curiously enough, we only hear of it once, and then it is not employed by Israelites.[6] But . . . we may take it for granted that the custom here mentioned was well known in Israel. And actually the Israelites made that psychic attack on the enemy which was inherent in the curse by the prayers for his defeat offered up in the temple.

The result aimed at by means of the curse might, however, be attained in other ways also. If the Israelites could strike terror directly to the soul of the enemy, it would become paralysed and divided, and the victory would be won. . . .

There is much evidence to show that noise played a great part in war, and also that it had its effect. *Terua,* the term for loud, uncontrolled clamour, which is also used about the shrill blast produced by the ram's horn bugle is inseparably bound up with warfare. The blare of the ram's horn bugle is the signal to make ready for battle and to break camp, but it also mingles with the shouting throughout the battle itself.

The noisy clamour of the fighters calls for no further explanation; it is a spontaneous expression of the spirit of the battling warriors. And as intensely as it rises out of the ecstatic certainty of victory, in the same degree will it be able to influence the enemy and weaken the firmness of his soul. . . .

During these times of political-military crisis the initial impetus toward the increase of psychic strength within Israel, so necessary to push back and confound the soul of the enemy, would often be provided by a charismatic figure known as a "judge." This leader, who emerged, as did Deborah, to call the people to covenant renewal

[6] *Cf.* The Bible, Num. 22.

The ram's horn, or shofar, has retained a place in Jewish tradition. It is blown in synagogues to herald in the Jewish New Year and on the Day of Atonement. (Louis Goldman from Rapho-Guillumette)

and war, whose conviction and enthusiasm seemed to be inspired, was believed to have a special gift or power received from Yahweh that gave him the right to lead. Such a figure, indeed, seemed possessed by the spirit of Yahweh, and on the basis of this apparent possession his authority was recognized by those outside his clan. Although he might on occasion preside over legal disputes, his main function—and thus the title judge—evolved from his being a representative of Yahweh's will; he judged Israel in relation to Yahweh's demands and, after the crisis, ruled for a time in Yahweh's name.

The office of the judge did not easily evolve into hereditary kingship, for the power and authority of *charisma* rested on the crisis that temporarily brought the normally independent tribes together. In times of peace Israel reverted to the autonomy of family and clan and, with the affirmation that "We have no king but Yahweh," reestablished patriarchal authority within the Israelite communities.

Our present understanding of the meaning and implications of *charisma* has been shaped by the work of the sociologist Max Weber (1864–1920). Weber distinguished three "models," or "ideal-types," of authority: traditional (principally patriarchal), charismatic, and legal-rational (bureaucratic).[7]

The General Character of Charisma
Max Weber[8]

Bureaucratic and patriarchal structures are antagonistic in many ways, yet they have in common a most important peculiarity: permanence. In this respect they are both institutitions of daily routine. Patriarchal power especially is rooted in the provisioning of recurrent and normal needs of the workaday life. Patriarchal authority thus has its original locus in the economy, that is, in those branches of the economy that can be satisfied by means of normal routine. The patriarch is the "natural leader" of the daily routine. And in this respect, the bureaucratic structure is only the counter-image of patriarchalism transposed into rationality. As a permanent structure with a system of rational rules, bureaucracy is fashioned to meet calculable and recurrent needs by means of a normal routine.

The provisioning of all demands that go beyond those of everyday routine has had, in principle, an entirely heterogeneous, namely, a *charismatic,* foundation; the further back we look in history, the more we find this to be the case. This means that the "natural" leaders—in times of psychic, physical, economic, ethical, religious, political distress—have been neither officeholders nor incumbents of an "occupation" in the present sense of the word, that is, men who have acquired expert knowledge and who serve for remuneration. The natural leaders in distress have been holders of specific gifts of the body and spirit; and these gifts have been believed to be supernatural, not accessible to everybody. The concept of "charisma" is here used in a completely "value-neutral" sense.

The capacity of the Irish culture hero, Cuchulain, or of the Homeric Achilles for heroic frenzy is a manic seizure, just as is that of the Arabian berserk who bites his shield like a mad dog—biting around until he darts off in raving bloodthirstiness. For a long time it has been maintained that the seizure of the berserk is artificially pro-

---

[7] The term ideal-type does not refer to a desirable condition but to a pure one. Such "models" never conform to specific historical examples, which either share aspects of two or more types or at least do not possess all the characteristics of one type.

[8] *From Max Weber: Essays in Sociology* edited and translated by H. H. Gerth and C. Wright Mills. Copyright 1946 by Oxford University Press, Inc. Reprinted by permission. Pp. 245–247.

duced through acute poisoning. In Byzantium, a number of "blond beasts" disposed to such seizures, were kept about, just as war elephants were formerly kept. Shamanist ecstasy is linked to constitutional epilepsy, the possession and the testing of which represents a charismatic qualification. Hence neither is "edifying" to our minds. They are just as little edifying to us as is the kind of "revelation," for instance, of the Sacred Book of the Mormons, which, at least from an evaluative standpoint, perhaps would have to be called a "hoax." But sociology is not concerned with such questions. In the faith of their followers, the chief of the Mormons has proved himself to be charismatically qualified, as have "heroes" and "sorcerers." All of them have practiced their arts and ruled by virtue of this gift (charisma) and, where the idea of God has already been clearly conceived, by virtue of the divine mission lying therein. This holds for doctors and prophets, just as for judges and military leaders, or for leaders of big hunting expeditions.

It is to his credit that Rudolf Sohm brought out the sociological peculiarity of this category of domination-structure for a historically important special case, namely, the historical development of the authority of the early Christian church. Sohm performed this task with logical consistency, and hence, by necessity, he was one-sided from a purely historical point of view. In principle, however, the very same state of affairs recurs universally, although often it is most clearly developed in the field of religion.

In contrast to any kind of bureaucratic organization of offices, the charismatic structure knows nothing of a form or of an ordered procedure of appointment or dismissal. It knows no regulated "career," "advancement," "salary," or regulated and expert training of the holder of charisma or his aids. It knows no agency of control or appeal, no local bailiwicks or exclusive functional jurisdictions; nor does it embrace permanent institutions like our bureaucratic "departments," which are independent of persons and of purely personal charisma.

Charisma knows only inner determination and inner restraint. The holder of charisma seizes the task that is adequate for him and demands obedience and a following by virtue of his mission. His success determines whether he finds them. His charismatic claim breaks down if his mission is not recognized by those to whom he feels he has been sent. If they recognize him, he is their master—so long as he knows how to maintain recognition through "proving" himself. But he does not derive his "right" from their will, in the manner of an election. Rather, the reverse holds: it is the *duty* of those to whom he addresses his mission to recognize him as their charismatically qualified leader.

In Chinese theory, the emperor's prerogatives are made dependent upon the recognition of the people. But this does not mean recognition of the sovereignty of the people any more than did the prophet's necessity of getting recognition from the believers in the early Christian community. The Chinese theory, rather, characterizes the charismatic nature of the *monarch's position*, which adheres to his *personal* qualification and to his *proved* worth.

Charisma can be, and of course regularly is, qualitatively particularized. This is an internal rather than an external affair, and results in the qualitative barrier of the charisma holder's mission and power. In meaning and in content the mission may be addressed to a group of men who are delimited locally, ethnically, socially, politically, occupationally, or in some other way. If the mission is thus addressed to a limited group of men, as is the rule, it finds its limits within their circle.

In its economic sub-structure, as in everything else, charismatic domination is the very opposite of bureaucratic domination. If bureaucratic domination depends upon regular income, and hence at least *a potiori* on a money economy and money taxes, charisma lives in, though not off, this world. This has to be properly understood. Frequently charisma quite deliberately shuns the possession of money and of pecuniary income *per se,* as did Saint Francis and many of his like; but this is of course not the rule. Even a pirate genius may exercise a "charismatic" domination, in the value-neutral sense intended here. Charismatic political heroes seek booty and, above all, gold. But charisma, and this is decisive, always rejects as undignified any pecuniary gain that is methodical and rational. In general, charisma rejects all rational economic conduct.

Charisma may sometimes be felt to reside in one who in more ordered times might exercise power through traditional or bureaucratic channels of authority—and thus be a "natural leader," easily elected or recognized. But it usually appears in one of the less distinguished members of the community, a person of low social rank, a member of a minority group, or a person with some handicap that is suddenly overcome at the moment he receives the *charisma*, a "miracle" that proves his authority and attracts the initial following.

The story of Gideon, one of the judges in Israel, provides a classic case of charismatic leadership. One of the least of his people, Gideon received "his calling" in the face of the inability of the traditional patriarchal leaders to defend the Israelite communities against the devastating raids of the Midianites from the Arabian desert. The account indicates the interrelation in the minds of the Israelites of the issues of political survival and religious assimilation.

THE STORY OF GIDEON[9]

6 The people of Israel did what was evil in the sight of the LORD; and the LORD gave them into the hand of Mid′i-an seven years. ² And the hand of Mid′ian prevailed over Israel; and because of Mid′ian the people of Israel made for themselves the dens which are in the mountains, and the caves and the strongholds. ³ For whenever the Israelites put in seed the Mid′ianites and the Amal′ekites and the people of the East would come up and attack them; ⁴ they would encamp against them and destroy the produce of the land, as far as the neighborhood of Gaza, and leave no sustenance in Israel, and no sheep or ox or ass. ⁵ For they would come up with their cattle and their tents, coming like locusts for number; both they and their camels could not be counted; so that they wasted the land as they came in. ⁶And Israel was brought very low because of Mid′ian; and the people of Israel cried for help to the LORD.

⁷ When the people of Israel cried to the LORD on account of the Mid′ianites, ⁸ the LORD sent a prophet to the people of Israel; and he said to them, "Thus says the LORD, the God of Israel: I led you up from Egypt, and brought you out of the house of bondage; ⁹ and I delivered you from the hand of the Egyptians, and from the hand of all who oppressed you, and drove them out

[9] The Bible, Judg. 6:1—8:28.

before you, and gave you their land; 10 and I said to you, 'I am the LORD your God; you shall not pay reverence to the gods of the Amorites, in whose land you dwell.' But you have not given heed to my voice."

11 Now the angel of the LORD came and sat under the oak at Ophrah, which belonged to Jo'ash the Abiez'rite, as his son Gideon was beating out wheat in the wine press, to hide it from the Mid'ianites. 12 And the angel of the LORD appeared to him and said to him, "The LORD is with you, you mighty man of valor." 13 And Gideon said to him, "Pray, sir, if the LORD is with us, why then has all this befallen us? And where are all his wonderful deeds which our fathers recounted to us, saying, 'Did not the LORD bring us up from Egypt?' But now the LORD has cast us off, and given us into the hand of Mid'ian." 14 And the LORD turned to him and said, "Go in this might of yours and deliver Israel from the hand of Mid'ian; do not I send you?" 15 And he said to him, "Pray, Lord, how can I deliver Israel? Behold, my clan is the weakest in Manas'seh, and I am the least in my family." 16 And the LORD said to him, "But I will be with you, and you shall smite the Mid'ianites as one man." 17 And he said to him, "If now I have found favor with thee, then show me a sign that it is thou who speakest with me. 18 Do not depart from here, I pray thee, until I come to thee, and bring out my present, and set it before thee." And he said, "I will stay till you return."

19 So Gideon went into his house and prepared a kid, and unleavened cakes from an ephah of flour; the meat he put in a basket, and the broth he put in a pot, and brought them to him under the oak and presented them. 20 And the angel of God said to him, "Take the meat and the unleavened cakes, and put them on this rock, and pour the broth over them." And he did so. 21 Then the angel of the LORD reached out the tip of the staff that was in his hand, and touched the meat and the unleavened cakes; and there sprang up fire from the rock and consumed the flesh and the unleavened cakes; and the angel of the LORD vanished from his sight. 22 Then Gideon perceived that he was the angel of the LORD; and Gideon said, "Alas, O Lord GOD! For now I have seen the angel of the LORD face to face." 23 But the LORD said to him, "Peace be to you; do not fear, you shall not die." 24 Then Gideon built an altar there to the LORD, and called it, The LORD is peace. To this day it still stands at Ophrah, which belongs to the Abiez'rites.

25 That night the LORD said to him, "Take your father's bull, the second bull seven years old, and pull down the altar of Ba'al which your father has, and cut down the Ashe'rah that is beside it; 26 and build an altar to the LORD your God on the top of the stronghold here, with stones laid in due order; then take the second bull, and offer it as a burnt offering with the wood of the Ashe'rah which you shall cut down." 27 So Gideon took ten men of his servants, and did as the LORD had told him; but because he was too afraid of his family and the men of the town to do it by day, he did it by night.

28 When the men of the town rose early in the morning, behold, the altar of Ba'al was broken down, and the Ashe'rah beside it was cut down, and the second bull was offered upon the altar which had been built. 29 And they said to one another, "Who has done this thing?" And after they had made search and inquired, they said, "Gideon the son of Jo'ash has done this thing." 30 Then the men of the town said to Jo'ash, "Bring out your son, that he may die, for he has pulled down the altar of

Ba′al and cut down the Ashe′rah beside it." 31 But Jo′ash said to all who were arrayed against him, "Will you contend for Ba′al? Or will you defend his cause? Whoever contends for him shall be put to death by morning. If he is a god, let him contend for himself, because his altar has been pulled down." 32 Therefore on that day he was called Jerubba′al, that is to say, "Let Ba′al contend against him," because he pulled down his altar.

33 Then all the Mid′ianites and the Amal′ekites and the people of the East came together, and crossing the Jordan they encamped in the Valley of Jezreel. 34 But the Spirit of the LORD took possession of Gideon; and he sounded the trumpet, and the Abiez′rites were called out to follow him. 35 And he sent messengers throughout all Manas′seh; and they too were called out to follow him. And he sent messengers to Asher, Zeb′ulun, and Naph′tali; and they went up to meet him.

36 Then Gideon said to God, "If thou wilt deliver Israel by my hand, as thou hast said, 37 behold, I am laying a fleece of wool on the threshing floor; if there is dew on the fleece alone, and it is dry on all the ground, then I shall know that thou wilt deliver Israel by my hand, as thou hast said." 38 And it was so. When he rose early next morning and squeezed the fleece, he wrung enough dew from the fleece to fill a bowl with water. 39 Then Gideon said to God, "Let not thy anger burn against me, let me speak but this once; pray, let me make trial only this once with the fleece; pray, let it be dry only on the fleece, and on all the ground let there be dew." 40 And God did so that night; for it was dry on the fleece only, and on all the ground there was dew.

7 Then Jerubba′al (that is, Gideon) and all the people who were with him rose early and encamped beside the spring of Harod; and the camp of Mid′ian was north of them, by the hill of Moreh, in the valley.

2 The LORD said to Gideon, "The people with you are too many for me to give the Mid′ianites into their hand, lest Israel vaunt themselves against me, saying, 'My own hand has delivered me.' 3 Now therefore proclaim in the ears of the people, saying, 'Whoever is fearful and trembling, let him return home.'" And Gideon tested them; twenty-two thousand returned, and ten thousand remained.

4 And the LORD said to Gideon, "The people are still too many; take them down to the water and I will test them for you there; and he of whom I say to you, 'This man shall go with you,' shall go with you; and any of whom I say to you, 'This man shall not go with you,' shall not go." 5 So he brought the people down to the water; and the LORD said to Gideon, "Every one that laps the water with his tongue, as a dog laps, you shall set by himself; likewise every one that kneels down to drink." 6 And the number of those that lapped, putting their hands to their mouths, was three hundred men; but all the rest of the people knelt down to drink water. 7 And the LORD said to Gideon, "With the three hundred men that lapped I will deliver you, and give the Mid′ianites into your hand; and let all the others go every man to his home." 8 So he took the jars of the people from their hands, and their trumpets; and he sent all the rest of Israel every man to his tent, but retained the three hundred men; and the camp of Mid′ian was below him in the valley.

9 That same night the LORD said to him, "Arise, go down against the camp; for I have given it into your hand. 10 But if you fear to go down, go down to the camp with Purah your servant; 11 and you shall hear

what they say, and afterward your hands shall be strengthened to go down against the camp." Then he went down with Purah his servant to the outposts of the armed men that were in the camp. 12 And the Mid′ianites and the Amal′ekites and all the people of the East lay along the valley like locusts for multitude; and their camels were without number, as the sand which is upon the seashore for multitude. 13 When Gideon came, behold a man was telling a dream to his comrade; and he said, "Behold, I dreamed a dream; and lo, a cake of barley bread tumbled into the camp of Mid′ian, and came to the tent, and struck it so that it fell, and turned it upside down, so that the tent lay flat." 14 And his comrade answered, "This is no other than the sword of Gideon the son of Jo′ash, a man of Israel; into his hand God has given Mid′ian and all the host."

15 When Gideon heard the telling of the dream and its interpretation, he worshiped; and he returned to the camp of Israel, and said, "Arise; for the LORD has given the host of Mid′ian into your hand." 16 And he divided the three hundred men into three companies, and put trumpets into the hands of all of them and empty jars, with torches inside the jars. 17 And he said to them, "Look at me, and do likewise; when I come to the outskirts of the camp, do as I do. 18 When I blow the trumpet, I and all who are with me, then blow the trumpets also on every side of all the camp, and shout, 'For the LORD and for Gideon.'"

19 So Gideon and the hundred men who were with him came to the outskirts of the camp at the beginning of the middle watch, when they had just set the watch; and they blew the trumpets and smashed the jars that were in their hands. 20 And the three companies blew the trumpets and broke the jars, holding in their left hands the torches, and in their right hands the trumpets to blow; and they cried, "A sword for the LORD and for Gideon!" 21 They stood every man in his place round about the camp, and all the army ran; they cried out and fled. 22 When they blew the three hundred trumpets, the LORD set every man's sword against his fellow and against all the army; and the army fled as far as Beth-shit′tah toward Zer′erah, as far as the border of A′bel-meho′lah, by Tabbath. 23 And the men of Israel were called out from Naph′tali and from Asher and from all Manas′seh, and they pursued after Mid′ian.

24 And Gideon sent messengers throughout all the hill country of E′phraim, saying, "Come down against the Mid′ianites and seize the waters against them, as far as Beth-bar′ah, and also the Jordan." So all the men of E′phraim were called out, and they seized the waters as far as Beth-bar′ah, and also the Jordan. 25 And they took the two princes of Mid′ian, Oreb and Zeeb; they killed Oreb at the rock of Oreb, and Zeeb they killed at the wine press of Zeeb, as they pursued Mid′ian; and they brought the heads of Oreb and Zeeb to Gideon beyond the Jordan.

8 And the men of E′phraim said to him, "What is this that you have done to us, not to call us when you went to fight with Mid′ian?" And they upbraided him violently. 2 And he said to them, "What have I done now in comparison with you? Is not the gleaning of the grapes of E′phraim better than the vintage of Abi-e′zer? 3 God has given into your hands the princes of Mid′ian, Oreb and Zeeb; what have I been able to do in comparison with you?" Then their anger against him was abated, when he had said this.

4 And Gideon came to the Jordan and

passed over, he and the three hundred men who were with him, faint yet pursuing. 5 So he said to the men of Succoth, "Pray, give loaves of bread to the people who follow me; for they are faint, and I am pursuing after Zebah and Zalmun′na, the kings of Mid′ian." 6And the officials of Succoth said, "Are Zebah and Zalmun′na already in your hand, that we should give bread to your army?" 7And Gideon said, "Well then, when the LORD has given Zebah and Zalmun′na into my hand, I will flail your flesh with the thorns of the wilderness and with briers." 8And from there he went up to Penu′el, and spoke to them in the same way; and the men of Penu′el answered him as the men of Succoth had answered. 9And he said to the men of Penu′el, "When I come again in peace, I will break down this tower."

10 Now Zebah and Zalmun′na were in Karkor with their army, about fifteen thousand men, all who were left of all the army of the people of the East; for there had fallen a hundred and twenty thousand men who drew the sword. 11And Gideon went up by the caravan route east of Nobah and Jog′behah, and attacked the army; for the army was off its guard. 12And Zebah and Zalmun′na fled; and he pursued them and took the two kings of Mid′ian, Zebah and Zalmun′na, and he threw all the army into a panic.

13 Then Gideon the son of Jo′ash returned from the battle by the ascent of Heres. 14And he caught a young man of Succoth, and questioned him; and he wrote down for him the officials and elders of Succoth, seventy-seven men. 15And he came to the men of Succoth, and said, "Behold Zebah and Zalmun′na, about whom you taunted me, saying, 'Are Zebah and Zalmun′na already in your hand, that we should give bread to your men who are faint?'" 16And he took the elders of the city and he took thorns of the wilderness and briers and with them taught the men of Succoth. 17And he broke down the tower of Penu′el, and slew the men of the city.

18 Then he said to Zebah and Zalmun′na, "Where are the men whom you slew at Tabor?" They answered, "As you are, so were they, every one of them; they resembled the sons of a king." 19And he said, "They were my brothers, the sons of my mother; as the LORD lives, if you had saved them alive, I would not slay you." 20And he said to Jether his firstborn, "Rise, and slay them." But the youth did not draw his sword; for he was afraid, because he was still a youth. 21 Then Zebah and Zalmun′na said, "Rise yourself, and fall upon us; for as the man is, so is his strength." And Gideon arose and slew Zebah and Zalmun′na; and he took the crescents that were on the necks of their camels.

22 Then the men of Israel said to Gideon, "Rule over us, you and your son and your grandson also; for you have delivered us out of the hand of Mid′ian." 23 Gideon said to them, "I will not rule over you, and my son will not rule over you; the LORD will rule over you." 24And Gideon said to them, "Let me make a request of you; give me every man of you the earrings of his spoil." (For they had golden earrings, because they were Ish′maelites.) 25And they answered, "We will willingly give them." And they spread a garment, and every man cast in it the earrings of his spoil. 26And the weight of the golden earrings that he requested was one thousand seven hundred shekels of gold; besides the crescents and the pendants and the purple garments worn by the kings of Mid′ian, and besides the collars that were about the necks of

their camels. ²⁷And Gideon made an ephod of it and put it in his city, in Ophrah; and all Israel played the harlot after it there, and it became a snare to Gideon and to his family. ²⁸ So Mid′ian was subdued before the people of Israel, and they lifted up their heads no more. And the land had rest forty years in the days of Gideon.

The charismatic leadership of the judges was a product of two separate but related pressures working upon Israel. Each appearance of charismatic leadership was, as Weber saw it, a reaction to an extreme political-military crisis that threatened the community, a crisis too difficult to be handled by the normal patriarchal authority of the clans and tribes. But it was also a reaction to acculturation, a time of religious renewal, inasmuch as the political-military danger was associated with religious apostasy. Initially this "return to Yahweh" may have been occasioned by a natural association of Yahweh with war, as Pedersen suggests. However, even the Song of Deborah reflects a concern over the Israelite adoption of Canaanite gods, and although the military crisis is not seen in this poem as a punishment inflicted by Yahweh, there is a feeling of guilt and insecurity at some of the results of acculturation. Under repeated military crises, during which the tribes united behind Yahwist religion, this sense of guilt for religious apostasy increased, and the crisis itself was more often seen as a *result* of apostasy, a punishment of Yahweh on his people. Such a view is taken in the present form of the story of Gideon.

In the face of continued military crises two solutions presented themselves. The traditional solution—a reactive adaptation—was to increase Israel's faithfulness to Yahweh and to the Covenant, and this solution was widely supported since it had sufficed to preserve Israel from the attacks of the Canaanites as well as the desert raiders from the east and south. However, the emergence of a new and stronger power in the west precipitated a second, nontraditional solution—a progressive adjustment—namely, to strengthen the governmental and military structures of Israelite society to the point where Israel's security would be assured through the normal channels of authority.

Shortly after 1200 B.C. a seafaring people known as the Philistines (from whom the name Palestine is derived) settled along the coastal region of Palestine. The Philistines seem to have been one of a number of "sea peoples" who poured out of the Aegean area onto the eastern shores of the Mediterranean, probably as part of the Indo-European migrations that inundated Greece and destroyed the Minoan civilization centered in Crete. The aggressive Philistines gradually penetrated inland, swept aside the remaining Canaanite resistance, and soon came into conflict with the Israelite tribes. Because the Philistines possessed great skill in making iron weapons, they proved far superior to the Israelites in battle. Under the impact of this new crisis the Israelites adopted the second solution to the problem of military attack and consequently transformed the political organization of Israel from a tribal confederacy into a national monarchy.

Because the tribal organization of the Israelite community had such deep roots, the transition from confederacy to monarchy was not completed without resistance. We have seen in the Gideon story how reluctant the judges were to create a monarchy. Faithful to the tribal tradition, Gideon had refused a hereditary kingship:

> Then the men of Israel said to Gideon, "Rule over us, you and your son and your grandson also; for you have delivered us out of the hand of Midian." Gideon said to them, "I will not rule over you, and my son will not rule over you; Yahweh will rule over you."[10]

This same reluctance is evident in Samuel, the last of the judges. Only with Samuel's successor, Saul, did the confederacy begin to take the form of a monarchy, but even then the tribal structure remained intact. After further military defeats and the death of Saul in battle, the task of re-

[10] The Bible, Judg. 8:22–23.

organizing the tribes into a cohesive monarchical state and driving back the Philistines fell to Saul's successor, David (1000–961 B.C.). Amid defeat and disorganization David forged the tribes into a centralized monarchy and decisively defeated the Philistines. David's son, Solomon (961–922 B.C.), inherited the task of completing the plans and dreams of his father.

Within two generations the tribal basis of Israel was transformed. Centralized political authority was vested in the king and implemented by a court bureaucracy centered in the new capital of Jerusalem. The army was organized into a permanent professional body directly under royal authority. To weaken tribal loyalties further, Israel was divided into twelve administrative districts, which did not necessarily coincide with the old tribal territories. Each district had its own royally appointed governor. Financial support for the centralized monarchy came from a taxation system based on the new administrative districts and census of their inhabitants. Symbolically, David moved the Ark of the Covenant from its confederate sanctuary at Shiloh to a royal shrine in Jerusalem. What David had begun, his son completed. Solomon inaugurated a great building program and a period of literary productivity. During his reign a magnificent Temple was built by Canaanite architects to house the Ark of the Covenant. At this time writing came into use and the books of the Pentateuch began to take written form based on material that for centuries had been handed down in oral tradition.

Solomon's rule brought prosperity and prestige to Israel but at a high price. High taxes, forced labor, tolerance of alien and Canaanite religions, and the extravagant life of the royal court led to political dissension. On the death of Solomon a revolution split the kingdom into a northern part (called Israel or Ephraim) and a southern part (called Judah). Israel survived until 722 B.C. and Judah until 586 B.C. Though the united kingdom of David had fallen, the principle of monarchy was firmly implanted. Both the Northern and Southern kingdoms soon developed into carbon copies of the Davidic monarchy. The division between Israel and Judah was, however, primarily political, for the two kingdoms were bound together always as one covenant people with a common religious tradition.

STUDY QUESTIONS

1. Would you consider Israelite culture to be open or closed, rigid or flexible? How would you apply these terms to Canaanite culture?

2. What boundary-maintaining mechanisms operated within Israelite culture? Do religion and/or morality serve that function, and, if so, how?

3. What self-correcting mechanisms were present in Israelite culture?

4. What effect did the desert experience have on Israel's adjustment to Canaanite culture?

5. To what degree is charismatic leadership a reactive adaptation? Need it always be so?

6. Were Israelite religion and morality reshaped as a result of assimilation and reactive adaptations?

7. To what degree can postconquest Palestine be considered an instance of stabilized pluralism?

8. How would you compare the rate of change for Israelite culture in the areas of economics, social structure, politics, religion, and morality?

9. What effect might the cycle of apostasy and renewal have upon religion and morality?

10. What impact did warfare have on Israelite religion?

11. Would the Israelites have seen any conflict between their acknowledgment of Yahweh's kingship and their support of autonomous patriarchal authority?

12. In what respects does Gideon fit Weber's description of charismatic authority?

13. What does the Song of Deborah suggest about the place of women in Israelite society? How does that picture compare with what is learned from Hebrew law?

For those who have used The Contribution of Ancient Greece *edited by Jacqueline Strain:*

14. Did war perform the same function for the Israelites as it did for the Homeric Greeks and for the Athenians during the Peloponnesian Wars? Compare the style and content of the Song of Deborah with the battle scenes of Homer's *Iliad*.

CHAPTER 4

POLITICAL DISINTEGRATION AND PROPHETIC RENEWAL:
The Deepening of the Ethical Conscience

The ethical code of Judaism is laid down, often in minute detail, in the Law. Such a scheme had manifest advantages. It ensured that the content of Jewish ethics was concrete and not merely abstract. After all, it is by their fruits that people are known. But it had its disadvantages. The emphasis was on outward observance, and that was compatible with decidedly unethical inner attitudes.

> *John Ferguson,* Moral Values in the Ancient World *(London: Methuen & Co., Ltd., 1958), pp. 208-209.*

The Judeo-Christian religious continuum is historically a synthesis of two main factors. First we have a developing pattern of Covenants between God and early Israel governing faith, ethics, and cult. Second we see the interaction of two distinct elements in periodic tension: an institutionalized hierarchy of religious functionaries and an upsurge of charismatic spiritual leaders. Because of this ever-renewed tension between hierarchy and charisma, the Judeo-Christian continuum has always been capable of periodic self-criticism—a process to which Western conscience owes its persistent revivals of sensitivity.

> *William F. Albright,* Samuel and the Beginnings of the Prophetic Movement *(Cincinnati: Hebrew Union College Press, 1961), p. 19.*

The prophetic orientation to man, nature and time has had a pervasive influence upon Western value orientations. . . . Man is conceived to be a significant actor on the stage of history who, upon divine command, is obligated to participate in the task of bringing about in time the Kingdom of God on earth.

Although Robert Oppenheimer's eminence as a physicist lends no weight to his views in other fields, the observations of a widely experienced, richly endowed and highly cultivated intellect may not be neglected. He finds in the European tradition but not in those of China and India two major traits of current significance: (1) a sense of responsibility to the present and future of human history manifested in the

Old Testament and the New which "is probably a decisive reason for the growth of . . . the modern world of science." And to the question why no such development occurred in China, India or the Mediterranean world of antiquity, Oppenheimer replies (2) "I believe that the idea of the improvement of human life on earth provided the air for the great fires of science." It seems to the present writer that both these traits, responsibility for history and the improvement of human life, ultimately derive from the Old Testament prophets, whereas no similar influence was able to make itself felt once mysticism had established itself in India and the Orient.

Isidor Thorner, "Prophetic and Mystic Experience," Journal for the Scientific Study of Religion, V (1965), 93.

The political transition from the charismatic leadership of the judges to centralized, monarchical government increased a psychological tension within the life of Israel that appears time and again in the prophetic books of the Old Testament. David's attempt to smooth the transition and make the position of his descendants secure by moving the Ark, the Tabernacle, and the priesthood to Jerusalem, thus associating religion with the monarchy and bringing it under royal control, only made the political and religious change more apparent. It was felt by many that:

> In this change something happened to the character of "Israel," to the structure of the community. No longer was Israel, the people of God, bound together on the basis of *covenant allegiance* to Yahweh at the central sanctuary; Israel was now bound together *politically*, on the basis of a covenant between king and people (II Sam. 5:3). As citizens of the state, the men of Israel owed allegiance to a king who could take a census, exact forced labor, and require submission to his power. Throughout the history of the monarchy there was a deep-seated conflict between these two conceptions of "Israel." As Israel became a state modeled after other oriental monarchies, more and more she lost her distinctive character and faced the danger of being swallowed up in the power-struggle and cultural stream of the Near East.[1]

Alongside the increasing conflict between the two conceptions of Israel there developed a separation between the two aspects of the authority of the charismatic judge. The judge had been a religious as well as a political-military leader. As a religious leader he had called for a return to Yahweh, and his political authority had been considered a result of his charisma. With the the establishment of the monarchy this combination of political and charismatic authority disappeared and, with it, the fusion of political and religious leadership. While the political authority of the judge devolved upon the monarchy, his religious authority was inherited by the prophets. Through this separation it became possible for the representative of religious renewal, the prophet, to criticize political action as well as apostasy and immorality. There thus developed an ongoing critique within Israelite society that could be applied not only to failure in observing the moral code but to the meaning of the moral code itself under the impact of changing social and economic conditions. As the instruments of that critique, the prophets made an incalculable contribution to the ethical development of monotheism. More precisely, the prophets were the authors of the Judeo-Christian notions of individual moral responsibility, a personal God, and a purposive understanding of history.

[1] Bernhard W. Anderson, *Understanding the Old Testament*, 2nd ed., © 1966, p. 150. Reprinted by permission of Prentice-Hall, Inc., Englewood Cliffs, New Jersey.

Modern Jerusalem still retains much of its ancient character. On the far edge of the city, overlooking the valley of Kidron, stands the Moslem Mosque of Omar on the site of the ancient temple. Behind it rises the Mount of Olives. (El Al Israel Airlines)

The prophetic tradition reached its peak in the two centuries lying between the decline of the Northern Kingdom and the Babylonian Exile, roughly between 750 and 550 B.C. For purposes of chronology, the prophets we will be considering can be grouped into those prophesying in the Northern Kingdom of Israel (Amos and Hosea) until its collapse in 722 B.C., those prophesying in the Southern Kingdom of Judah until its collapse in 586 B.C. (Isaiah and Jeremiah), and those prophesying during the Babylonian Exile (Ezekiel and the Second Isaiah).

To open the discussion on the age of prophecy several questions require answering. Who were the prophets? What cultural function did they perform? What is the nature of prophecy? It appears more than likely that the conquering Israelite tribes quite early acquired the art of ecstatic prophecy from the Canaanites. People known as soothsayers, seers, or miracle-workers formed a distinctive social group in most ancient Near Eastern civilizations. Ecstasy, frenzy, astrology, divination by magical formula were the common property and trademark of the Near Eastern priestly orders. The Old Testament is full of references to such priests or prophets. In the period of the early monarchy both the Baal and Israelite prophets wandered about in companies delivering oracles to those seeking answers from their god. Elijah seems to have been a leader of one such prophetic group or community. Even earlier some of the judges possessed prophetic qualities as a manifestation of their charismatic authority. Samuel and his successor Saul were regarded not only as political leaders but also as prophets. In this sense there is a close affinity between charismatic and prophetic power; the military leader and the prophet were both possessed by Yahweh's spirit (*ruach*).

Some of the Hebrew prophets—called cultic prophets—attached themselves to religious sanctuaries, temples, and royal courts to augment the priests in performing religious ceremonies. By means of their special talent of prayer the cultic prophets were able to communicate divine answers to those petitioning Yahweh and were, therefore, regarded as the spokesmen of Yahweh. Because of this unique gift prophets tended to take on a more significant role than priests in Hebrew religion. Priests could only conduct sacred services, inculcate religious traditions to the youth, and answer formal religious questions. Prophets, alone, were under the direct influence of Yahweh's spirit and hence were able to interpret events and reveal Yahweh's will.

During the monarchical period of the tenth and ninth centuries B.C., the cultic prophets were professionally trained and tended to transmit their craft from generation to generation through guild organizations. In this way prophecy became something of a religious office, closely associated with the priests who were appointed by the king to manage the Temple. Because of the association of the cultic prophets with the priesthood and monarchy, they seldom criticized government policy or contrasted the will of Yahweh with that of the king. Consequently, when troubled times approached, the institutionalized religion of the Temple seemed unable to give meaning to the historical events that were befalling Israel.

Out of this situation there arose in the eighth century B.C. a new emphasis in prophecy in which

> divination and miracle working were virtually eliminated. . . . The ecstatic element continued, but the prophets began to utilize and perfect another medium by which to convince their fellow Israelites of the truth of their teachings. To achieve this effect they began to rely more and more on the eloquence and logic of their literary compositions. . . . Although it should not be overlooked that several of the earlier prophets had produced important literary compositions, the later prophets fully merit the characterization of "literary" or "rhapsodic," to distinguish them from their predecessors. This title, however, must not be allowed to obscure the far more important fact that this elevation of style reflects a sublimated moral and religious experience, free from the least trace of magic. It is this elevated character which fundamentally dis-

tinguishes the "literary" prophets from their precursors.[2]

The following discussion focuses upon the nature of this new prophetic medium, which came to provide the dynamic thrust in Hebrew religion for two centuries.

THE NATURE OF PROPHECY
J. Lindblom[3]

When most people speak of prophets, they think of the prophets of ancient Israel, whose work and utterances are familiar to us from the Scriptures of the Old Testament. The modern study of the psychology and history of religion, however, has shown that prophets are found in many provinces of the world of religion, in modern as well as in ancient times. Among men and women who can be characterized as *homines religiosi* [religious men], we distinguish a special type which can be called *the prophetic type*. What are the characteristics of this prophetic type?

It is often said that the prophet is a person who has the gift of foretelling the future. The word "prophet" itself seems to support this definition. Yet, as has been shown, *pro* in the Greek term *prophetes* does not mean "before" but "forth." Thus the Greek term indicates that the prophet is a preacher, a *forth*teller rather than a *fore*teller. In reality men and women who belong to the prophetic type have been, in the first place, persons who have had something to proclaim, something to announce publicly (their message has of course frequently also been about future events).

Thus the first thing we have to say about the prophets is that they are *homines religiosi*. The prophet is not in himself a politician, a social reformer, a thinker, or a philosopher; nor is he in the first place a poet, even though he often puts his sayings in a poetical form. The special gift of a prophet is his ability to experience the divine in an original way and to receive revelations from the divine world. The prophet belongs entirely to his God; his paramount task is to listen to and obey his God. In every respect he has given himself up to his God and stands unreservedly at His disposal.

There are *homines religiosi* to whom religious experiences as such are the essence of their religious life. Personal communion with God, prayer, devotion, moral submission to the divine will are the principal traits in their religious attitude. That which distinguishes a prophet from other *homines religiosi* is that he never keeps his experiences to himself; he always feels compelled to announce to others what he has seen and heard. The prophet is a man of the public word. He is a speaker and a preacher.

The prophet is an inspired man. He claims to share in a particular divine inspiration. He always refers to another who stands behind him and tells him what he must say. A mighty power deals with him and speaks through him. The prophet knows that his thoughts and words never come from himself: they are given him. The philosopher works in the laboratory

---

[2] Harry M. Orlinsky, *Ancient Israel* (Ithaca, N.Y.: Cornell University Press, 1964), pp. 125–127. These later prophets, beginning with Amos, are sometimes called "writing prophets" because their words were preserved in writing, often as they were uttered. Amos was the first prophet whose oracles survived in written form. Prophets who preceded Amos are known to us only through oral tradition as it was later recorded.

[3] J. Lindblom, *Prophecy in Ancient Israel* (Oxford, Eng.: Basil Blackwell & Mott, Ltd., 1962), pp. 1–2, 4–6.

of the intellect. His task is to combine various thoughts in a logical connection, and from given premises to draw the right conclusions. The prophet does not philosophize, does not muse or speculate; his privilege is to receive, to receive thoughts, visions, and words as wonderful gifts from heaven. The prophet is, in short, a proclaimer of divine revelations.

In this respect the prophet plainly differs from the religious teacher or pedagogue who methodically instructs his pupils according to didactic rules. The prophet is compelled by the spirit; and he knows no other rules than the force and the guidance of the divine impulse.

As one compelled by the divine power, the prophet lives under a divine constraint. He has lost the freedom of the ordinary man and is forced to follow the orders of the deity. He must say what has been given him to say and go where he is commanded to go. Few things are so characteristic of the prophets, wherever we meet them in the world of religion, as the feeling of being under a superhuman and supernatural constraint.

In the experience of inspiration and the feeling of necessity and constraint there is a kinship between the prophet and the poet. The prophet, as we have said, is not in himself a poet; but from a psychological point of view there is a great similarity between the two types. The poet, too, often speaks of inspiration and of a sort of abnormal force which compels him to write. Of course, not all the poets are inspired or even pretend to be inspired. Plato and Aristotle distinguished between poets who worked rationally and methodically and others who composed their verses in a state of mania. But many poets of all ages have been familiar with this peculiar state of irresistible inspiration which, for instance, characterized Aeschylus, of whom it was said that he composed his tragedies as in a state of intoxication. . . .

An inspired poet is not in himself a prophet, but from a psychological point of view we have much to learn from the descriptions of what the poet experiences in the divinely endowed moments of highest inspiration. This feeling of personal passivity and absolute dependence on a higher power is extremely typical of the "prophets," too, wherever we meet them in various parts of the world.

When inspiration strongly intensifies it turns into ecstasy. Ecstasy belongs to the psychical phenomena the definition of which has varied from time to time and from one author to another. Sometimes the etymology of the word has been followed. Then ecstasy has been defined as a mental state in which one has a feeling that the soul leaves the body and goes off to distant regions, and the bond with this world is temporarily cut off. However, this definition is too narrow. Phenomena which are commonly called ecstatic are not always combined with such a conception of the relation between soul and body as is here described; they also appear in connection with other more or less violent alterations in the ordinary spiritual life.

The term "ecstasy" has also been used to denote the culminating point of religious experience whereby perfect union with God is realized in direct though ineffable experience. Ecstasy in this sense is often described in the works of the great mystics. . . . This *unio mystica* [mystical union] as an act of the highest grace, according to the estimate of the mystics themselves, is a special kind of ecstasy. But firstly, many mystics have had ecstatic experiences without having attained the highest degree of perfect absorption in the divinity, wherein the human personality is dissolved and merged in God; and secondly, ecstatic phenomena are not necessarily associated with religion at all. For this reason it is necessary to find a wider definition, a definition which covers the whole field of experiences which are usually called ecstatic.

Modern psychologists rightly take the term "ecstasy" in a wider sense. Following scholars . . . who have thoroughly studied ecstatic experience, I prefer to define ecstasy as an abnormal state of consciousness in which one is so intensely absorbed by one single idea or one single feeling, or by a group of ideas or feelings, that the normal stream of psychical life is more or less arrested. The bodily senses cease to function; one becomes impervious to impressions from without; consciousness is exalted above the ordinary level of daily experience; unconscious mental impressions and ideas come to the surface in the form of visions and auditions. Consequently ecstasy can rightly be described as a kind of monoideism. Such ecstasy is, of course, not peculiar to religious men. Any person so predisposed, who concentrates upon one idea or feeling, easily passes into a sort of trance, however trivial the idea may be which gains possession of his consciousness. Ecstasy in this sense merely indicates the presence of certain abnormal psycho-physical conditions, an alteration of the normal equilibrium, a shifting of the threshold of consciousness. Of course the worth of ecstasy depends entirely on the objective value of the dominating idea or feeling.

In religious ecstasy, consciousness is entirely filled with the presence of God, with ideas and feelings belonging to the divine sphere. The soul is lifted up into the exalted region of divine revelation, and the lower world with its sensations momentarily disappears. There are various means to induce such a mental rapture: intoxication of different kinds, fasts, flagellation, dancing, music and so on. On a higher level, prayer and meditation are well-known means of attaining ecstatic experiences. Ecstasy in this sense can be communicated by direct contagion. In the history of religion there have been many instances of psychical epidemics.

It must be kept in mind that ecstasy has many degrees. There is an ecstasy which involves a total extinction of the normal consciousness, a complete insensibility and anaesthesia. There is also an ecstasy which approximates to a normal fit of absence of mind or intense excitement. This observation is very important for the study of the psychology of the prophets. Inspiration or psychical exaltation is characteristic of all men and women who belong to the prophetic type. But this inspired exaltation has in the prophets a tendency to pass over into a real ecstasy of a more or less intense nature, lethargic or orgiastic.

In the foregoing it has been established that the following attributes are characteristic of the prophetic class among *homines religiosi*. They are entirely devoted, soul and body, to the divinity. They are inspired personalities who have the power to receive divine revelations. They act as speakers and preachers who publicly announce what they have to say. They are compelled by higher powers and kept under divine constraint. The inspiration which they experience has a tendency to pass over into real ecstasy.

One further attribute may be added: the

special call. A prophet knows that he has never chosen his way himself: he has been chosen by the deity. He points to a particular experience in his life through which it has become clear to him that the deity has a special purpose with him and has designated him to perform a special mission. The call often takes him by surprise. He sometimes offers resistance, but is vanquished by the deity and makes an unconditional surrender. The call has the character of a supernatural experience. It exceeds all human reason. It is often accompanied by physical and psychical phenomena. The call is frequently met with fear and trembling; but it is always regarded as an act of divine grace.

The prophets who exhibited the new medium of expression were rarely professionally trained and often came from very humble backgrounds. Such was Amos who, along with Hosea, prophesied in the Northern Kingdom during the middle decades of the eighth century, B.C. While the prophets from Amos on should not be considered enemies of the priests and cultic prophets, they were frequently critical of their religious teaching and practices. We hear Amos revealing Yahweh's stern warning:

> I hate, I despise your feasts,
>   and I take no delight in your solemn assemblies.
> Even though you offer me your burnt offerings and cereal offerings,
>   I will not accept them,
> and the peace offerings of your fatted beasts
>   I will not look upon.
> Take away from me the noise of your songs;
>   to the melody of your harps I will not listen.
> But let justice roll down like waters,
>   and righteousness like an ever-flowing stream.   —Amos 5:21–24

Amos and Hosea did not reserve their condemnation for the cultic prophets and priests only. They criticized the Northern Kingdom as a whole because of the effects which a growing material prosperity and increased political importance had wrought in social relationships and religious practices. Because of economic prosperity the distinction between the rich and poor had widened, and the covenant requirement of charity was not being fulfilled. In addition, the Northern Kingdom had entered into alliances with other Near Eastern powers, and as a result cultural outlooks and religious practices alien to Israel's tradition had been introduced. Amos and Hosea were convinced that under such political and social conditions Israel could not endure. Both Amos and Hosea interpreted these circumstances as a rejection by Israel of its covenant with Yahweh.

The consequence of Israel's action, as the prophets saw it, was political and moral destruction. From the north the Assyrians were advancing across the Fertile Crescent toward Egypt, and Palestine lay in their path. To the prophets the Assyrian menace meant something far more serious than a political power struggle. It was a clear indication of Yahweh's handiwork. If Israel did not return to Yahweh and keep the covenant, Yahweh would use the Assyrians to chastise them. As we know, the Northern Kingdom, being no match for the mighty Assyrian Empire, fell in 722 B.C., while the smaller Southern Kingdom of Judah maintained some semblance of political independence within the sphere of the Assyrian Empire.

For the full meaning of the breaking of the covenant—its ethical and religious implications—we must turn to the words of Amos and Hosea. In their interpretation of historical events these two prophets revealed to Israel a deeper meaning of the covenant relationship with Yahweh than she had previously known. The selections that follow, taken from the books of Amos and Hosea, were not written by the prophets themselves. Rather, they represent a compilation of their preaching as it was passed down in oral tradition. Consequently there is a certain amount of repetition and an almost continual alternation between condemnation and forgiveness.

AMOS: THE CALL FOR SOCIAL JUSTICE[4]

1 The words of Amos, who was among the shepherds of Teko'a, which he saw concerning Israel in the days of Uzzi'ah king of Judah and in the days of Jerobo'am the son of Jo'ash, king of Israel, two years before the earthquake. ²And he said:
"The LORD roars from Zion,
  and utters his voice from Jerusalem;
the pastures of the shepherds mourn,
  and the top of Carmel withers." . . .

[4] The Bible, Amos 1:1-2; 2:4—3:8; 3:13—4:13; 5:10-15, 18-24.

2 . . . ⁴ Thus says the LORD:
"For three transgressions of Judah,
  and for four, I will not revoke the punishment;
because they have rejected the law of the LORD,
  and have not kept his statutes,
but their lies have led them astray,
  after which their fathers walked.
⁵ So I will send a fire upon Judah,
  and it shall devour the strongholds of Jerusalem."

⁶ Thus says the LORD:
"For three transgressions of Israel,
  and for four, I will not revoke the punishment;
because they sell the righteous for silver,
  and the needy for a pair of shoes—

Assyrian cavalrymen, from a relief in the palace of Sennacherib, 705-681 B.C. (The Metropolitan Museum of Art, Gift of John D. Rockefeller, Jr., 1932)

⁷ they that trample the head of the poor
    into the dust of the earth,
  and turn aside the way of the afflicted;
a man and his father go in to the same
    maiden,
  so that my holy name is profaned;
⁸ they lay themselves down beside every
    altar
  upon garments taken in pledge;
and in the house of their God they drink
  the wine of those who have been
    fined.

⁹ "Yet I destroyed the Amorite before
    them,
  whose height was like the height of
    the cedars,
  and who was as strong as the oaks;
I destroyed his fruit above,
  and his roots beneath.
¹⁰ Also I brought you up out of the land
    of Egypt,
  and led you forty years in the wilder-
    ness,
  to possess the land of the Amorite.
¹¹ And I raised up some of your sons for
    prophets,
  and some of your young men for
    Nazirites.
Is it not indeed so, O people of Is-
    rael?"
                                says the LORD.

¹² "But you made the Nazirites drink
    wine,
  and commanded the prophets,
    saying, 'You shall not prophesy.'
¹³ "Behold, I will press you down in
    your place,
  as a cart full of sheaves presses
    down.
¹⁴ Flight shall perish from the swift,
  and the strong shall not retain his
    strength,
  nor shall the mighty save his life;
¹⁵ he who handles the bow shall not
    stand,
  and he who is swift of foot shall not
    save himself,
  nor shall he who rides the horse save
    his life;
¹⁶ and he who is stout of heart among
    the mighty
  shall flee away naked in that day,"
                                says the LORD.

3 Hear this word that the LORD has spoken against you, O people of Israel, against the whole family which I brought up out of the land of Egypt:
  ² "You only have I known
    of all the families of the earth;
  therefore I will punish you
    for all your iniquities.

  ³ "Do two walk together,
    unless they have made an appoint-
      ment?
  ⁴ Does a lion roar in the forest,
    when he has no prey?
  Does a young lion cry out from his den,
    if he has taken nothing?
  ⁵ Does a bird fall in a snare on the earth,
    when there is no trap for it?
  Does a snare spring up from the ground,
    when it has taken nothing?
  ⁶ Is a trumpet blown in a city,
    and the people are not afraid?
  Does evil befall a city,
    unless the LORD has done it?
  ⁷ Surely the Lord GOD does nothing,
    without revealing his secret
    to his servants the prophets.
  ⁸ The lion has roared;
    who will not fear?
  The Lord GOD has spoken;
    who can but prophesy?" . . .

¹³ "Hear, and testify against the house
    of Jacob,"

says the Lord GOD, the God of hosts,
¹⁴ "that on the day I punish Israel for his transgressions,
I will punish the altars of Bethel,
and the horns of the altar shall be cut off and fall to the ground.
¹⁵ I will smite the winter house with the summer house;
and the houses of ivory shall perish,
and the great houses shall come to an end,"
                                says the LORD.

4 "Hear this word, you cows of Bashan,
    who are in the mountain of Samar'ia,
who oppress the poor, who crush the needy,
    who say to their husbands, 'Bring, that we may drink!'
² The Lord GOD has sworn by his holiness
    that, behold, the days are coming upon you,
when they shall take you away with hooks,
    even the last of you with fishhooks.
³ And you shall go out through the breaches,
    every one straight before her;
and you shall be cast forth into Harmon,"
                                says the LORD.

⁴ "Come to Bethel, and transgress;
    to Gilgal, and multiply transgression;
bring your sacrifices every morning,
    your tithes every three days;
⁵ offer a sacrifice of thanksgiving of that which is leavened,
    and proclaim freewill offerings, publish them;
for so you love to do, O people of Israel!"
                           says the Lord GOD.

⁶ "I gave you cleanness of teeth in all your cities,
    and lack of bread in all your places,
yet you did not return to me,"
                                says the LORD.

⁷ "And I also withheld the rain from you
    when there were yet three months to the harvest;
I would send rain upon one city,
    and send no rain upon another city;
one field would be rained upon,
    and the field on which it did not rain withered;
⁸ so two or three cities wandered to one city
    to drink water, and were not satisfied;
yet you did not return to me,"
                                says the LORD.

⁹ "I smote you with blight and mildew;
    I laid waste your gardens and your vineyards;
your fig trees and your olive trees
    the locust devoured;
yet you did not return to me,"
                                says the LORD.

¹⁰ I sent among you a pestilence after the manner of Egypt;
    I slew your young men with the sword;
I carried away your horses;
    and I made the stench of your camp go up into your nostrils;
yet you did not return to me,"
                                says the LORD.

¹¹ "I overthrew some of you,
    as when God overthrew Sodom and Gomor'rah,
and you were as a brand plucked out of the burning;
yet you did not return to me,"
                                says the LORD.

12 "Therefore thus I will do to you, O Israel;
because I will do this to you,
prepare to meet your God, O Israel!"

13 For lo, he who forms the mountains,
and creates the wind,
and declares to man what is his thought;
who makes the morning darkness,
and treads on the heights of the earth—
the LORD, the God of hosts, is his name! . . .

5 . . . 10 They hate him who reproves in the gate,
and they abhor him who speaks the truth.
11 Therefore because you trample upon the poor
and take from him exactions of wheat,
you have built houses of hewn stone,
but you shall not dwell in them;
you have planted pleasant vineyards,
but you shall not drink their wine.
12 For I know how many are your transgressions,
and how great are your sins—
you who afflict the righteous, who take a bribe,
and turn aside the needy in the gate.
13 Therefore he who is prudent will keep silent in such a time;
for it is an evil time.
14 Seek good, and not evil,
that you may live;
and so the LORD, the God of hosts, will be with you,
as you have said.
15 Hate evil, and love good,
and establish justice in the gate;
it may be that the LORD, the God of hosts,
will be gracious to the remnant of Joseph. . . .

18 Woe to you who desire the day of the LORD!
Why would you have the day of the LORD?
It is darkness, and not light;
19 as if a man fled from a lion,
and a bear met him;
or went into the house and leaned with his hand against the wall,
and a serpent bit him.
20 Is not the day of the LORD darkness, and not light,
and gloom with no brightness in it?
21 "I hate, I despise your feasts,
and I take no delight in your solemn assemblies.
22 Even though you offer me your burnt offerings and cereal offerings,
I will not accept them,
and the peace offerings of your fatted beasts
I will not look upon.
23 Take away from me the noise of your songs;
to the melody of your harps I will not listen.
24 But let justice roll down like waters,
and righteousness like an ever-flowing stream.

HOSEA: THE CALL FOR COVENANT FIDELITY[5]

1 The word of the LORD that came to Hose′a the son of Be-e′ri, in the days of Uzzi′ah, Jotham, Ahaz, and Hezeki′ah,

[5] The Bible, Hos. 1:1—4:19; 5:15—6:6; 7:8—8:14; 10:11—11:12; 14:1–9.

kings of Judah, and in the days of Jerobo′am the son of Jo′ash, king of Israel.

² When the LORD first spoke through Hose′a, the LORD said to Hose′a, "Go, take to yourself a wife of harlotry and have children of harlotry, for the land commits great harlotry by forsaking the LORD." ³ So he went and took Gomer the daughter of Dibla′im, and she conceived and bore him a son.

⁴ And the LORD said to him, "Call his name Jezreel; for yet a little while, and I will punish the house of Jehu for the blood of Jezreel, and I will put an end to the kingdom of the house of Israel. ⁵ And on that day, I will break the bow of Israel in the valley of Jezreel."

⁶ She conceived again and bore a daughter. And the LORD said to him, "Call her name Not pitied, for I will no more have pity on the house of Israel, to forgive them at all. ⁷ But I will have pity on the house of Judah, and I will deliver them by the LORD their God; I will not deliver them by bow, nor by sword, nor by war, nor by horses, nor by horsemen."

⁸ When she had weaned Not pitied, she conceived and bore a son. ⁹ And the LORD said, "Call his name Not my people, for you are not my people and I am not your God."

¹⁰ Yet the number of the people of Israel shall be like the sand of the sea, which can be neither measured nor numbered; and in the place where it was said to them, "You are not my people," it shall be said to them, "Sons of the living God." ¹¹ And the people of Judah and the people of Israel shall be gathered together, and they shall appoint for themselves one head; and they shall go up from the land, for great shall be the day of Jezreel.

2 Say to your brother, "My people," and to your sister, "She has obtained pity."

² "Plead with your mother, plead—
for she is not my wife,
and I am not her husband—
that she put away her harlotry from her face,
and her adultery from between her breasts;
³ lest I strip her naked
and make her as in the day she was born,
and make her like a wilderness,
and set her like a parched land,
and slay her with thirst.
⁴ Upon her children also I will have no pity,
because they are children of harlotry.
⁵ For their mother has played the harlot;
she that conceived them has acted shamefully.
For she said, 'I will go after my lovers,
who give me my bread and my water,
my wool and my flax, my oil and my drink.'
⁶ Therefore I will hedge up her way with thorns;
and I will build a wall against her,
so that she cannot find her paths.
⁷ She shall pursue her lovers,
but not overtake them;
and she shall seek them,
but shall not find them.
Then she shall say, 'I will go
and return to my first husband,
for it was better with me then than now.'
⁸ And she did not know
that it was I who gave her
the grain, the wine, and the oil,
and who lavished upon her silver
and gold which they used for Ba′al.
⁹ Therefore I will take back

    my grain in its time,
      and my wine in its season;
    and I will take away my wool and my
      flax,
    which were to cover her nakedness.
10 Now I will uncover her lewdness
    in the sight of her lovers,
      and no one shall rescue her out of
      my hand.
11And I will put an end to all her mirth,
    her feasts, her new moons, her sabbaths,
    and all her appointed feasts.
12And I will lay waste her vines and
    her fig trees,
    of which she said,
'These are my hire,
    which my lovers have given me.'
I will make them a forest,
    and the beasts of the field shall devour them.
13And I will punish her for the feast
    days of the Ba'als
    when she burned incense to them
and decked herself with her ring and
    jewelry,
    and went after her lovers,
    and forgot me, says the LORD.
14 "Therefore, behold, I will allure her,
    and bring her into the wilderness,
    and speak tenderly to her.
15And there I will give her her vineyards,
    and make the valley of Achor a door
    of hope.
And there she shall answer as in the
    days of her youth,
    as at the time when she came out of
    the land of Egypt.
16 "And in that day, says the LORD, you will call me, 'My husband,' and no longer will you call me, 'My Ba'al.' 17 For I will remove the names of the Ba'als from her mouth, and they shall be mentioned by name no more. 18And I will make for you a covenant on that day with the beasts of the field, the birds of the air, and the creeping things of the ground; and I will abolish the bow, the sword, and war from the land; and I will make you lie down in safety. 19And I will betroth you to me for ever; I will betroth you to me in righteousness and in justice, in steadfast love, and in mercy. 20 I will betroth you to me in faithfulness; and you shall know the LORD.

21 "And in that day, says the LORD,
    I will answer the heavens
      and they shall answer the earth;
22 and the earth shall answer the grain,
    the wine, and the oil,
    and they shall answer Jezreel;
23 and I will sow him for myself in the land.
And I will have pity on Not pitied,
    and I will say to Not my people,
    'You are my people';
    and he shall say, "Thou art my God."'

3 And the LORD said to me, "Go again, love a woman who is beloved of a paramour and is an adultress; even as the LORD loves the people of Israel, though they turn to other gods and love cakes of raisins." 2 So I bought her for fifteen shekels of silver and a homer and a lethech of barley. 3And I said to her, "You must dwell as mine for many days; you shall not play the harlot, or belong to another man; so will I also be to you." 4 For the children of Israel shall dwell many days without king or prince, without sacrifice or pillar, without ephod or teraphim. 5Afterward the children of Israel shall return and seek the LORD their God, and David their king; and they shall come in fear to the LORD and to his goodness in the latter days.

4 Hear the word of the LORD, O people of Israel;
   for the LORD has a controversy with the inhabitants of the land.
There is no faithfulness or kindness,
   and no knowledge of God in the land;
² there is swearing, lying, killing, stealing, and committing adultery;
   they break all bounds and murder follows murder.
³ Therefore the land mourns,
   and all who dwell in it languish,
and also the beasts of the field,
   and the birds of the air;
   and even the fish of the sea are taken away.

⁴ Yet let no one contend,
   and let none accuse,
   for with you is my contention, O priest.
⁵ You shall stumble by day,
   the prophet also shall stumble with you by night;
   and I will destroy your mother.
⁶ My people are destroyed for lack of knowledge;
   because you have rejected knowledge,
   I reject you from being a priest to me.
And since you have forgotten the law of your God,
   I also will forget your children.
⁷ The more they increased,
   the more they sinned against me;
   I will change their glory into shame.
⁸ They feed on the sin of my people;
   they are greedy for their iniquity.
⁹ And it shall be like people, like priest;
   I will punish them for their ways,
   and requite them for their deeds.
¹⁰ They shall eat, but not be satisfied;
   they shall play the harlot, but not multiply;
because they have forsaken the LORD
   to cherish harlotry.
¹¹ Wine and new wine
   take away the understanding.
¹² My people inquire of a thing of wood,
   and their staff gives them oracles.
For a spirit of harlotry has led them astray,
   and they have left their God to play the harlot.
¹³ They sacrifice on the tops of the mountains,
   and make offerings upon the hills,
under oak, poplar, and terebinth,
   because their shade is good.

Therefore your daughters play the harlot,
   and your brides commit adultery.
¹⁴ I will not punish your daughters when they play the harlot,
   nor your brides when they commit adultery;
for the men themselves go aside with harlots,
   and sacrifice with cult prostitutes,
and a people without understanding shall come to ruin.

¹⁵ Though you play the harlot, O Israel,
   let not Judah become guilty.
Enter not into Gilgal,
   nor go up to Beth-a'ven,
   and swear not, "As the LORD lives."
¹⁶ Like a stubborn heifer
   Israel is stubborn;
can the LORD now feed them
   like a lamb in a broad pasture?

¹⁷ E'phraim is joined to idols,
   let him alone.
¹⁸ A band of drunkards, they give themselves to harlotry;

they love shame more than their
     glory.
19 A wind has wrapped them in its
     wings,
  and they shall be ashamed because
     of their altars. . . .

5 . . . 15 I will return again to my place,
  until they acknowledge their guilt
     and seek my face,
  and in their distress they seek me,
     saying,
6 "Come, let us return to the LORD;
  for he has torn, that he may heal us;
  he has stricken, and he will bind us
     up.
2 After two days he will revive us;
  on the third day he will raise us up,
     that we may live before him.
3 Let us know, let us press on to know
     the LORD;
  his going forth is sure as the dawn;
  he will come to us as the showers,
  as the spring rains that water the
     earth."

4 What shall I do with you, O E'phraim?
  What shall I do with you, O Judah?
  Your love is like a morning cloud,
     like the dew that goes early away.
5 Therefore I have hewn them by the
     prophets,
  I have slain them by the words of my
     mouth,
  and my judgment goes forth as the
     light.
6 For I desire steadfast love and not
     sacrifice,
  the knowledge of God, rather than
     burnt offerings. . . .

7 . . . 8 E'phraim mixes himself with
     the peoples;

E'phraim is a cake not turned.
9 Aliens devour his strength,
  and he knows it not;
gray hairs are sprinkled upon him,
  and he knows it not.
10 The pride of Israel witnesses against
     him;
  yet they do not return to the LORD
     their God,
  nor seek him, for all this.
11 E'phraim is like a dove,
  silly and without sense,
  calling to Egypt, going to Assyria.
12 As they go, I will spread over them
     my net;
  I will bring them down like birds of
     the air;
  I will chastise them for their wicked
     deeds.
13 Woe to them, for they have strayed
     from me!
  Destruction to them, for they have
     rebelled against me!
  I would redeem them,
  but they speak lies against me.
14 They do not cry to me from the heart,
  but they wail upon their beds;
for grain and wine they gash themselves,
  they rebel against me.
15 Although I trained and strengthened
     their arms,
  yet they devise evil against me.
16 They turn to Ba'al;
  they are like a treacherous bow,
their princes shall fall by the sword
  because of the insolence of their
     tongue.
This shall be their derision in the land
     of Egypt.

8 Set the trumpet to your lips,
  for a vulture is over the house of the
     LORD,

because they have broken my covenant,
  and transgressed my law.
² To me they cry,
  My God, we Israel know thee.
³ Israel has spurned the good;
  the enemy shall pursue him.

⁴ They made kings, but not through me.
  They set up princes, but without my
    knowledge.
With their silver and gold they made
    idols
  for their own destruction.
⁵ I have spurned your calf, O Samar′ia.
  My anger burns against them.
How long will it be
  till they are pure ⁶ in Israel?

A workman made it;
  it is not God.
The calf of Samar′ia
  shall be broken to pieces.

⁷ For they sow the wind,
  and they shall reap the whirlwind.
The standing grain has no heads,
  it shall yield no meal;
if it were to yield,
  aliens would devour it.
⁸ Israel is swallowed up;
  already they are among the nations
  as a useless vessel.
⁹ For they have gone up to Assyria,
  a wild ass wandering alone;
  E′phraim has hired lovers.
¹⁰ Though they hire allies among the
    nations,
  I will soon gather them up.
And they shall cease for a little while
  from anointing king and princes.
¹¹ Because E′phraim has multiplied al-
    tars for sinning,
  they have become to him altars for
    sinning.

¹² Were I to write for him my laws by
    ten thousands,
  they would be regarded as a strange
    thing.
¹³ They love sacrifice;
  they sacrifice flesh and eat it;
  but the Lord has no delight in them.
Now he will remember their iniquity,
  and punish their sins;
  they shall return to Egypt.
¹⁴ For Israel has forgotten his Maker,
  and built palaces;
and Judah has multiplied fortified cities;
  but I will send a fire upon his cities,
  and it shall devour his strong-
    holds. . . .

10 . . . "E′phraim was a trained heifer
    that loved to thresh,
  and I spared her fair neck;
but I will put E′phraim to the yoke,
  Judah must plow,
  Jacob must harrow for himself.
¹² Sow for yourselves righteousness,
  reap the fruit of steadfast love;
  break up your fallow ground,
for it is the time to seek the Lord,
  that he may come and rain salvation
    upon you.
¹³ You have plowed iniquity,
  you have reaped injustice,
  you have eaten the fruit of lies.
Because you have trusted in your char-
    iots
  and in the multitude of your war-
    riors,
¹⁴ therefore the tumult of war shall
    arise among your people,
  and all your fortresses shall be de-
    stroyed,
as Shalman destroyed Betharbel on the
    day of battle;
  mothers were dashed in pieces with
    their children.

15 Thus it shall be done to you, O house of Israel,
   because of your great wickedness.
In the storm the king of Israel
   shall be utterly cut off.

11 When Israel was a child, I loved him,
   and out of Egypt I called my son.
2 The more I called them,
   the more they went from me;
they kept sacrificing to the Ba'als,
   and burning incense to idols.
3 Yet it was I who taught E'phraim to walk,
   I took them up in my arms;
   but they did not know that I healed them.
4 I led them with cords of compassion,
   with the bands of love,
and I became to them as one
   who eases the yoke on their jaws,
   and I bent down to them and fed them.
5 They shall return to the land of Egypt,
   and Assyria shall be their king,
   because they have refused to return to me.
6 The sword shall rage against their cities,
   consume the bars of their gates,
   and devour them in their fortresses.
7 My people are bent on turning away from me;
   so they are appointed to the yoke,
   and none shall remove it.

8 How can I give you up, O E'phraim!
   How can I hand you over, O Israel!
How can I make you like Admah!
   How can I treat you like Zeboi'im!
My heart recoils within me,
   my compassion grows warm and tender.
9 I will not execute my fierce anger,
   I will not again destroy E'phraim;
for I am God and not man,
   the Holy One in your midst,
   and I will not come to destroy.
10 They shall go after the LORD,
   he will roar like a lion;
yea, he will roar,
   and his sons shall come trembling from the west;
11 they shall come eagerly like birds from Egypt,
   and like doves from the land of Assyria;
   and I will return them to their homes, says the LORD.
12 E'phraim has encompassed me with lies,
   and the house of Israel with deceit;
but Judah is still known by God,
   and is faithful to the Holy One. . . .

14 Return, O Israel, to the LORD your God,
   for you have stumbled because of your iniquity.
2 Take with you words
   and return to the LORD;
say to him,
   "Take away all iniquity;
accept that which is good
   and we will render
   the fruit of our lips.
3 Assyria shall not save us,
   we will not ride upon horses;
and we will say no more, 'Our God,'
   to the work of our hands.
In thee the orphan finds mercy."

4 I will heal their faithlessness;
   I will love them freely,
   for my anger has turned from them.
5 I will be as the dew to Israel;
   he shall blossom as the lily,

he shall strike root as the poplar;
⁶ his shoots shall spread out;
    his beauty shall be like the olive,
    and his fragrance like Lebanon.
⁷ They shall return and dwell beneath my shadow,
    they shall flourish as a garden;
they shall blossom as the vine,
    their fragrance shall be like the wine of Lebanon.

⁸ O E′phraim, what have I to do with idols?
It is I who answer and look after you.
I am like an evergreen cypress,
    from me comes your fruit.

⁹ Whoever is wise, let him understand these things;
    whoever is discerning, let him know them;
for the ways of the LORD are right,
    and the upright walk in them,
    but transgressors stumble in them.

After the Northern Kingdom fell to the Assyrians in 722 B.C., the Southern Kingdom of Judah maintained a precarious existence for another century. At times during this century Judah was little more than an Assyrian satellite. Assyrian domination led to the introduction of alien cultural influences into the more backward Judah. With the gradual eclipse of Assyrian power during the last half of the seventh century B.C., however, Judah, during the reign of Josiah (640–609 B.C.), once again reasserted its power, finally winning independence around 620 B.C. Having capitalized upon Assyria's political weakness, Josiah quickly removed every vestige of alien cultural influence within his kingdom. This cultural purification is known as the Deuteronomic Reformation, since it was aided by the discovery in the Temple of a code of laws now contained in the book of Deuteronomy. Through the revival of the Mosaic Torah, or Law, and the renewed importance of the first commandment, Assyrian and Canaanite cultic practices that had persisted were forbidden.

The reforms of Josiah, as it turned out, were short-lived. By a complex turn of events Judah's independence was again jeopardized, this time by the rising power of Babylon under the leadership of Nebuchadnezzar (605–562 B.C.). Caught up in the nationalistic fervor which the Deuteronomic Reform had nurtured, Judah rashly challenged the great power of Babylon. The outcome was catastrophic for the future of Judah. What had begun in the last quarter of the seventh century B.C. as a new golden age, much in the tradition of the Davidic kingdom, ended during the first quarter of the sixth century B.C. with the Babylonian Exile when Nebuchadnezzar forced Judah into submission. To insure its political dependence, Nebuchadnezzar exiled the elite of Judah (including the prophet Ezekiel) to Babylon in 597 B.C. Unrest continued, however, and in 588 B.C. Judah revolted and Nebuchadnezzar's army laid siege to Jerusalem. After a long and savage battle Jerusalem capitulated in 586 B.C.

To make certain that revolt would never again occur, Nebuchadnezzar destroyed Jerusalem and exiled the remaining elite to Egypt and Babylonia, leaving the poorer elements of the population in Palestine. Those in Egypt, although they continued to cherish their Judean ancestry and traditions, adopted many practices and beliefs from their new social and religious environment. Few of these returned to Judea. The Jews[6] in Babylonia, however, not only maintained the orthodox Mosaic tradition but developed it in such a way that when they were allowed to return to Palestine the priests and the Torah became the most important religious element within the life of post-Exilic Judaism.

Nebuchadnezzar had not intended the Exile as a punishment but rather as a means of removing the elements in Jewish society who de-

---

[6] The term Jew is far more limited than the terms Hebrew and Israelite. It properly refers to the Judean population that retained its blood purity and religious faith.

sired to reestablish their political autonomy. However, for the two great prophets who lived through the crisis that engulfed Judah—Jeremiah, whose prophetic career (626–586 B.C.) paralleled the collapse of Judah, and Ezekiel, whose prophetic career (593–573 B.C.) spanned the early decades of the Exile in Babylon—the catastrophe decidedly was a punishment. For Jeremiah, as for Amos a century and a half earlier, the political calamity that Israel was

An inscribed cylinder from sixth-century Babylonia. (City Art Museum of Saint Louis)

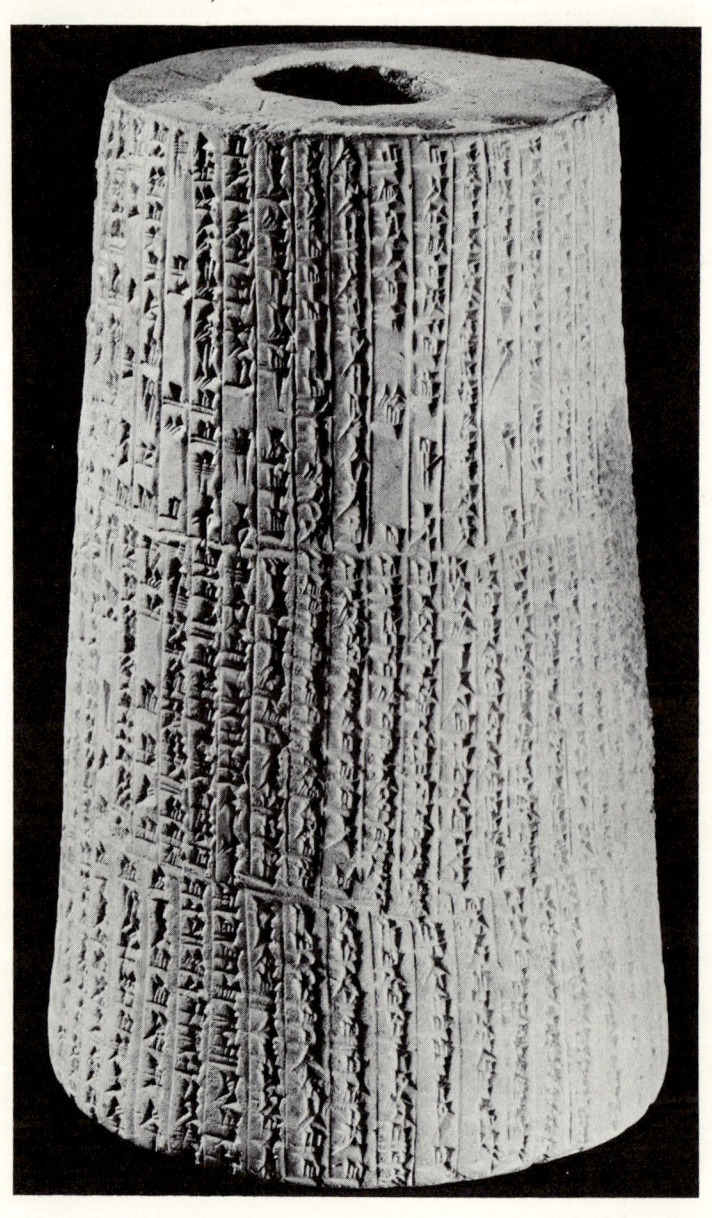

experiencing had but one explanation: the Israelites had forsaken Yahweh and had failed to fulfill their ethical commitments.

5 Run to and fro through the streets of
   Jerusalem,
  look and take note!

A reconstruction of Babylon as seen from the Ishtar Gate; to the right are the Hanging Gardens and, beyond them, the Tower of Babel. (The Oriental Institute, University of Chicago)

The remains of Babylon. (The Matson Photo Service, Alhambra, California)

Search her squares to see if you can find a man,
  one who does justice and seeks truth;
  that I may pardon her.
2 Though they say, "As the Lord lives,"
  yet they swear falsely.
3 O Lord, do not thy eyes look for truth?
Thou hast smitten them,
  but they felt no anguish;
thou hast consumed them,
  but they refused to take correction.
They have made their faces harder than rock;
  they have refused to repent. . . .

26 For wicked men are found among my people;
  they lurk like fowlers lying in wait.
They set a trap;
  they catch men.
27 Like a basket full of birds,
  their houses are full of treachery;
therefore they have become great and rich,

²⁸ they have grown fat and sleek.
They know no bounds in deeds of wickedness;
   they judge not with justice
the cause of the fatherless, to make it prosper,
   and they do not defend the rights of the needy.⁷

And again, echoing Amos (5:21-24) and Hosea (6:6), Jeremiah stressed that Israel had lost sight of the spiritual nature of the covenant relationship with Yahweh.

   7 . . . ²¹ Thus says the Lord of hosts, the God of Israel: "Add your burnt offerings to your sacrifices, and eat the flesh. ²² For in the day that I brought them out of the land of Egypt, I did not speak to your fathers or command them concerning burnt offerings and sacrifices. ²³ But this command I gave them, 'Obey my voice, and I will be your God, and you shall be my people; and walk in all the way that I command you, that it may be well with you.' ²⁴ But they did not obey or incline their ear, but walked in their own counsels and the stubbornness of their evil hearts, and went backward and not forward. ²⁵ From the day that your fathers came out of the land of Egypt to this day, I have persistently sent all my servants the prophets to them, day after day; ²⁶ yet they did not listen to me, or incline their ear, but stiffened their neck. They did worse than their fathers." . . .

   9 . . . ²³ Thus says the Lord: "Let not the wise man glory in his wisdom, let not the mighty man glory in his might, let not the rich man glory in his riches; ²⁴ but let him who glories glory in this, that he understands and knows me, that I am the Lord who practice kindness [*chesed*], justice, and righteousness in the earth; for in these things I delight, says the Lord."

   ²⁵ Behold, the days are coming, says the Lord, when I will punish all those who are circumcised but yet uncircumcised—²⁶ Egypt, Judah, Edom, the sons of Ammon, Moab, and all who dwell in the desert that cut the corners of their hair; for all these nations are uncircumcised, and all the house of Israel is uncircumcised in heart."⁸

True to the Deuteronomic Reformation, Jeremiah also sought a revival of the Mosaic past, the "ancient paths":

   6 . . . ¹⁶ Thus says the Lord:
"Stand by the roads, and look,
   and ask for the ancient paths,
where the good way is; and walk in it,
   and find rest for your souls.
But they said, 'We will not walk in it.' " ⁹

In these particular prophetic themes of Jeremiah we see nothing essentially new. Yet there are aspects of later prophecy that express new perspectives and ideas of crucial importance to ethics. The first of these is the increasing tendency, especially evident in Jeremiah and Ezekiel, to place moral responsibility with the individual rather than with the group. This change in ethical perspective resulted in part from the increased urbanization of Israelite society in the seventh century B.C. Jerusalem was no longer an Israelite town that had grown large by supplying the needs of the royal court and the Temple. It was a commercial city with a religiously mixed population where ties of family and kin were less meaningful than political alliances and trade agreements. Moreover, its style of life and its attitudes tended to influence the rest of Judea. In such an urban climate the traditional Hebraic conceptions of God and of moral responsibility, derived as they were from the Mosaic covenant and rooted in a communal or corporate way of life, seemed monstrous and unjust to the sophisticated citizen who could no longer accept a concept of a wrathful God and corporate moral responsibility. Under the traditional observances and rites, the society of Jerusalem grew skeptical and religiously indifferent. Jeremiah and Ezekiel attempted to overcome such apathy and skepticism, to effect a

---

⁷ The Bible, Jer. 5:1-3, 26-28.

⁸ The Bible, Jer., 7:21-26; 9:23-26.
⁹ The Bible, Jer. 6:16.

return to Yahweh, by revising the understanding of Yahweh and his ethical demands.

Jeremiah, Ezekiel: Yahweh's Covenant with the Individual

Jeremiah[10]

31 ... 27 "Behold, the days are coming, says the LORD, when I will sow the house of Israel and the house of Judah with the seed of man and the seed of beast. 28 And it shall come to pass that as I have watched over them to pluck up and break down, to overthrow, destroy, and bring evil, so I will watch over them to build and to plant, says the LORD. 29 In those days they shall no longer say:

'The fathers have eaten sour grapes,
 and the children's teeth are set on edge.'

30 But every one shall die for his own sin; each man who eats sour grapes, his teeth shall be set on edge.

31 "Behold, the days are coming, says the LORD, when I will make a new covenant with the house of Israel and the house of Judah, 32 not like the covenant which I made with their fathers when I took them by the hand to bring them out of the land of Egypt, my covenant which they broke, though I was their husband, says the LORD. 33 But this is the covenant which I will make with the house of Israel after those days, says the LORD: I will put my law within them, and I will write it upon their hearts; and I will be their God, and they shall be my people. 34 And no longer shall each man teach his neighbor and each his brother, saying, 'Know the LORD,' for they shall all know me, from the least of them to the greatest, says the LORD; for I will forgive their iniquity, and I will remember their sin no more." ...

Ezekiel[11]

18 The word of the LORD came to me again: 2 "What do you mean by repeating this proverb concerning the land of Israel, 'The fathers have eaten sour grapes, and the children's teeth are set on edge'? 3 As I live, says the Lord GOD, this proverb shall no more be used by you in Israel. 4 Behold, all souls are mine; the soul of the father as well as the soul of the son is mine: the soul that sins shall die.

5 "If a man is righteous and does what is lawful and right—6 if he does not eat upon the mountains or lift up his eyes to the idols of the house of Israel, does not defile his neighbor's wife or approach a woman in her time of impurity, 7 does not oppress anyone, but restores to the debtor his pledge, commits no robbery, gives his bread to the hungry and covers the naked with a garment, 8 does not lend at interest or take any increase, withholds his hand from iniquity, executes true justice between man and man, 9 walks in my statutes, and is careful to observe my ordinances—he is righteous, he shall surely live, says the Lord GOD.

10 "If he begets a son who is a robber, a shedder of blood, who does none of these duties, 11 but eats upon the mountains, defiles his neighbor's wife, 12 oppresses the poor and needy, commits robbery, does not restore the pledge, lifts up his eyes to the idols, commits abomination, 13 lends at interest, and takes increase; shall he then live? He shall not live. He has done all these abominable things; he

---

[10] The Bible, Jer. 31:27-34.

[11] The Bible, Ezek. 18:1-32.

shall surely die; his blood shall be upon himself.

14 "But if this man begets a son who sees all the sins which his father has done, and fears, and does not do likewise, 15 who does not eat upon the mountains or lift up his eyes to the idols of the house of Israel, does not defile his neighbor's wife, 16 does not wrong anyone, exacts no pledge, commits no robbery, but gives his bread to the hungry and covers the naked with a garment, 17 withholds his hand from iniquity, takes no interest or increase, observes my ordinances, and walks in my statutes; he shall not die for his father's iniquity; he shall surely live. 18 As for his father, because he practiced extortion, robbed his brother, and did what is not good among his people, behold, he shall die for his iniquity.

19 "Yet you say, 'Why should not the son suffer for the iniquity of the father?' When the son has done what is lawful and right, and has been careful to observe all my statutes, he shall surely live. 20 The soul that sins shall die. The son shall not suffer for the iniquity of the father, nor the father suffer for the iniquity of the son; the righteousness of the righteous shall be upon himself, and the wickedness of the wicked shall be upon himself.

21 "But if a wicked man turns away from all his sins which he has committed and keeps all my statutes and does what is lawful and right, he shall surely live; he shall not die. 22 None of the transgressions which he has committed shall be remembered against him; for the righteousness which he has done he shall live. 23 Have I any pleasure in the death of the wicked, says the Lord God, and not rather that he should turn from his way and live? 24 But when a righteous man turns away from his righteousness and commits iniquity and does the same abominable things that the wicked man does, shall he live? None of the righteous deeds which he has done shall be remembered; for the treachery of which he is guilty and the sin he has committed, he shall die.

25 "Yet you say, 'The way of the Lord is not just.' Hear now, O house of Israel: Is my way not just? Is it not your ways that are not just? 26 When a righteous man turns away from his righteousness and commits iniquity, he shall die for it; for the iniquity which he has committed he shall die. 27 Again, when a wicked man turns away from the wickedness he has committed and does what is lawful and right, he shall save his life. 28 Because he considered and turned away from all the transgressions which he had committed, he shall surely live, he shall not die. 29 Yet the house of Israel says, 'The way of the Lord is not just.' O house of Israel, are my ways not just? Is it not your ways that are not just?

30 "Therefore I will judge you, O house of Israel, every one according to his ways, says the Lord God. Repent and turn from all your transgressions, lest iniquity be your ruin. 31 Cast away from you all the transgressions which you have committed against me, and get yourselves a new heart and a new spirit! Why will you die, O house of Israel? 32 For I have no pleasure in the death of anyone, says the Lord God; so turn, and live."

The insistence on individual moral responsibility expressed in these two prophets was not exclusively a reaction to the charge of the skeptics that "the way of the Lord is not just." It was also a product of an increasing sense of personal individuality, as the following selection makes clear.

The Emergence of the Individual Through the Prophetic Consciousness
H. Wheeler Robinson[12]

It was characteristic that the national unity of Israel should have been created and sustained by its religion. It was equally characteristic that the fuller sense of individuality should be a product of the prophetic consciousness. This fuller sense came through the religious experience of men who believed that they stood in an individual relation both to God and the nation. They were the eyes of the people toward God and the mouth of God toward the people (Isa. 29:10, Jer. 15:19). From their individual call onward, their experience and their message alike isolated them in greater or less degree; thus the prophet Jeremiah cries to God, "I sat not in the assembly of them that make merry, nor rejoiced: I sat alone because of thy hand" (15:17). No man can be forced into such isolation from the natural fellowships of life without one of two things happening. Either he will become sullen and embittered, or else he will find consolation and compensation in a deeper sense of God. The God of Israel was always conceived as a Person, and there is no surer way of deepening our own personality than fellowship with a greater one. In discovering what the greater personality is, we discover our own. The process by which the prophet came to reflect the thought and feeling of God exalted him into a new consciousness of individual worth to God. This initial factor made the prophets pioneers of a richer sense of individual personality and able to leave behind them a legacy which has become part of the spiritual inheritance of the world.

But the initial factor, their own relation to God, was reinforced by the very demands they made of Israel in the name of God. "Cease to do evil, learn to do well; seek justice, make the violent keep straight; give judgment for the orphan, support the cause of the widow" (Isa. 1:16-17). Their message was to the nation, but they asked justice and mercy from the individual Israelite toward his neighbor as the true and essential fulfilment of God's desires, without which the ritual of worship became a mockery. This social ethic was the direct development of the old nomadic clan spirit, purified and enlightened, and raised to the level of a religious offering to God. The corporate personality of Israel could not stand in a right relation to God unless it approached Him in this unity of internal and individual fellowship. Such a demand, so conceived, even when presented to the nation, became inevitably a demand for an *individual* response to it. Moreover, it became increasingly a demand for something more than the *external* reformation of conduct. Hosea saw that what was wrong with Israel was its inner spirit of infidelity (4:12, 5:4). The only fulfilment of God's law was love. The book of Deuteronomy, largely influenced by Hosea's teaching, proclaimed, "Thou shalt love Yahweh thy God" (6:5), and justified the paradox of a law to love by presenting Yahweh as a lovable, because a redeeming, God (6:21 ff.). Jeremiah, saying, "Thou art near in their mouth and far from their affections"

---

[12] H. Wheeler Robinson, *Corporate Personality in Ancient Israel* (Philadelphia: Fortress Press, 1964), pp. 28-31.

(12:2), is contrasting the common shout of praise with the individual motive to thanksgiving. This new emphasis on motive went far to individualize the relation of the Israelite to Yahweh.

But the religious experience of the prophets went farther still in this process of individualization. They were themselves sustained in their mission by the personal fellowship of God, the experience of which one of them wrote, "morning by morning He wakeneth mine ear to hear as a disciple" (Isa. 50:4). Some of them came to see that they were making a demand on the individual Israelites which could be fulfilled only by divine aid, God's acts of individualizing grace. So we have the promise of a "new covenant" through Jeremiah, which should be individualized and internalized, in contrast with all previous covenants which had been national and expressed in external forms: "I will put my law in their inward parts, and in their heart will I write it" (31:31 ff.). It is still a covenant "with the house of Israel," but it is accomplished through a new and more searching relation of God to each member of that house. So also with the promise of grace through Jeremiah's younger contemporary, Ezekiel (36:26–27): "A new heart will I give you, and a new spirit will I put within you; and I will take away the stony heart out of your flesh, and I will give you a heart of flesh. And I will put my spirit within you, and cause you to walk in my statutes."

This new individualization of the relation of Israel to God is confirmed by the fact that Ezekiel (chap. 18) proclaims individual moral responsibility in sharper terms than anyone before him. "The soul that sinneth, *it* shall die"—not others also, as the older conception of corporate personality had demanded from Achan's family (Josh. 7:24 ff.).

If we think of the prophets of Israel as a spiritual aristocracy, then we may say that what they hoped for was a democratization of their own relation to God, when all the Lord's people would be prophets (Num. 11:29), and God would pour out his spirit upon all flesh (Joel 2:28). Indeed, we may say in general of the "great men" of Israel, those outstanding personalities which are so prominent in her history, that they are what they are precisely in this way. Their human personality is again and again shown to be achieved as a response to the call and influence of divine personality. It might well be argued, even on purely philosophical grounds, that no profounder interpretation of human personality could ever be given.

The prophetic message, especially of the later prophets, presupposed a particular view of historical development. For the Hebrew at the time of the conquest and settlement of Palestine the "past" consisted of tribal traditions and the mighty acts of Yahweh which could, in a sense, be relived or made present in cultic ceremony. There was, however, no sense of a developing plan or a particular divine purpose beyond the simple ethnocentric belief that Yahweh protected his people. During the period of the confederacy and monarchy, the pattern of apostasy, chastisement, and repentance which repeated itself so frequently suggested to some that there was a predictable correlation between apostasy and chastisement, that Yahweh allowed Israel to be attacked by enemies in order to renew her faith. Around this simple view of the past as an oscillation between covenant fidelity and infidelity grew up an idea of historical development. The later prophets felt that there was a purpose in God's continued concern for Israel, that the creation of the Covenant and the concern for obedience to it implied a plan in which Israel played a significant part. Moreover, this plan was working itself out in a particular direction, namely the conversion of all nations to Yahweh. Thus within the prophetic tradition there emerged a linear conception of historical events which were simultaneously acknowledged to be the working out of a divine plan. That view of history was passed on to Christianity and became a fundamental presupposition of historical thinking well into the modern age. It has, however, undergone radical revision since the end of the nineteenth century. Few historians today are willing to acknowledge supernatural causation. Yet the questions of meaning, direction, and purpose often reenter historical discussion, albeit divested of their theological garb. The linear, purposive view of history which Western civilization received from the Judeo-Christian tradition has remained the cornerstone for our notions of historical development, even in their modern, secularized versions. The following selection by a historian of religions indicates the scope of the Hebrew view of history.

The Prophetic Understanding of History
Mircea Eliade[13]

Among the Hebrews, every new historical calamity was regarded as a punishment inflicted by Yahweh, angered by the orgy of sin to which the chosen people had abandoned themselves. No military disaster seemed absurd, no suffering was vain, for, beyond the "event," it was always possible to perceive the will of Yahweh. Even more: these catastrophes were, we may say, necessary, they were foreseen by God so that the Jewish people should not contravene its true destiny by alienating the religious heritage left by Moses. Indeed, each time that history gave them the opportunity, each time that they enjoyed a period of comparative peace and economic prosperity, the Hebrews turned from Yahweh and to the Baals and Astartes of their neighbors. Only historical catastrophes brought them back to the right road by forcing them to look toward the true God. Then "they cried unto the Lord, and said, We have sinned, because we have forsaken the Lord, and have served Baalim and Ashtaroth: but now deliver us out of the hand of our enemies, and we will serve thee" (I Samuel 12:10). This return to the true God in the hour of disaster reminds us of the desperate gesture of the primitive, who, to rediscover the existence of the Supreme Being, requires the extreme of peril and the failure of all addresses to other divine forms (gods, ancestors, demons). Yet the Hebrews, from the moment the great military Assyro-Babylonian empires appeared on their historical horizon, lived constantly under the threat proclaimed by Yahweh: "But if ye will not obey the voice of the Lord, then shall the hand of the Lord be against you, as it was against your fathers" (I Samuel 12:15).

Through their terrifying visions, the prophets but confirmed and amplified Yahweh's ineluctable chastisement upon his people who had not kept the faith. And it is only insofar as such prophecies were ratified by catastrophes (as, indeed, was the case from Elijah to Jeremiah) that historical events acquired religious significance; i.e., that they clearly appeared as punishments inflicted by the Lord in return for the impiousness of Israel. Because of the prophets, who interpreted contemporary events in the light of a strict faith,

---
[13] Mircea Eliade, *Cosmos and History: The Myth of the Eternal Return* (New York: Harper and Row, 1959), pp. 102–104; copyright 1954 by Bollingen Foundation, Inc.

these events were transformed into "negative theophanies," into Yahweh's "wrath." Thus they not only acquired a meaning... but they also revealed their hidden coherence by proving to be the concrete expression of the same single divine will. Thus, for the first time, the prophets placed a value on history, succeeded in transcending the traditional vision of the cycle (the conception that ensures all things will be repeated forever), and discovered a one-way time. This discovery was not to be immediately and fully accepted by the consciousness of the entire Jewish people, and the ancient conceptions were still long to survive.

But, for the first time, we find affirmed, and increasingly accepted, the idea that historical events have a value in themselves, insofar as they are determined by the will of God. This God of the Jewish people is no longer an Oriental divinity, creator of archetypal gestures, but a personality who ceaselessly intervenes in history, who reveals his will through events (invasions, sieges, battles, and so on). Historical facts thus become "situations" of man in respect to God, and as such they acquire a religious value that nothing had previously been able to confer on them. It may, then, be said with truth that the Hebrews were the first to discover the meaning of history as the epiphany of God, and this conception, as we should expect, was taken up and amplified by Christianity.

In the prophetic understanding of history there was a clear causal relationship between Israel's action, Yahweh's will, and the great events of their history. Amos declared:

3 . . . ³ Do two walk together,
   unless they have made an appointment?
⁴ Does a lion roar in the forest,
   when he has no prey?
Does a young lion cry out from his den,
   If he has taken nothing?
⁵ Does a bird fall in a snare on the earth,
   when there is no trap for it?
Does a snare spring up from the ground,
   when it has taken nothing?
⁶ Is a trumpet blown in a city,
   and the people are not afraid?
Does evil befall a city,
   unless the Lord has done it?
⁷ Surely the Lord God does nothing,
   without revealing his secret to his servants the prophets.
⁸ The lion has roared;
   who will not fear?
The Lord God has spoken;
   who can but prophesy? [14]

The linear and purposive view of history developed by the later prophets was not a history with an open and indefinite future. These prophets felt that Yahweh would not allow the pattern of apostasy, chastisement, and repentance to continue indefinitely. With the fall of the Northern Kingdom and the possibility of a similar catastrophe befalling the Southern Kingdom, the prophets called for a complete return to Yahweh, a once-and-for-all repentance. To underscore the finality of Yahweh's requirements, the prophets increasingly spoke of a *future* and *final* chastisement and salvation. Chastisement was to fall on the nation as a whole for the apostasy of those who had broken the Covenant. Salvation was usually reserved for those few who had remained faithful. This emphasis on a future and final time of condemnation and salvation, be it personal or collective, religious or political, is termed eschatological (literally, concerned with last things).

Eschatology can best be understood, perhaps, from the analogy of myth. Myth gives its symbolic picture of unknown origins and the unknown past. Eschatology is that form of myth which accounts for the unknown future. Men walk in a here and now whose extent varies somewhat with their historical

[14] The Bible, Amos 3:3–8.

and geographical observation. Beyond the limited bounds of that here and now, in any stage of culture, they must fall back on an imaginative picture of what preceded the known and what is to follow it. They usually foreshorten the disappearing continuity of past and future, and construct in either case a mythical beginning and a mythical end which serve to focus in themselves all the past and all the future, and which become the termini of temporal experience.

Enlightened epochs are not free from this necessity. Our myth will differ but our representation of origins and of the future will still partake of the nature of myth. Prophecies of a world-state, a perfect society, the superman, evolutionary mutations, successive world-crises are of the nature of eschatological myth just as much as were the prophecies of the Millennium and the Judgment. Our doctrine of progress is a kind of contemporary messianism, and in so far as it is held to be inevitable, rests on as unethical presumptions as much ancient messianism.

If eschatology is of the nature of myth we must look to it for similar value. The world's greatest myths have always been summary representations of essential truths. They objectify in a unique way the nature and soul of a people or the race. The story of the Fall in Genesis is such a myth and witnesses to the origin and nature of the moral sense in a way unaffected by later views of social development.

Now Jewish eschatology is such a myth and carries a weight of spiritual truth such as only the greatest art can convey. It is an artificial schema, indeed, in its later form; it became a dogma with fixed detail. But it had behind it as creative and shaping and inspiring force a profound and true intuition with regard to the future. The best spiritual experience of the Hebrews persuaded them of coming creative change in human nature and society.[15]

[15] Amos N. Wilder, "The Nature of Jewish Eschatology," *Journal of Biblical Literature*, L (1931), pp. 201-202. This material is thoroughly copyrighted by *The Journal of Biblical Literature*, which protection is not lessened by reproduction in this volume.

The increasing importance of the eschatological dimension in the Hebraic understanding of history can be seen in the changing meaning attached to the phrase the Day of Yahweh. A major implication of the covenant concept in Israel's history was that if the people were faithful to Yahweh, Yahweh in turn would shower blessings upon them. If political and economic disorders were the results of a loss of faith, then political prestige and economic security were the products of faithfulness to the Covenant. The complete and final success of Yahweh's people was the Day of Yahweh. It was one of the achievements of Amos to show that economic prosperity and political security were not always caused by faithfulness to the Covenant. The wicked might also prosper. The analysis of Amos takes dramatic form by changing the definition of the Day of Yahweh from ultimate victory and blessing to condemnation and punishment.

> 5 . . . [18] Woe to you who desire the day of the Lord!
> Why would you have the day of the Lord?
> It is darkness, and not light;
> [19] as if a man fled from a lion, and a bear met him;
> Or went into the house and leaned with his hand against the wall,
> and a serpent bit him.
> [20] Is not the day of the Lord darkness, and not light,
> and gloom with no brightness in it? [16]

This eschatological judgment was followed by God's promise of a future salvation, as in Jeremiah's prophecy of a "New Covenant."

The eschatological interpretation of history that grew out of the experience of the prophets during the collapse of the two kingdoms was intensified during the period of exile after the fall of Jerusalem in 586 B.C. Because the exiled Jews in Babylonia were allowed a high degree of social freedom and economic opportunity, an increased need for preserving national and religious identity was felt. The heightening of national and religious consciousness was achieved

[16] The Bible, Amos 5:18-20.

by such prophets as Ezekiel and Second Isaiah as well as by the priests who during this period edited and organized the Pentateuch and made the Torah the heart of the Jewish religious faith. It was probably also during this time of separation from the Temple in Jerusalem that the synagogue was created as a place to gather for communal worship.

This rejuvenated national consciousness was translated into religious terms by an unknown prophet in exile who gave a new meaning to the understanding of Israel's special role in *world history*. For convenience sake this prophet is called Second Isaiah (or Deutero-Isaiah) because his prophecy appears in the Book of Isaiah, chapters 40–55.[17] Second Isaiah prophesied as Babylon was being overshadowed by the rising Persian empire of Cyrus, a fact that undoubtedly accounts for the optimistic tone of his poetry. The prophet foretold the defeat of the Babylonians and hailed Cyrus as Yahweh's "shepherd" who would allow the Chosen People to return to Jerusalem and rebuild the Temple. Yet this prophecy was not merely a nationalistic hope for the restoration of political freedom and independence, for Israel was not destined to return to her old ways. She now stood at the dawn of a new age. In imagery drawn from Israel's Exodus experience of old, Second Isaiah portrayed her imminent liberation from Babylonian bondage and triumphant return to the Promised Land.

> 40 Comfort, comfort my people,
>   says your God.
> 2 Speak tenderly to Jerusalem,
>   and cry to her
> that her warfare is ended,
>   that her iniquity is pardoned,
>   that she has received from the LORD's hand
>   double for all her sins.
>
> 3 A voice cries:
> "In the wilderness prepare the way of the
>   LORD,
>   make straight in the desert a highway for
>   our God.
> 4 Every valley shall be lifted up,
>   and every mountain and hill be made low;
> the uneven ground shall become level,
>   and the rough places a plain.
> 5 And the glory of the LORD shall be revealed,
>   and all flesh shall see it together,
>   for the mouth of the LORD has spoken." . . .
>
> 9 Get you up to a high mountain,
>   O Zion, herald of good tidings;
> lift up your voice with strength,
>   O Jerusalem, herald of good tidings,
>   lift it up, fear not;
> say to the cities of Judah,
>   "Behold your God!"
> 10 Behold, the Lord GOD comes with might,
>   and his arm rules for him;
> behold, his reward is with him,
>   and his recompense before him.
> 11 He will feed his flock like a shepherd,
>   he will gather the lambs in his arms,
> he will carry them in his bosom,
>   and gently lead those that are with
>   young. . . .
>
> 27 Why do you say, O Jacob,
>   and speak, O Israel,
> "My way is hid from the LORD,
>   and my right is disregarded by my God"?
> 28 Have you not known? Have you not heard?
>   The LORD is the everlasting God,
>   The Creator of the ends of the earth.
> He does not faint or grow weary,
>   his understanding is unsearchable.
> 29 He gives power to the faint,
>   and to him who has no might he increases
>   strength.
> 30 Even youths shall faint and be weary,
>   and young men shall fall exhausted;
> 31 but they who wait for the LORD shall renew their strength,

---

[17] Scholars generally regard the Book of Isaiah as made up of the writings of three prophets from three different periods. Chapters 1–39 are the work of the great prophet Isaiah of the eighth century B.C., after whom the book is named; chapters 40–55 belong to the unknown Second Isaiah who prophesied in Babylon in 540 B.C.; and chapters 56–66 are attributed to an unknown Third Isaiah, probably a disciple of the Second Isaiah, who wrote in the late sixth century after the return from exile to Jerusalem.

they shall mount up with wings like eagles,
they shall run and not be weary,
they shall walk and not faint.[18]

Second Isaiah prophesied a "new Exodus," a new national beginning, a future more glorious than the past. And as redemption neared, Yahweh would offer Israel a new covenant, an "everlasting covenant," to accompany the new Exodus. The glad tidings of this prophet thus carried with them a new historical or eschatological dimension.

51 . . . [9]Awake, awake, put on strength,
O arm of the LORD;
awake, as in days of old,
the generations of long ago.
Was it not thou that didst cut Rahab in pieces,
that didst pierce the dragon?
[10] Was it not thou that didst dry up the sea,
the waters of the great deep;
that didst make the depths of the sea a way
for the redeemed to pass over?
[11]And the ransomed of the LORD shall return,
and come to Zion with singing;
everlasting joy shall be upon their heads;
they shall obtain joy and gladness,
and sorrow and sighing shall flee away.

52 . . . [11] Depart, depart, go out thence,
touch no unclean thing;
go out from the midst of her, purify yourselves,
you who bear the vessels of the LORD.
[12] For you shall not go out in haste,
and you shall not go in flight,
for the LORD will go before you,
and the God of Israel will be your rear guard.

55 "Ho, every one who thirsts, come to the waters;
and he who has no money,
come, buy and eat!
Come, buy wine and milk
without money and without price.
[2] Why do you spend your money for that which is not bread,

and your labor for that which does not satisfy?
Hearken diligently to me, and eat what is good,
and delight yourselves in fatness.
[3] Incline your ear, and come to me;
hear, that your soul may live;
and I will make with you an everlasting covenant,
my steadfast, sure love for David.
[4] Behold, I made him a witness to the peoples,
a leader and commander for the peoples.
[5] Behold, you shall call nations that you know not,
and nations that knew you not shall run to you,
because of the LORD your God, and of the Holy One of Israel,
for he has glorified you.

[6] "Seek the LORD while he may be found,
call upon him while he is near;
[7] let the wicked forsake his way,
and the unrighteous man his thoughts;
let him return to the LORD, that he may have mercy on him,
and to our God, for he will abundantly pardon.
[8] For my thoughts are not your thoughts,
neither are your ways my ways, says the LORD.
[9] For as the heavens are higher than the earth,
so are my ways higher than your ways
and my thoughts than your thoughts.

[10] "For as the rain and the snow come down from heaven,
and return not thither but water the earth,
making it bring forth and sprout,
giving seed to the sower and bread to the eater,
[11] so shall my word be that goes forth from my mouth;
it shall not return to me empty,
but it shall accomplish that which I purpose,
and prosper in the thing for which I sent it.

[12] "For you shall go out in joy,
and be led forth in peace;
the mountains and the hills before you

[18] The Bible, Isa. 40:1-5; 9-11, 27-31.

shall break forth into singing,
and all the trees of the field shall clap their hands.
¹³ Instead of the thorn shall come up the cypress;
instead of the brier shall come up the myrtle;
and it shall be to the LORD for a memorial,
for an everlasting sign which shall not be cut off." [19]

Second Isaiah understood Yahweh's kingdom to be a universal kingdom. God did not manipulate history in favor of Israel only; his concerns were much wider than one nation. His self-revelation through historical events was directed to all nations. Israel still had a unique role to play, but it was now the role of a missionary who has suffered in the past and will continue to suffer in the future while taking the message of Yahweh's universal rule to the corners of the earth.

42 Behold my servant, whom I uphold,
my chosen, in whom my soul delights;
I have put my spirit upon him,
he will bring forth justice to the nations.
² He will not cry or lift up his voice,
or make it heard in the street;
³ a bruised reed he will not break,
and a dimly burning wick he will not quench;
he will faithfully bring forth justice.
⁴ He will not fail or be discouraged
till he has established justice in the earth;
and the coastlands wait for his law.

⁵ Thus says God, the LORD,
who created the heavens and stretched them out,
who spread forth the earth and what comes from it,
who gives breath to the people upon it
and spirit to those who walk in it:
⁶ "I am the LORD, I have called you in righteousness,
I have taken you by the hand and kept you;
I have given you as a covenant to the people,
a light to the nations,
⁷ to open the eyes that are blind,
to bring out the prisoners from the dungeon,
from the prison those who sit in darkness.[20]

[19] The Bible, Isa. 51:9-11; 52:11-12; 55:1-13.

[20] The Bible, Isa. 42:1-7.

STUDY QUESTIONS

1. What is the nature of prophecy and what cultural function does it perform?

2. What influence has the prophetic tradition made upon Western culture?

3. What is the relationship between ecstasy and religion?

4. In what respects do the prophets reflect the continuing pressures of acculturation?

5. What was the reason for Amos' condemnation of Israel's priests and cultic prophets, and what ethical demands were placed on Israel?

6. What analogies did Hosea use to describe the broken relationship between Israel and Yahweh, and what were the sources and implications of those analogies?

7. What is the relationship between the ethical precepts and sanctions given in the Decalogue and those proclaimed by Amos and Hosea?

8. Did the Israelite prophets alter

or develop the Hebrew understanding of God?

9. Did Amos and Hosea express their charisma in a purely religious form, and, if so, why?

10. Did Jeremiah and Ezekiel make any lasting changes in the traditional means of enforcing standards of conduct?

11. How would you compare the kind of individualized morality proclaimed by the prophets with the individualized morality of the twentieth century?

12. What effect did the eschatological understanding of history have upon the ethical teaching of later prophecy?

13. In what ways is the modern view of history and ethics still influenced by the Judeo-Christian view?

For those who have used The Contribution of Ancient Greece *edited by Jacqueline Strain:*

14. Compare and contrast the effects of urbanization and commercialism on the concept of corporate moral responsibility or inherited guilt in Greek and Hebrew cultures.

15. Compare the role and function of prophecy in Greek and Hebrew cultures.

CHAPTER 5

LEGALISM, SEPARATISM, AND ESCHATOLOGICAL WITHDRAWAL:
Post-Exilic Judaism

Modern research has demonstrated that the messianic hope was one characteristic expression of Jewish religious faith, but that it had no uniform structure or dogmatic authorization. It was based fundamentally on the Old Testament, with its eschatological view of history, its teleology, its unfulfilled promises of a glorious future which stood out in ever stronger contrast with the increasing difficulties and disasters which Israel faced in its actual history, from the Exile onward. That it strongly influenced early Christianity and in fact conditioned its rise does not prove that Judaism as a whole was oriented in this direction. But it enables us somewhat better to understand the shift in emphasis which Christianity represented, and the consequent tensions between Jews and Christians, especially in their interpretation of the Old Testament and their view of the future destiny of Israel.

Frederick C. Grant, Ancient Judaism and the New Testament *(New York: The Macmillan Company, 1959), p. 83.*

The concept of salvation is clearly one of very wide and diverse connotation. Even if kept within the context of religion, its application ranges from the idea of safety from disease and misfortune, engendered by demoniac agency, to that of deliverance from some form of eternal damnation. And the means by which such various kinds of salvation have been thought to be effected are equally diverse—indeed from the magical amulet to the divine saviour. This complex diversity, however, can be conveniently simplified to reveal what is surely the quintessence of the idea of salvation.

Human consciousness, inhering essentially in awareness of the three temporal categories of past, present and future, causes man to know that he is mortal. Hence in each individual there is a fundamental sense of insecurity; for, whatever be his present fortune, each knows that he is subject to time that brings old age, decay and death. The realization that such is the nature of human destiny has provoked from mankind a varied pattern of reaction which has found expression in its many religions. With a few exceptions, in this reaction there has been a common factor, namely, the quest for the assurance of *post-mortem* security by attaching oneself to, or associating with, some eternal or life-giving entity.

S. G. F. Brandon, "The Ritual Technique of Salvation in the Ancient Near East" in S. G. F. Brandon, ed., The Saviour God (Manchester, England: Manchester University Press, 1963), pp. 17–18.

The portion of the wicked shall be [to be afflicted with pain]s in their bones and to be a reproach to all flesh;
but the righteous [shall be destined to en]joy the rich delights of heaven and to be [glut]ted on the yield of the earth.

[Thou wilt distinguish between the right]eous and the wicked.
Thou wilt give the wicked as our [ran]som, and the faithless [in exchange for us].

[Thou wilt make] an end of all that oppress us;
and we shall give thanks unto Thy name for ever [and bless Thee alway;]
for this it is for which Thou hast created us, and that it is that [beseemeth] Thee.

From The Dead Sea Scriptures, *p. 311, translated by Theodor H. Gastner. Copyright © 1956, 1964 by Theodor H. Gastner. Reprinted by permission of Doubleday & Company, Inc.*

At the end of Chapter 4 the concept of eschatology was introduced in the context of the prophetic view of historical development. Eschatology, however, is far more than simply a view of history that asserts the dawn of a new age. The glorious future, the new order of things that is soon to come, invariably produces or is precipitated by the disappearance of the present order. Within eschatological thinking the termination of present suffering and injustice is as important as the expectation of the new age.

Eschatology, moreover, is not a poetic device used exclusively by the later prophets to reassure a suppressed and discouraged people. It is a universal phenomenon that can be found in some form in every society. The expectation need not restrict itself to a fringe group, nor need it always envisage a cataclysmic end to the present order. Eschatology may describe a belief accepted generally throughout a society or a belief held by only a few individuals within that society; its content may consist only in the positive features of the new age into which all shall pass smoothly, or it may be filled with the gruesome and terrifying details of the destruction that will accompany the end of the present age in which most shall perish; it may be generalized in such a way that the expectation can maintain itself for centuries in the face of little or no apparent change in the present order, or it may require an immediate end to the world according to a predictable schedule of events. But whatever its content, whatever its form, eschatology is seldom the conception of one isolated individual: it can be and usually is a shared belief, a group myth.

As Amos N. Wilder has suggested, the term eschatology can be used in a broad sense to cover anyone's view of and attitude toward the future. As a society-wide belief it may express the general desires and goals of the society or it may aid the society in adjusting to otherwise unacceptable conditions. However, the term is more frequently used to describe a belief in the destruction of the present world in the immediate future. In such cases the expectation will be intense and will either reorganize the society or will separate out a portion of that society into a smaller group for whom the eschatological myth is the one important reality without which life would become unbearable and the group inevitably disintegrate. It is this last situation that is properly termed an eschatological movement. Such a group does not tolerate the conditions that brought it into existence but rather withdraws from the society, attempts to totally restructure the society, or attempts to destroy the present order and thus initiate the new age.

While eschatology has the power to attract and motivate, thus increasing the size of the group or movement, it should be realized that eschatology is also a *creation* of the group, not something that just "happens" to the group. At the earliest stage, the eschatology of a movement may be the thought of one individual whose insight into the immediate future, through a dream or an increasingly certain awareness of an imminent and total change, spreads rapidly, with missionary zeal, among like-minded persons. His insight into future events is, for the group, a major sign of his charismatic authority. In fact, the program of a charismatic leader is of necessity eschatological in character.

There are several factors that cause eschatology to move from the individual to the group and from a mild hope for better times to a firm belief in an imminent holocaust that will engulf all peoples. Eschatology can appear as a means of adjusting to or, more frequently, of rejecting the processes of acculturation. This is especially true where the previous adoption of alien elements has seemingly led to political and economic disaster for the society. If the influences of acculturation cannot be excluded through the erection of barriers or by shifting the location of the group, then stronger solutions may be adopted, one of the most common being the expectation that divine powers will intervene to protect or reestablish the smooth, ongoing life of the community.

Another and stronger factor is a sense of deprivation, a sense of an intolerable gap between expectation and reality, that cannot be adequately corrected or compensated within the normal political and social channels. We have already examined, in Chapter 3, the reactions of a society undergoing acculturation; the following selection will analyze the concept of relative deprivation as a major cause of eschatological movements.

Relative Deprivation and Eschatological Movements
David F. Aberle[1]

Relative deprivation[2] is defined as a negative discrepancy between legitimate expectation and actuality. Where an individual or a group has a particular expec-

---

[1] David F. Aberle, "A Note on Relative Deprivation as Applied to Millenarian and Other Cult Movements," in Sylvia L. Thrupp, ed., *Comparative Studies in Society and History*, Supplement II (New York: Cambridge University Press, 1962), pp. 209–211, 213–214.

[2] Aberle subsequently expanded his definition as follows: "Relative deprivation is defined as a negative discrepancy between legitimate expectation and actuality, or between legitimate expectation and anticipated actuality, or both" (David F. Aberle, 1966, *The Peyote Religion Among the Navaho*. Chicago: Aldine Publishing Company, p. 323). This change circumvents the problem raised by his speaking of reference points for judging relative deprivation as including "one's present versus one's future circumstances," since such a negative discrepancy is not a difference between legitimate expectation and current actuality.

tation and furthermore where this expectation is considered to be a proper state of affairs and where something less than that expectation is fulfilled, we may speak of relative deprivation. It is important to stress that deprivation *is* relative and not absolute. To a hunting and gathering group with an expectation of going hungry one out of four days, failure to find game is not a relative deprivation, although it may produce marked discomfort. It is a truism that for a multi-millionnaire to lose all but his last million in a stock market crash *is* a major deprivation. The deprivation, then, is not a particular objective state of affairs, but a difference between an anticipated state of affairs and a less agreeable actuality. We must furthermore consider the expectations as *standards,* rather than merely as prophecies of what will happen tomorrow.

The discovery of what constitutes serious deprivation for particular groups or individuals is a difficult empirical problem. It requires careful attention to the reference points that people employ to judge their legitimate expectations, as well as to their actual circumstances. Among the obvious reference points that can be, and are used for such judgments are: (1) one's past versus one's present circumstances; (2) one's present versus one's future circumstances; (3) one's own versus some one else's present circumstances. . . .

It is where conditions decline by comparison with the past, where it is expected that they will decline, in the future by comparison with the present, and where shifts in the relative conditions of two groups occur, that the deprivation experience becomes significant for efforts at remedial action. Indeed it is change itself that creates discrepancies between *legitimate* expectations and actuality, either by worsening the conditions of a group, or by exposing a group to new standards. . . .

It is not necessary . . . to assume that all deprivation experiences are primarily concerned with [material] goods. I have attempted a rough classification of types of deprivation. They fall into four groups: possessions, status, behavior, and worth. They may furthermore be classified as *personal* and *group* or *category* experiences. A man whose house is destroyed by fire experiences a personal deprivation of possessions—since this is *not* an experience most of us plan on. An American Indian tribe expropriated from its land, experiences group deprivation of possessions. . . .

We can, however, eliminate the purely personal deprivations. If the individual does not find that there are others in like circumstances, their significance for social movements, millenarian[3] or other, political or religious, would appear to be trivial. I will attempt to illustrate the others, using Navaho examples and only one frame of reference for comparison: present (undesirable) versus past (desirable). Navahos who had large herds in the 1920's lost them through livestock reduction in the 1930's. Those with such herds constituted a category, and their loss of stock adversely affected other Navahos who had benefitted from their generosity, so that the Navahos as a group or set of groups experienced deprivation of possessions, with respect to diet, trade goods procured through sale of animal products, etc. In addition, the large owners suffered deprivation of status. The society was reduced to far more egalitarian relationships; the man who had had followers to herd for him, gratitude for generosity, and

---

[3] A term used in Christian eschatology that has been applied to all eschatological movements.

standing because of his wealth now was almost as badly off as any other Navaho. His comparison here was to his past status in *his* group, not vis-à-vis the outside world. These were among the key deprivations experienced by Navahos during this period.

With the decline in livestock holdings came a necessary decline in certain types of behavior viewed as desirable by Navahos. Kin did not fulfill their obligation to kin, neighbors to neighbors, "rich" to poor, because the wherewithal for reciprocity and generosity was no longer there. There was a pervasive feeling that people did not *behave* as they should, or as they once did, and this I would call a deprivation in the area of behavior. This particular type of deprivation can be equally well illustrated by a shift to a different frame of reference for deprivation. With continued exposure to Americans, under circumstances which make Americans a model, some Navahos have come to feel that they do not behave as they should, by comparison with Americans: they are dirty, or superstitious, or eat "bad" foods (e.g., prairie dogs).

Finally, I come to worth, which is to some degree a residual category. It refers to a person's experience of others' estimation of him on grounds over and above his alterable characteristics—of possessions, status, and behavior. It is best illustrated again by those Navahos who use the outside world as a point of reference. Navahos with most contact have come to realize that to some degree neither wealth, occupational status, nor "proper" behavior can alter the fact that they are Navahos, and that they are therefore regarded as inferior and undesirable. Their total worth, then, is not what they feel it should be, and they experience a sense of deprivation in this regard. . . .

I conceive of any of these types of deprivation . . . to be the possible basis for efforts at remedial action to overcome the discrepancy between actuality and legitimate aspiration. . . . But the fact of deprivation is clearly an insufficient basis for predicting whether remedial efforts will occur, and, if they occur, whether they will have as aims changing the world, transcending it, or withdrawing from it, whether the remedy will be sought in direct action or ritual, and whether it will be sought with the aid of supernatural powers or without. . . .

It is fair to say that millenarian [and other such movements] do not arise under circumstances where the members of a group think that the world is so nearly perfect that transformation or translation must be just around the corner. . . .

[Rather], the millenarian ideology often justifies the *removal* of the participants in the movement from the ordinary spheres of life. Indeed, this removal is frequently not only social but spatial, whether it takes the form of withdrawal or of wandering. I would suggest that the deprivations which form the background for the movement not only involve the sense of blockage to which I have referred earlier, which leads to resort to supernaturalism, but also the sense of a social order which cannot be reconstituted to yield the satisfactions desired. The millenarian ideology justifies the removal of the participants from that social order, by reassuring them that the order itself will not long continue, and frees them to indulge in phantasy about the ideal society, or to attempt to build it in isolation or through violent attempts against the existing order. Those who suf-

142 Post-Exilic Judaism

fer from acute deprivation and cannot withdraw from the world can only constitute sects of the elect, or utilize devices to compensate for deprivation. The millenarian ideology justifies withdrawal, and that is its functional significance.

Post-Exilic Judaism knew the problems of both acculturation and deprivation, and these forces shaped Jewish society and religion in the centuries immediately preceding the appearance of Christianity. At the beginning of this five-hundred-year period the future seemed to bode well for the Jews. The Babylonian empire, to which they had been exiled, barely survived the death of its founding emperor Nebuchadnezzar, and a new power arose amid the political disorder that followed his death. Within a decade and a half the Persians, under the leadership of Cyrus, conquered most of the Near East including Babylon, which fell to their armies in 539

The Persians, who controlled the Near East in the fifth century, adopted many of the artistic patterns of the Assyrians. This gold drinking cup from Iran is representative of the Persian art of this period. (The Metropolitan Museum of Art, Fletcher Fund, 1954)

B.C. The Persians reversed the Assyrian and Babylonian "scorched earth" policy, which tried to achieve internal stability by displacing the smaller national groups within its boundaries, and instead gave such groups as the Jews permission to return to their homeland, where they were given a certain degree of political autonomy.

When the Jews began to return to Judea in 538 B.C., they erected a small theocracy headed jointly by the high priest and a civil leader of the Davidic line. Under their supervision the Temple and the walls of Jerusalem were rebuilt, and a strict conformity to the Law was required. Although such was definitely not the original intention of the priests who urged obedience to the Law, in time a legalism and ritualism developed similar to that which the earlier prophets had condemned. To the degree that Judaism came to be defined as obedience to the Law and ability to trade on one's Jewish ancestry (intermarriage being strictly prohibited), a wall of exclusiveness was erected against the immediate neighbors of the Jews such as the Samaritans,[4] a wall based on birth and religious conformity. This is illustrated in the Book of Ezra:

> 9 . . . [10] We have forsaken thy commandments, [11] which thou didst command by thy servants the prophets, saying, "The land which you are entering, to take possession of it, is a land unclean with the pollutions of the peoples of the lands, with their abominations which have filled it from end to end with their uncleanness. [12] Therefore give not your daughters to their sons, neither take their daughters for your sons, and never seek their peace or prosperity, that you may be strong, and eat the good of the land, and leave it for an inheritance to your children for ever." [13] And after all that has come upon us for our evil deeds and for our great guilt, seeing that thou, our God, has punished us less than our iniquities deserved and hast given us such a remnant as this, [14] shall we break thy commandments again and intermarry with the peoples who practice these abominations? Wouldst thou not be angry with us till thou wouldst consume us, so that there should be no remnant, nor any to escape? [15] O Lord the God of Israel, thou art just, for we are left a remnant that has escaped, as at this day. Behold, we are before thee in our guilt, for none can stand before thee because of this.[5]

The two centuries of Persian domination during which Jewish legalism became more rigid came to an abrupt end with the spectacular conquest of the Near East in 334–330 B.C. by Alexander the Great. After Alexander's death in 323 B.C. his empire was divided into three great Hellenistic monarchies: the Ptolemaic, encompassing Egypt; the Seleucid, comprising Syria and Mesopotamia; and the Antigonid, centered in Macedonia. Initially the Jews received the same kind of treatment from their Greek rulers as they had from the Persians. Alexander and his successors, the Ptolemies who controlled Palestine as part of their Egyptian monarchy, granted limited self-government and religious toleration to the Jews.

Under the Ptolemies the Jews were for the first time brought into contact with Hellenistic culture, and Greek practices began to permeate the Jewish community. It became fashionable for Jews to take Greek names, wear Greek dress, follow Greek customs, read Greek literature, and attend or take part in Greek games. Some Jews even had recourse to surgery to remove the marks of circumcision. The upper classes, including the ruling priestly class, were most deeply influenced by Hellenistic culture. Such flirting with Hellenism could only lead to religious, and hence political, tension. In reaction to the processes of acculturation, a strong conservative faction arose called the Hasidim, or "pious ones."

---

[4] The Samaritans were a mixture of the poorer elements of Israelite society who were left by the Assyrians after the fall of Samaria, the capital of the Northern Kingdom, in 722 B.C. and the other peoples who had moved there. The Jews rejected them because of their mixed blood and because they had assimilated elements of other cultures.

[5] The Bible, Ezra 9:10–15.

In the second century B.C., as had happened so often in the past, Palestine was caught in a power struggle between her more powerful neighbors. After long warfare between Ptolemaic Egypt and Seleucid-ruled Syria-Mesopotamia, the Seleucid king Antiochus IV (Epiphanes) (175–164 B.C.) drove the Ptolemies out of Palestine and reversed the long-standing policy of religious toleration. As an enthusiastic missionary of Hellenism, Antiochus was determined to stamp out the Jewish religion and thereby bring the troublesome Jews under his political control. To this end he sided with a faction of Jews who had become Hellenized and forbade all Jews within his territory under penalty of death to worship their God or celebrate religious festivals. Those found in possession of the Torah were to be punished. As a final attack on the Jewish religion Antiochus had erected in the Temple in Jerusalem an altar to Zeus on which swine were sacrificed. As might be expected this attempt to eradicate Judaism by attacking its traditions led many Jews to support the Hasidim and resulted in the insurrection known as the Maccabean Revolt. Under the leadership of the Hasidic Judas Maccabeus (after whom the revolt was named) the pious Jews fled to the hills and conducted successful guerrilla warfare against the Seleucids. In 165 B.C. the Jews succeeded in obtaining religious freedom from the Seleucids, and, finally, some thirty years later they won their political independence.

The Maccabean family became, for all practical purposes, hereditary high priests or rulers of Palestine, until in 67 B.C. a dispute arose between two heirs over the succession to the high office. In the resultant political confusion, Pompey, the Roman general who had just subdued Syria, was asked by a faction of Jews to intercede. Arriving in Jerusalem in 63 B.C., Pompey reestablished political order and appointed a high priest to govern under Roman authority. In this way Palestine passed under Roman rule. After the establishment of the imperial system of government, Palestine was ruled by appointed governors, or procurators, of whom the most successful was the Jew, Herod, who ruled at the time of Jesus' birth. The popular picture of the Jews being suppressed by the harsh rule of Roman governors is greatly overdrawn. Roman administration of Palestine was remarkably efficient during this period. Local customs were rarely interfered with, and governors were directed to permit as much freedom as possible. In the province of Judea political and judicial power was largely vested in the Sanhedrin, or Jewish religious court under priestly control. Yet, despite the relative liberality of the Romans, the Jews never accepted Roman rule, and many found the political situation intolerable.

The shifting fortunes of the Jewish people from the Exile to Roman rule and the frequency with which they found themselves under the authority of a foreign nation had profound effects upon Jewish society and religion. In light of the prophetic message, political suppression was interpreted by many as a result of religious disobedience, so obedience to Yahweh's law became the obvious means of ensuring political independence and cultural survival. The ethnocentrism and legalism characteristic of the Jewish upper classes in the post-Exilic period, the increase in boundary-maintaining mechanisms (to use our earlier terminology), were among the major reactions to the events that befell the Jewish people. The effects of such attempts at compensation and correction can be seen in the reaction to the Babylonian Exile out of which emerged the major attitudes and institutions of post-Exilic Judaism.

Post-Exilic Judaism
Howard Clark Kee, Franklin W. Young, and Karlfried Froehlich[6]

When the leaders of the Jews [returning from the Babylonian Captivity] tried to understand just how the people had sinned

[6] Howard Clark Kee, Franklin W. Young and Karlfried Froehlich, *Understanding the New Testament*, 2nd ed., © 1965, pp. 31–34. Reprinted by permission of Prentice-Hall, Inc., Englewood Cliffs, New Jersey.

and had brought down the judgment of God, they emphasized three major failures: First, the Jews had succumbed to idolatry and had turned to foreign gods rather than to Jehovah alone. Second, they had not worshiped Jehovah in purity but had permitted their worship to become corrupted by all manner of foreign practices. Third, they had not obeyed the commandments that he had given them. With these failures in mind, the post-exilic Jews determined to guard against any intrusion into their religious belief and life that might turn them from worshiping God as he ought to be worshiped. They realized that all through their history God had been seeking to lead them to what they fully came to understand only through the Babylonian captivity. They had been chosen by the one true God to know him, to worship him, and to live according to his commandments.

These convictions led to what has been called Jewish "particularism" or "exclusivism." It was not merely their belief that they were God's Chosen People that set the Jews apart from all other people. Given their firm conviction that belief, conduct, and worship were all of one piece, it was inevitable that they would seek to separate themselves from any mode of life that threatened the purity of any of the three. The book of Ezra shows the lengths to which this particularism was carried, for in it the Jews returning to Judaea after the captivity are forbidden to marry foreigners, and those who have married non-Jews are asked to put them aside. Such exclusivism can be understood only in the light of the religious zeal that prompted it—the earnest desire to avoid at all costs the disloyalty of their fathers. And since loyalty to Jehovah involved every aspect of life, it was dangerous to enter into close relations with those who lived in accordance with other ways. This exclusivism at its worst could become a cloak for the derision and hatred of other peoples. But at its best it was the Jews' testimony to the reality of the God they worshiped and the way of life into which faithfulness to him inescapably led them.

In the Hellenistic age, when polytheism and idolatry were commonplace, and when religion and morality were not so clearly related as they were in Judaism, the exclusivism of the Jews stood out sharply against the pagan world. Concerted efforts to Hellenize the Jews, by such rulers as Antiochus Epiphanes, drove loyal Jews to defiance, since they felt that their way of life had been given by God himself, in the form of the Jewish Law. More than anything else, it was the Law that provided the bond between Jews and that distinguished them as a community from all other people.

The Jews were convinced that to avoid the recurrence of such a tragedy as the Babylonian exile, they must know God's will as revealed in the Law of Moses and live in accordance with it. The Jews fervently believed that his Law had been given by divine revelation through Moses and was contained in the Pentateuch (the first five books of the Old Testament). It is now common knowledge that these books contain materials that were gradually brought together over many centuries and that it was not until the end of the fifth century B.C. that they reached their present state.

By the end of the third century B.C., the prophetic books (Amos, Hosea, Isaiah, and so forth) had also assumed the form in which they now appear and had been accepted as part of God's divine revelation to his people. In the New Testament, the phrase "the Law and the Prophets" is a reference to God's revelation to his people as it was contained in these holy scriptures. By the end of the first century B.C., all the books in the Old Testament, except for a very few, were regarded as divine revelation.

The English term *law* is not a precise equivalent of the Hebrew word *Torah*, a fact that is obvious to anyone who reads the Pentateuch carefully. For the Pentateuch contains a great deal of legend, history, and myth, as well as specific rules or regulations. To the Jews, Torah was a very inclusive term that referred to all that God had revealed about himself, their history, and the conduct that was required of them. In time, the entire written revelation came to be referred to as Torah, though in the more narrow sense Torah always meant the Pentateuch, and often specifically God's commandments.

It is this centrality of the Torah in Judaism that accounts for the rise of a body of Jewish scholars known as the Scribes (*Sopherim*). Since knowledge of the Torah was so essential, there had to be authorities who were competent to interpret the meaning of Torah to the people. In the early post-exilic period, the priests had been the learned men who were looked to as authorities. By the end of the third century B.C., some laymen had become Scribes charged with the responsibility of preserving the writings and giving the official interpretation of them. The conviction had arisen by that time that God was no longer revealing his will through the prophets but that the authority for understanding and interpreting God's will now resided largely with the Scribes, who accordingly thought of themselves as the successors to the prophets. . . .

The Torah, then, provided the basis for the common belief and conduct that characterized Jewish life and bound Jews together wherever they might be. But no institution in Judaism was more important in transmitting knowledge of the Torah and in nurturing deep reverence for it than the synagogue (transliterated from a Greek word meaning *assembly*). It is impossible to speak with certainty of the precise origins of the synagogue. It may have had its inception during the exile in Babylonia, when the Temple no longer stood and the Jews, far from their home, came together for worship, deliberation, and mutual support. Long before the end of the first century B.C., the synagogue had become a well-established institution, though its significance had evolved gradually. Not only in Palestine, but wherever Jews lived throughout the Graeco-Roman world, the synagogue served as the center of Jewish life and thought. Indeed, the term *synagogue* referred not so much to a place of meeting as to the coming together of Jews in any locality. It was an assembly for worship for Jews who had no temple, an occasion to read and interpret the Torah in the presence of the community. And it was in the synagogue that the "elders," the respected counselors of the local Jewish community, sought ways in which the Jews could adjust to an alien environment without being unfaithful to the Torah. When the Romans destroyed the Temple in A.D. 70, the Synagogue continued as the vital center of Jewish faith and life.

When the Jews returned to Jerusalem from the exile after 538 B.C., one of the first things they did was to rebuild the Temple. This step was in keeping with

Post-Exilic Judaism · 147

their strong desire to re-institute the proper worship of God. The priests who did the final editing of the Law of Moses (Torah) were careful to include specific instructions on the temple structure and the form of temple worship. The Temple itself consisted of a series of courts; the innermost court was the Holy of Holies, which only the High Priest was permitted to enter. This secret chamber was the

The Jewish reverence for the Torah is reflected in the elaborate cases made to preserve copies in synagogues. This silver Torah case comes from eighteenth-century Persia. (Courtesy of the Jewish Museum, New York)

The mosaic floor of the synagogue of the fourth century A.D. at Tiberias in Galilee contains many of the symbols of the Jewish faith: the menorah, or seven-branched candelabrum, the palm branch, the incense shovel, the shofar, or ram's horn, and, on the left edge, the Ark of the Covenant. (Israel Information Services)

place where God dwelled, and it symbolized his presence with his people. Naturally enough, the Holy of Holies provoked endless curiosity among non-Jews, who circulated scandalous rumors about the contents of the room and what went on inside.

The heart of the temple worship consisted of sacrificial offerings, including daily sacrifices morning and evening, and special sacrifices and more elaborate rituals on festival occasions. Then there were daily private offerings by individuals to cover the multitude of sacrifices required by Torah. Consequently, the temple area was constantly crowded with priests and Jews making offerings, and with the sacrificial animals and the men who sold them. In addition, money-changers were always on hand, since Torah required that financial transactions in the Temple could be carried on only with a particular kind of coin.

It is hard to tell just what meaning the sacrifices had for the average Jew at the end of the first century B.C. But there is no doubt about one point: the whole sacrificial system was essential to Jewish worship, for it was required by Torah itself.

To officiate at the numerous sacrificial rites there were multitudes of priests from a long line of priestly families whose genealogies were recorded in the Torah. Admission to the priesthood was carefully controlled, since the Jews were determined that worship be conducted only by properly qualified men. Only descendants from the sons of Aaron could be priests, although descendants from the line of Levi could perform restricted functions alongside the priests. The Torah's regulations to insure the purity of the priests were meticulously observed, as was the Torah's requirement that the priests and the Levites be supported from offerings made by the people.

At the head of the priesthood was the High Priest, an office that seems to have emerged during the Persian period. As the titular head of the Jewish people, the High Priest carried on negotiations with the various governments to which the Jews were subject. From the beginning, this meant that the High Priest, together with the other priests whom he represented, exercised unusual authority in the community. By the second century B.C., and perhaps earlier, he served as head of the Sanhedrin, a court that handled cases involving infraction of the Torah. Since the Jews made no distinction between civil and religious law, the Sanhedrin could control every aspect of the daily life of the Jewish people. In practice, however, the Sanhedrin concerned itself with only the most obvious infractions of Torah. Since the Romans recognized the Sanhedrin as the ruling body over the Jews, except in matters of treason, the Sanhedrin with the High Priest at its head wielded a great deal of authority.

In the Temple itself, the High Priest's importance was most dramatically symbolized on the Day of Atonement (Yom Kippur), when he entered into the Holy of Holies, into the very presence of God, as the representative of all the Jews. There he offered sacrifices for all the unwitting sins committed by the people during the year, and in response God assured the Jews of his continuing presence and love.

Although the High Priest and the priesthood continued to occupy a place of great importance up to the time of the destruction of the Temple in A.D. 70, their influence had begun to wane. Since the families

Post-Exilic Judaism

from which the High Priests came were typically wealthy and aristocratic, they were separated in sympathy and understanding from the masses of the people. Probably the most important factor in the decline of the priesthood was the rising influence of the Pharisees, who were in dispute with the priests on many points of interpreting the Torah and who usually represented a position more sympathetic toward the people.

It is around the interpretation of the Torah, more especially the understanding of the relation between the written Torah and the oral tradition, that most of the sects and institutions of Judaism in the two centuries before Christ can

The Wailing Wall in Jerusalem, part of the western wall of the Temple area. Since the Middle Ages, Jews have come to this wall, believed to be a section of the original wall of Solomon's Temple, to lament the destruction of the Temple and to pray for the restoration of the Jewish people. Individual prayers are often written on slips of paper and inserted in the crevices of the stones. (Louis Goldman from Rapho-Guillumette)

be grouped. In this period the oral law became increasingly important.

This tradition or oral law was simply the consequence of the ingrained confidence that all of God's revelation was contained in the written law. It was there, but it was often so compressed, so terse or so hidden, that it was intelligible only to the closest and most reverent study. And this the scribes, who were the scholars and teachers of Israel, sought to provide. Thus through the years—as new occasions taught new duties and historical changes brought new problems and their solutions—the mass of oral law grew and became the actual source of orderly life in the Jewish world. In theory the Constitution is the source of law and order in the United States; but it is the Constitution as interpreted and applied by the legislatures and the court decisions that governs American life. So it was in Palestine. The oral law was not regarded as an addition to the Scripture but the legitimate interpretation of what the Scriptures contained. Thus year by year the material increased and was passed on by teacher to student.

Eventually in the second century [A.D.] this tradition came to be reduced to written form. We call the results the rabbinical literature. . . .

While the reduction of all this material to writing took place after Christianity had begun, the process of creation was going on much earlier. It was the consequence of the fundamental conviction that God had revealed in the Torah his whole will. Given this assumption of an unchanging law in a changing society, only two courses of action were possible. One was to retreat from the new society, to retire to the wilderness and to refuse to have anything to do with the newfangled ways. In essence that is what the so-called ascetic sects, like the Essenes [the semimonastic community associated with the Dead Sea Scrolls] and Therapeutae, and more particularly the Covenanters of Damascus, sought to do. In their camps and communities they sought to relive the days of the wilderness experience of Israel. It may also be remarked that in the course of this fancied "reliving" they introduced many ascetic notions quite alien to the genius of Judaism. But by and large these groups exerted little influence. The other and important answer to this problem of a static law in a dynamic society was given by the Pharisees.

This Pharisaic answer was to adapt and modify the law to make it workable, to fit it to new conditions and experiences. Of course they did not think of themselves as innovators; indeed they could have been—and often were—scandalized by the charge. Yet it was because of this willingness to "modernize" the law that the Pharisees became the religious leaders of Israel. . . .

The Sadducees, aristocratic and stand-pat supporters of the *status quo* in both religion and politics, simply refused to see the need for change. They closed their eyes in the fashion of fundamentalists of every age, and the problem conveniently vanished. When their temple crashed about their ears in A.D. 70, they never emerged from the wreckage.

The Pharisees honestly sought to adapt the old law to new ways, or as they would have phrased it, sought to find the answers to the new problems in the old law. Much that is adverse has been written about their casuistry and hairsplitting (cf. Matt. 15:1–9). There may well have been many Pharisees of harsh and unlovely disposition, . . . But this was not the genius of Pharisaism. . . . The aim of the Pharisee was to simplify the meaning of the will of God, not to complicate it. "Remember the sabbath day to keep it holy" is easily said. How did that apply in contemporary Jerusalem? What was work? Fine-spun distinctions as to what was, what was not, to be counted within the permitted maximum of two thousand cubits for a sabbath day's journey; the seeming fussiness about the ceremonial washing of hands—all this and the hundreds of other niceties which to many modern men seem so absurd and burdensome, were prompted solely by the desire to preserve God's law intact and to make its observance possible.

Thus in the case of the rule "Abide ye every man in his place, let no man go out of his place on the seventh day" (Exod. 16:29)—by interpreting the word "place" as meaning "city," not a particular house, the scribes were able to permit a man to cross the whole of Jerusalem and to continue nearly a mile beyond its border without incurring the onus of being a law-breaker. The emphasis upon

The destruction of the Temple in A.D. 70 was one of the most tragic results of the Jewish Revolt that began in A.D. 66. The four-year war ended in Roman victory, celebrated by the issuing of coins with the legend *Judaea capta* (Judea seized). (Photograph by Alfred Bernheim from the book, *Thesaurus of Judaean Coins*, published by the Bialik Institute)

the washing of hands, against which thoughtless criticism has so often been raised, was an attempt to remove the hardship entailed in the older law which demanded not merely the bathing of the whole body but the lapse of time until sunset before the man would again be Levitically clean. These few examples are representative of the whole. The Pharisees' aim, at times of course not attained, was not to devise new and hampering restrictions in addition to those already present in the old law, but to make that law apply in circumstances far different from those which had existed in the hoary past of its origin.[7]

Although the Pharisees represented to those of their own day a liberal, modernizing element that made the literal observance of the Law a practical possibility for the average Jew, they at no time intended to imply that the Law could be altered or was only partially applicable. The Pharisees, along with the Sadducees, supported ethnocentrism and legalism within the Jewish community. This position was, in part, a reaction to the pressures of acculturation. It was also for the Pharisees eschatological, for they believed that once the Law was fulfilled the day of Israel's redemption would come and suffering would cease. The number of people required to obey and the duration of their complete obedience were sharply debated, but it was the observance of the Law that would precipitate divine action and usher in the new age.

Into their view of the future and the world beyond, the Pharisees, despite their ethnocentrism, had incorporated elements from other religious sources, notably Persian. They affirmed a spirit world peopled with angels and other beings, a life after death in which good and evil actions would find retribution, and a bodily resurrection precedent to a final judgment. Such beliefs marked an important departure from earlier Jewish tradition and are quite closely associated with a developing eschatology in the post-Exilic period. Both the concept of an afterlife and the eschatological hope depict a future judgment that lies beyond the world of sense experience. These beliefs arose not only from cultural borrowing but also from psychological changes within the social group itself. At the root of almost any concept of the afterlife, including the Pharisaic, lies the belief in the immortality of the self. This belief seems to be an almost inevitable consequence of the realization of the ego, or consciousness of self, and it has even been seen as an expression of the biological organism's craving for survival and growth.

We find that it is extremely difficult to imagine ourselves as non-existent. We may envisage our own death and even our own funeral, but it is *we* who do the envisaging. *We* are there witnessing the events *after* our death. No matter how far forward we reach with our imaginations into the future or how far back into the past, we ourselves inevitably remain the audience at the passing pageant. The egocentric predicament holds us fast in its clutches; and it lures on the unsophisticated to a spontaneous belief in unending life. Then . . . there is the innate animal impulse to cling to life and flee from death with all the accumulated determination of the species' age-long struggle to survive. Other emotions may now and then force this will to live into the background, but in ordinary circumstances it is a ruling passion. Under its impulsion the conscious man, seeing ultimate death written indelibly on the horizon, attempts to dodge his fate by taking refuge in a transcendental self-preservation beyond the grave.[8]

To this idea of a simple personality survival is usually added the idea of some eternal retribution, compensating the individual or group for its sense of deprivation and injustice. The concepts of heaven and hell, of a judgment after death, and of a reversal of the inequalities of this life have an origin almost identical with that of eschatology. Indeed, one might argue that a

---

[7] Morton Enslin, "New Testament Times II: Palestine," in *The Interpreter's Bible*, Volume VII, pp. 111-112. Copyright 1951 by Pierce and Smith. Used by permission of Abingdon Press.

[8] Corliss Lamont, *The Illusion of Immortality* (4th ed.; New York: Ungar Publications, 1965), pp. 8-9.

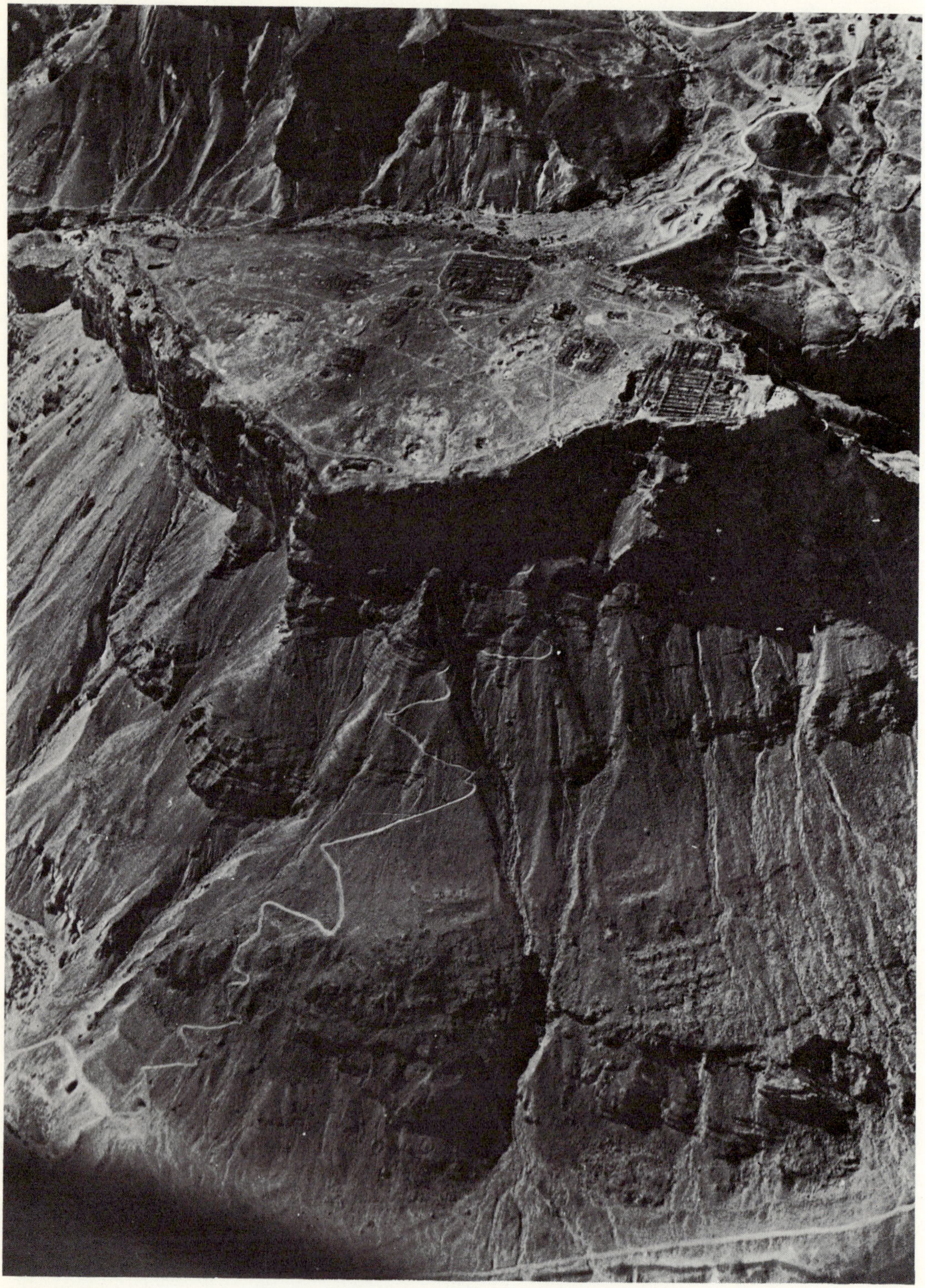

Post-Exilic Judaism 155

(*Below and opposite*) One of the last outposts to fall to the Roman legions was the fortress of Masada, near the Dead Sea. On this flat rock, surrounded on three sides by steep cliffs, 950 Jewish zealots defended their stronghold against the Romans for three years and in the end committed mass suicide rather than be captured. (*Below*, El Al Israel Airlines. *Opposite*, courtesy of the State of Israel Government Press Office)

heightened eschatology represents an unconscious attempt to shrink the time between the present suffering and the final retribution. As the sense of injustice becomes increasingly intolerable, retribution cannot be delayed nor can it take place in some "other" realm beyond sense experience. It cries out to be redressed immediately, before the living as well as the dead.

In Pharisaic thought this belief in eternal retribution took the form of a belief in the resurrection of the body. This concept was probably not stimulated by the thought that to "feel" punishment or reward a physical body was necessary, but rather was adopted from outside Judaism because it fitted the Hebraic view of man as a psychophysical unity.

On the questions of the oral law, the afterlife, and eschatology the Pharisees stood midway between the conservative Sadducees and such extremist groups as the Essenes, and the Pharisaic answers to these questions are expressive of one consistent viewpoint. The Sadducees, representative of the privileged elements within Jewish society, found little difficulty in cooperating with the Roman authorities and prospering under their protection. Occupying an established position within their own world, the Sadducees were antagonistic toward political or social change, and they likewise showed little sympathy toward the anxious eschatological expectation of less satisfied groups.

By contrast, the Pharisees expected some eventual political change, were concerned in providing the common people with a means of fulfilling the Law, believed in an afterlife where resurrected bodies would undergo a final judgment, and awaited the spilling-over of that "other" world into the present age, bringing Yahweh's justice and righteousness to the defense of his people. Conditions were not, however, from the Pharisaic point of view, so intolerable that one should withdraw from society or take revolutionary action. The Pharisees were willing to await the action of Yahweh, and, being willing to live with things as they were, they preferred to build barriers between Judaism and surrounding cultures rather than withdraw from the Jewish community itself. The Pharisaic eschatology gave meaning and shape to everyday life; it justified a policy of passive expectation.

Other groups, however, found the present order less tolerable and were unwilling to await the Day of Yahweh as participants in what they viewed to be an immoral and unrighteous society. They saw their age on the threshold of an imminent and final conflict between the forces of good and evil, light and darkness, and the imagery of that conflict became a major motif of their thought and literature. The increase in apocalyptic literature, that is, image-filled speculations on *how* the end of the present age would come, is a marked feature of post-Exilic Judaism. This heightened eschatology, although it developed out of the milder, prophetic eschatology, undermined the basic prophetic understanding of Israel's future.

The eschatology of the prophets is usually described as this-worldly, arising out of the flow of history. History is the vehicle of the kingdom; God will act through historical personages, nations, and events to accomplish his redemptive purpose. The messianic personage, when one appears, is a king of the seed of David who will arise from among men to rule over the restored earthly kingdom.

The "prophetic" hope of an earthly kingdom within history was not realized; and the post-prophetic eschatological literature postulated a kingdom different in kind. The apocalyptic writers came to despair of history. The sufferings of God's people were so inexplicable that they concluded history was utterly abandoned to evil and could no longer be the vehicle of the kingdom. Salvation would come only beyond history, in a transcendental world which would be inaugurated by a cosmic catastrophe terminating history and introducing an entirely different order of existence. This apocalyptic eschatology in its most developed form is basically dualistic. Existence is divided into two ages which are fundamentally different both as to their ethical character and their very mode of existence. In the coming age, not only will righteousness prevail, but earthly historical existence will be displaced by a transcendental heavenly world. This transcendental kingdom will be ushered in by a pre-existent, supernatural, heavenly Son of man who will come from heaven to judge the wicked and to bring the righteous into the kingdom of glory. In this apocalyptic eschatology, the kingdom is entirely beyond history in a new and different world.[9]

Prophetic and apocalyptic eschatology differ not only in the way in which the promise will be fulfilled, that is, in history or beyond history, but in the degree of elaborate and fantastic imagery associated with the coming age. This distinction can perhaps best be seen by comparing the eschatology of the Book of Daniel, composed sometime during the Maccabean revolt, with prophetic eschatology.

The Apocalypse of Daniel[10]

7 In the first year of Belshaz′zar king of Babylon, Daniel had a dream and visions of his head as he lay in his bed. Then he wrote down the dream, and told the sum of the matter. ²Daniel said, "I saw in my vision by night, and behold, the four winds of heaven were stirring up the great sea. ³And four great beasts came up out of the sea, different from one another. ⁴ The first was like a lion and had eagles' wings. Then as I looked its wings were plucked off, and it was lifted up from the ground and made to stand upon two feet like a man; and the mind of a man was given to it. ⁵And behold, another beast, a second one, like a bear. It was raised up on one side; it had three ribs in its mouth between its teeth; and it was told, 'Arise, devour much flesh.' ⁶After this I looked, and lo, another, like a leopard, with four wings of a bird on its back; and the beast had four heads; and dominion was given to it. ⁷After this I saw in the night visions, and behold, a fourth beast, terrible and dreadful and exceedingly strong; and it had great iron teeth; it devoured and broke in pieces, and stamped the residue with its feet. It was different from all the beasts that were before it; and it had ten horns. ⁸ I considered the horns, and behold, there came up among them another horn, a little one, before which three of the first horns were plucked up by the roots; and behold, in this horn were eyes like the eyes of a man, and a mouth speaking great things. ⁹As I looked,

> thrones were placed
>   and one that was ancient of days took his seat;
> his raiment was white as snow,
>   and the hair of his head like pure wool;
> his throne was fiery flames,
>   its wheels were burning fire.
> ¹⁰A stream of fire issued
>   and came forth from before him;
> a thousand thousands served him,
>   and ten thousand times ten thousand stood before him;
> the court sat in judgment,
>   and the books were opened.

¹¹ I looked then because of the sound of the great words which the horn was speaking. And as I looked, the beast was slain, and its body destroyed and given over to be burned with fire. ¹²As for the rest of the beasts, their dominion was taken away, but

---

[9] George Eldon Ladd, "Why Not Prophetic-Apocalyptic?" *Journal of Biblical Literature,* LXXVI (1957), 193. This material is thoroughly copyrighted by the *Journal of Biblical Literature,* which protection is not lessened by reproduction in this volume.

[10] The Bible, Dan. 7:1–28.

their lives were prolonged for a season and a time. ¹³ I saw in the night visions,
   and behold, with the clouds of heaven
     there came one like a son of man,
   and he came to the Ancient of Days
     and was presented before him.
¹⁴And to him was given dominion
     and glory and kingdom,
   that all peoples, nations, and languages should serve him;
   his dominion is an everlasting dominion, which shall not pass away,
   and his kingdom one
     that shall not be destroyed.

¹⁵ "As for me, Daniel, my spirit within me was anxious and the visions of my head alarmed me. ¹⁶ I approached one of those who stood there and asked him the truth concerning all this. So he told me, and made known to me the interpretation of the things. ¹⁷ 'These four great beasts are four kings who shall arise out of the earth. ¹⁸ But the saints of the Most High shall receive the kingdom, and possess the kingdom for ever, for ever and ever.'

¹⁹ "Then I desired to know the truth concerning the fourth beast, which was different from all the rest, exceedingly terrible, with its teeth of iron and claws of bronze; and which devoured and broke in pieces, and stamped the residue with its feet; ²⁰ and concerning the ten horns that were on its head, and the other horn which came up and before which three of them fell, the horn which had eyes and a mouth that spoke great things, and which seemed greater than its fellows. ²¹As I looked, this horn made war with the saints, and prevailed over them, ²² until the Ancient of Days came, and judgment was given for the saints of the Most High, and the time came when the saints received the kingdom.

²³ "Thus he said: 'As for the fourth beast,
   there shall be a fourth kingdom on earth,
     which shall be different from all the kingdoms,
   and it shall devour the whole earth,
     and trample it down, and break it to pieces.
²⁴As for the ten horns,
   out of this kingdom
     ten kings shall arise,
     and another shall arise after them;
   he shall be different from the former ones,
     and shall put down three kings.
²⁵ He shall speak words against the Most High,
   and shall wear out the saints of the Most High,
   and shall think to change the times and the law;
   and they shall be given into his hand
     for a time, two times, and a half a time.
²⁶ But the court shall sit in judgment,
   and his dominion shall be taken away,
     to be consumed and destroyed to the end.
²⁷And the kingdom and the dominion
   and the greatness of the kingdoms under the whole heaven
   shall be given to the people of the saints of the Most High;
   their kingdom shall be an everlasting kingdom,
   and all dominions shall serve and obey them.

²⁸ "Here is the end of the matter. As for me, Daniel, my thoughts greatly alarmed me, and my color changed; but I kept the matter in my mind.''

Unlike prophetic eschatology, apocalyptic eschatology can seldom be separated from a group or movement. It is born directly out of the tensions of acculturation or, more frequently, a sense of deprivation. Its appeal is always to those whose stake in the present world is so small that they passionately adopt the idea of a totally new world. These movements, frequently termed eschatological movements, nativistic movements, messianic movements, or charismatic movements, are part of a larger phenomenon known as revitalization movements. Such groups attempt to solve the problems facing them by reorganizing their life and worldview. Occasionally the majority of members of a given society take part in such a reorganization. But every movement of revitalization begins with a small group whose successful reorganization may result in a total "reformation," but who more often meet with only partial success, break off from the larger social body, and form sects. Christianity was just such a movement of revitalization which, regardless of its ultimate success in reshaping Roman civilization, failed to reshape the Jewish society within which it developed and which it attempted to reform. There were probably many such attempts at revitalization—eschatological movements that tried to alter Jewish society and ultimately broke off. Before we look at one of those movements, some consideration should be given to the causes and mechanisms of movements of revitalization.

Revitalization Movements
Anthony Wallace[11]

A revitalization movement is defined as a deliberate, organized, conscious effort by members of a society to construct a more satisfying culture. Revitalization is thus, from a cultural standpoint, a special kind of culture change phenomenon: the persons involved in the process of revitalization must perceive their culture, or some major areas of it, as a system (whether accurately or not); they must feel that this cultural system is unsatisfactory; and they must innovate not merely discrete items, but a new cultural system, specifying new relationships as well as, in some cases, new traits. The classic processes of culture change (evolution, drift, diffusion, historical change, acculturation) all produce changes in cultures as systems; however, they do not depend on deliberate intent by members of a society, but rather on a gradual chain-reaction effect: introducing A induces change in B; changing B affects C; when C shifts, A is modified; this involves D . . . and so on *ad infinitum*. This process continues for years, generations, centuries, millennia, and its pervasiveness has led many cultural theorists to regard culture change as essentially a slow, chain-like, self-contained procession of superorganic inevitabilities. In revitalization movements, however, A, B, C, D, E . . . N are shifted into a new *Gestalt* [form] abruptly and simultaneously in intent; and frequently within a few years the new plan is put into effect by the participants in the movement. . . .

It is therefore functionally necessary for every person in society to maintain a mental image of the society and its culture, as well as of his own body and its behavioral regularities, in order to act in ways which reduce stress at all levels of the system. The person does, in fact, maintain such an image. This mental image I have called "the mazeway," since as a model of the cell - body - personality - nature - culture - society system or field, organized by the individual's own experience, it includes perceptions of both the maze of physical objects of the environment (internal and external, human and nonhuman) and also of the ways in which this maze can be

[11] Anthony F. C. Wallace, "Revitalization Movements," reproduced by permission of the American Anthropological Association from the *American Anthropologist:* Vol. 58, 1956, pp. 265-268.

manipulated by the self and others in order to minimize stress. The mazeway is nature, society, culture, personality, and body image, as seen by one person. . . .

We may now see more clearly what "revitalization movements" revitalize. Whenever an individual who is under chronic, physiologically measurable stress, receives repeated information which indicates that his mazeway does not lead to action which reduces the level of stress, he must choose between maintaining his present mazeway and tolerating the stress, or changing the mazeway in an attempt to reduce the stress. Changing the mazeway involves changing the total *Gestalt* of his image of self, society, and culture, of nature and body, and of ways of action. It may also be necessary to make changes in the "real" system in order to bring mazeway and "reality" into congruence. The effort to work a change in mazeway and "real" system together so as to permit more effective stress reduction is the effort at revitalization; and the collaboration of a number of persons in such an effort is called a revitalization movement.

The term revitalization movement thus denotes a very large class of phenomena. Other terms are employed in the existing literature to denote what I would call subclasses, distinguished by a miscellany of criteria. "Nativistic movements," for example, are revitalization movements characterized by strong emphasis on the elimination of alien persons, customs, values, and/or materiel from the mazeway. . . . "Revivalistic" movements emphasize the institution of customs, values, and even aspects of nature which are thought to have been in the mazeway of previous generations but are not now present. . . . "Cargo cults" emphasize the importation of alien values, customs, and materiel into the mazeway, these things being expected to arrive as a ship's cargo. . . . "Vitalistic movements" emphasize the importation of alien elements into the mazeway but do not necessarily invoke ship and cargo as the mechanism. "Millenarian movements" emphasize mazeway transformation in an apocalyptic world transformation engineered by the supernatural. "Messianic movements" emphasize the participation of a divine savior in human flesh in the mazeway transformation. . . . These and parallel terms do not denote mutually exclusive categories, for a given revitalization movement may be nativistic, millenarian, messianic, and revivalistic all at once; and it may (in fact, usually does) display ambivalence with respect to nativistic, revivalistic, and importation themes.

Revitalization movements are evidently not unusual phenomena, but are recurrent features in human history. Probably few men have lived who have not been involved in an instance of the revitalization process. They are, furthermore, of profound historical importance. Both Christianity and Mohammedanism, and possibly Buddhism as well, originated in revitalization movements. Most denominational and sectarian groups and orders budded or split off after failure to revitalize a traditional institution. One can ask whether a large proportion of religious phenomena have not originated in personality transformation dreams or visions characteristic of the revitalization process. Myths, legends, and rituals may be relics, either of the manifest content of vision-dreams or of the doctrines and history of revival and import cults, the circumstances of whose origin have been distorted and forgotten, and whose connection with dream states is now ignored. Myths in particular have long been noted to possess a dream-like quality, and have been more or less speculatively interpreted according to the principles of symptomatic dream interpretation. It is tempting to suggest that myths and, often, even legends, read like dreams because they *were* dreams when they were first told. It is tempting to argue further that culture heroes represent a condensation of the figures of the prophet and of the supernatural being of whom he dreamed.

In fact, it can be argued that all organized religions are relics of old revitalization movements, surviving in routinized form in stabilized cultures, and that religious phenomena per se originated (if it is permissible still in this day and age to talk about the "origins" of major elements of culture) in the revitalization process—i.e., in visions of a new way of life by individuals under extreme stress.

Withdrawal from the existing social order, a stage in the development of many revitalization movements that are unsuccessful in reorganizing the larger society, often involves a tendency to view the world, indeed the cosmos, as the battleground of a war between the forces of good (identified with light) and the forces of evil (equated with darkness). The imagery of such dualism, reflected in Daniel and other post-Exilic Jewish sources, seems to have been imported into Judaism from Persian religious thought, although the dualism itself lies at the very heart of most apocalyptic movements. The leader of such an eschatological or apocalyptic movement will be charismatic and in communication with the forces of good, namely God or some supernatural messenger of God. The relationship between the charismatic leader and the forces of good may vary from that of prophet or spokesman to complete identification, and the shift that sometimes occurs from prophet to savior may not only indicate a change in the psychology of the leader but also the pressures upon the group—the growing need for direct cosmic remedial action. The concept of a savior, common to many religious movements, seems to be born out of this need to communicate with and be joined to the world beyond.

The saviour is an essential factor in religion, because many religious people are convinced that the domain of men and the world of the gods are separated by a deep cleft. In order to link up these two worlds a bridge must be laid across the cleft. Man is unable to perform this act. It should be done by a creature who unites the two worlds by his nature. That is the saviour. He is a divine or semi-divine being, who descends from the domain of the gods to the dwelling-places of men, or who operates through other gods for the benefit of men. The figure of the saviour shows many varieties. As he combines in himself a human and a divine element, the emphasis may alternatively be put on the one or the other side of his nature. Saviours, in whom the human factor dominates, are the sacral king, the hero, the prophet, the sage and the saint. It is evident that in the saviour-god, i.e., the god who functions as saviour, the divine nature fully prevails. Yet the human factor is not absolutely absent. It finds its expression on the one hand in the human feelings which the god displays and on the other side in his interest in the destiny of men. Moreover, he often passes a severe trial, so that he is a consoling example to suffering humanity, and he conquers death, so that in man the hope of immortality awakens. The saviour-god thus shows two striking and nearly related features: he is a dynamic personality and he cares for the well-being of men, indeed he sometimes takes part in human sufferings.[12]

While the shift from prophet to savior may occur within the psychology of the leader, such "divinization" is usually accomplished by his followers whose expectation of a supernatural figure, a savior or messiah who will appear and

[12] C. J. Bleeker, "Isis as Saviour Goddess" in S. G. F. Brandon, ed., *The Saviour God* (Manchester, England: Manchester University Press, 1963), p. 2.

162 Post-Exilic Judaism

effect the end of the existing social order, becomes fused with their devotion to their leader. Wallace has suggested, however, that "successful prophets . . . usually do not believe that they are the supernatural, only that they have communicated with him (although their followers may freely deify them). Prophets do not lose their sense of personal identity . . . ."[13]

Of several eschatological movements in the post-Exilic period the most familiar to us now,

[13] Wallace, p. 272.

A triad of Egyptian gods: Osiris, Isis, and Horus. The mystery cult of Isis and her consort Osiris follows the pattern of the ancient fertility cults of death and renewal, while portraying Isis as a divine saviour. (The Metropolitan Museum of Art, Rogers Fund, 1942)

A portion of the Thanksgiving Scroll, primarily a collection of hymns similar to those found in the Psalms. (The Israel Museum, Jerusalem)

through the discovery of the Dead Sea Scrolls in 1947, is the Essene community at Qumran. The Essenes were an apocalyptic group, Hasidic in outlook, which, probably under the pressures of Hellenization, withdrew to the desert area at the northwest corner of the Dead Sea to await the Day of the Lord in the purity of obedience to the Torah. In this manner they survived into the early Christian period, possibly having some effect on the thought of Jesus and his disciples. This Essene community seems to have been organized as a military group ready to take part in the final war between light and darkness. It was composed of priests and laymen, and accepted both celibate groups and families. Many of its institutions seem to represent a return to the organization of Israel during the sojourn in the wilderness—an idealization of the strength and sanctity of the Jewish people immediately after the Exodus and the giving of the Law. This attitude was sustained by the annual covenant-renewal ceremony in which all members of the community participated. Other aspects of the life of the Essenes, however, were of a more recent origin and represented an apocalyptic outlook, such as the initiation ceremony of baptism, the ritual washings, the common, sacramental meal, and the firm messianic expectation. In reading the following selections from the Dead Sea Scrolls, the various aspects of revitalization and apocalyptic dualism should be kept in mind.

THE DEAD SEA SCROLLS[14]

THE MANUAL OF DISCIPLINE

Of the Commitment (i, 1–15)

Everyone who wishes to join the community must pledge himself to respect God and man; to live according to the communal rule; to seek God [   ]; to do what is good and upright in His sight,

[14] From *The Dead Sea Scriptures,* pp. 39–40, 43–46 translated by Theodor H. Gastner. Copyright © 1956, 1964 by Theodor H. Gastner. Reprinted by permission of Doubleday & Company, Inc.

in accordance with what He has commanded through Moses and through His servants the prophets; to love all that He has chosen and hate all that He has rejected; to keep far from all evil and to cling to all good works; to act truthfully and righteously and justly on earth and to walk no more in the stubbornness of a guilty heart and of lustful eyes, doing all manner of evil; to bring into a bond of mutual love all who have declared their willingness to carry out the statutes of God; to join the formal community of God; to walk blamelessly before Him in conformity with His various laws and dispositions; to love all the children of light, each according to his stake in the formal community of God; and to hate all the children of darkness, each according to the measure of his guilt, which God will ultimately requite.

All who declare their willingness to serve God's truth must bring all of their mind, all of their strength, and all of their wealth into the community of God, so that their minds may be purified by the truth of His precepts, their strength controlled by His perfect ways, and their wealth disposed in accordance with His just design. They must not deviate by a single step from carrying out the orders of God at the times appointed for them; they must neither advance the statutory times nor postpone the prescribed seasons. They must not turn aside from the ordinances of God's truth either to the right or to the left. . . .

Of the two spirits in man (iii, 13–iv, 26)

This is for the man who would bring others to the inner vision, so that he may understand and teach to all the children of light the real nature of men, touching the different varieties of their temperaments with the distinguishing traits thereof,

The painstaking process of unfolding pieces of parchment of one of the Dead Sea Scrolls. (Israel Information Services)

touching their actions throughout their generations, and touching the reason why they are now visited with afflictions and now enjoy periods of well-being.

All that is and ever was comes from a God of knowledge. Before things came into existence He determined the plan of them; and when they fill their appointed roles, it is in accordance with His glorious design that they discharge their functions. Nothing can be changed. In His hand lies the government of all things. God it is that sustains them in their needs.

Now, this God created man to rule the world, and appointed for him two spirits after whose direction he was to walk until the final Inquisition. They are the spirits of truth and of perversity.

The origin of truth lies in the Fountain of Light, and that of perversity in the Wellspring of Darkness. All who practice righteousness are under the domination of the Prince of Lights, and walk in ways of light; whereas all who practice perversity are under the domination of the Angel of Darkness and walk in ways of darkness. Through the Angel of Darkness, however, even those who practice righteousness are made liable to error. All their sin and their iniquities, all their guilt and their deeds of transgression are the result of his domination; and this, by God's inscrutable design, will continue until the time appointed by Him. Moreover, all men's afflictions and all their moments of tribulation are due to this being's malevolent sway. All of the spirits that attend upon him are bent on causing the sons of light to stumble. Howbeit, the God of Israel and the Angel of His truth are always there to help the sons of light. It is God that created these spirits of light and darkness and made them the basis of every act, the [instigators] of every deed and the directors of every thought. The one He loves to all eternity, and is ever pleased with its deeds; but any association with the other He abhors, and He hates all its ways to the end of time.

This is the way those spirits operate in the world. The enlightenment of man's heart, the making straight before him all the ways of righteousness and truth, the implanting in his heart of fear for the judgments of God, of a spirit of humility, of patience, of abundant compassion, of perpetual goodness, of insight, of perception, of that sense of the Divine Power that is based at once on an apprehension of God's works and a reliance on His plenteous mercy, of a spirit of knowledge informing every plan of action, of a zeal for righteous government, of a hallowed mind in a controlled nature, of abounding love for all who follow the truth, of a self-respecting purity which abhors all the taint of filth, of a modesty of behavior coupled with a general prudence and an ability to hide within oneself the secrets of what one knows—these are the things that come to men in this world through communion with the spirit of truth. And the guerdon [reward] of all that walk in its ways is health and abundant well-being, with long life and fruition of seed along with eternal blessings and everlasting joy in the life everlasting, and a crown of glory and a robe of honor, amid light perpetual.

But to the spirit of perversity belong greed, remissness in right-doing, wickedness and falsehood, pride and presumption, deception and guile, cruelty and abundant insolence, shortness of temper and profusion of folly, arrogant passion, abominable acts in a spirit of lewdness, filthy ways in the thralldom of unchastity, a blasphemous tongue, blindness of eyes, dullness of ears, stiffness of neck and hardness of heart, to the end that a man walks

The remains of a table from the library of Qumran where scribes copied the sacred texts. (By courtesy of the Israel Department of Antiquities and Museums)

entirely in ways of darkness and of evil cunning. The guerdon of all who walk in such ways is multitude of afflictions at the hands of all the angels of destruction, everlasting perdition through the angry wrath of an avenging God, eternal horror and perpetual reproach, the disgrace of final annihilation in the Fire, darkness throughout the vicissitudes of life in every generation, doleful sorrow, bitter misfortune and darkling ruin—ending in extinction without remnant or survival.

It is to these things that all men are born, and it is to these that all the host of them are heirs throughout their generations. It is in these ways that men needs must walk and it is in these two divisions, according as a man inherits something of each, that all human acts are divided throughout all the ages of eternity. For God has appointed these two things to obtain in equal measure until the final age. . . . But [when the time] of Inquisition [comes], He will determine the fate of every living being in accordance with which of the [two spirits he has chosen to follow].

THE ZADOKITE DOCUMENT[15]
Of the Remnant (v, 17–vi, 11)
When, in antiquity, Israel was first delivered, Moses and Aaron still continued in their charge, through the help of the Angel of Lights, even though Belial in his cunning had set up Jannes and his brother in opposition to them.

Similarly, at the time when the land was destroyed, men arose who removed the ancient landmarks and led Israel astray; and it was, indeed, because they uttered sedition against the commandments of God which He had given through Moses and through His holy anointed priest Aaron, and because they gave forth false prophecies in order to subvert Israel from God, that the land was laid utterly waste. Nevertheless, God still remembered the Covenant which He had made with their forbears and raised from the priesthood men of discernment and from the laity men of wisdom, and He made them hearken to Him. And these men "dug the well." . . . The "well" in question is the Law. They that "digged" are those of Israel who repented and departed from the land of Judah to sojourn in "the land of Damascus."[16] . . . Without such "implements," they would, indeed, never achieve their goal until such time as the true Expositor arises at the end of days.

Of the obligation of the Covenant (vi, 11–vii, 6a)
All that enter the covenant with no intention of going into the sanctuary to keep the flame alive on the altar do so in vain. They have as good as shut the door. Of them God has said: "Who is there among you that would shut the door, and who of you would not keep alive the flame upon Mine altar?" In vain [Mal. 1.10] [are all their deeds] if, in an era of wickedness, they do not take heed

to act in accordance with the explicit injunctions of the Law;

to keep away from men of ill-repute;

to hold themselves aloof from ill-gotten gain;

not to defile themselves by laying hands on that which has been vowed or devoted to God or on the property of the sanctuary;

not to rob the poor of God's people;

not to make widows their prey or murder the fatherless;

---

[15] *Ibid.*, pp. 67–70, 72–74.

[16] In this document "Damascus" stands for obedience to the New Covenant.

to distinguish between unclean and clean and to recognize holy from profane;
to keep the sabbath in its every detail, and the festivals and fasts in accordance with the practice laid down originally by the men who entered the covenant in "the land of Damascus;"
to pay their required dues in conformity with the detailed rules thereof;
to love each man his neighbor like himself;
to grasp the hand of the poor, the needy and the stranger;
to seek each man the welfare of his fellow;
to cheat not his own kin;
to abstain from whoredom, as is meet;
to bring no charge against his neighbor except by due process, and not to nurse grudges from day to day;
to keep away from all unclean things, in accordance with what has been prescribed in each case and with the distinctions which God Himself has drawn for them;
not to sully any man the holy spirit within him.

Howbeit, for all that perform these rules in holiness unimpaired, according to all the instruction that has been given them—for them will God's Covenant be made good, that they shall be preserved for a thousand generations, even as it is written: "He keepeth Covenant and loyalty with them that love Him and keep His commandments, even unto a thousand generations" [Deut. 7.9].

Of family life (vii, 6a–9)

If members of the community happen to be living in encampments, in accordance with a usage which obtains in this country, and if they marry and beget children, they are [in such matters] to follow the precepts of the Law [*Torah*] and the disciplinary regulations therein prescribed for the relationship of husband to wife and of father to child.

Of the future requital of the disobedient (vii, 9–viii, 21)

All those that entered into the new covenant in "the land of Damascus" but subsequently relapsed and played false and turned away from the well of living waters shall not be reckoned as of the communion of the people nor inscribed in the roster of it throughout the period from the time the teacher of the community is gathered to his rest until that in which the lay and the priestly Messiah [anointed] assume their office.

The same applies also to all that entered the company of the "specially holy and blameless" but were loath to carry out the rules imposed upon the upright. Every such man is, as it were, like "one molten in the furnace" [Ez. 22.22]. When his deeds come clearly to light, he shall be cast out of that company as being one who has no share among the disciples of God. Men of knowledge shall reprove him according to his perfidy until he repent and thereby resume his place among the specially holy and blameless—that is, until it become clear that his actions are again in accordance with the interpretation of the Law adopted by the specially holy and blameless. Meanwhile, no man shall have commerce with him in matters either of property or of employment, for he has been cursed by all the holy ones of God on high.

The same applies again—in the future as it did in the past—to all who commit their hearts to idolatry and walk in the stubbornness of their hearts. All such have no portion in the household of the Law [*Torah*].

The same applies, once again, to all of their fellows that relapse in the company of scoffers. These too shall be judged; for they will have spoken error against the righteous ordinances and have rejected the Covenant of God and the pledge which they swore in "the land of Damascus"—that is, the new covenant. Neither they nor their families shall have a portion in the household of the Law [*Torah*].

About forty years will elapse from the death of the teacher of the community until all the men who take up arms and relapse in the company of the Man of Falsehood are brought to an end. At that time, the wrath of God will be kindled against Israel, and that will ensue which is described by the prophet when he says: "No king shall there be nor priest nor judge nor any that reproves aright" [cf. Hos. 3.4].

But they of Jacob that have repented, that have kept the Covenant of God, shall then speak each to his neighbor to bring him to righteousness, to direct his steps upon the way. And God will pay heed to their words and hearken, and He will draw up a record of those that fear Him and esteem His name, to the end that salvation shall be revealed for all God-fearing men. Then ye shall again distinguish the righteous from the wicked, him that serves God from him that serves Him not. And God will "show mercy unto thousands, unto them that love Him and keep His commandments"—yea, even unto a thousand generations.

The divisive elements that, in the era of Israel's perfidy, when it defiled the sanctuary, indeed went out from the holy city and placed their reliance on God and returned to God, but through whose wrangles the people were thrown into discord—these shall be subjected to judgment at the hands of the sacred council, each according to his attitude.

Those, however, who had entered the covenant but subsequently broke through the bounds of the Law—all of those shall be "cut off from the midst of the camp" at the time when God's glory is made manifest to Israel. And along with them shall go those that sought to turn Judah to wickedness in the days when it was being put to the test.

Of the future reward of the faithful
(B. xx, 27–34)

Howbeit, all that hold fast to these enactments, going and coming in accordance with the Law; that hearken to the voice of the Teacher; that make confession before God, saying: Just and truthful are Thy judgments against us, for we have done wickedly, both we and our fathers, in that we have gone contrary to the statutes of the Covenant; all who raise not their hands against His holy statutes or His righteous judgments or His truthful ordinances; all who learn the lessons of the former judgments wherewith the men of the community were adjudged in time past; all who give ear to him who imparts the true interpretation of the Law and who do not controvert the right ordinances when they hear them—all of these shall rejoice and their hearts shall be strong, and they shall prevail over all that dwell in the world. And God will accept their atonement, and because they took refuge in His holy name they shall indeed see salvation at His hand.

THE WAR OF THE SONS OF
LIGHT AND THE SONS OF DARKNESS[17]

[Prologue] (i, 1–17)

The first engagement of the Sons of Light against the Sons of Darkness—that is, against the army of Belial—shall be an attack on the troop of Edom, Moab, the Ammonites and the Philistine area and

[17] From *The Dead Sea Scriptures,* pp. 281–282, translated by Theodor H. Gastner. Copyright © 1956, 1964 by Theodor H. Gastner. Reprinted by permission of Doubleday & Co., Inc.

The entrance to the catacombs of Beth She'arim, not far from modern Haifa. This burial place contains the remains of a Jewish community that lived here from the second to the fourth century A.D. (El Al Israel Airlines)

The menorah carved in the wall of the Beth She'arim catacombs seems to have had an importance for this community similar to the cross in Christian catacombs. (Israel Information Services)

upon that of the Kittians of Assyria, and of those violators of the Covenant who give them aid. When the Sons of Light who are now in exile return from the "desert of the nations" to pitch camp in the desert of Judah, the children of Levi, Judah and Benjamin, who are now among those exiles, shall wage war against these peoples —that is, against each and every one of their troops.

After that battle they shall advance upon the [king of] the Kittians of Egypt. In due time, he will sally forth in high fury to wage war against the kings of the north, being minded in his anger to destroy his enemies and cut down their power. This, however, will be the time of salvation for the people of God, the critical moment when those that have cast their lot with Him will come to dominion, whereas those that have cast it with Belial shall be doomed to eternal extinction. [Great] havoc shall then beset the descendants of Japheth: Assyria shall fall, with none to help her, and the dominion of the Kittians shall depart. Wickedness will thus be humbled and left without remnant, and no survivor shall remain of the Sons of Darkness.

[Streaks of lightn]ing will flash from one end of the world to the other, growing ever brighter until the era of darkness is brought utterly to an end. Then, in the era of God, His exalted grandeur will give light for [evermore,] shedding on all the Sons of Light peace and blessing, gladness and length of days.

On the day the Kittians fall, there shall be mighty combat and carnage in the presence of the God of Israel, for that is the day which He appointed of old for the final battle against the Sons of Darkness. Thereon the company of the divine and the congregation of the human shall engage side by side in combat and carnage, the Sons of Light doing battle against the Sons of Darkness with a show of godlike might, amid uproarious tumult, amid the war-cries of gods and men, in a veritable day of havoc. It will be, indeed, a "time of [   ] tribulation" for "the people redeemed of God," but, unlike all their previous tribulations, this one will come to a speedy end in a redemption which shall last for ever.

When they engage the Kittians, [amid all the combat and car]nage of battle, the Sons of Light shall have luck three times in discomfiting the forces of wickedness; but three times the host of Belial shall brace themselves to turn back the tide. At this, the squadrons of the infantry shall become faint-hearted, but the power of God shall strengthen their hearts, and on the seventh occasion the great hand of God shall finally subdue [the army of Belial. For will He summon] all the angels of His dominion and all the humans [that are bound to His communion] [   ] [and amid] the Holy Beings He Himself will appear to give aid [   ], [and He will make] the truth [to shine forth,] bringing doom upon the Sons of Darkness [   ] [and] they shall surrender....

The Essenes were only one of several apocalyptic groups that existed in the century or two immediately preceding the birth of Christianity. As such they represent one of the most important reactions to the social, economic, and religious disorders of that period.

> Late Jewish and early Christian eschatologies, as we find them in the major figures and documents, are conditioned by crisis situations, ... and it is not enough to identify these with either political persecution or economic pressures on the one hand or with "religious" factors on the other. The crises were religio-cultural whether in Palestine or in the Hellenistic pagan setting. The fan-

tasy-like but yet often healthy projection of dramatic symbol suggesting the dissolution of the usual categories of time, space, and causation reflect social-cultural incoherence, anomie and loss of meaning. . . . Eschatological conceptions arise in this kind of situation. The eschatological mood represents a radical spiritual and cultural effort of a group (or an individual) to overcome disorder and to define meaning, and to give body to possibilities and to the future, as well as to come to terms with dynamic and radical changes in the conditions of existence. The background for this in the centuries before and after Christ was the loss of meaning and relationship of many groups, whether in Jewish or pagan life. . . . Such elements as poverty, slavery, class or social frustration, persecution, were only elements in the more general crisis. The hopes defined in the inevitably symbolic way were not escapist fantasies but were healthy and creative just as they were grounded in the social traditions of Jewish covenant theology, which, indeed, was later fused with Gentile civic and imperial ideals.[18]

[18] Amos N. Wilder, "Social Factors in Early Christian Eschatology" in *Early Christian Origins*, Alan Wikgren, ed. (Chicago: Quadrangle Books, 1961), pp. 75–76.

STUDY QUESTIONS

1. What are the possible causes of an eschatological worldview? Which factors seem the most important?

2. What aspects of post-Exilic Judaism can be explained as rejections of acculturation or attempts to offset a feeling of deprivation? What aspects cannot be so easily explained in this way?

3. To what degree is a concept of future judgment necessary to an ethical system? How do the sanctions of the Decalogue differ from those of the Pharisaic ethic or of the Essene ethic?

4. Is the concept of a savior or a messiah a necessary part of eschatology? What functions does it perform? Does the presence of a messiah-concept indicate anything about the degree or the nature of the pressures on an individual or group?

5. What is the effect of eschatology on ethics? What effect did the type of eschatology have on the various groups within post-Exilic Judaism?

6. What was the Essenes' understanding of evil? How was this understanding related to the post-Exilic experiences of the Jews?

7. What is the effect of a strong cosmic dualism on ethics?

8. How did the Essenes use and interpret the Torah? What restrictions, if any, did they place on the commandment to love one's neighbor?

9. Was post-Exilic Judaism overly "legalistic"?

For those who have used The Contribution of Ancient Greece *edited by Jacqueline Strain:*

10. Compare and contrast the reaction of the Jewish nation and the reaction of the Greek city-states to the loss of political autonomy in the Hellenistic age.

CHAPTER 6

FROM CORPORATE RIGHTEOUSNESS TO INDIVIDUAL SALVATION:
Eschatology and Ethics in the Teaching of Jesus

The Sermon on the Mount . . . has been variously assessed. Some have found it a pernicious document, which, by presenting an utterly impossible ethic, has wrought incalculable harm in personal, social and international life. An exceptional English jurist in the last century claimed it to be "not only imprudent but unjust." Others have seen in it the finest statement of the highest ethic that mankind has known. The words of a recent commentator, that "These chapters have won universal recognition as the supreme statement of the ethical duties of man," are typical. Different as are these estimates, however, they share one common assumption, namely, that Matthew v–vii can be regarded as a single entity, which has its own unified secret to reveal, and that this secret is the ethical teaching of Jesus of Nazareth. But it is precisely this assumption that modern critical studies have made dubious.

> *W. D. Davies,* The Setting of the Sermon on the Mount *(Cambridge, Eng.: Cambridge University Press, 1964), p. 1.*

. . . the New Testament documents are suffused with eschatological figures, expressions, and hopes. It is no longer possible to expunge this element from the records as extraneous. It was the lasting service of Albert Schweitzer to force New Testament scholarship to face this fact squarely. It may be accepted as axiomatic, therefore, that the message and any account of it must deal with the problem of eschatology.

> *Donald J. Selby, "Changing Ideas in New Testament Eschatology,"* Harvard Theological Review, *L (1957) p. 21.*

Too often it has been assumed that apocalyptic was the outcome of a mere escapism, and it was often possible to dismiss it with the condescension, if not contempt, with which moderns usually dismiss the more bizarre forms of the Second Advent Hope. In view of this, allied to the sharp distinction which was usually drawn between the sober Pharisee and the fiery, day-dreaming Apocalyptist, it was not recognized that apocalyptic was the outcome of a profound ethical seriousness, which was usually no less concerned with the observance of the Torah than was Pharisaism, and that the Messianic hope was relevant for ethics.

W. D. Davies, *The Setting of the Sermon on the Mount, (Cambridge, Eng.: Cambridge University Press, 1964), p. 447.*

Perhaps the most important development in the religious and moral conceptions of the Judeo-Christian tradition occurred in the teachings of Jesus of Nazareth as they were known and interpreted by the Christian Church that developed from among his immediate disciples and followers. The moral conceptions, according to the Church's traditional view, are best expressed in the Sermon on the Mount (Matt., chaps. 5-7), which supposedly attacks Jewish legalism and proclaims the commandment of love. The religious conceptions, however, grew less out of the teachings of Jesus than out of his actions, actions in which the Church saw not only the practice of the ethic he proclaimed, but which made Jesus rather than his message the object of belief and adoration, thus forming a new religion. It is the task of this chapter to examine the religious and moral ideas stemming from Jesus' ministry, especially as expressed in the Sermon on the Mount. In order to understand those ideas properly it is necessary, at the beginning, to consider certain issues and problems that modern scholars of the New Testament have raised.

The first problem that faces the student is the present impossibility of constructing a historically accurate biography of Jesus.

No one is any longer in the position to write a life of Jesus. This is the scarcely questioned and surprising result today of an enquiry which for almost two hundred years has devoted prodigious and by no means fruitless effort to regain and expound the life of the historical Jesus, freed from all embellishment by dogma and doctrine. At the end of this research on the life of Jesus stands the recognition of its own failure. Albert Schweitzer, in his classic work, *The Quest of the Historical Jesus,* has erected its memorial, but at the same time has delivered its funeral oration.

Why have these attempts failed? Perhaps only because it became alarmingly and terrifyingly evident how inevitably each author brought the spirit of his own age into his presentation of the figure of Jesus. In point of fact the changing pictures of the innumerable "Lives" of Jesus are not very encouraging, confronting us as they do with now the "enlightened" teacher of God, virtue, and immortality, now the religious genius of the Romantics, now the teacher of ethics in Kant's sense, now the protagonist of social theory. . . . In truth this state of affairs has deeper causes, and compels us to affirm the futility of any renewal of attempts at Lives of Jesus now or in the future.

This judgment is based on the special nature and character of the sources to which we owe almost exclusively our historical knowledge of Jesus. These are the Gospels of the New Testament, mainly the first three (Mark, Matthew, Luke). We call them commonly the synoptic Gospels because they are interconnected and interdependent, a fact which becomes evident as their respective records are looked at "synoptically." The Gospel according to John has so different a character in comparison with the other three, and is to such a degree the product of a developed theological reflection, that we can only treat it as a secondary source. Admittedly the synoptic Gospels themselves are not simply historical sources which the historian, enquiring after Jesus of Nazareth as a figure of the past, could use without examination and criticism. Although their relation to history is a different one from that of John, they none the less unite to a remarkable degree both record of Jesus Christ and witness to him, testimony of the Church's faith in him and narration of his history.

Both should be continually distinguished in the understanding of the Gospels and in each individual part of their tradition; on the other hand, both are so closely interwoven that it is often exceedingly hard to say where one ends and the other begins. Mathematical certainty in the exposition of a bare history of Jesus, unembellished by faith, is unobtainable, in spite of the fact that the critical discernment of older and more recent layers of tradition belongs to the work of research. We possess no single word of Jesus and no single story of Jesus, no matter how incontestably genuine they may be, which do not contain at the same time the confession of the believing congregation or at least are embedded therein. This makes the search after the bare facts of history difficult and to a large extent futile.[1]

The New Testament is, therefore, a product of the early Christian Church, not its cause. The earliest documents in the New Testament, namely the letters of the Apostle Paul, were written in the third decade of the life of the Church, that is, toward the end of the first generation, and reflect the needs and conceptions of that community rather than the immediate experience of the life and death of Jesus. The gospels were all composed later, in the last three decades of the first century A.D., and the earliest of them, the Gospel of Mark, was written more than forty years after the crucifixion of Jesus. The New Testament is, therefore, not a contemporary biographical account of the life of Jesus and the early Church but rather the recorded memory of the Christian community as it entered its second generation. While many of the original words and actions of Jesus may have been preserved within oral tradition, it is extremely difficult to ascertain the degree, if any, to which a particular passage preserves the original wording and setting within the life of Jesus.

The difficulty of discovering the historical Jesus is further complicated by the fact that the gospels and the letters of Paul reflect the early Church's theological interpretation of Jesus and his ministry; that is, they proclaim that Jesus was the Messiah, or Christ, and that in his death and resurrection the crucial eschatological event, the arrival of the Kingdom, had taken place. Therefore, the New Testament documents do not speak of the "historical" events of the life of Jesus of Nazareth, but rather proclaim the Christ of faith. This message proclaimed by the early Church is termed *kerygma*,[2] and it is sharply distinguished from simple fact-reporting or teaching, known as *didache*.[3] This *kerygma* is the main content of the New Testament; it represents the Church's view of Jesus and, as such, reflects the life and problems of Christian congregations in the second half of the first century.

Because of the difficulty in penetrating back to the original figure of Jesus of Nazareth, many New Testament scholars and theologians have chosen to concentrate on the Christ of faith to the exclusion of the Jesus of history. The leading figure in this movement is Rudolf Bultmann, a New Testament scholar and existentialist thinker at the University of Marburg, Germany, whose opinion has been influential in America as well as in Europe. A non-Bultmannian but no less critical German scholar has described the meaning of Bultmann's "critical" theology:

> After a hundred and fifty years of preoccupation with the historical Jesus, critical theology came to recognize that it had undertaken an impossible task; it had the courage to acknowledge this fact openly, and with banners flying went over into the enemy camp. It

---

[1] From pp. 13–14 *Jesus of Nazareth* by Günther Bornkamm. Copyright © 1960 by Hodder & Stoughton Ltd and Harper & Row, Publishers, Incorporated.

[2] kẽ·rǐg·mä—accent on middle syllable.
[3] dǐ·dä·kā—accent on last syllable.

turned its back on its history . . . it declared its preoccupation with the historical Jesus to have been an insoluble and fruitless undertaking, and it withdrew into the invulnerable bastion of the kerygma, the proclamation about Christ. . . .

Now it is not as if the sources left us entirely in the lurch, says critical theology. The time is past when an unscientific skepticism could doubt whether Jesus had ever lived at all. On the contrary, we can gain considerable information about Jesus himself and also about his proclamation. But what we arrive at when we analyze the sources with the tools of historical research, says critical theology, yields nothing that would be of significance for faith. For this Jesus of Nazareth was a Jewish prophet. To be sure, he was a prophet who, since he demanded absolute obedience, saw mankind as totally sinful, and proclaimed divine forgiveness to men, had apprehended "the Jewish conception of God in its purity and consistency." He was indeed a prophet who claimed that a man's attitude toward His word determined his attitude toward God. But, for all that, he remained within the framework of Judaism. What he preached was a more radicalized form of Old Testament, Jewish faith in God. For Bultmann, the history of Jesus is part of the history of Judaism, not of Christianity. To be sure, this Jewish prophet is of historical interest for New Testament theology, but he neither has, nor can have, significance for Christian faith, since (and here we have an astonishing thesis) Christianity first began at Easter. Here a decisive point has been reached. Who would ever think of saying that Islam began after Mohammed's death, or Buddhism after the death of Buddha? If we accept the thesis that Christianity began at Easter with the proclamation about the risen Christ, then indeed the logical inference is that, since Jesus was only a Jewish prophet, he does not belong to Christianity. "The message of Jesus," so runs the opening sentence of Bultmann's *Theology of the New Testament,* "belongs to the presuppositions of the theology of the New Testament and is not a part of that theology itself." [4]

Since 1953, however, there has been an attempt among certain students of Bultmann to reopen the question of the historical Jesus. They have not endeavored to resume the old quest but rather to relate the Christ of faith to the Jesus of Nazareth about whom even Bultmann admitted we do possess a little historical knowledge. Admittedly this attempt has been motivated in part by a fear among Christian scholars of loosing the historic foundations of Christianity. For the historian, however, it has meant that we may be able to speak, however cautiously, of Jesus of Nazareth and his teaching.

Although few, the biographical details of the life of Jesus that are now generally accepted are nonetheless significant.

> The home of Jesus is the semi-pagan, despised Galilee. His native town is Nazareth. His family certainly belonged to the Jewish part of the population which, since the times of the Maccabees, had reattached themselves to the temple cult in Jerusalem and the legal practices of Judaism. Only a criticism blinded by racial ideologies could deny the Jewish origin of Jesus. Jesus' father was a carpenter, and possibly he himself was too. . . . Jesus' mother tongue is the Aramaic of Galilee, the same dialect by which the servants of the high priest recognise Peter when he denies his Master in Jerusalem (Matth. xxvi.73). Hebrew was at that time no longer a spoken language, but rather only the language of religion and of scholars . . . . As a Jewish rabbi he must have been able to understand the ancient language of the Bible. On the other hand, we do not know to what extent he and his disciples knew Greek, widely used in administration and commerce. At any rate we find in Jesus no trace of the influence of Greek philosophy or of the Greek manner of living, just as nothing is known of activity on his part in the Hellenistic towns of the country.

[4] Joachim Jeremias, *The Problem of the Historical Jesus* (Philadelphia: Fortress Press, 1964), pp. 7–9.

The Sea of Galilee as seen from the surrounding hills. (Israel Government Tourist Office)

The synagogue at Capernaum was familiar to Jesus during his early ministry around Galilee. Much of the present structure dates from the third century of the Christian era, reflecting the Imperial style in its Corinthian columns. (Israel Information Services)

Rather we hear of his activity in the smaller hamlets and villages—Bethsaida, Chorazin, Capernaum—in the hill country and round the Sea of Galilee.

According to an isolated note in Luke, Jesus' public ministry begins, following the work of John the Baptist, at about his thirtieth year. His own baptism by John is one of the most certainly verified occurrences of his life. Tradition, however, has altogether transformed the story into a testimony to the Christ, so that we cannot gather from it what baptism meant for Jesus himself, for his decisions and for his inner development. But that this event was of far-reaching importance nobody will deny. It is all the more important that Jesus, without ever questioning the mission and the authority of the Baptist, nevertheless does not continue the work of the Baptist and his followers in the Jordan valley, but starts his own work in Galilee—like John, as a prophet of the coming kingdom of God. The instrument of his activity, however, is no longer baptism, but his spoken word and helping hand. We can no longer say with certainty how long Jesus' activity lasted. The first three Gospels create the impression that it lasted but a year. But they do not give a reliable chronology. We learn a great deal about his preaching, the conflict with his opponents, his healing and the additional help he granted the suffering, and the powerful influence which went forth from him. The people flock to him. Disciples follow him, but his enemies also arise and increase.... The last decisive turning point in his life is the resolution to go to Jerusalem with his disciples in order to confront the people there with his message in face of the coming kingdom of God. At the end of this road is his death on the cross.[5]

The second problem facing the student concerns the eschatological elements in the New Testament, elements that are now accepted by all scholars as an essential part of the life and teachings of Jesus. However, it is difficult if not impossible to determine what elements in the eschatology belong to the teaching of Jesus and what elements belong to the affirmation of the early Church. This eschatological problem was one of the major reasons for abandoning the original quest for the historical Jesus, a quest

[5] Bornkamm, *Jesus of Nazareth*, pp. 53–55.

Early ornamentation on a stone from the synagogue at Capernaum. On the far left is the six-sided star later adapted as the Star of David. (J. Leonard Hornstein, Jersey City)

The Via Dolorosa in Jerusalem along which Jesus is believed to have walked from the house of Pilate to the Mount of Calvary, where he was crucified. (The Matson Photo Service, Alhambra, California)

that ran aground on the seeming inconsistency between the ethical teaching of Jesus and his messianic claim. If Jesus were to be seen only as the great teacher whose ethical humanitarianism was contained in the gospels, a rabbi or prophet who condemned the religious superficiality of his time and taught the fatherhood of God and the brotherhood of man, then his claim to messiahship and the eschatological elements in the gospels had to be viewed as a later interpolation of the Church. However, the eschatology is too central to the New Testament to be dismissed simply as the superimposition of an ideology foreign to the teaching of Jesus. The question is no longer whether Jesus' teaching was eschatological, but rather whether Jesus' eschatological teaching differed from that of contemporary Judaism and the early Church.

The first question, then, within the problem of New Testament eschatology is the nature of Jesus' eschatology. Was Jesus a Jewish apocalyptic prophet or was he a rabbi opposed to apocalypse? The second and more important question is the role Jesus felt himself to play within that eschatology. Does the Church's affirmation that Jesus was the Messiah find its origin in Jesus' own messianic consciousness, or is it only part of the Church's post-Easter faith? Did Jesus preach the future advent of the eschatological kingdom or its realization during his ministry? This eschatological kingdom, referred to as the Kingdom of God or the Kingdom of Heaven, seems at times to lie in the future and, at such points, Jesus speaks of the coming of the Son of Man. Elsewhere the Kingdom is spoken of as a present reality, and in this context Jesus seems to refer to himself as the Messiah. The first tendency of scholarship was to interpret the former as the teaching of Jesus and the latter as the interpolation of the early Church. Such was the view of Albert Schweitzer, which has been summarized as follows:

> Jesus began his ministry proclaiming the near advent of the catastrophic Judgment and the Kingdom of God, and calling upon men to repent in view of them. He was already conscious of his Messiahship, a humble and unrecognized Messiahship, a mystery that only a few were called to recognize. But he anticipated his own metamorphosis with the coming of the Kingdom. So soon was the Son of Man to appear that Jesus could tell them [the disciples] that they would not have passed through the cities of Israel before that event. When their preaching tour had taken place and they had returned, all things continuing as they had, Jesus was led to revise his outlook. Whereas in sending out the Twelve he had anticipated that they like himself would have to endure the immediate messianic woes, he now sees that he himself shall bear those woes alone, "for many," that is, for the predestined elect. It is now that there comes to Jesus the daring thought that since the Kingdom delays its coming, he will precipitate it. He will take hold of the great wheel of destiny, of the eschatological train of events, and fling it around, even if he be crushed in his venture. The "dogmatic history" of the eschatological outlook Jesus will introduce by faith into real history. His astounding act of faith issued in despair on the cross. But from him have flowed streams of spiritual power in the life of humanity.[6]

For Schweitzer, then, the Kingdom was a future event that Jesus fully expected but that never arrived. Schweitzer's view has been superseded not only because he ignored the references in the gospels to the Kingdom as a present reality, but because Biblical criticism has shown that many of his examples came from the life of the early Church rather than from the life of Jesus. The seeming discrepancy between the future Kingdom and the realized Kingdom has been solved by seeing the future cataclysm as a future event whose reality has overflowed into the present. To put it more simply, Jesus taught both a "realized" and a "future" eschatology, that the Kingdom of God, whose fulfillment lay

[6] From pp. 37–38 in *Eschatology and Ethics in the Teaching of Jesus*, Revised Ed. by Amos N. Wilder. Copyright 1939, 1950 by Harper & Row, Publishers, Incorporated.

in the future, was in small measure present and active in the world through Jesus and his disciples.

The problem of uncovering the authentic teaching of Jesus and the eschatological worldview of the teaching that can be so authenticated raises serious questions for our understanding of the ethics of Jesus and in particular our understanding of the meaning of the Sermon on the Mount. Initially, Biblical criticism was led to a very skeptical view of the authenticity of the Sermon on the Mount.

> The views propounded by scholars in our day about the contents and structure of Matth. v-vii seem to compel the conclusion that the whole section is merely a collection of unrelated sayings of diverse origins, a patchwork, which cannot possibly retain the preeminence once accorded to it as the authoritative source for the teaching of Jesus. To embark critically on the interpretation of the Sermon on the Mount is inevitably to encounter the "frustration" of that honest dissection which, in New Testament scholarship, as in other spheres, so often seems to end in murder.[7]

Such skepticism has, however, been mitigated by recent studies of the Sermon on the Mount which have revealed not only an overall structure, provided most likely by the author or authors of the Gospel of Matthew, but also particular fragments of teaching that now appear to be authentic. It is around such fragments that students of Bultmann have begun to reconstruct the teaching of Jesus.

Apart from the problem of authenticating the separate parts of the Sermon on the Mount, such ethical teaching found there and elsewhere seems in any case negated by the eschatological worldview that pervades the New Testament. Schweitzer considered the ethics of Jesus, especially as reflected in the Sermon on the Mount, to be an "interim ethic," valid for, in fact created for, those few weeks and months before the end of the world. The ethical code was rigorous, demanding, and total in the obedience it required to God's will just because it was to be practiced only a short time during the "last days." If, as more recent scholars have suggested, Jesus believed that the Kingdom had begun with his ministry, does this in any way alter the fact that Jesus' ethic was an interim ethic?

Before discussing further the ethical teaching of Jesus, the pertinent sections of the Gospel of Matthew should be read, keeping in mind the problems and questions that have been raised thus far. The following reading includes the baptism of Jesus by John the Baptist, the Sermon on the Mount, the parables of the Kingdom, and the apocalyptic expectation.

THE GOSPEL ACCORDING TO MATTHEW[8]

3 In those days came John the Baptist, preaching in the wilderness of Judea, 2 "Repent, for the kingdom of heaven is at hand." 3 For this is he who was spoken of by the prophet Isaiah when he said,

"The voice of one crying in the wilderness:
Prepare the way of the Lord,
make his paths straight."

4 Now John wore a garment of camel's hair, and a leather girdle around his waist; and his food was locusts and wild honey. 5 Then went out to him Jerusalem and all Judea and all the region about the Jordan, 6 and they were baptized by him in the river Jordan, confessing their sins.

7 But when he saw many of the Pharisees and Sad'ducees coming for baptism, he said to them, "You brood of vipers! Who warned you to flee from the wrath to come? 8 Bear fruit that befits repentance,

---

[7] W. D. Davies, *The Setting of the Sermon on the Mount* (Cambridge, Eng.: Cambridge University Press, 1964), p. 1.

[8] The Bible, Matt. 3:1–17; 4:12–7:29; 10:1–23, 34–39; 12:1–13:58; 22:34–40; 24:3–44.

⁹ and do not presume to say to yourselves, 'We have Abraham as our father'; for I tell you, God is able from these stones to raise up children to Abraham. ¹⁰ Even now the ax is laid to the root of the trees; every tree therefore that does not bear good fruit is cut down and thrown into the fire.

¹¹ "I baptize you with water for repentance, but he who is coming after me is mightier than I, whose sandals I am not worthy to carry; he will baptize you with the Holy Spirit and with fire. ¹² His winnowing fork is in his hand, and he will clear his threshing floor and gather his wheat into the granary, but the chaff he will burn with unquenchable fire."

¹³ Then Jesus came from Galilee to the Jordan to John, to be baptized by him.

The River Jordan in which Jesus was baptized. (Israel Government Tourist Office)

14 John would have prevented him, saying, "I need to be baptized by you, and do you come to me?" 15 But Jesus answered him, "Let it be so now; for thus it is fitting for us to fulfil all righteousness." Then he consented. 16 And when Jesus was baptized, he went up immediately from the water, and behold, the heavens were opened and he saw the Spirit of God descending like a dove, and alighting on him; 17 and lo, a voice from heaven, saying, "This is my beloved Son, with whom I am well pleased." . . .

4 . . . 12 Now when he heard that John had been arrested, he withdrew into Galilee; 13 and leaving Nazareth he went and dwelt in Caper'na-um by the sea, in the territory of Zeb'ulun and Naph'tali, 14 that what was spoken by the prophet Isaiah might be fulfilled:

15 "The land of Zeb'ulun and the land of Naph'tali,
toward the sea, across the Jordan,
Galilee of the Gentiles—
16 the people who sat in darkness
have seen a great light,
and for those who sat in the region and shadow of death
light has dawned."

17 From that time Jesus began to preach, saying, "Repent, for the kingdom of heaven is at hand."

18 As he walked by the Sea of Galilee, he saw two brothers, Simon who is called Peter and Andrew his brother, casting a net into the sea; for they were fishermen. 19 And he said to them, "Follow me, and I will make you fishers of men." 20 Immediately they left their nets and followed him. 21 And going on from there he saw two other brothers, James the son of Zeb'edee and John his brother, in the boat with Zeb'edee their father, mending their nets, and he called them. 22 Immediately they left the boat and their father, and followed him.

23 And he went about all Galilee, teaching in their synagogues and preaching the gospel of the kingdom and healing every disease and every infirmity among the people. 24 So his fame spread throughout all Syria, and they brought him all the sick, those afflicted with various diseases and pains, demoniacs, epileptics, and paralytics, and he healed them. 25 And great crowds followed him from Galilee and the Decap'olis and Jerusalem and Judea and from beyond the Jordan.

5 Seeing the crowds, he went up on the mountain, and when he sat down his disciples came to him. 2 And he opened his mouth and taught them, saying:

3 "Blessed are the poor in spirit, for theirs is the kingdom of heaven.

4 "Blessed are those who mourn, for they shall be comforted.

5 "Blessed are the meek, for they shall inherit the earth.

6 "Blessed are those who hunger and thirst for righteousness, for they shall be satisfied.

7 "Blessed are the merciful, for they shall obtain mercy.

8 "Blessed are the pure in heart, for they shall see God.

9 "Blessed are the peacemakers, for they shall be called sons of God.

10 "Blessed are those who are persecuted for righteousness' sake, for theirs is the kingdom of heaven.

11 "Blessed are you when men revile you and persecute you and utter all kinds of evil against you falsely on my account. 12 Rejoice and be glad, for your reward is great in heaven, for so men persecuted the prophets who were before you.

13 "You are the salt of the earth; but if

salt has lost its taste, how shall its saltness be restored? It is no longer good for anything except to be thrown out and trodden under foot by men.

14 "You are the light of the world. A city set on a hill cannot be hid. 15 Nor do men light a lamp and put it under a bushel, but on a stand, and it gives light to all in the house. 16 Let your light so shine before men, that they may see your good works and give glory to your Father who is in heaven.

Traditional methods of fishing are sometimes still used along the shores of the Sea of Galilee. (Israel Government Tourist Office)

17 "Think not that I have come to abolish the law and the prophets; I have come not to abolish them but to fulfil them. 18 For truly, I say to you, till heaven and earth pass away, not an iota, not a dot, will pass from the law until all is accomplished. 19 Whoever then relaxes one of the least of these commandments and teaches men so, shall be called least in the kingdom of heaven; but he who does them and teaches them shall be called great in the kingdom of heaven. 20 For I tell you, unless your righteousness exceeds that of the scribes and Pharisees, you will never enter the kingdom of heaven.

21 "You have heard that it was said to the men of old, 'You shall not kill; and whoever kills shall be liable to judgment.' 22 But I say to you that every one who is angry with his brother shall be liable to judgment; whoever insults his brother shall be liable to the council, and whoever says, 'You fool!' shall be liable to the hell of fire. 23 So if you are offering your gift at the altar, and there remember that your brother has something against you, 24 leave your gift there before the altar and go; first be reconciled to your brother, and then come and offer your gift. 25 Make friends quickly with your accuser, while you are going with him to court, lest your accuser hand you over to the judge, and the judge to the guard, and you be put in prison; 26 truly, I say to you, you will never get out till you have paid the last penny.

27 "You have heard that it was said, 'You shall not commit adultery.' 28 But I say to you that every one who looks at a woman lustfully has already committed adultery with her in his heart. 29 If your right eye causes you to sin, pluck it out and throw it away; it is better that you lose one of your members than that your whole body be thrown into hell. 30 And if your right hand causes you to sin, cut it off and throw it away; it is better that you lose one of your members than that your whole body go into hell.

31 "It was also said, 'Whoever divorces his wife, let him give her a certificate of divorce.' 32 But I say to you that every one who divorces his wife, except on the ground of unchastity, makes her an adulteress; and whoever marries a divorced woman commits adultery.

33 "Again you have heard that it was said to the men of old, 'You shall not swear falsely, but shall perform to the Lord what you have sworn.' 34 But I say to you, Do not swear at all, either by heaven, for it is the throne of God, 35 or by the earth, for it is his footstool, or by Jerusalem, for it is the city of the great King. 36 And do not swear by your head, for you cannot make one hair white or black. 37 Let what you say be simply 'Yes' or 'No'; anything more than this comes from evil.

38 "You have heard that it was said, 'An eye for an eye and a tooth for a tooth.' 39 But I say to you, Do not resist one who is evil. But if any one strikes you on the right cheek, turn to him the other also; 40 and if any one would sue you and take your coat, let him have your cloak as well; 41 and if any one forces you to go one mile, go with him two miles. 42 Give to him who begs from you, and do not refuse him who would borrow from you.

43 "You have heard that it was said, 'You shall love your neighbor and hate your enemy.' 44 But I say to you, Love your enemies and pray for those who persecute you, 45 so that you may be sons of your Father who is in heaven; for he makes his sun rise on the evil and on the good, and sends rain on the just and on

the unjust. ⁴⁶ For if you love those who love you, what reward have you? Do not even the tax collectors do the same? ⁴⁷ And if you salute only your brethren, what more are you doing than others? Do not even the Gentiles do the same? ⁴⁸ You, therefore, must be perfect, as your heavenly Father is perfect.

6 "Beware of practicing your piety before men in order to be seen by them; for then you will have no reward from your Father who is in heaven.

² "Thus, when you give alms, sound no trumpet before you, as the hypocrites do in the synagogues and in the streets, that they may be praised by men. Truly, I say to you, they have their reward. ³ But when you give alms, do not let your left hand know what your right hand is doing, ⁴ so that your alms may be in secret; and your Father who sees in secret will reward you.

⁵ "And when you pray, you must not be like the hypocrites; for they love to stand and pray in the synagogues and at the street corners, that they may be seen by men. Truly, I say to you, they have their reward. ⁶ But when you pray, go into your room and shut the door and pray to your Father who is in secret; and your Father who sees in secret will reward you.

⁷ "And in praying do not heap up empty phrases as the Gentiles do; for they think that they will be heard for their many words. ⁸ Do not be like them, for your Father knows what you need before you ask him. ⁹ Pray then like this:

Our Father who art in heaven,
Hallowed be thy name.
¹⁰Thy kingdom come,
Thy will be done,
 On earth as it is in heaven.
¹¹ Give us this day our daily bread;
¹² And forgive us our debts,

 As we also have forgiven our debtors;
¹³ And lead us not into temptation,
 But deliver us from evil.

¹⁴ For if you forgive men their trespasses, your heavenly Father also will forgive you; ¹⁵ but if you do not forgive men their trespasses, neither will your Father forgive your trespasses.

¹⁶ "And when you fast, do not look dismal, like the hypocrites, for they disfigure their faces that their fasting may be seen by men. Truly, I say to you, they have their reward. ¹⁷ But when you fast, anoint your head and wash your face, ¹⁸ that your fasting may not be seen by men but by your Father who is in secret; and your Father who sees in secret will reward you.

¹⁹ "Do not lay up for yourselves treasures on earth, where moth and rust consume and where thieves break in and steal, ²⁰ but lay up for yourselves treasures in heaven, where neither moth nor rust consumes and where thieves do not break in and steal. ²¹ For where your treasure is, there will your heart be also.

²² "The eye is the lamp of the body. So, if your eye is sound, your whole body will be full of light; ²³ but if your eye is not sound, your whole body will be full of darkness. If then the light in you is darkness, how great is the darkness!

²⁴ "No one can serve two masters; for either he will hate the one and love the other, or he will be devoted to the one and despise the other. You cannot serve God and mammon.

²⁵ "Therefore I tell you, do not be anxious about your life, what you shall eat or what you shall drink, nor about your body, what you shall put on. Is not life more than food, and the body more than clothing? ²⁶ Look at the birds of the air: they neither sow nor reap nor gather into barns,

and yet your heavenly Father feeds them. Are you not of more value than they? 27 And which of you by being anxious can add one cubit to his span of life? 28 And why are you anxious about clothing? Consider the lilies of the field, how they grow; they neither toil nor spin; 29 yet I tell you, even Solomon in all his glory was not arrayed like one of these. 30 But if God so clothes the grass of the field, which today is alive and tomorrow is thrown into the oven, will he not much more clothe you, O men of little faith? 31 Therefore do not be anxious, saying, 'What shall we eat?' or 'What shall we drink?' or 'What shall we wear?' 32 For the Gentiles seek all these things; and your heavenly Father knows that you need them all. 33 But seek first his kingdom and his righteousness, and all these things shall be yours as well.

34 "Therefore do not be anxious about tomorrow, for tomorrow will be anxious for itself. Let the day's own trouble be sufficient for the day.

7 "Judge not, that you be not judged. 2 For with the judgment you pronounce you will be judged, and the measure you give will be the measure you get. 3 Why do you see the speck that is in your brother's eye, but do not notice the log that is in your own eye? 4 Or how can you say to your brother, 'Let me take the speck out of your eye,' when there is the log in your own eye? 5 You hypocrite, first take the log out of your own eye, and then you will see clearly to take the speck out of your brother's eye.

6 "Do not give dogs what is holy; and do not throw your pearls before swine, lest they trample them underfoot and turn to attack you.

7 "Ask, and it will be given you; seek and you will find; knock, and it will be opened to you. 8 For every one who asks receives, and he who seeks finds, and to him who knocks it will be opened. 9 Or what man of you, if his son asks him for a loaf, will give him a stone? 10 Or if he asks for a fish, will give him a serpent? 11 If you then, who are evil, know how to give good gifts to your children, how much more will your Father who is in heaven give good things to those who ask him? 12 So whatever you wish that men would do to you, do so to them; for this is the law and the prophets.

13 "Enter by the narrow gate; for the gate is wide and the way is easy, that leads to destruction, and those who enter by it are many. 14 For the gate is narrow and the way is hard, that leads to life, and those who find it are few.

15 "Beware of false prophets, who come to you in sheep's clothing but inwardly are ravenous wolves. 16 You will know them by their fruits. Are grapes gathered from thorns, or figs from thistles? 17 So, every sound tree bears good fruit, but the bad tree bears evil fruit. 18 A sound tree cannot bear evil fruit, nor can a bad tree bear good fruit. 19 Every tree that does not bear good fruit is cut down and thrown into the fire. 20 Thus you will know them by their fruits.

21 "Not every one who says to me, 'Lord, Lord,' shall enter the kingdom of heaven, but he who does the will of my Father who is in heaven. 22 On that day many will say to me, 'Lord, Lord, did we not prophesy in your name, and cast out demons in your name, and do many mighty works in your name?' 23 And then will I declare to them, 'I never knew you; depart from me, you evildoers.'

24 "Every one then who hears these words of mine and does them will be like a wise man who built his house upon the

rock; 25 and the rain fell, and the floods came, and the winds blew and beat upon that house, but it did not fall, because it had been founded on the rock. 26And every one who hears these words of mine and does not do them will be like a foolish man who built his house upon the sand; 27 and the rain fell, and the floods came, and the winds blew and beat against that house, and it fell; and great was the fall of it."

28And when Jesus finished these sayings, the crowds were astonished at his teaching, 29 for he taught them as one who had authority, and not as their scribes. . . .

10 And he called to him his twelve disciples and gave them authority over unclean spirits, to cast them out, and to heal every disease and every infirmity. 2 The names of the twelve apostles are these: first, Simon, who is called Peter, and Andrew his brother; James the son of Zeb'edee, and John his brother; 3 Philip and Bartholomew; Thomas and Matthew the tax collector; James the son of Alphaeus, and Thaddaeus; 4 Simon the Cananaean, and Judas Iscariot, who betrayed him.

5 These twelve Jesus sent out, charging them, "Go nowhere among the Gentiles, and enter no town of the Samaritans, 6 but go rather to the lost sheep of the house of Israel. 7And preach as you go, saying, 'The kingdom of heaven is at hand.' 8 Heal the sick, raise the dead, cleanse lepers, cast out demons. You received without pay, give without pay. 9 Take no gold, nor silver, nor copper in your belts, 10 no bag for your journey, nor two tunics, nor sandals, nor a staff; for the laborer deserves his food. 11And whatever town or village you enter, find out who is worthy in it, and stay with him until you depart. 12As you enter the house, salute it. 13And if the house is worthy, let your peace come upon it; but if it is not worthy, let your peace return to you. 14And if any one will not receive you or listen to your words, shake off the dust from your feet as you leave that house or town. 15 Truly, I say to you, it shall be more tolerable on the day of judgment for the land of Sodom and Gomor'rah than for that town.

16 "Behold, I send you out as sheep in the midst of wolves; so be wise as serpents and innocent as doves. 17Beware of men; for they will deliver you up to councils, and flog you in their synagogues, 18and you will be dragged before governors and kings for my sake, to bear testimony before them and the Gentiles. 19 When they deliver you up, do not be anxious how you are to speak or what you are to say; for what you are to say will be given to you in that hour; 20 for it is not you who speak, but the Spirit of your Father speaking through you. 21 Brother will deliver up brother to death, and the father his child, and children will rise against parents and have them put to death; 22 and you will be hated by all for my name's sake. But he who endures to the end will be saved. 23 When they persecute you in one town, flee to the next; for truly, I say to you, you will not have gone through all the towns of Israel, before the Son of man comes. . . .

34 "Do not think that I have come to bring peace on earth; I have not come to bring peace, but a sword. 35 For I have come to set a man against his father, and a daughter against her mother, and a daughter-in-law against her mother-in-law; 36 and a man's foes will be those of his own household. 37 He who loves father or mother more than me is not worthy of me; and he who loves son or daughter more

than me is not worthy of me; 38 and he who does not take his cross and follow me is not worthy of me. 39 He who finds his life will lose it, and he who loses his life for my sake will find it. . . .

12 At that time Jesus went through the grainfields on the sabbath; his disciples were hungry, and they began to pluck ears of grain and to eat. 2 But when Pharisees saw it, they said to him, "Look, your disciples are doing what is not lawful to do on the sabbath." 3 He said to them, "Have you not read what David did, when he was hungry, and those who were with him: 4 how he entered the house of God and ate the bread of the Presence, which it was not lawful for him to eat nor for those who were with him, but only for the priest? 5 Or have you not read in the law how on the sabbath the priests in the temple profane the sabbath, and are guiltless? 6 I tell you, something greater than the temple is here. 7 And if you had known what this means, 'I desire mercy, and not sacrifice,' you would not have condemned the guiltless. 8 For the Son of man is lord of the sabbath."

9 And he went on from there, and entered their synagogue. 10 And behold, there was a man with a withered hand. And they asked him, "Is it lawful to heal on the sabbath?" so that they might accuse him. 11 He said to them, "What man of you, if he has one sheep and it falls into a pit on the sabbath, will not lay hold of it and lift it out? 12 Of how much more value is a man than a sheep! So it is lawful to do good on the sabbath." 13 Then he said to the man, "Stretch out your hand." And the man stretched it out, and it was restored, whole like the other. 14 But the Pharisees went out and took counsel against him, how to destroy him.

15 Jesus, aware of this, withdrew from there. And many followed him, and he healed them all, 16 and ordered them not to make him known. 17 This was to fulfil what was spoken by the prophet Isaiah:
18 "Behold, my servant whom I have chosen,
my beloved with whom my soul is well pleased.
I will put my Spirit upon him,
and he shall proclaim justice to the Gentiles.
19 He will not wrangle or cry aloud,
nor will any one hear his voice in the streets;
20 he will not break a bruised reed
or quench a smoldering wick,
till he brings justice to victory;
21 and in his name will the Gentiles hope."

22 Then a blind and dumb demoniac was brought to him, and he healed him, so that the dumb man spoke and saw. 23 And all the people were amazed, and said, "Can this be the Son of David?" 24 But when the Pharisees heard it they said, "It is only by Be-el'zebul, the prince of demons, that this man casts out demons." 25 Knowing their thoughts, he said to them, "Every kingdom divided against itself is laid waste, and no city or house divided against itself will stand; 26 and if Satan casts out Satan, he is divided against himself; how then will his kingdom stand? 27 And if I cast out demons by Be-el'zebul, by whom do your sons cast them out? Therefore they shall be your judges. 28 But if it is by the Spirit of God that I cast out demons, then the kingdom of God has come upon you. 29 Or how can one enter a strong man's house and plunder his goods, unless he first binds the strong man? Then indeed he may plunder his house. 30 He who is not with me is against me, and he who does

not gather with me scatters. ³¹ Therefore I tell you, every sin and blasphemy will be forgiven men, but the blasphemy against the Spirit will not be forgiven. ³² And whoever says a word against the Son of man will be forgiven; but whoever speaks against the Holy Spirit will not be forgiven, either in this age or in the age to come.

³³ "Either make the tree good, and its fruit good; or make the tree bad, and its fruit bad; for the tree is known by its fruit. ³⁴ You brood of vipers! how can you speak good, when you are evil? For out of the abundance of the heart the mouth speaks. ³⁵ The good man out of his good treasure brings forth good, and the evil man out of his evil treasure brings forth evil. ³⁶ I tell you, on the day of judgment men will render account for every careless word they utter; ³⁷ for by your words you will be justified, and by your words you will be condemned."

³⁸ Then some of the scribes and Pharisees said to him, "Teacher, we wish to see a sign from you." ³⁹ But he answered them, "An evil and adulterous generation seeks for a sign; but no sign shall be given to it except the sign of the prophet Jonah. ⁴⁰ For as Jonah was three days and three nights in the belly of the whale, so will the Son of man be three days and three nights in the heart of the earth. ⁴¹ The men of Nin'eveh will arise at the judgment with this generation and condemn it; for they repented at the preaching of Jonah, and behold, something greater than Jonah is here. ⁴² The queen of the South will arise at the judgment with this generation and condemn it; for she came from the ends of the earth to hear the wisdom of Solomon, and behold, something greater than Solomon is here.

⁴³ "When the unclean spirit has gone out of a man, he passes through waterless places seeking rest, but he finds none. ⁴⁴ Then he says, 'I will return to my house from which I came.' And when he comes he finds it empty, swept, and put in order. ⁴⁵ Then he goes and brings with him seven other spirits more evil than himself, and they enter and dwell there; and the last state of that man becomes worse than the first. So shall it be also with this evil generation."

⁴⁶ While he was still speaking to the people, behold, his mother and his brothers stood outside, asking to speak to him. ⁴⁸ But he replied to the man who told him, "Who is my mother, and who are my brothers?" ⁴⁹ And stretching out his hand toward his disciples, he said, "Here are my mother and my brothers! ⁵⁰ For whoever does the will of my Father in heaven is my brother, and sister, and mother."

13 That same day Jesus went out of the house and sat beside the sea. ² And great crowds gathered about him, so that he got into a boat and sat there; and the whole crowd stood on the beach. ³ And he told them many things in parables, saying: "A sower went out to sow. ⁴ And as he sowed, some seeds fell along the path, and the birds came and devoured them. ⁵ Other seeds fell on rocky ground, where they had not much soil, and immediately they sprang up, since they had no depth of soil, ⁶ but when the sun rose they were scorched; and since they had no root they withered away. ⁷ Other seeds fell upon thorns, and the thorns grew up and choked them. ⁸ Other seeds fell on good soil and brought forth grain, some a hundredfold, some sixty, some thirty. ⁹ He who has ears, let him hear."

¹⁰ Then the disciples came and said to him, "Why do you speak to them in parables?" ¹¹ And he answered them, "To you it has been given to know the secrets of

the kingdom of heaven, but to them it has not been given. 12 For to him who has will more be given, and he will have abundance; but from him who has not, even what he has will be taken away. 13 This is why I speak to them in parables, because seeing they do not see, and hearing they do not hear, nor do they understand. 14 With them indeed is fulfilled the prophecy of Isaiah which says:

'You shall indeed hear but never understand,
and you shall indeed see but never perceive.
15 For this people's heart has grown dull,
and their ears are heavy of hearing,
and their eyes they have closed
lest they should perceive with their eyes,
and hear with their ears,
and understand with their heart,
and turn for me to heal them.'

16 But blessed are your eyes, for they see, and your ears, for they hear. 17 Truly, I say to you, many prophets and righteous men longed to see what you see, and did not see it, and to hear what you hear, and did not hear it.

18 "Hear then the parable of the sower. 19 When any one hears the word of the kingdom and does not understand it, the evil one comes and snatches away what is sown in his heart; this is what was sown along the path. 20 As for what was sown on rocky ground, this is he who hears the word and immediately receives it with joy; 21 yet he has no root in himself, but endures for a while, and when tribulation or persecution arises on account of the word, immediately he falls away. 22 As for what was sown among thorns, this is he who hears the word, but the cares of the world and the delight in riches choke the word, and it proves unfruitful. 23 As for what was sown on good soil, this is he who hears the word and understands it; he indeed bears fruit, and yields, in one case a hundredfold, in another sixty, and in another thirty."

24 Another parable he put before them, saying, "The kingdom of heaven may be compared to a man who sowed good seed in his field; 25 but while men were sleeping, his enemy came and sowed weeds among the wheat, and went away. 26 So when the plants came up and bore grain, then the weeds appeared also. 27 And the servants of the householder came and said to him, 'Sir, did you not sow good seed in your field? How then has it weeds?' 28 He said to them, 'An enemy has done this.' The servants said to him, 'Then do you want us to go and gather them?' 29 But he said, 'No; lest in gathering the weeds you root up the wheat along with them. 30 Let both grow together until the harvest; and at harvest time I will tell the reapers, Gather the weeds first and bind them in bundles to be burned, but gather the wheat into my barn.'"

31 Another parable he put before them, saying, "The kingdom of heaven is like a grain of mustard seed which a man took and sowed in his field; 32 it is the smallest of all seeds, but when it has grown it is the greatest of shrubs and becomes a tree, so that the birds of the air come and make nests in its branches."

33 He told them another parable. "The kingdom of heaven is like leaven which a woman took and hid in three measures of meal, till it was all leavened."

34 All this Jesus said to the crowds in parables; indeed he said nothing to them without a parable. 35 This was to fulfil what was spoken by the prophet:

"I will open my mouth in parables,
I will utter what has been hidden since the foundation of the world."

36 Then he left the crowds and went into the house. And his disciples came to him, saying, "Explain to us the parable of the weeds of the field." 37 He answered, "He who sows the good seed is the Son of man; 38 the field is the world, and the good seed means the sons of the kingdom; the weeds are the sons of the evil one, 39 and the enemy who sowed them is the devil; the harvest is the close of the age, and the reapers are angels. 40 Just as the weeds are gathered and burned with fire, so will it be at the close of the age. 41 The Son of man will send his angels, and they will gather out of his kingdom all causes of sin and all evildoers, 42 and throw them into the furnace of fire; there men will weep and gnash their teeth. 43 Then the righteous will shine like the sun in the kingdom of their Father. He who has ears, let him hear.

44 "The kingdom of heaven is like treasure hidden in a field, which a man found and covered up; then in his joy he goes and sells all that he has and buys that field.

45 "Again, the kingdom of heaven is like a merchant in search of fine pearls, 46 who, on finding one pearl of great value went and sold all that he had and bought it.

47 "Again, the kingdom of heaven is like a net which was thrown into the sea and gathered fish of every kind; 48 when it was full, men drew it ashore and sat down and sorted the good into vessels but threw away the bad. 49 So it will be at the close of the age. The angels will come out and separate the evil from the righteous, 50 and throw them into the furnace of fire; there men will weep and gnash their teeth.

51 "Have you understood all this?" They said to him, "Yes." 52 And he said to them, "Therefore every scribe who has been trained for the kingdom of heaven is like a householder who brings out of his treasure what is new and what is old."

53 And when Jesus had finished these parables, he went away from there, 54 and coming to his own country he taught them in their synagogue, so that they were astonished, and said, "Where did this man get this wisdom and these mighty works? 55 Is not this the carpenter's son? Is not his mother called Mary? And are not his brothers James and Joseph and Simon and Judas? 56 And are not all his sisters with us? Where then did this man get all this?" 57 And they took offense at him. But Jesus said to them, "A prophet is not without honor except in his own country and in his own house." 58 And he did not do many mighty works there, because of their unbelief. . . .

22 . . . 34 But when the Pharisees heard that he had silenced the Sad′ducees, they came together. 35 And one of them, a lawyer, asked him a question, to test him. 36 "Teacher, which is the great commandment in the law?" 37 And he said to him, "You shall love the Lord your God with all your heart, and with all your soul, and with all your mind. 38 This is the great and first commandment. 39 And a second is like it, You shall love your neighbor as yourself. 40 On these two commandments depend all the law and the prophets." . . .

24 . . . 3 As he sat on the Mount of Olives, the disciples came to him privately, saying, "Tell us, when will this be, and what will be the sign of your coming and of the close of the age?" 4 And Jesus answered them, "Take heed that no one leads you astray. 5 For many will come in

The Mount of Olives, across the Kidron Valley from the Temple in Jerusalem, was the scene of much of Jesus' activity in the last week of his life. The Garden of Gethsemane is at the foot of the hill. (George Rodger from Magnum)

my name, saying, 'I am the Christ,' and they will lead many astray. 6 And you will hear of wars and rumors of wars, see that you are not alarmed; for this must take place, but the end is not yet. 7 For nation will rise against nation, and kingdom against kingdom, and there will be famines and earthquakes in various places: 8 all this is but the beginning of the sufferings.

9 "Then they will deliver you up to tribulation, and put you to death; and you will be hated by all nations for my name's sake. 10 And then many will fall away, and betray one another, and hate one another. 11 And many false prophets will arise and lead many astray. 12 And because wickedness is multiplied, most men's love will grow cold. 13 But he who endures to the end will be saved. 14 And this gospel of the kingdom will be preached throughout the whole world, as a testimony to all nations; and then the end will come.

15 "So when you see the desolating sacrilege spoken of by the prophet Daniel, standing in the holy place (let the reader understand), 16 then let those who are in Judea flee to the mountains; 17 let him who is on the housetop not go down to take what is in his house; 18 and let him who is in the field not turn back to take his mantle. 19 And alas for those who are with child and for those who give suck in those days! 20 Pray that your flight may not be in winter or on a sabbath. 21 For then there will be great tribulation, such as has not been from the beginning of the world until now, no, and never will be. 22 And if those days had not been shortened, no human being would be saved; but for the sake of the elect those days will be shortened. 23 Then if any one says to you, 'Lo, here is the Christ!' or 'There he is!' do not believe it. 24 For false Christs and false prophets will arise and show great signs and wonders, so as to lead astray, if possible, even the elect. 25 Lo, I have told you beforehand. 26 So, if they say to you, 'Lo, he is in the wilderness,' do not go out; if they say, 'Lo, he is in the inner rooms,' do not believe it. 27 For as the lightning comes from the east and shines as far as the west, so will be the coming of the Son of man. 28 Wherever the body is, there the eagles will be gathered together.

29 "Immediately after the tribulation of those days the sun will be darkened, and the moon will not give its light, and the stars will fall from heaven, and the powers of the heavens will be shaken; 30 then will appear the sign of the Son of man in heaven, and then all the tribes of the earth will mourn, and they will see the Son of man coming on the clouds of heaven with power and great glory; 31 and he will send out his angels with a loud trumpet call, and they will gather his elect from the four winds, from one end of heaven to the other.

32 "From the fig tree learn its lesson: as soon as its branch becomes tender and puts forth its leaves, you know that summer is near. 33 So also, when you see all these things, you know that he is near, at the very gates. 34 Truly, I say to you, this generation will not pass away till all these things take place. 35 Heaven and earth will pass away, but my words will not pass away.

36 "But of that day and hour no one knows, not even the angels of heaven, nor the Son, but the Father only. 37 As were the days of Noah, so will be the coming of the Son of man. 38 For as in those days before the flood they were eating and drinking, marrying and giving in marriage, until the day when Noah entered the ark, 39 and

they did not know until the flood came and swept them all away, so will be the coming of the Son of man. ⁴⁰ Then two men will be in the field; one is taken and one is left. ⁴¹ Two women will be grinding at the mill; one is taken and one is left. ⁴² Watch therefore, for you do not know on what day your Lord is coming. ⁴³ But know this, that if the householder had known in what part of the night the thief was coming, he would have watched and would not have let his house be broken into. ⁴⁴ Therefore you also must be ready; for the Son of man is coming at an hour you do not expect.

Only a small portion of the ethical teaching of Jesus can be considered unique to him, for much of it, whether spoken by Jesus or not, belongs to the Old Testament, to the general wisdom literature of the period, or to rabbinic teaching. For example, the commandment to love one's neighbor as one's self is rabbinic and based on Old Testament teaching (Lev. 19:18). Some of the ethical teaching, however, is less common and more controversial, such as the sixth antithesis (Matt. 5:43-44), which is directed against the Essenes and others like them who restricted the commandment of love to the community of the elect. But at several points Jesus sets his own authority not against sectarian Jewish communities but against the authority of Moses, and in so doing he sets himself off from the entire Old Testament tradition. It is the radical and unique quality of such teaching, a radicalness the gospels often try to tone down, that seems to many scholars to ensure the authenticity of these fragments. This applies especially to the first, second, and fourth antitheses (Matt. 5:21-22, 27-28, 33-34), where Jesus places his own authority over against that of Moses and expands the prohibitions on murder, adultery, and oath breaking into prohibitions on anger, lust, and swearing of oaths.

In fact, these words are among the most astonishing to be found anywhere in the Gospels. In their form, they elaborate the wording of the Torah as a rabbi interpreting the sense of the Scripture might have done. The determining factor however, is that the words "But I say" embody a claim to an authority which rivals and challenges that of Moses. But anyone who claims an authority rivalling and challenging Moses has *ipso facto* set himself above Moses; he has ceased to be a rabbi, for a rabbi's authority only comes to him as derived from Moses. Rabbis may oppose each other in debate by the use of the formula 'But *I* say'; but this is only a formal parallel, because, in the case we are discussing, it is not another rabbi but the Scriptures and Moses himself who constitute the other party. To this there are no Jewish parallels, nor indeed can there be. For the Jew who does what is done here has cut himself off from the community of Judaism—or else he brings the Messianic Torah and is therefore the Messiah. Even the prophet does not stand alongside Moses but under him. The unheard-of implication of the saying testifies to its genuineness. It proves, secondly, that while Jesus may have made his appearance in the first place in the character of a rabbi or a prophet, nevertheless his claim far surpasses that of any rabbi or prophet; and thirdly, that he cannot be integrated into the background of the Jewish piety of his time. Certainly he was a Jew and made the assumptions of Jewish piety, but at the same time he shatters this framework with his claim. The only category which does justice to his claim (quite independently of whether he used it himself and required it of others) is that in which his disciples themselves placed him—namely, that of the Messiah.

This passage is not an isolated one so far as the Synoptists are concerned. The same dialectical relationship to the law, seeking the will of God and, in pursuit of it, shattering the letter of the law, is reflected in the attitude to the Sabbath commandment and the prescriptions for ceremonial purity. We can hardly say here that Jesus has left the law as such untouched and merely made its demands more radical. This is certainly Matthew's understanding of what happened. But the history of the Gospel is always at the same time a history of misunderstandings, as the Synoptists themselves frequently show us. And the majesty of Jesus is most plainly revealed when we see his first disciples already feeling that they must soften or correct his words, because otherwise they could not endure him.

. . . The community embarked on this process of watering-down the saying because, while it might credit its Lord with the freedom he had assumed, it was not prepared to allow it to all men. Its members felt themselves more tightly bound by the law than he had been and, as the subsequent pericope [section] about the healing on the sabbath shows, they exercised their freedom only in exceptional cases and not as a matter of principle; and certainly not in that spirit of unforced responsibility to God, which was Jesus' legacy to them. The greatness of his gift causes the community to take fright.

The same process may also be observed in the conflict over the law of purification. Again, Matthew obviously thought that Jesus was only attacking the rabbinate and Pharisaism with their heightening of the demands of the Torah. But the man who denies that impurity from external sources can penetrate into man's essential being is striking at the presuppositions and the plain verbal sense of the Torah and at the authority of Moses himself. Over and above that, he is striking at the presuppositions of the whole classical conception of cultus with its sacrificial and expiatory system. To put this in another way, he is removing the distinction (which is fundamental to the whole of ancient thought) between the *temenos*, the realm of the sacred, and the secular, and it is for this reason that he is able to consort with sinners. For Jesus, it is the heart of man which lets impurity loose upon the world. . . . Finally, by this saying, Jesus destroys the basis of classical demonology which rests on the conception that man is threatened by the powers of the universe and thus at bottom fails to recognize the threat which is offered to the universe by man himself. . . . Jesus felt himself in a position to override, with an unparalleled and sovereign freedom, the words of the Torah and the authority of Moses. This sovereign freedom not merely shakes the very foundations of Judaism and causes his death, but, further, it cuts the ground from under the feet of the ancient world-view with its antithesis of sacred and profane and its demonology.[9]

Other scholars have seen in the Sermon on the Mount not a rejection of the Mosaic Torah from the standpoint of prophecy, but rather the fulfillment or transformation of the Law under the impact of the dawning new age. If the contrast between priest and prophet, between cult and charisma, has been sometimes overdrawn in Old Testament studies so that their frequent relation and cooperation has not been appreciated, so perhaps has the contrast between the Mosaic Law and the teaching of Jesus. The following comments on the "antitheses" of the Sermon on the Mount are made by a scholar who sees in Matthew's account the proclamation of the Messianic Torah, the New Law proclaimed from the New Sinai by the New Moses, Jesus.

In none of the antitheses is there an intention to annul the provisions of the Law but only to carry them to their ultimate meaning. . . . "The Matthaean form is far milder, less revolutionary, than one might incline to believe . . . ; these declarations, 'Ye have heard—But I say unto you,' are intended to prove Jesus the Law's upholder, not destroyer. The relationship between the two members of the form is not one of pure contrast; the demand that you must not be angry with your brother is not thought of as utterly irreconcilable with the prohibition of killing. On the contrary, wider and deeper though it may be, it is

[9] Ernst Käsemann, *Essays on New Testament Themes* ("Studies in Biblical Theology," No. 41; Naperville, Ill.: Alec R. Allenson, Inc., 1964), pp. 37–40. Reprinted by permission of SCM Press, Ltd.

thought of as, in a sense, resulting from and certainly including the old rule; it is the revelation of a fuller meaning for a new age. The second member unfolds rather than sweeps away the first."[10] To interpret on the side of stringency is not to annul the Law, but to change it in accordance with its own intention. From this point of view . . . we cannot speak of the Law being annulled in the antitheses, but only of its being intensified in its demand, or reinterpreted in a higher key.[11]

Was Jesus a charismatic leader bent on overthrowing the Law and founding a new faith on his own authority, or was he a Jewish prophet proclaiming the fulfillment of the Law? The answer to this question is obviously difficult, and it is further complicated by the problem of the relation of eschatology and ethics in the teaching of Jesus. The nature of the problem and one possible solution is suggested in the following selection. In reading this section, it is important to distinguish the way in which eschatology affects the sanctions of an ethic from the way in which it affects the content of that ethic.

Eschatology and Ethics in the Teaching of Jesus
A. N. Wilder[12]

[What is] the nature of the sanctions invoked by Jesus for his ethical summons, whether in his call to repentance generally or in his particular precepts?

The nearness of the Kingdom of Heaven, viewed both as promise and as menace, is the dominant sanction for righteousness.

---

[10] D. Daube, *The New Testament and Rabbinic Judaism* (London: University of London Press, 1956), p. 60.
[11] Davies, *The Setting of the Sermon on the Mount*, p. 102.
[12] From pp. 133-137, 140-141, 145-147, 160-162 in *Eschatology and Ethics in the Teaching of Jesus,* Revised Ed. by Amos N. Wilder. Copyright 1939, 1950 by Harper & Row, Publishers, Incorporated.

This dominant eschatological sanction is, however, a formal sanction only, secondary to, if closely related to, the essential sanction.

The essential sanction for righteousness is the nature of God.

The essential sanction represents an appeal simply to the reason and discernment, to the God-conscious moral nature of men, assisted by the witness of Scripture and the example and authority of Jesus.

The formal sanction represents an appeal to self-interest in view of the rewards and punishments that are to follow on the Judgment; and, incidentally, that are to be present in a degree in the present interim, which is a phase of the messianic times, in which the Kingdom of God is already present in a sense. . . .

In the eschatological tableau the Jewish mind was—in a way most suitable to its Weltanschauung—dramatizing its conviction of the holiness of God in its dealing with men. . . .

The apocalyptic ideas are "fictions." They are fictions naïvely held; that is, they are not conscious symbol and deliberate metaphor. As fictions, it follows that, however vividly they might compel the imagination of the eschatologist, they could never serve as a final and determinative sanction. A fiction however vivid and compelling has not the substance to serve this purpose. The only exception here is when it has grown so impoverished and conventionalized that men begin to take it with a crass literalism. We are not surprised, therefore, to find that the eschatological sanction, in the vital and creative stage in which it appears in our gospels, is always in the form of a fictional or formal sanction. But what real force there is in this sanction, properly enough, springs out of its immediate relation to that from which the fiction springs, that is, the experience of the holiness and power of God. For our gospels, indeed, it must be recognized that the eschatology falls sometimes below this level of creative power. The original creative symbol or "fiction," the true heart of all apocalyptic, here as elsewhere has advanced some steps on the way of literary crystallization. . . .

In the gospels both the original and the conventionalized or impoverished stages of conception are found, and these in varying degrees. The former are pervasive enough to save the whole from misrepresenting the teaching of Jesus. Behind Mt.'s elaborations of the judgment motif and his constant invocation of penalty, for instance, we feel the fresh religious experience of the early church animating and validating these. . . .

Examination of Jesus' teaching permits us to catch in the moment of transition this tendency we have indicated to pass from one type of sanction to the other. Jesus says: do so and so because such and such is the evident nature of man, the world and God. But such a grounding of ethical choice and conduct, if in the least developed, seems immediately to involve a reflection upon consequences of conduct in a world where the realities are such as Jesus describes. But *consequences are most naturally conceived in the light of rewards and punishments among those for whom the personal rule of God is so much an axiom. By these stages we thus pass from the sphere of essential sanction to that of retributive sanction, and from disinterested or impulsive virtue to calculative virtue.* Jesus himself and the people to whom he talked were not dialectical enough to raise the issue discussed in the *Republic* as to disinterested virtue. The rabbis indeed warned against obedience for the sake of reward.

But the Jewish mind as we have seen conceived of right conduct as obedience to the will of a gracious Jahweh, and intrinsic and extrinsic sanctions were confused and mingled.

Jesus' essential appeal to the nature of God and man and their relation as the ground of his ethical demands led, then, immediately to the envisagement of consequences as a further sanction. . . .

In fact, any appeal to reason and conscience like that of Jesus necessarily evokes a moral order in which consequences are patent and inescapable. It was a reminder that the nature of man, the world and God and their relation were such and such, and that this nature demanded such and such attitudes and actions, and penalized the actions of folly and blindness. Such insight into moral consequences is found in the Old Testament in various forms. Sometimes we find it, here in the least developed stage, in the form of a wise aphorism, like the many found in the Wisdom Literature, where merely the natural this-worldly consequences of conduct are pointed out. Jesus' saying concerning those that take the sword falls in this class. Not far from it are such sayings as, "Blessed are the merciful for they shall obtain mercy," and "With what measure ye mete, it shall be measured to you again." Similarly with the parable of the two builders. In such ethical teaching, the appeal to the moral sense and moral insight has compelled recognition of the moral order conditioning conduct. Then, at a deeper stage of insight, this merely sapiential sanction, a discernment of natural and social consequences, begins to pass over into a truly religious sanction, a discernment of divine retributions. The important reality conditioning conduct is now the majestic God of righteousness. The further step is when this sanction becomes dramatized and perhaps eventually dogmatized in a scheme of eschatological rewards and punishments. . . .

The portrayal of divine reward and punishment is, therefore, inevitable for the religious consciousness when it is in any degree ethicized. . . .

As regards the sanction of the ethics, Jesus' teaching concerning the future is by no means of first importance. The announcements of rewards and punishments may be ubiquitous and highly colored; certainly Mt. has lent this motive to righteousness more weight than the other gospels. Yet this should not blind us to the fact that even in this gospel the fundamental motives are religious-prophetic. What Sevenster says of the synoptic gospels generally is true here: "We can conclude then that by far the larger portion of the synoptic ethics brings no interim ethics, not even eschatologically conditioned ethics, but common religious ethics." . . .[13]

Our first part has dealt with the sanction aspect of the relation of eschatology to ethics. We have to turn now to an even more significant aspect. How did the eschatological conception affect the content and nature of the ethics, if at all? Does Jesus call for a different righteousness, and if so, how is it related to the conception of the end?

In the first section we have assumed that eschatology meant an event still in the future. As long as we thus confine ourselves to the thought of the coming Judgment with its rewards and penalties, our problem is comparatively simple. The coming event is, then, motive for repentance and for urgency in doing righteousness, and the particular demands are looked on as conditions of entrance to the future Kingdom. If this were all, the problem would be much simplified. Then the Baptist and Jesus would be prophetic exponents of the law in its inner meaning, calling the nation to prepare itself by righteousness for the coming day of Jehovah.

But . . . the eschatology taught by Jesus . . . includes elements anterior to the parousia [second coming of Christ] and Judgment. The eschatological period begins with the proclamation of the Baptist and the work of Jesus, and goes on through the death and resurrection of the latter to the coming of the Son of Man. . . .

This fact presents us with a new aspect of the relation of eschatology to ethics and opens up an essentially different problem. The eschatological period is already present. It is now not the sanction of the ethical teaching that is in question, but its very content. How is the ethic affected by the fact of the present eschatological situation? This new situation is constituted by the presence of the Kingdom in its first and humbler manifestation, with its accompanying benefits and powers, and by the activity of Jesus, whose humble role was none the less closely related to the coming of the Son of Man in power. In these circumstances it is not surprising to find that a correspondently modified ethic is taught. . . .

We take it that it is not an interim ethic. The new situation is not *essentially* characterized by the fact that it is a respite before the terrors of the Judgment. The new situation is rather the anticipated time of

---

[13] G. Sevenster, *Ethiek en Eschatologie in de Synoptische Evangelien* (Leiden, 1929), p. 195.

salvation in which men are no longer hard-hearted, in which they become God's sons in a full sense, receive forgiveness on the occasion of the Great Repentance, know the Spirit, and recognize the overthrow of Satan and the demons. It is the time in which God is enacting his great deliverance, and in which he is drawing near to men in a way he had not done since the time of Moses, and is making a new covenant with them, not as the covenant which he made with them in the time of Moses, which they had broken. The feature that Jesus is present as herald of this gospel, and as central evidence of this new situation, is subsidiary to the main fact of God's action.

Thus the ethic is not an interim ethic. It is not even a repentance ethic in the sense of an extreme renunciation or asceticism as penance for the emergency. It *is* a repentance ethic in the sense that it calls for "fruits worthy of repentance," i.e., conduct evidencing the changed disposition. Rather, it can be best designated as an ethic of the present Kingdom of God or a new-covenant ethic. It is not primarily an ethic for the relations and conduct of the future transcendental Kingdom. Nor is it a Kingdom ethic in the sense that its practice would admit to the Kingdom nor that it would "build" the Kingdom. It is a Kingdom ethic in the sense that it represents the righteousness of those living in the days of the new covenant and empowered and qualified by the reconciliation and redemption of that age.

But what of the transcendental Kingdom? It is true that Jesus taught that the new era is to have its all-important manifestation in a supernatural way: advent of the Son of Man, Judgment and the miraculously instituted Kingdom. And it is true that Jesus cast his ethic, with the repentance it involves, in the form of entrance conditions to that Kingdom. The point is, *the conception of that eschatological culmination so partook of the nature of myth or poetry that it did not other than formally determine the ethic.* The conception of the Judgment and the supernatural rewards, including the Kingdom, stand to Jesus and to the community as *representations,* with full validity and credibility, indeed, of the unprophesiable, unimaginable but certain, God-determined future. This future and God's action in it lend immense weight and urgency to their present moral responsibility. Yet this temporal imminence of God is but a function of his spiritual imminence, and it is this latter which really determines conduct. It is not a dualistic other-worldliness that meets us in Jesus' inattention to property, family ties and citizenship, but a selective valuation and a particular focus of concern consequent upon immediate confrontation with God. The sense of the divinely determined future, however apocalyptically it may be formulated, does not in actual fact put an end to the this-worldly concern of Jesus and the church. Reserves may be made for the evidences of true interim phenomena of the early church, but these are not typical. The radical character of Jesus' ethics does not spring from the shortness of the time but from the new relation to God in the time of salvation. The sanction for it is not the sanction of imminent supernatural retributions—except formally—but the appeal to the God-enlightened moral discernment recognizing the nature and will of God and inferring consequences (thence eschatologically dramatized).

What these ethics were we can only suggest. Jesus virtually supersedes the law by the lengths he goes in appealing to its deeper principles. We can see that the dispute as to whether he did or did not overthrow the law is ambiguous. Many scribes exercised their judgment in discriminating the weightier or more central demands of the law; and it can well be said that Jesus upheld by saying and act the word of God in the law. But we are satisfied to rest the case for his *virtual setting aside of the law on the degree of independent interpretation he exercises. He goes so far beyond such scribes in matters of emphasis and spirit that the difference in degree becomes a difference in kind,* and confirmation of this is found in the attitude to him of the scribes and Pharisees.

Going on we note further as to the ethics that Jesus goes back to the great principles of the prophets, judgment, mercy and truth, but he sees these in a religious background different from that of the prophets, namely, his new portrayal of the nature of God. The ethics are conceived as responses to the nature of God, along emphatically positive lines. God's generosity, his forgiveness become determinative. Purity, sincerity and unreserved devotion answer all to another main aspect of his religious conception, the fact of such full sonship as implies immediate relation of obedience and response. The full personal will of the individual is therefore in play. ... Ethics is now unqualifiedly the relation of the heart to God, person to Person, and this is ever present and controlling in the relation of man to man.

The ethical demand in the teaching of Jesus and its eschatological dramatization do not seem to have been directed toward the entire population of Palestine. Both were representative of the rural population of northern Palestine, a group without the social, economic, and political power of the Jerusalem nobility. The following selection examines the agrarian background of the eschatology and ethics of Jesus.

THE AGRARIAN FOCUS OF NEW TESTAMENT ETHICS
F. C. Grant[14]

The "ethics" of the gospel are Jewish through and through. Not that they are identical with those of the Pharisees, or of any one Pharisaic teacher; Jesus was an individual, and unique. The ethics of Jesus are, in fact, agrarian—whereas, ... those of the Pharisees were mainly urban. But the background of Judaism as a whole, especially as it is reflected in the Old Testament, was agarian, and had been so for a thousand years; before that, it had been nomadic—anything but urban. The unworkableness or "impracticality" (impracticability) of the gospel, of which so much is heard today, is true only in our overgrown urban and industrial society; in a purely rustic society like that of most of Galilee in the first century the charge could not be made. ...

The agrarian background of Jesus' ethic (or what [has been] called the "patriarchal" background) is reflected even in the metaphors and similes that he used. In the selection from his teaching—sayings, parables, expositions of the Law, eschatological warnings, and "beatitudes" or macarisms —which Matthew gives in the Sermon on the Mount this is perfectly clear. The fig-

[14] From *An Introduction to New Testament Thought* by F. C. Grant, pp. 303, 307–309, 312–314, 316–317, 320. Copyright 1950 by Pierce and Smith. Used by permission of Abingdon Press.

ures of speech, the examples selected, the persons addressed by the Teacher all belong to the Galilean village or countryside: the tasteless salt flung into the street, the single lamp that lights up the whole house, the village blasphemer with his string of oaths and terms of abuse, the temple pilgrim setting out with his one gift to present before the altar, the village judge and the jailor, the local ruffian and hoodlum swift to strike, the king's man or garrison trooper who compels the peasant to carry his baggage or to yield up his mantle, the sinner's field wet with the same rain that falls on his righteous neighbor's, the local tax collector, the birds of the air and the lilies of the field (the bright anemones springing up in profusion beside the country lane), the child crying to be fed, the fruitful trees and the unfruitful, the two housebuilders, one wise and one foolish. There is nothing here about kings and their councils, let alone parliaments and assemblies; nothing about armies and tribute, not even about the Roman army of occupation in Palestine, and the question of submission to this invasion and denial of the theocratic rule assumed in the Torah; nothing about civil or criminal law, the administration of government, the function of courts, the rights of the people, the duties of statesmen and administrators, the merits of various constitutions! Aristotle would have been greatly puzzled by these chapters, supposing he had thought them worthy of examination.

Jesus was no philosopher investigating the logical bases of ethics, or endeavoring to work out a system which should be applicable to all men everywhere, in every age, under whatever conditions of society, of political organization or of economic order, might then prevail. Instead he was carrying on the tradition of biblical ethics, enriching, deepening, and "completing" the teaching of the Law and the prophets (Matt. 5:17). The biblical ethics, as we have seen, was fundamentally agrarian, not urban, with many surviving traces of nomadic ethics. It was among the "poor of the land" that he lived and worked. His trade of "carpenter" not only was that of builder ... but also included that of smith, joiner, and village artisan.... By trade and vocation, and also by his own interest, he was associated with agricultural life. The farms and meadows of Galilee were not in some remote region, but came up to the edge of the village; thus the village was in closest contact with rural life. The same outlook was found, for the most part, in the older elements of the wisdom tradition as it circulated in Judaism—as it had circulated, in fact, for two thousand years or more throughout Egypt and the Near East, an international fund of ethical lore. It is significant that the subject matter of Jesus' ethical teaching is identical with that of the Jewish wisdom teachers, and of the early scribes....

The fundamentally agrarian outlook of the Old Testament, of Judaism, and of Jesus is found also in the apocalyptic literature and its traditions. The very language of the apocalyptic hope is rural, and the conceptions of coming bliss are the reverse of conditions now prevailing. (*a*) The calendar has gone wrong, in Enoch (I En. 80:2–8), as was natural and inevitable since twelve lunar months do not make a solar year. But the grave seriousness of the situation was not apparent in the cities, where the traders with their goods and their contracts carried on as usual; the real crisis faced the farmer, for the seasons were awry, the harvest now came when the seeding should begin, and the festivals (still basically agricultural) were all at the wrong time of year. Something had gone wrong in the heavens—the moon had slowed down, or the stars were slipping from their accustomed courses! This was surely a naïve, rustic explanation; a little astronomy, and an intercalary month, could have cured the trouble—and did cure it, in due course, when the added month was more scientifically devised and made official—not in the country but at Jerusalem. So likewise (*b*) with the pictures of imagined bliss in the Age to Come; these are fundamentally agrarian, and the reverse of the conditions now prevalent. Instead of poor harvests, abundance; instead of blight, murrain, and mildew, sound ears in every sheaf; instead of a brief, toilsome life for the tillers of the soil, a long life, like that of the patriarchs, or even that of the men of old who lived before the Flood; instead of painful childbearing, and the hazards of infancy, and barren wedlock—fatal to the countryman —there would be abundance of offspring, born without pain, and maturing with amazing health and vigor. The crops, the herds, the flocks would all exemplify the changed conditions. And instead of war, that ancient curse to the dweller on the soil, who was always the first to suffer from invasion and pillage, peace would prevail over the whole earth. It takes no great gift of imagination to understand the conditions of life among those who dreamed these dreams, or to interpret their vision of the blissful future as the compensating reversal of present ills in the great age about to come.

The ethics which accompany these agrarian dreams are the traditional rustic virtues with their usual sanctions and imperatives—as old as the Egyptian moralists, or Hesiod, or the oldest portions of Proverbs, or the still older ethical elements in the popular traditions underlying the Old Testament as a whole. This was not a scientific, philosophical ethics, but popular, age-old and fundamentally religious: Do good and you will prosper, because God is in control of things! Or, if you are not prospering, find out what is wrong; examine your ways and your doings! This message the prophets had driven home to their contemporaries through century after century. But the apocalyptists opened up still another alternative—nature itself might be under a curse. Their clue they found in the verse of Genesis, "Cursed is the ground for thy sake"—for man's sake, or perhaps on account of the demons (3:17). Then pray God that the demons may speedily be vanquished and his world brought back to its original, pristine state as soon as possible! Or pray that he will soon take his great power and reign, and establish the New Age at once—"in your days, in the days of your children" as the familiar synagogue prayer phrased it! The precise "time of the end" was variously calculated, by "weeks of years," or by decades, or in other ways; but the basic and dominant character of all apocalyptic was the reversal, or the abolition, of the present world order and the inauguration of one completely under the control of the divine sovereignty. . . .

Jesus widens the idea of God's kingdom to include many who were looked upon as hopeless outcasts by the religious authorities of his day. He may even have drawn a wider circle—the evidence shows that he did so, on occasion—to include devout pagans and heathen. . . . The new messianic community, the group specially devoted to preparation for the coming of God's kingdom, had its own requirements, some of which were stricter and more severe than those of ordinary Judaism. To the scandal of the scribes, he insisted that family loyalty might have to yield to a higher loyalty to the kingdom of God (Luke 14:26). At the same time he stressed care of parents in the face of certain *ex parte* rules (e.g. Corban, Mark 7:9–13) which absolved sons from the care of their dependent fathers or mothers. . . . Yet over all the sayings of the gospel—even over such sayings as "How hard it will be for those who have riches to enter the kingdom!" (Mark 10:23–27), "Sell all that you have, . . . and come, follow me" (Mark 10:21), "He who loves father or mother more than me is not worthy of me" (Matt. 10:37)—over all these sayings with their implied duties of renunciation and sacrifice stands the gracious assurance, "Fear not, little flock, for it is your Father's good pleasure to *give* you the kingdom" (Luke 12:32). This is the heart of Jesus' ethics, and the mainspring or central motive of all his revision, re-interpretation, or re-emphasis of the traditional round of duties. If the kingdom and its requirements are superior to the ties and duties of kindred, family, and home, it is only because the kingdom is itself a more perfect family, the reign of God our Father. . . .

Associated with this religious-ethical attitude is a whole group of virtues: humility, single-mindedness, sincerity, honesty, responsiveness, purity of heart, poverty in spirit, peaceableness, generosity, readiness to forgive, contentedness, trust in God, mildness of speech, restraint in judgment, nonresentment, love of neighbor, and love even of enemies. The whole round of terms descriptive of the character requisite in those who are to enter God's kingdom (the new "righteousness" of the Sermon on the Mount) is derived mainly from the Old Testament and the old Jewish piety; what is distinctive is the selection, the emphasis, and the setting—that is, in relation to the approaching kingdom. True, Jesus had nothing to say to the judge on the bench or the Roman procurator or the tax collector about their duties. Jesus was concerned with the men he knew, in the circle of their environment, faced with their problems and responsibilities. He lived among the lowly, the *am ha-aretz*, the "people of the land," and to them he devoted himself—"the lost sheep of the house of Israel" (Matt. 15:24; cf. 10:6).

STUDY QUESTIONS

1. In what ways was Christianity a revitalization movement? Was it successful?

2. What did Jesus mean to that portion of the early Christian community reflected in the Gospel of Matthew? Was Jesus seen as a heavenly Messiah, a prophet announcing the Last Days, or a new lawgiver, a second Moses?

3. Do eschatology and apocalypticism have an ethic inherent within them?

4. Was Jesus' eschatology apocalyptic or anti-apocalyptic? To what degree

or in what way did Jewish apocalyptic thinking, as seen in the Essene community, contribute to the teachings of Jesus?

5. Is the ethic of the Sermon on the Mount radically different from that given in the Decalogue? How does it relate to the ethical teaching of the prophets? What concept of the will and conscience is operative here, if any?

6. To what degree is the ethic of the Sermon on the Mount shaped by an eschatological worldview? Is that ethic valid apart from the eschatology, that is, is it a realistic ethic for one who does not believe in the imminent end of the world? Does an ethic based on an extreme eschatology disintegrate when the eschatology begins to fade or continues to be unrealized?

7. What is the effect of eschatology on the content of ethics? In what ways does eschatology determine "what" one is to do? What does "right action" mean according to the ethic of the Sermon on the Mount? What does the term righteous mean in the teaching of Jesus? Is its content identical with the Old Testament concept of righteousness?

8. What is the effect of eschatology on the retributive ethical sanctions, on the motivation for ethical action? In what ways does eschatology determine "why" one should do such and such? Is the sanction of the ethics in the teaching of Jesus the fear of eternal damnation, the promise of an eternal reward in the form of a compensatory share in the new age about to dawn, or an altruistic response to a realization of God's love?

9. What does "being saved" mean in the teaching of Jesus, and what must one do to be "saved"? Does salvation act as a retributive sanction for ethical action, or is the ethical action the result of disinterested love for God, born out of belonging to a community that automatically guarantees salvation?

10. To what degree is the ethic of Jesus an individualistic ethic? Does Jesus call for corporate righteousness or individual salvation? If the demand of God is directed toward the individual, is this unique in Jesus' teaching or is it a development of the period?

11. Is the ethic of the Sermon on the Mount a general ethic or is it directed toward an agrarian community as opposed to urban? If the ethic is agrarian, how is it applicable for a nonagrarian world?

12. Does Jesus teach absolute precepts governing ethical behavior in any situation, or is ethical behavior determined by the particular situation in which it must operate? Is the ethic absolute or situational?

13. Is the ethic of the Sermon on the Mount impossible and harmful, or is it the highest ethical achievement of mankind? Would the wholesale adoption of the Christian ethic bring in a utopian world? Specifically, is the commandment to love one's enemies the heart of the "Christian" ethic and, if so, can it really be implemented?

14. What merit, if any, lies in the observation of Nietzsche that the ethical system of Christianity, which accords highest value to the poor, the weak, the lowly, the sick, and the suffering, and condemns wealth, power, prestige, and physical strength, was devised by the "priestly" nation of the Jews as a revenge

against their enemies, the strong and aristocratic elements of society? Has Western culture suffered for two millenniums under what Nietzsche termed "this Jewish transvaluation" or "the revolt of the slaves"?

For those who have used The Contribution of Ancient Greece *edited by Jacqueline Strain:*

15. In what ways is the ethical teaching of Jesus related to that of Socrates or of Aristotle? In what ways does it differ?

The cross, the instrument of Jesus' death, quickly became the symbol of his sacrifice and victory over death. One of the earliest representations of the cross was found in the chapel of a villa belonging to a wealthy Roman in Herculaneum, a town buried by the eruption of Vesuvius in A.D. 79. (Rev. Raymond V. Schoder, S.J.)

CHAPTER 7

THE INSTITUTIONALIZATION OF CHARISMA AND THE TRANSFORMATION OF THE JUDEO-CHRISTIAN ETHIC:
Paul and the Early Church

[The increasing time-span between the Resurrection of Jesus and the Second-Coming] involves other factors than linear development. There is a change in the ethical emphasis. Whereas [immediately after the experience of the Resurrection] the cry was "repent" as though the very hour had arrived, now the ethical teaching became more concerned with day to day problems. It may not be amiss to assume that the great body of ethical teaching in the New Testament achieved its importance —hence its preservation in the context [of this later period]. This, of course, is not to say that eschatology had become more ethical, for eschatology was always ethical to the core.... But it does mean that as the "final hour" receded into a more indefinite and distant future, ethics became more concerned with practical living and less with last-minute preparation for judgment.

D. J. Selby, "Changing Ideas in the New Testament Eschatology," Harvard Theological Review, *L (1957), 34*

Christianity is sociologically understandable only in terms of community. What is the essence of the Christian doctrine, if we strip it of all accessories? Surely this: that the clan of Adam fell through the sin of Adam, as the clan of Ham fell through the sin of Ham; in other words, that by dint of the fundamental and indissoluble unity of the social whole, the fate of one is the fate of all. And further: that the family of Christ, incorporated in the Church, rose through the merits of Christ, the new Adam, because the deed of one is in its effects the salvation of all. Take away the basic ontology of community, and the doctrine dissolves: keep to that ontology, and all difficulties of the faith vanish. In the Christian religion which conceives all men as one lineage, bound together for better and worse, bound together both in sin and salvation, the principle of community has found its finest incarnation.

Werner Stark, "The Sociology of Knowledge and the Problem of Ethics," Transactions of the Fourth World Congress of Sociology, *Milan, 1959 (Louvain, 1961), Vol. IV, p. 91.*

212   Paul and the Early Church

> A new commandment I give to you, that you love one another; even as I have loved you, that you also love one another. By this all men will know that you are my disciples, if you have love for one another.
>
> *John 13:34–35*

A group of those most closely associated with Jesus during his lifetime remained in and around Jerusalem after his death, in spite of the scandal of his crucifixion as a criminal guilty of blasphemy for messianic pretensions and under the threat of further repression from the political and religious leaders of Jewish society. In the days and weeks following the crucifixion, there

The Sign of the Cross with the alpha and omega on a tomb, *ca.* first century A.D., discovered at St. Bertrand de Cominges, France. (Boudot-Lamotte)

developed a strong sense of Jesus' continuing presence amid his followers, born of their belief in his resurrection from the dead, increased by his appearances to various disciples, and finally confirmed through an intense awareness of a "spirit" that so enriched their sense of community and mission that this small group of disciples began to attract a committed and ever-increasing following.

The culminating event that gave the disciples the impetus to spread the "gospel" of their Lord, the "good news" that the Kingdom had arrived, came at the Jewish Feast of Weeks, fifty days after the second day of Passover. At the celebration of this feast, known as Pentecost, the disciples became aware of an intense spirit within the group, which they identified as the Holy Spirit. This Spirit became the essential sign of the life-force of the Christian community, and Pentecost, the day on which the gift of the Spirit was received, was looked back on as the birthday of the Church.

The event of the Kingdom's arrival, confirmed for the disciples by the resurrection of Jesus and

Early Christian symbols of fish and cross, *ca.* first to third century A.D. (Boudot-Lamotte)

the gift of the Spirit, became the message that not only transformed them into missionary apostles or evangelists but transformed the meaning of—and thus their memory of—the years of discipleship with Jesus that had preceded these events. From the very beginning the message of the apostles was an interpretation of historical event and religious experience. The needs and experiences of the early Church in the years and decades following Pentecost further transformed the belief and ethic of the Christian community. As we have seen, the Gospel of Matthew already cast the person and message of Jesus in legal terms, and while some justification for this may have existed within the teaching of Jesus, this tendency to make the message a prescriptive and practicable law was amplified by the early Church. The Church expanded and elevated the view of Jesus as the Christ or Messiah, understanding his role and message increasingly in terms of law, ignoring or reinterpreting the more difficult aspects of the ethic, and amplifying the reward motif. Such a transformation was not sudden; it was a slow process that developed across the first centuries of Christianity.

The change that took place in Christianity in terms of religious belief and ethical action was only part of a larger process whereby a small eschatological community became an established Church, a process which took centuries to complete and which progressed at different rates at various levels of society and in various geographical areas. The process by which a charismatic movement becomes institutionalized so that it develops a bureaucracy and a prescribed system of doctrine and ritual, is considered by sociologists to be an inevitable step that ensures the preservation of the community. Such a process has been termed the "routinization of charisma," that is, a process by which the charismatic inspiration and leadership of the movement becomes rationalized or traditionalized so as to protect and perpetuate the group in a predictable manner. Some aspects of this process are considered in the following selection.

The Institutionalization of Religion
Thomas F. O'Dea[1]

In the first or charismatic period in the development of founded religions, usually to be seen in the relationship between a charismatic leader and his disciples, the motivation of the active participants tends to be characterized by considerable single-mindedness. The religious movement does satisfy complex needs for its adherents, but such needs are focused upon religious values as these are proclaimed and embodied by the charismatic leader. With institutionalization, however, an important innovation is introduced.

Institutionalization involves a stable set of statuses and roles, defined in terms of functions, upon which are encumbent rights and obligations. There arises a structure of offices which involves a stratified set of rewards in terms of prestige, life opportunities, and material compensations.

This process is clearly to be observed in the emergence of specifically religious organizations. The stable structure which thus develops becomes capable of eliciting a wide range of individual motives and of focusing diverse motivations behind the goals of the organization as specified in prescribed role behavior. This process has the strategic functional significance of providing stability, since the organization no longer has to depend upon disinterested motivation. Institutionalization mobilizes behind institutionalized expectations . . . both disinterested and interested

[1] Thomas F. O'Dea, *The Sociology of Religion,* © 1966, pp. 91–95. Reprinted by permission of Prentice-Hall, Inc., Englewood Cliffs, New Jersey.

motivation. However, this mobilization of a variety of motives in support of the goals and values of the organization can, and often does, result in the subtle transformation of the goals and values themselves. When a professional clergy emerges in the church, there comes into existence a body of men for whom the clerical life offers not simply the "religious" satisfactions of the earlier charismatic period, but also prestige and respectability, power and influence, in both church and society, and satisfactions derived from the use of personal talents in teaching, leadership, etc. Moreover, the *maintenance* of the situation in which these rewards are forthcoming tends to become an element in the motivation of the group.

[There are] . . . numerous examples of the kinds of changes which such developments introduce into the church and the way that they affect the relationship of the church and society. The higher clergy in Christian history became important functionaries and dignitaries in society, with all the rewards and benefits accruing to people in such positions. The higher clergy, in terms of both church office and of non-ecclesiastical governmental functions, became part of the ruling and dominant classes in society, and their interests fused with those of such classes. These new interests of the clergy often deviated from the goals and values of the church. The church was transformed in a subtle way. It became secularized; the clergy became "worldly." Since it is the clergy who interpret the church's teachings, these come to be understood and applied in ways which tend to express and maintain the interests of the clerical stratum itself. Thus while mixed motivation, introduced by institutionalization, enhances stability and contributes to the survival of the organization, it also represents a source of serious transformation in the goals and values of the church.

This development of mixed motivation is most significant with respect to leadership roles, but it is to be seen in the rank and file as well. As "born members" replaced people who had been converted, a different kind of motivation and identification came to prevail in the church. As the laity became a more passive element in the church, lay people tended to develop a different kind of identification, and their motives for participation changed as well. Already in the second century there appears a prophetic literature denouncing the resulting lukewarmness of many in the church. . . .

To retain the original experience, with its supraempirical relation to the ultimate and the sacred, it must be given expression in symbolic forms which are themselves empirical and profane, and which with repetition become prosaic and everyday in character. Hence the use of symbols in order to make possible . . . apprehensions of the sacred can be a first step in routinization. . . .

Ritual is expressive in a logical rather than a psychological sense. Ritual represents an objectified order of symbols which elicits and articulates attitudes and feelings, molding the personal dispositions of the worshipers after its own model. This objectification is a requisite for continuity, and for sharing within the religious group. Without such objectification and sharing, collective worship would be impossible. . . .

The routinization of charisma often gives rise to formal organization with bureaucratic structure. New offices tend to develop as new functions arise. Moreover, precedents established in action lead to a transformation of existing offices. The general contours of the administrative structure tend to reflect the problems and functions in response to which the structure developed. There are several factors which tend to render such bureaucratic structures disfunctional. Structures which emerge in one set of conditions and in response to one set of problems may turn out later to be unwieldly instruments for handling new problems under new conditions. Functional precedents established in handling earlier problems can become disfunctional in later situations, and can even become formidable obstacles blocking any forthright action. . . .

To affect the lives of men, the original religious message must be stated in terms that have relevance to the everyday activities and concerns of people. Moreover, to preserve the import of the message, it must be protected against interpretations which would transform it in ways conflicting with its inner ethos. These needs are characteristic of both the religious message and the ethic implied in it. Both of these needs constitute a strong pressure for definition. Thus in the history of the Christian church we see a continual process in which doctrine is defined in response to interpretations felt to be heretical. Moreover, with respect to the Christian ethic, it was soon found that its implications had to be spelled out in some detail for the new converts made among the gentiles. This involved both the utilization of elements of Hebraic law—the Ten Commandments, especially, . . . and the natural law of Greek philosophy, especially as formulated by the Stoics. Such definition was also a process of concretization, and it was a functional necessity without which the church could hardly have maintained its religious insights and its organizational integrity.

This process of definition and concretization is at the same time a relativization of the religious and ethical message—a rendering of it relevant to the new circumstances of life of the religious group—and therefore involves the risk of making everyday and prosaic what was originally a call to the extraordinary. Moreover, implications drawn in concrete form under particular circumstances may come to be accepted in a literalist manner, in which the original scope of the implications of the religious message may be lost. The problem may be seen quite clearly in the sphere of the religious ethic. The original ethical insight is translated into a set of rules to bring it within the grasp of new converts. These rules give the original ethical insight a kind of "operational definition" comprehensible to the average man. Yet rules, however elaborate they may become, cannot make explicit all that was implied in the original insight itself, and run the risk of losing its spirit. Rules specify, and thereby substitute for the original insight specific items of prescribed or proscribed behavior. Thus there can develop a complicated set of legalistic formulations.

The transformation of Christianity through the routinization of charisma and the accompanying changes in religious and ethical thinking were stimulated initially by the delay in the total entrance of the Kingdom of God into history, an entrance that was understood as the return of the "Son of Man" and the destruction of the present world. The delay in the return of Christ to fulfill the eschatological Kingdom necessitated a moral code covering the aspects of daily life that had previously seemed insignificant under the threat of the final holocaust. As was pointed out in Chapter 6, the ethic of Jesus provided some foundation for this "revision," since it was not conditioned solely by the sanctions of reward and punishment that accompanied the imminent Kingdom. Certain aspects of that ethic seemed applicable to a non-eschatological age. Nor, on the other hand, did the Christian Church throughout its history completely forsake the eschatological hope in Christ's return. However, a shift in ethical motivation did take place as the eschatological expectations faded.

While there was always a ready explanation for the delay in Christ's second coming, the nature of the Christian community was undergoing continual change which made it increasingly unnecessary to explain that delay. While Christianity first spread among the Jews in Palestine and other areas of the Near East, by the middle of the first century it began to attract Gentiles who did not share the Jewish apocalyptic tradition out of which Christianity emerged, and were not motivated toward so strong an eschatological hope. This shift, perhaps the most important one in the life of the early Church, grew out of the very missionary zeal with which the first disciples and apostles spread the message of the advent of the Kingdom. The following selection describes this transition from a Jewish sect centered in Jerusalem to a Gentile religion known throughout the Roman Empire.

THE SPREAD OF CHRISTIANITY INTO THE NON-JEWISH WORLD
Kenneth Scott Latourette[2]

The complete story of the spread of Christianity in its first five centuries cannot be told, for we do not possess sufficient data to write it.... The documents which have been preserved make much of the spread of the faith from the church in Jerusalem and especially of the missionary labours of Paul. It was natural that the initial centre of Christianity should be in Jerusalem. Here was the geographic focus of Judaism. Here Jesus had been crucified and raised from the dead, and here, at his express command, the main nucleus of his followers had waited until the Pentecost experience brought them a compelling dynamic. Peter was their acknowledged spokesman, but before many years, presumably as his missionary travels carried him ever more frequently away from Jerusalem, James the brother of Jesus became the head of the community.... To their neighbours these early followers of Jesus, for they did not yet bear the distinctive designation of Christian, must have appeared another sect of Judaism, predominantly Galilean in membership, distinguished from other Jews by their belief that Jesus was the Messiah and by their expectation of the early return of their Lord. Their leader, James, appears to have been especially conservative in his loyalty to Jewish customs. They continued to use the temple as a place of worship and observed the Jewish law, including its ceremonies, circumcision, and the dietary regulations. Even some of the Pharisees joined them. So far as we know, their numbers were recruited entirely from Jews and proselytes to Judaism....

Outstanding in carrying the faith into the non-Jewish, and especially the Hellenistic world was a Jew whose conversion is closely associated with the death of Stephen [the first Christian martyr]. This was Saul, or, to use the name by which he is best remembered, Paul. We know more about Paul than we do of any other Chris-

[2] From pp. 65, 67–69, 72–74, *A History of Christianity* by Kenneth Scott Latourette. Copyright 1953 by Harper & Row, Publishers, Incorporated.

tian of the first century. Not only does *The Acts of the Apostles* make him and his mission its main theme, but we also have, most fortunately, a number of his letters which give us intimate pictures of him. . . .

It is clear that Paul was of pure Jewish stock, that his father had that highly prized privilege, Roman citizenship, that the son was born and reared at Tarsus, a Hellenistic city in what we now call Asia Minor, a stronghold of Greek learning. However, far from conforming to the Greek pattern, Paul had been carefully nurtured in Phariseeism. While probably not highly educated in Greek philosophy and literature, he was thoroughly at home in the Greek language, did not use it crudely, and was steeped in the Septuagint, the famous Greek translation of the Jewish scriptures. He also knew Aramaic and his training in Phariseeism made him think naturally in the methods of interpreting the sacred books which were current in that school of thought. Ardent by disposition, the young Paul may have been all the more loyal and dogmatic in the strict adherence to the Jewish law and customs entailed by his Phariseeism because of his consciousness of the paganism which was all about him in Tarsus. As a youth he went to Jerusalem, the citadel of his religion, to study at the feet of Gamaliel, one of the outstanding teachers in Pharisaic circles. Here he came in touch with the followers of Jesus and joined in persecuting them. He stood by when Stephen was stoned and was sent to Damascus with letters from the high priest to the synagogues in that city with instructions to have arrested and brought to Jerusalem for trial those who were adherents of the Nazarene heresy.

While on his way to Damascus, just as he was nearing that city, Paul was smitten by a vision which changed his life. He believed that the risen Jesus appeared to him and spoke with him, and was convinced that the experience was as authentic as those which had earlier come to Peter, James, and the others. . . . The conviction came to Paul that his mission was to be to the Gentiles, the non-Jews. He was to be a pioneer. The universalism of the Gospel which may have been one of the causes of his original antagonism had gripped him. . . .

Paul gave his chief attention to cities [in Asia Minor, Macedonia, and Greece]. Much, perhaps most of the time he supported himself by working at his trade of tent-maker. He took satisfaction in not preaching where other men had preached and in not being dependent upon his converts for his livelihood. His was an arduous life. Celibate by conviction, Paul devoted himself entirely to his mission, untrammeled by family ties. We hear of his spending months in one or another of the larger centres. Much of the time he was travelling. He speaks of shipwreck, of perils from rivers and from robbers, of hunger and thirst, of beatings, and of being stoned. Upon him weighed the care of the many churches which he helped to bring into being. He kept in touch with them by oral messages and by letters. A few of the latter survive and give evidence of the white heat and the pressure under which they were written. Although possessing enormous vitality and astounding powers of endurance, Paul had some persistent physical or nervous weakness which he described as a "thorn in the flesh" and which was to him a heavy burden. He met with bitter opposition, not only from Jews and other non-

Christians, but also from other Christians and within some of the churches which he had nurtured. Yet after some years he could say that from Jerusalem as far as Illyricum, on the east coast of the Adriatic, he had "fully preached the Gospel of Christ."

Then came seeming disaster, and in an undertaking to which a sense of duty called him. For some time Paul had been gathering from his churches in the Gentile world a fund to give to the poor among the Christians in Jerusalem. He planned to go to Spain from Jerusalem, on the way visiting the Christians in Rome. It became clear that the mission to Jerusalem would be fraught with peril, for he was to be there at the Passover season and was regarded by many loyal Jews who would be flocking there at that high feast from many parts of the Empire as one who was threatening Judaism and the temple. Characteristically, Paul insisted on making the journey. While he was in the temple some Jews from Asia Minor who had been angered by what they had heard of his attitude towards Judaism aroused a tumult against him. A mob was seeking to kill him when the Roman guard intervened. There followed arrest, judicial hearings, detention of at least two years, an appeal by Paul to Caesar, as was his right as a Roman citizen, the journey to Rome under guard, a shipwreck in which the prisoner took command, the survival of himself and the ship's company, the completion of the journey, and a stay of at least two years in Rome, presumably still technically as a prisoner, but with considerable freedom to receive visitors and to present to them the Christian message. Then the curtain falls and assured information fails. The fact of eventual martyrdom in Rome seems to be well established.

The first stage in the spread of Christianity from an eschatological movement to an institutionalized Church was achieved by the apostle Paul. It was primarily Paul who took Christianity into the Greek-speaking communities of Asia Minor and Greece, and who founded churches whose strength and growth were crucial in the rapid spread of Christianity in that area, effecting within a few generations a geographical shift in power and leadership in the Church from Palestine to Asia Minor. Secondly, as part of that shift, Paul concentrated his efforts on the urban centers of Asia Minor and Greece, thus helping to effect a socioeconomic shift in the appeal of Christianity from the rural villages of Palestine to the commercial centers of the Greco-Roman world. Thirdly, by concentrating much of his time and energy on the Gentile populations of these centers, Paul aided in a shift in the composition of the Christian Church from Jewish to Gentile and, in doing so, unwittingly aided in the transformation of Christianity from a Jewish messianic sect to a separate, universal and institutionalized religion.

This last transformation was certainly never the intention of Paul who, although the self-proclaimed apostle to the Gentiles, was as Jewish in background and outlook as Peter or James. Far from separating himself from Judaism, Paul wished to incorporate the Gentiles into the realization of God's promise to the Jews and to give them their rightful place within the messianic kingdom. The ultimate inclusion of some Gentiles within the Promise of Yahweh was an accepted tradition within Judaism since Second Isaiah, and the conflict between Paul and the Church leaders at Jerusalem (Acts, chap. 15) was not whether the Gentiles should be included but when and on what terms.

The original Jewish content of much of Paul's thinking has been lost in the last nineteen hundred years as each generation interpreted his words according to their own particular needs. This is especially true of two contrasts which Paul continually makes, that between flesh and spirit and that between law and grace (or law and gospel). The terms flesh and spirit in Paul should not be understood in the Greek sense of body and soul. Paul, as a Hebrew, did not make such a distinction. Flesh and spirit should rather be taken as a distinction between the lower and higher motivations in the whole man, between what in rabbinic circles was called an evil impulse and a good impulse. Similarly, the second contrast is equally Jewish. By freedom from the law Paul did not mean freedom from the Decalogue but rather from the restrictions that accentuated Jewish exclusiveness such as circumcision and dietary laws. Grace, while expressing God's mercy, was for Paul the incorporation of a person into the Church, the mystical body of Christ. This is the meaning of Paul's statement to Christians: "You are not under law but under grace" (Rom. 6:14).

This emphasis on corporate unity is a theme that runs throughout the writings of Paul, and although it is reminiscent of—and in part derived from—the Old Testament concept of Yahweh's covenant with Israel, it represents a definite shift in emphasis in comparison with the teaching of Jesus. Jesus' call to righteousness was directed toward the individual and often urged him to forsake family and friends for the sake of his own salvation. The emphasis in Jesus on the fatherhood of God and the expression of love even toward strangers suggests that the Kingdom is to be something of a spiritual family, but this thought motif seems secondary to his call for individual righteousness and for individual commitment to Jesus' messiahship.

In the letters of Paul and in the Gospel of John, however, the emphasis is firmly on corporate unity, where all Christians belong to one body.

15. . . . [4]Abide in me, and I in you. As the branch cannot bear fruit by itself, unless it abides in the vine, neither can you, unless you abide in me. [5] I am the vine, you are the branches. He who abides in me, and I in him, he it is that bears much fruit, for apart from me you can do nothing. [6] If a man does not abide in me, he is cast forth as a branch and withers; and the branches are gathered, thrown into the fire and burned. [7] If you abide in me, and my words abide in you, ask whatever you will, and it shall be done for you. [8] By this my Father is glorified, that you bear much fruit, and so prove to be my disciples. . . .

[16] You did not choose me, but I chose you and appointed you that you should go and bear fruit and that your fruit should abide; so that whatever you ask the Father in my name, he may give it to you. [17] This I command you, to love one another.[3]

For Paul this sense of corporate unity is so strong that it is not undermined by the increasing rationalization and bureaucratization of the religion. In fact, Paul redefined the charismatic or spiritual gifts in such a way as to limit their unrestricted power and to underscore an increasing administrative diversification within the Church. The routinization of charisma and the development of rationalized leadership was justified by Paul by attributing to every office some charismatic power. Various functions within the life of the Church were ranked in order of importance, but the test of any office or function was its contribution to the health and welfare of the Church. It is in the context of his discussion of charisma and office that Paul outlines his view of the Church as a corporate unity, the body of Christ, in which all members are bound together by one spirit in the bond of love.

Paul's Concept of the Church[4]

12 . . . [4]Now there are varieties of gifts, but the same Spirit; [5] and there are varieties of service, but the same Lord; [6] and there are varieties of working, but it is the

---

[3] The Bible, John 15:4-8, 16-17.
[4] The Bible, I Cor. 12:4—14:40.

same God who inspires them all in every one. 7 To each is given the manifestation of the Spirit for the common good. 8 To one is given through the Spirit the utterance of wisdom, and to another the utterance of knowledge according to the same Spirit, 9 to another faith by the same Spirit, to another gifts of healing by the one Spirit, 10 to another the working of miracles, to another prophecy, to another the ability to distinguish between spirits, to another various kinds of tongues, to another the interpretation of tongues. 11 All these are inspired by one and the same Spirit, who apportions to each one individually as he wills.

12 For just as the body is one and has many members, and all the members of the body, though many, are one body, so it is with Christ. 13 For by one Spirit we were all baptized into one body—Jews or Greeks, slaves or free—and all were made to drink of one Spirit.

14 For the body does not consist of one

The mosaic in the vault of the crypt in the Church of Santa Costanza in Rome was allowed to remain when the building was adapted from pagan to Christian use. The motif of the vine and branches, expressive of the close association of Christ and his followers, became a symbolic image of the Church. Christians, therefore, had little difficulty in finding religious meaning in Bacchic representations of grape harvesting and wine making. (André Held, Paris)

A detail from the Sarcophagus of the Three Shepherds (end of the third century A.D.). The Good Shepherd of Paradise, often depicted on Christian sarcophagi alongside the Praying Soul (*Orans*) and True Philosophy, is placed here within the imagery of the vintage. (Boudot-Lamotte)

member but of many. 15 If the foot should say, "Because I am not a hand, I do not belong to the body," that would not make it any less a part of the body. 16 And if the ear should say, "Because I am not an eye, I do not belong to the body," that would not make it any less a part of the body. 17 If the whole body were an eye, where would be the hearing? If the whole body were an ear, where would be the sense of smell? 18 But as it is, God arranged the organs in the body, each one of them, as he chose. 19 If all were a single organ, where would the body be? 20 As it is, there are many parts, yet one body. 21 The eye cannot say to the hand, "I have no need for you," nor again the head to the feet, "I have no need of you." 22 On the contrary, the parts of the body which seem to be weaker are indispensable, 23 and those parts of the body which we think less honorable we invest with the greater honor, and our unpresentable parts are treated with greater modesty, 24 which our more presentable parts do not require. But God has so adjusted the body, giving the greater honor to the inferior part, 25 that there may be no discord in the body, but that the members may have the same care for one another. 26 If one member suffers, all suffer together; if one member is honored, all rejoice together.

27 Now you are the body of Christ and individually members of it. 28 And God has appointed in the church first apostles, second prophets, third teachers, then workers of miracles, then healers, helpers, administrators, speakers in various kinds of tongues. 29 Are all apostles? Are all prophets? Are all teachers? Do all work miracles? 30 Do all possess gifts of healing? Do all speak with tongues? Do all interpret? 31 But earnestly desire the higher gifts.

And I will show you a still more excellent way.

13 If I speak in the tongues of men and of angels, but have not love, I am a noisy gong or a clanging cymbal. 2 And if I have prophetic powers, and understand all mysteries and all knowledge, and if I have all faith, so as to remove mountains, but have not love, I am nothing. 3 If I give away all I have, and if I deliver my body to be burned, but have not love, I gain nothing.

4 Love is patient and kind; love is not jealous or boastful; 5 it is not arrogant or rude. Love does not insist on its own way; it is not irritable or resentful; 6 it does not rejoice at wrong, but rejoices in the right. 7 Love bears all things, believes all things, hopes all things, endures all things.

8 Love never ends; as for prophecy, it will pass away; as for tongues, they will cease; as for knowledge, it will pass away. 9 For our knowledge is imperfect and our prophecy is imperfect; 10 but when the perfect comes, the imperfect will pass away. 11 When I was a child, I spoke like a child, I thought like a child, I reasoned like a child; when I became a man, I gave up childish ways. 12 For now we see in a mirror dimly, but then face to face. Now I know in part; then I shall understand fully, even as I have been fully understood. 13 So faith, hope, love abide, these three; but the greatest of these is love.

14 Make love your aim, and earnestly desire the spiritual gifts, especially that you may prophesy. 2 For one who speaks in a tongue speaks not to men but to God; for no one understands him, but he utters mysteries in the Spirit. 3 On the other hand, he who prophesies speaks to men for their upbuilding and encouragement and consolation. 4 He who speaks in a tongue edifies himself, but he who prophesies edifies the church. 5 Now I want you all to speak in tongues, but even more to prophesy. He who prophesies is greater than he who speaks in tongues, unless some one

interprets, so that the church may be edified.

6 Now, brethren, if I come to you speaking in tongues, how shall I benefit you unless I bring you some revelation or knowledge or prophecy or teaching? 7 If even lifeless instruments, such as the flute or the harp, do not give distinct notes, how will anyone know what is played? 8 And if the bugle gives an indistinct sound, who will get ready for battle? 9 So with yourselves; if you in a tongue utter speech that is not intelligible, how will anyone know what is said? For you will be speaking into the air. 10 There are doubtless many different languages in the world, and none is without meaning; 11 but if I do not know the meaning of the language, I shall be a foreigner to the speaker and the speaker a foreigner to me. 12 So with yourselves; since you are eager for manifestations of the Spirit, strive to excel in building up the church.

13 Therefore, he who speaks in a tongue should pray for the power to interpret. 14 For if I pray in a tongue, my spirit prays but my mind is unfruitful. 15 What am I to do? I will pray with the spirit and I will pray with the mind also; I will sing with the spirit and I will sing with the mind also. 16 Otherwise, if you bless with the spirit, how can any one in the position of an outsider say the "Amen" to your thanksgiving when he does not know what you are saying? 17 For you may give thanks well enough, but the other man is not edified. 18 I thank God that I speak in tongues more than you all; 19 nevertheless, in church I would rather speak five words with my mind, in order to instruct others, than ten thousand words in a tongue.

20 Brethren, do not be children in your thinking; be babes in evil, but in thinking be mature. 21 In the law it is written, "By men of strange tongues and by the lips of foreigners will I speak to this people, and even then they will not listen to me, says the Lord." 22 Thus, tongues are a sign not for believers but for unbelievers, while prophecy is not for unbelievers but for believers. 23 If, therefore, the whole church assembles and all speak in tongues, and outsiders or unbelievers enter, will they not say that you are mad? 24 But if all prophesy, and an unbeliever or outsider enters, he is convicted by all, he is called to account by all, 25 the secrets of his heart are disclosed; and so, falling on his face, he will worship God and declare that God is really among you.

26 What then, brethren? When you come together, each one has a hymn, a lesson, a revelation, a tongue, or an interpretation. Let all things be done for edification. 27 If any speak in a tongue, let there by only two or at most three, and each in turn; and let one interpret. 28 But if there is no one to interpret, let each of them keep silence in church and speak to himself and to God. 29 Let two or three prophets speak, and let the others weigh what is said. 30 If a revelation is made to another sitting by, let the first be silent. 31 For you can all prophesy one by one, so that all may learn and all be encouraged; 32 and the spirits of prophets are subject to prophets. 33 For God is not a God of confusion but of peace.

As in all the churches of the saints, 34 the women should keep silence in the churches. For they are not permitted to speak, but should be subordinate, as even the law says. 35 If there is anything they desire to know, let them ask their husbands at home. For it is shameful for a woman to speak in church. 36 What! Did the word of God originate with you, or are you the only ones it has reached?

Paul and the Early Church 225

37 If any one thinks that he is a prophet, or spiritual, he should acknowledge that what I am writing to you is a command of the Lord. 38 If any one does not recognize this, he is not recognized. 39 So, my brethren, earnestly desire to prophesy, and do not forbid speaking in tongues; 40 but all things should be done decently and in order.

Order within community perhaps best summarizes Paul's view of the Christian life. The Church was to have the same order within a

The family unit retains its importance in the Christian Church. The bottom of this fourth-century A.D. glass bowl depicts a Christian marriage or betrothal scene. The inscription reads *Vivatis in Deo*, "May you live in God." (The Metropolitan Museum of Art, Rogers Fund, 1915)

community of love that typified the ideal family relationship for Paul. This emphasis on community and family is far stronger in Paul's letters than in the teaching of Jesus. Among those to whom Jesus preached, the corporate unity of the family was an accepted fact, and Jesus, especially in the areas of religion and ethics, appealed to a need for greater individual expression, even to the point of forsaking family. Paul, by contrast, seems to have responded to the needs of the urban society of Asia Minor and Greece, which called for a greater sense of community and family. The shift is dramatic. In Paul's letters the Kingdom had now become the Church, and discipleship received definition and regulation as the obligations incumbent upon a member of the "family of God" or the "body of Christ." This concept of the corporate unity of the family is basic to Paul's ethics.

The central emphasis is to be found in the idea of the church, which is the "family of

A fourth-century A.D. sarcophagus with a medallion of a Christian husband and wife, surrounded by scenes from the Old and New Testaments. (Boudot-Lamotte)

God," from whom every fatherhood—or family, *patria*—"in heaven and on earth is named" (Eph. 3:15); it is "the household of faith" (Gal. 6:10); it is the "body of Christ"—but Christians may be "members" of this body, as they are members of a family. And the duties that go with such membership are family duties, raised to a new and transcendent level. As Christ loved the church and gave himself up for it, so Christians must be prepared to lay down their lives—if that is required—"for the brethren" (Eph. 5:25; I John 3:16). All the way up to that high, heroic motive of utter love and self-abandonment the Christian scale of values in human conduct springs from this central idea of union and communion with Christ, who is "the head over all things for the church, which is his body, the fullness of him who fills all in all" (Eph. 1:22-23).

And yet rules are necessary, in human life, even in the transfigured life of the "family of God." Paul's converts probably needed more rules than he realized—and he gave them, in the end. The Gospels, especially Matthew, show how the sayings of the Lord were taken as rules, codified, classified, and given specific application. The "hortatory" parts of other New Testament writings reflect the same tendency, and need. All this was perfectly natural and inevitable, as the church grew into an institution separate from the synagogue.[5]

This corporate unity in which every person and every office finds a place is not restricted by Paul to the organization of the Church or the keeping of order within its meetings. For Paul, all men are bound together in such a way that both sin and righteousness can be transferred or inherited.

15 . . . [21] For as by a man came death, by a man has come also the resurrection of the dead. [22] For as in Adam all die, so also in Christ shall all be made alive.[6]

At the center of Paul's view of the unity within the Church as well as the unity of all mankind stands the figure of Christ whose death was a cosmic event reversing the course of history and whose presence after death expresses itself as the life-force of the Church. Paul's interest in the life and teachings of Jesus was minimal, at least as far as can be determined from his letters. His writings are dominated rather by the figure of the risen Christ, whose victory over death and ongoing activity were of ultimate importance both to the Church and to the world. Paul went far in shaping the Church's concentration on the Christ of faith, heightening the Christology and emphasizing the cosmic significance of Christ's death and resurrection.

5 . . . [16] From now on, therefore, we regard no one from a human point of view; even though we once regarded Christ from a human point of view, we regard him thus no longer. [17] Therefore, if any one is in Christ, he is a new creation; the old has passed away, behold, the new has come. [18] All this is from God, who through Christ reconciled us to himself and gave us the ministry of reconciliation; [19] that is, God was in Christ reconciling the world to himself, not counting their trespasses against them, and entrusting to us the message of reconciliation. [20] So we are ambassadors for Christ, God making his appeal through us. We beseech you on behalf of Christ, be reconciled to God. [21] For our sake he made him to be sin who knew no sin, so that in him we might become the righteousness of God.[7]

2 . . . [5] Have this mind among yourselves, which you have in Christ Jesus, [6] who, though he was in the form of God, did not count equality with God a thing to be grasped, [7] but emptied himself, taking the form of a servant, being born in the likeness of men.

---

[5] From *An Introduction to New Testament Thought* by F. C. Grant, pp. 317-318. Copyright 1950 by Pierce and Smith. Used by permission of Abingdon Press.

[6] The Bible, I Cor. 15:21-22.
[7] The Bible, II Cor. 5:16-21.

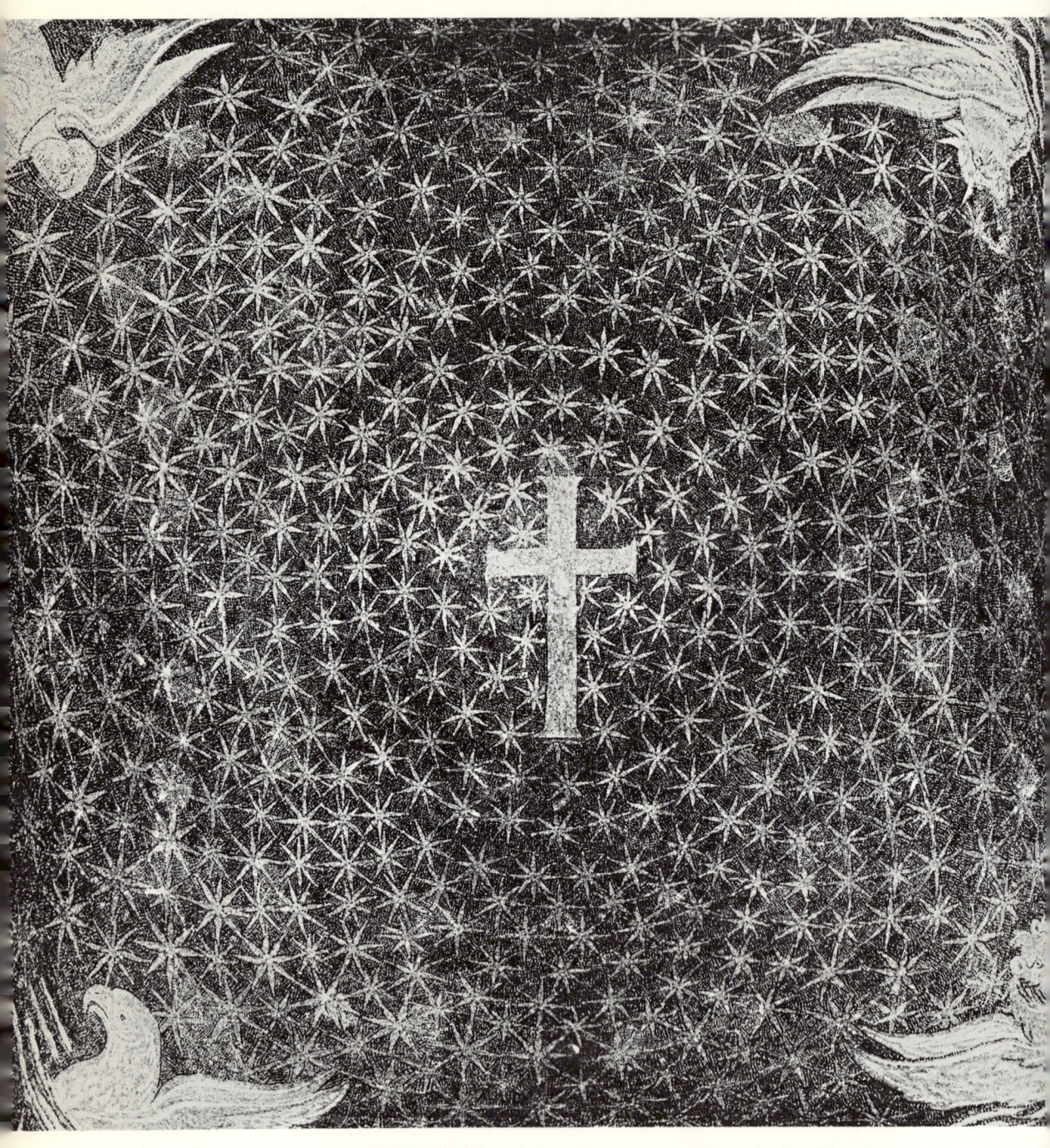

The centrality and cosmic importance of the empty cross was later depicted in many vault mosaics by placing the cross at the center of a starry heaven to represent Christ in Glory. One of the loveliest is the fifth-century cupola mosaic in the so-called mausoleum of Galla Placidia in Ravenna. (Alinari)

⁸And being found in human form he humbled himself and became obedient unto death, even death on a cross. ⁹ Therefore God has highly exalted him and bestowed on him the name which is above every name, ¹⁰ that at the name of Jesus every knee should bow, in heaven and on earth and under the earth, ¹¹ and every tongue confess that Jesus Christ is Lord, to the glory of God the Father.⁸

The corporate unity of mankind and the significance of the death of Christ for all history were given the fullest development by Paul in his letter to the Christians at Rome. Of all Paul's letters, the one to the Church at Rome is unique because it was written to a Church Paul had neither founded nor yet visited, and because it gives the fullest exposition of Paul's theology and ethics. Paul wrote the letter in preparation for his visit to Rome, as a means of introducing himself and his thought to the Christian community there. The letter represents the first consistent expression of Christian doctrine, one which deals with the nature and destiny of man within the plan of God.

PAUL'S LETTER TO THE ROMANS⁹

1 Paul, a servant of Jesus Christ, called to be an apostle, set apart for the gospel of God ² which he promised beforehand through his prophets in the holy scriptures, ³ the gospel concerning his Son, who was descended from David according to the flesh ⁴ and designated Son of God in power according to the Spirit of holiness by his resurrection from the dead, Jesus Christ our Lord, ⁵ through whom we have received grace and apostleship to bring about the obedience of faith for the sake of his name among all the nations, ⁶ including yourselves who are called to belong to Jesus Christ;

⁸ The Bible, Phil. 2:5–11.
⁹ The Bible, Rom, 1–8.

⁷ To all God's beloved in Rome, who are called to be saints:
Grace to you and peace from God our Father and the Lord Jesus Christ.
⁸ First, I thank my God through Jesus Christ for all of you, because your faith is proclaimed in all the world. ⁹ For God is my witness, whom I serve with my spirit in the gospel of his Son, that without ceasing I mention you always in my prayers, ¹⁰ asking that somehow by God's will I may now at last succeed in coming to you. ¹¹ For I long to see you, that I may impart to you some spiritual gift to strengthen you, ¹² that is, that we may be mutually encouraged by each other's faith, both yours and mine. ¹³ I want you to know, brethren, that I have often intended to come to you (but thus far have been prevented), in order that I may reap some harvest among you as well as among the rest of the Gentiles. ¹⁴ I am under obligation both to Greeks and to barbarians, both to the wise and to the foolish: ¹⁵ so I am eager to preach the gospel to you also who are in Rome.

¹⁶ For I am not ashamed of the gospel: it is the power of God for salvation to every one who has faith, to the Jew first and also to the Greek. ¹⁷ For in it the righteousness of God is revealed through faith for faith; as it is written, "He who through faith is righteous shall live."

¹⁸ For the wrath of God is revealed from heaven against all ungodliness and wickedness of men who by their wickedness suppress the truth. ¹⁹ For what can be known about God is plain to them, because God has shown it to them. ²⁰ Ever since the creation of the world his invisible nature, namely, his eternal power and deity, has been clearly perceived in the things that have been made. So they

are without excuse; 21 for although they knew God they did not honor him as God or give thanks to him, but they became futile in their thinking and their senseless minds were darkened. 22 Claiming to be wise, they became fools, 23 and exchanged the glory of the immortal God for images resembling mortal man or birds or animals or reptiles.

24 Therefore God gave them up in the lusts of their hearts to impurity, to the dishonoring of their bodies among themselves, 25 because they exchanged the truth about God for a lie and worshiped and served the creature rather than the Creator, who is blessed for ever! Amen.

26 For this reason God gave them up to dishonorable passions. Their women exchanged natural relations for unnatural, 27 and the men likewise gave up natural relations with women and were consumed with passion for one another, men committing shameless acts with men and receiving in their own persons the due penalty for their error.

28 And since they did not see fit to acknowledge God, God gave them up to a base mind and to improper conduct. 29 They were filled with all manner of wickedness, evil, covetousness, malice. Full of envy, murder, strife, deceit, malignity, they are gossips, 30 slanderers, haters of God, insolent, haughty, boastful, inventors of evil, disobedient to parents, 31 foolish, faithless, heartless, ruthless. 32 Though they know God's decree that those who do such things deserve to die, they not only do them but approve those who practice them.

2 Therefore you have no excuse, O man, whoever you are, when you judge another; for in passing judgment upon him you condemn yourself, because you, the judge, are doing the very same things. 2 We know that the judgment of God rightly falls upon those who do such things. 3 Do you suppose, O man, that when you judge those who do such things and yet do them yourself, you will escape the judgment of God? 4 Or do you presume upon the riches of his kindness and forbearance and patience? Do you not know that God's kindness is meant to lead you to repentance? 5 But by your hard and impenitent heart you are storing up wrath for yourself on the day of wrath when God's righteous judgment will be revealed. 6 For he will render to every man according to his works: 7 to those who by patience in well-doing seek for glory and honor and immortality, he will give eternal life; 8 but for those who are factious and do not obey the truth, but obey wickedness, there will be wrath and fury. 9 There will be tribulation and distress for every human being who does evil, the Jew first and also the Greek, 10 but glory and honor and peace for every one who does good, the Jew first and also the Greek. 11 For God shows no partiality.

12 All who have sinned without the law will also perish without the law, and all who have sinned under the law will be judged by the law. 13 For it is not the hearers of the law who are righteous before God, but the doers of the law who will be justified. 14 When Gentiles who have not the law do by nature what the law requires, they are a law to themselves, even though they do not have the law. 15 They show that what the law requires is written on their hearts, while their conscience also bears witness and their conflicting thoughts accuse or perhaps excuse them 16 on that day when, according to my gospel, God judges the secrets of men by Christ Jesus.

17 But if you call yourself a Jew and rely upon the law and boast of your relation to

God ¹⁸ and know his will and approve what is excellent, because you are instructed in the law, ¹⁹ and if you are sure that you are a guide to the blind, a light to those who are in darkness, ²⁰ a corrector of the foolish, a teacher of children, having in the law the embodiment of knowledge and truth—²¹ you then who teach others, will you not teach yourself? While you preach against stealing, do you steal? ²² You who say that one must not commit adultery, do you commit adultery? You who abhor idols, do you rob temples? ²³ You who boast in the law, do you dishonor God by breaking the law? ²⁴ For, as it is written, "The name of God is blasphemed among the Gentiles because of you."

²⁵ Circumcision indeed is of value if you obey the law; but if you break the law, your circumcision becomes uncircumcision. ²⁶ So, if a man who is uncircumcised keeps the precepts of the law, will not his uncircumcision be regarded as circumcision? ²⁷ Then those who are physically uncircumcised but keep the law will condemn you who have the written code and circumcision but break the law. ²⁸ For he is not a real Jew who is one outwardly, nor is true circumcision something external and physical. ²⁹ He is a Jew who is one inwardly, and real circumcision is a matter of the heart, spiritual and not literal. His praise is not from men but from God.

3 Then what advantage has the Jew? Or what is the value of circumcision? ² Much in every way. To begin with, the Jews are entrusted with the oracles of God. ³ What if some were unfaithful? Does their faithlessness nullify the faithfulness of God? ⁴ By no means! Let God be true though every man be false, as it is written,

"That thou mayest be justified in thy words,
and prevail when thou art judged."

⁵ But if our wickedness serves to show the justice of God, what shall we say? That God is unjust to inflict wrath on us? (I speak in a human way.) ⁶ By no means! For then how could God judge the world? ⁷ But if through my falsehood God's truthfulness abounds to his glory, why am I still being condemned as a sinner? ⁸ And why not do evil that good may come?—as some people slanderously charge us with saying. Their condemnation is just.

⁹ What then? Are we Jews any better off? No, not at all; for I have already charged that all men, both Jews and Greeks, are under the power of sin, ¹⁰ as it is written:

"None is righteous, no, not one;
¹¹ no one understands, no one seeks for God.
¹² All have turned aside, together they have gone wrong;
no one does good, not even one."
¹³ "Their throat is an open grave,
they use their tongues to deceive."
"The venom of asps is under their lips."
¹⁴ "Their mouth is full of curses and bitterness."
¹⁵ "Their feet are swift to shed blood,
¹⁶ in their paths are ruin and misery,
¹⁷ and the way of peace they do not know."
¹⁸ "There is no fear of God before their eyes."

¹⁹ Now we know that whatever the law says it speaks to those who are under the law, so that every mouth may be stopped, and the whole world may be held accountable to God. ²⁰ For no human being will be justified in his sight by works of the law, since through the law comes knowledge of sin.

²¹ But now the righteousness of God has been manifested apart from law, although

the law and the prophets bear witness to it, 22 the righteousness of God through faith in Jesus Christ for all who believe. For there is no distinction; 23 since all have sinned and fall short of the glory of God, 24 they are justified by his grace as a gift, through the redemption which is in Christ Jesus, 25 whom God put forward as an expiation by his blood, to be received by faith. This was to show God's righteousness, because in his divine forbearance he had passed over former sins; 26 it was to prove at the present time that he himself is righteous and that he justifies him who has faith in Jesus.

27 Then what becomes of our boasting? It is excluded. On what principle? On the principle of works? No, but on the principle of faith. 28 For we hold that a man is justified by faith apart from works of law. 29 Or is God the God of Jews only? Is he not the God of Gentiles also? Yes, of Gentiles also, 30 since God is one; and he will justify the circumcised on the ground of their faith and the uncircumcised through their faith. 31 Do we then overthrow the law by this faith? By no means! On the contrary, we uphold the law.

4 What then shall we say about Abraham, our forefather according to the flesh? 2 For if Abraham was justified by works, he has something to boast about, but not before God. 3 For what does the scripture say? "Abraham believed God, and it was reckoned to him as righteousness." 4 Now to one who works, his wages are not reckoned as a gift but as his due. 5 And to one who does not work but trusts him who justifies the ungodly, his faith is reckoned as righteousness. 6 So also David pronounces a blessing upon the man to whom God reckons righteousness apart from works:

7 "Blessed are those whose iniquities are forgiven, and whose sins are covered;

8 blessed is the man against whom the Lord will not reckon his sin."

9 Is this blessing pronounced only upon the circumcised, or also upon the uncircumcised? We say that faith was reckoned to Abraham as righteousness. 10 How then was it reckoned to him? Was it before or after he had been circumcised? It was not after, but before he was circumcised. 11 He received circumcision as a sign or seal of the righteousness which he had by faith while he was still uncircumcised. The purpose was to make him the father of all who believe without being circumcised and who thus have righteousness reckoned to them, 12 and likewise the father of the circumcised who are not merely circumcised but also follow the example of the faith which our father Abraham had before he was circumcised.

13 The promise to Abraham and his descendants, that they should inherit the world, did not come through the law but through the righteousness of faith. 14 If it is the adherents of the law who are to be the heirs, faith is null and the promise is void. 15 For the law brings wrath, but where there is no law there is no transgression.

16 That is why it depends on faith, in order that the promise may rest on grace and be guaranteed to all his descendants—not only to the adherents of the law but also to those who share the faith of Abraham, for he is the father of us all, 17 as it is written, "I have made you the father of many nations"—in the presence of the God in whom he believed, who gives life to the dead and calls into existence the things that do not exist. 18 In hope he believed against hope, that he should become the

father of many nations; as he had been told, "So shall your descendants be." [19] He did not weaken in faith when he considered his own body, which was as good as dead because he was about a hundred years old, or when he considered the barrenness of Sarah's womb. [20] No distrust made him waver concerning the promise of God, but he grew strong in his faith as he gave glory to God, [21] fully convinced that God was able to do what he had promised. [22] That is why his faith was "reckoned to him as righteousness." [23] But the words, "it was reckoned to him," were written not for his sake alone, [24] but for ours also. It will be reckoned to us who believe in him that raised from the dead Jesus our Lord, [25] who was put to death for our trespasses and raised for our justification.

5 Therefore, since we are justified by faith, we have peace with God through our Lord Jesus Christ. [2] Through him we have obtained access to this grace in which we stand, and we rejoice in our hope of sharing the glory of God. [3] More than that, we rejoice in our sufferings, knowing that suffering produces endurance, [4] and endurance produces character, and character produces hope, [5] and hope does not disappoint us, because God's love has been poured into our hearts through the Holy Spirit which has been given to us.

[6] While we were yet helpless, at the right time Christ died for the ungodly. [7] Why, one will hardly die for a righteous man—though perhaps for a good man one will dare even to die. [8] But God shows his love for us in that while we were yet sinners Christ died for us. [9] Since, therefore, we are now justified by his blood, much more shall we be saved by him from the wrath of God. [10] For if while we were enemies we were reconciled to God by the death of his Son, much more, now that we are reconciled, shall we be saved by his life. [11] Not only so, but we also rejoice in God through our Lord Jesus Christ, through whom we have now received our reconciliation.

[12] Therefore as sin came into the world through one man and death through sin, and so death spread to all men because all men sinned—[13] sin indeed was in the world before the law was given, but sin is not counted where there is no law. [14] Yet death reigned from Adam to Moses, even over those whose sins were not like the transgression of Adam, who was a type of the one who was to come.

[15] But the free gift is not like the trespass. For if many died through one man's trespass, much more have the grace of God and the free gift in the grace of that one man Jesus Christ abounded for many. [16] And the free gift is not like the effect of that one man's sin. For the judgment following one trespass brought condemnation, but the free gift following many trespasses brings justification. [17] If, because of one man's trespass, death reigned through that one man, much more will those who receive the abundance of grace and the free gift of righteousness reign in life through the one man Jesus Christ.

[18] Then as one man's trespass led to condemnation for all men, so one man's act of righteousness leads to acquittal and life for all men. [19] For as by one man's disobedience many were made sinners, so by one man's obedience many will be made righteous. [20] Law came in, to increase the trespass; but where sin increased, grace abounded all the more, [21] so that, as sin reigned in death, grace also might reign through righteousness to eternal life through Jesus Christ our Lord.

6 What shall we say then? Are we to continue in sin that grace may abound? 2 By no means! How can we who died to sin still live in it? 3 Do you not know that all of us who have been baptized into Christ Jesus were baptized into his death? 4 We were buried therefore with him by baptism into death, so that as Christ was raised from the dead by the glory of the Father, we too might walk in newness of life.

5 For if we have been united with him in a death like his, we shall certainly be united with him in a resurrection like his. 6 We know that our old self was crucified with him so that the sinful body might be destroyed, and we might no longer be enslaved to sin. 7 For he who has died is freed from sin. 8 But if we have died with Christ, we believe that we shall also live with him. 9 For we know that Christ being raised from the dead will never die again; death no longer has dominion over him. 10 The death he died he died to sin, once for all, but the life he lives he lives to God. 11 So you also must consider yourselves dead to sin and alive to God in Christ Jesus.

12 Let not sin therefore reign in your mortal bodies, to make you obey their passions. 13 Do not yield your members to sin as instruments of wickedness, but yield yourselves to God as men who have been brought from death to life, and your members to God as instruments of righteousness. 14 For sin will have no dominion over you, since you are not under law but under grace.

15 What then? Are we to sin because we are not under law but under grace? By no means! 16 Do you not know that if you yield yourselves to any one as obedient slaves, you are slaves of the one whom you obey, either of sin, which leads to death, or of obedience, which leads to righteousness? 17 But thanks be to God, that you who were once slaves of sin have become obedient from the heart to the standard of teaching to which you were committed, 18 and, having been set free from sin, have become slaves of righteousness. 19 I am speaking in human terms, because of your natural limitations. For just as you once yielded your members to impurity and to greater and greater iniquity, so now yield your members to righteousness for sanctification.

20 When you were slaves of sin, you were free in regard to righteousness. 21 But then what return did you get from the things of which you are now ashamed? The end of those things is death. 22 But now that you have been set free from sin and have become slaves of God, the return you get is sanctification and its end, eternal life. 23 For the wages of sin is death, but the free gift of God is eternal life in Christ Jesus our Lord.

7 Do you not know, brethren—for I am speaking to those who know the law—that the law is binding on a person only during his life? 2 Thus a married woman is bound by law to her husband as long as he lives; but if her husband dies she is discharged from the law concerning the husband. 3 Accordingly, she will be called an adulteress if she lives with another man while her husband is alive. But if her husband dies she is free from that law, and if she marries another man she is not an adulteress.

4 Likewise, my brethren, you have died to the law through the body of Christ, so that you may belong to another, to him who has been raised from the dead in order that we may bear fruit for God. 5 While we were living in the flesh, our sinful pas-

sions, aroused by the law, were at work in our members to bear fruit for death. 6 But now we are discharged from the law, dead to that which held us captive, so that we serve not under the old written code but in the new life of the Spirit.

7 What then shall we say? That the law is sin? By no means! Yet, if it had not been for the law, I should not have known sin. I should not have known what it is to covet if the law had not said, "You shall not covet." 8 But sin, finding opportunity in the commandment, wrought in me all kinds of covetousness. Apart from the law sin lies dead. 9 I was once alive apart from the law, but when the commandment came, sin revived and I died; 10 the very commandment which promised life proved to be death to me. 11 For sin, finding opportunity in the commandment, deceived me and by it killed me. 12 So the law is holy, and the commandment is holy and just and good.

13 Did that which is good, then, bring death to me? By no means! It was sin, working death in me through what is good, in order that sin might be shown to be sin, and through the commandment might become sinful beyond measure. 14 We know that the law is spiritual; but I am carnal, sold under sin. 15 I do not understand my own actions. For I do not do what I want, but I do the very thing I hate. 16 Now if I do what I do not want, I agree that the law is good. 17 So then it is no longer I that do it, but sin which dwells within me. 18 For I know that nothing good dwells within me, that is, in my flesh. I can will what is right, but I cannot do it. 19 For I do not do the good I want, but the evil I do not want is what I do. 20 Now if I do what I do not want, it is no longer I that do it, but sin which dwells within me.

21 So I find it to be a law that when I want to do right, evil lies close at hand. 22 For I delight in the law of God, in my inmost self, 23 but I see in my members another law at war with the law of my mind and making me captive to the law of sin which dwells in my members. 24 Wretched man that I am! Who will deliver me from this body of death? 25 Thanks be to God through Jesus Christ our Lord! So then, I of myself serve the law of God with my mind, but with my flesh I serve the law of sin.

8 There is therefore now no condemnation for those who are in Christ Jesus. 2 For the law of the Spirit of life in Christ Jesus has set me free from the law of sin and death. 3 For God has done what the law, weakened by the flesh, could not do: sending his own Son in the likeness of sinful flesh and for sin, he condemned sin in the flesh, 4 in order that the just requirement of the law might be fulfilled in us, who walk not according to the flesh but according to the Spirit. 5 For those who live according to the flesh set their minds on the things of the flesh, but those who live according to the Spirit set their minds on the things of the Spirit. 6 To set the mind on the flesh is death, but to set the mind on the Spirit is life and peace. 7 For the mind that is set on the flesh is hostile to God; it does not submit to God's law, indeed it cannot: 8 and those who are in the flesh cannot please God.

9 But you are not in the flesh, you are in the Spirit, if the Spirit of God really dwells in you. Any one who does not have the Spirit of Christ does not belong to him. 10 But if Christ is in you, although your bodies are dead because of sin, your spirits are alive because of righteousness. 11 If the Spirit of him who raised Jesus from the

dead dwells in you, he who raised Christ Jesus from the dead will give life to your mortal bodies also through his Spirit which dwells in you.

12 So then, brethren, we are debtors, not to the flesh, to live according to the flesh— 13 for if you live according to the flesh you will die, but if by the Spirit you put to death the deeds of the body you will live. 14 For all who are led by the Spirit of God are sons of God. 15 For you did not receive the spirit of slavery to fall back into fear, but you have received the spirit of sonship. When we cry, "Abba! Father!" 16 it is the Spirit himself bearing witness with our spirit that we are children of God, 17 and if children, then heirs, heirs of God and fellow heirs with Christ, provided we suffer with him in order that we may also be glorified with him.

18 I consider that the sufferings of this present time are not worth comparing with the glory that is to be revealed to us. 19 For the creation waits with eager longing for the revealing of the sons of God; 20 for the creation was subjected to futility, not of its own will but by the will of him who subjected it in hope; 21 because the creation itself will be set free from its bondage to decay and obtain the glorious liberty of the children of God. 22 We know that the whole creation has been groaning in travail together until now; 23 and not only the creation, but we ourselves, who have the first fruits of the Spirit, groan inwardly as we wait for adoption as sons, the redemption of our bodies. 24 For in this hope we were saved. Now hope that is seen is not hope. For who hopes for what he sees? 25 But if we hope for what we do not see, we wait for it with patience.

26 Likewise the Spirit helps us in our weakness; for we do not know how to pray as we ought, but the Spirit himself intercedes for us with sighs too deep for words. 27 And he who searches the hearts of men knows what is the mind of the Spirit, because the Spirit intercedes for the saints according to the will of God.

28 We know that in everything God works for good with those who love him, who are called according to his purpose. 29 For those whom he foreknew he also predestined to be conformed to the image of his Son, in order that he might be the first-born among many brethren. 30 And those whom he predestined he also called; and those whom he called he also justified; and those whom he justified he also glorified.

31 What then shall we say to this? If God is for us, who is against us? 32 He who did not spare his own Son but gave him up for us all, will he not also give us all things with him? 33 Who shall bring any charge against God's elect? It is God who justifies; 34 who is to condemn? Is it Christ Jesus, who died, yes, who was raised from the dead, who is at the right hand of God, who indeed intercedes for us? 35 Who shall separate us from the love of Christ? Shall tribulation, or distress, or persecution, or famine, or nakedness, or peril, or sword? 36 As it is written,

"For thy sake we are being killed all the day long;
we are regarded as sheep to be slaughtered."

37 No, in all these things we are more than conquerors through him who loved us. 38 For I am sure that neither death, nor life, nor angels, nor principalities, nor things present, nor things to come, nor powers, 39 nor height, nor depth, nor anything else in all creation, will be able to separate us from the love of God in Christ Jesus our Lord.

This love of which Paul speaks is the foundation for his ethics. It developed from the concept of love within the family and, by analogy, within the covenant, the family of God, although it owed much to the unrestricted, unbounded devotion toward others already seen in the teaching of Jesus. This "altruistic" love, based on a denial of self and expressed even toward enemies, became the heart of the Christian ethic, and Paul was instrumental in its dissemination. Initially, this concept of love derived from the Old Testament concept of *chesed* (usually translated "steadfast love"), which, like the Christian word *agape*,[10] described God's love for those who shared the covenant with him. For Christians, the term *agape* also came to express love toward one's fellow man.

Behind the commandment of love, however, lies the problem of the will and the moral conscience, that is, the problem of knowing when and how ethical rules are to be applied in specific situations and having sufficient control of the will to transform intention into action. The concept of conscience is intimately tied up with the concepts of sin and will. In the popular, modern view, "conscience" has primarily a predictive function. "Wherever two courses of action are possible, conscience tells me which is right, and to choose the other is sin."[11] We are often admonished to let conscience be our guide, but within Greek thought and within the New Testament the term conscience has a retrodictive function; it evaluates past action.

Conscience in Greek and the N.T. does not look to the future: its reference is to acts at least begun, if not irrevocably completed, in the past. It tells me that what I have done is sin: whether its absence can be taken to tell me that what I have done is righteousness may be thought debatable, . . . but there is no question about the tense of the action referred to. . . .

The pain of conscience [is] that combination of fear and shame which is called *guilt*—but not guilt legalistically conceived. The guilt which paralyses and *destroys,* and is internally effective whether it be externally declared or not, is a phenomenon familiar to modern psychopathology. It is only too rightly called a *disease,* and he who suffers from it truly can never be called happy.

If the pain of conscience is rightly so described, then it follows that it may produce physical symptoms: these will vary all but infinitely from person to person.

Conscience is the reaction of the whole man to his own wrong acts. It is a moral reflex action, parallel, but also akin, to those reactions that make a man drop a red hot poker or spew out a poison, long before conscious reasoning has been brought to bear on those objects. The absolute pitch of the trained musician is likewise akin to the moral "absolute pitch" of the trained Christian: the wrong note—be it never so little wrong—causes immediate pain.[12]

Paul introduced this concept of conscience into Christianity. However, it was, for him, a common experience of mankind—not a matter of divine revelation. The limits Paul placed on conscience as a guide to behavior grew out of his reaction to certain members of the church in Corinth, who justified their immorality by appealing to a clear conscience. For Paul, the conscience could be misled through wrong information or through habitual wrong-doing.

Paul would have granted that, for all its liability to error, conscience must be obeyed: but he would never have added "for man has no other guide." He is definite that conscience only comes into play after at least the initiation of a wrong act; when it does not come into play, it may mean that the act committed is not wrong, but equally it may mean that the reactions are defective—either handicapped by wrong information, wrong en-

---

[10] ä·gä·pā—accent on the middle syllable.

[11] Bertrand Russell, *History of Western Philosophy* (New York: Simon and Schuster, Inc., 1945), p. 200.

[12] *Conscience in the New Testament* by C. A. Pierce ("Studies in Biblical Theology," first series, no. 15), pp. 112-113, 114-115. London: SCM Press; Naperville, Ill.: Alec R. Allenson, Inc., 1955.

vironment or wrong habit, or made sluggish by sin, repeated and unrepented. In any case it can never mean that the action was more than "not wrong"—that it was "right" in the sense, even, of the only or best possible in the circumstances; still less can conscience have anything to say directly about future acts. There are many means by, and grounds on, which an assessment may be hazarded of the heat of bath water; the man's nature itself will not so react as to show whether it is too hot for him to get in, until he gets in.

To some extent its fallible, and, to a far greater extent, its negative character account for St. Paul's lack of enthusiasm for this Gentile experience, although he recognised it as valid, and good so far as it went. . . . The main reason for the minor place he allots it in his Christian scheme is, that, in Christ, having died to sin, a man should be free from conscience. He himself was forced to face the fact that the Christian did not automatically become sinless at the moment of Baptism; but he did not think it a gross optimism to expect a Christian's behaviour to be, even when not ideal, at least sufficiently within the limits of his nature as created, to avoid the reaction that results from the attempt to exceed them. Later Christian experience may have had also to revise this expectation as still too optimistic—but not for a considerable time, and then with no little reluctance.[13]

For Paul, then, conscience serves the limited function of evaluating past action, provided that one knows what constitutes acceptable behavior. Knowledge of God and of his demands is revealed, in part, through nature to all men (Rom. 1:18-20). A far more explicit knowledge of God's demands is given in the Decalogue and the teaching of the Church. However, knowing the natural and revealed law of God is not sufficient for Paul. The will must be able to act, but it is frequently hindered in so doing by the influence of the "evil impulse"—what Paul sometimes calls the "flesh" or "sin."

[13] *Ibid.*, pp. 109-110.

Thus it is that we owe to Paul that classic description of the impotence of the human will that seems so un-Greek: "I do not understand my own actions. For I do not do what I want, but I do the very thing I hate" (Rom. 7:15). Paul did not mean to imply by this statement that his will—or any will—is unable to act, unable to fulfill the demands of the Law, and therefore that he is forced to live under an intolerable burden of guilt. On the basis of the Hebrew tradition Paul dismisses the idea of a "guilty conscience." In general he felt he had had no difficulty in fulfilling the commandments of the Law before he became a Christian, and his inability to do so now and then was blamed on the "evil impulse" in man. "Now if I do what I do not want, it is no longer I that do it, but sin which dwells within me" (Rom. 7:20).

Regardless of the effect of this passage on the development of the introspective moral conscience in the West, Paul meant only to show that the Law itself was not responsible for man's failure to fulfill its demands.[14] Romans 7:13-25 is part of a long and intricate argument through which Paul intended to show the place of the Law before and after Christ, and consequently the role played by the Law in the evangelization and incorporation of the Gentiles into the dawning Kingdom of God. Paul's emphasis in his letter to the Romans and elsewhere was not on individual moral or immoral acts in their own right, but rather on what they indicated about the religious status of the person, that is, whether he was a healthy member of the Body of Christ. For Paul, "sin" was a term for the "evil impulse" in man, and the sinner was one who was dominated by that evil impulse, a state particularly descriptive of man's life outside the Church, outside the New Covenant between God and his "chosen people." Once a man was engrafted into the Body of Christ he became a "new man," whose shortcomings or vices could be easily corrected. If, on the other hand, the

[14] For a discussion of this issue, see Krister Stendahl, "The Apostle Paul and the Introspective Conscience of the West," *Harvard Theological Review*, LVI (1963), 199-213.

"life in Christ" did not cure his immorality, he was driven from the Church, since his actions indicated that he was not of the community of God. Short of gross immorality, however, which resulted in temporary or permanent expulsion from the Church, the moral failings of early Christians were not concentrated on in such a way as to produce extreme anxiety and guilt.

The ethical needs of a continuing community, however, changed in the face of the delay in the return of Christ and the end of the existing order. As an administrative structure became necessary for the expansion and continuation of the community, so a specified ethical code became necessary in order to define the life and activity of that community. Paul continued to share with other early Christians the belief in the imminent return of Christ, but he was also disturbed by the fact that the first generation of Christians began to die before the end had arrived. Paul's solution to this problem, his rationalization for the delay, was that it was first necessary that the proclamation of the gospel reach throughout the Greco-Roman world, so that before the end all might have an opportunity to accept or reject the messiahship of Jesus. With this in mind, he attempted to divert apocalyptic speculations, such as were prevalent in the church at Thessalonica, into ethical action and evangelization.

4 . . . 13 But we would not have you ignorant, brethren, concerning those who are asleep, that you may not grieve as others do who have no hope. 14 For since we believe that Jesus died and rose again, even so, through Jesus, God will bring with him those who have fallen asleep. 15 For this we declare to you by the word of the Lord, that we who are alive, who are left until the coming of the Lord, shall not precede those who have fallen asleep. 16 For the Lord himself will descend from heaven with a cry of command, with the archangel's call, and with the sound of the trumpet of God. And the dead in Christ will rise first; 17 then we who are alive, who are left, shall be caught up together with them in the clouds to meet the Lord in the air; and so we shall always be with the Lord. 18 Therefore comfort one another with these words.

5 But as to the times and the seasons, brethren, you have no need to have anything written to you. 2 For you yourselves know well that the day of the Lord will come like a thief in the night. 3 When people say, "There is peace and security," then sudden destruction will come upon them as travail comes upon a woman with child, and there will be no escape.[15]

2 Now concerning the coming of our Lord Jesus Christ and our assembling to meet him, we beg you, brethren, 2 not to be quickly shaken in mind or excited, either by spirit or by word, or by letter purporting to be from us, to the effect that the day of the Lord has come. 3 Let no one deceive you in any way; for that day will not come, unless the rebellion comes first, and the man of lawlessness is revealed, the son of perdition, 4 who opposes and exalts himself against every so-called god or object of worship, so that he takes his seat in the temple of God, proclaiming himself to be God. 5 Do you not remember that when I was still with you I told you this? 6 And you know what is restraining him now so that he may be revealed in his time. 7 For the mystery of lawlessness is already at work; only he who now restrains it will do so until he is out of the way. 8 And then the lawless one will be revealed, and the Lord Jesus will slay him with the breath of his mouth and destroy him by his appearing and his coming. 9 The coming of the lawless one by the activity of Satan will be with all power and with pretended signs and wonders, 10 and with all wicked deception for those who are to perish, because they refused to love the truth and so be saved. 11 Therefore God sends upon them a strong delusion, to make them believe what is false, 12 so that all may be condemned who did not believe the truth but had pleasure in unrighteousness.[16]

[15] The Bible, I Thess. 4:13—5:3.
[16] The Bible, II Thess. 2:1-12.

240 Paul and the Early Church

Although Paul never abandoned his eschatological hope, he found it increasingly necessary to make the ethical demands of Christianity explicit for the early Christian communities. Some of those ethical demands presuppose the imminent end of the present world, in the face of which Paul urged a continuation of existing social inequalities, tempered by the spirit of love.

7 . . . [17] Only, let every one lead the life which the Lord has assigned to him, and in

The resurrection of Tabitha (third to fourth century A.D.). The belief in the eventual resurrection of Christians continued to be a major part of the Church's expectation, in spite of the delay in the Second Coming. (Boudot-Lamotte)

which God has called him. This is my rule in all the churches. . . .

[20] Every one should remain in the state in which he was called. [21] Were you a slave when called? Never mind. But if you can gain your freedom, avail yourself of the opportunity. [22] For he who was called in the Lord as a slave is a freedman of the Lord. Likewise he who was free when called is a slave of Christ. [23] You were bought with a price; do not become slaves of men. [24] So, brethren, in whatever state each was called, there let him remain with God.[17]

6 . . . [5] Slaves, be obedient to those who are your earthly masters, with fear and trembling, in singleness of heart, as to Christ; [6] not in the way of eye-service, as men-pleasers, but as servants of Christ, doing the will of God from the heart, [7] rendering service with a good will as to the Lord and not to men, [8] knowing that whatever good any one does, he will receive the same again from the Lord, whether he is a slave or free. [9] Masters, do the same to them, and forbear threatening, knowing that he who is both their Master and yours is in heaven, and that there is no partiality with him.[18]

In much the same way, Paul's eschatology shaped his attitude toward sex and marriage. In addition to sharing with most of his contemporaries the belief in the inferior nature of women, he placed strong curbs on sexual activity and, in view of the imminent Second Coming, discouraged marriage. The problem of sexual immorality, which ranked at the top of Paul's list of vices, was especially strong at Corinth, even within the Christian community there.

6 . . . [9] Do you not know that the unrighteous will not inherit the kingdom of God? Do not be deceived; neither the immoral, nor idolaters, not adulterers, nor homosexuals, [10] nor thieves, nor the greedy, nor drunkards, nor revilers, nor robbers will inherit the kingdom of God. [11] And such were some of you. But you were washed, you were sanctified, you were justified in the name of the Lord Jesus Christ and in the Spirit of our God.

[12] "All things are lawful for me," but not all things are helpful. . . . The body is not meant for immorality, but for the Lord, and the Lord for the body. [14] And God raised the Lord and will also raise us up by his power. [15] Do you not know that your bodies are members of Christ? Shall I therefore take the members of Christ and make them members of a prostitute? Never! [16] Do you not know that he who joins himself to a prostitute becomes one body with her? For, as it is written, "The two shall become one." [17] But he who is united to the Lord becomes one spirit with him. [18] Shun immorality. Every other sin which a man commits is outside the body; but the immoral man sins against his own body. [19] Do you not know that your body is a temple of the Holy Spirit within you, which you have from God? You are not your own; [20] you were bought with a price. So glorify God in your body.

7 Now concerning the matters about which you wrote. It is well for a man not to touch a woman. [2] But because of the temptation to immorality, each man should have his own wife and each woman her own husband. [3] The husband should give to his wife her conjugal rights, and likewise the wife to her husband. [4] For the wife does not rule over her own body, but the husband does; likewise the husband does not rule over his own body, but the wife does. [5] Do not refuse one another except perhaps by agreement for a season, that you may devote yourselves to prayer; but then come together again, lest Satan tempt you through lack of self-control. [6] I say this by way of concession, not of command. [7] I wish that all were as I myself am. But each has his own special gift from God, one of one kind and one of another.

---

[17] The Bible, I Cor. 7:17, 20–24.
[18] The Bible, Eph. 6:5–9. Although the Letter to the Ephesians is probably not an authentic letter of Paul, it does represent his viewpoint.

⁸ To the unmarried and the widows I say that it is well for them to remain single as I do. ⁹ But if they cannot exercise self-control, they should marry. For it is better to marry than to be aflame with passion.

¹⁰ To the married I give charge, not I but the Lord, that the wife should not separate from her husband ¹¹ (but if she does, let her remain single or else be reconciled to her husband)—and that the husband should not divorce his wife.

¹² To the rest I say, not the Lord, that if any brother has a wife who is an unbeliever, and she consents to live with him, he should not divorce her. ¹³ If any woman has a husband who is an unbeliever, and he consents to live with her, she should not divorce him. ¹⁴ For the unbelieving husband is consecrated through his wife, and the unbelieving wife is consecrated through her husband. Otherwise, your children would be unclean, but as it is they are holy. ¹⁵ But if the unbelieving partner desires to separate, let it be so; in such a case the brother or sister is not bound. For God has called us to peace. ¹⁶ Wife, how do you know whether you will save your husband? Husband, how do you know whether you will save your wife? . . .

²⁵ Now concerning the unmarried, I have no command of the Lord, but I give my opinion as one who by the Lord's mercy is trustworthy. ²⁶ I think that in view of the impending distress it is well for a person to remain as he is. ²⁷ Are you bound to a wife? Do not seek to be free. Are you free from a wife? Do not seek marriage. ²⁸ But if you marry, you do not sin, and if a girl marries she does not sin. Yet those who marry will have worldly troubles, and I would spare you that. ²⁹ I mean, brethren, the appointed time has grown very short; from now on, let those who have wives live as though they had none, ³⁰ and those who mourn as though they were not mourning, and those who rejoice as though they were not rejoicing, and those who buy as though they had no goods, ³¹ and those who deal with the world as though they had no dealings with it. For the form of this world is passing away.

³² I want you to be free from anxieties. The unmarried man is anxious about the affairs of the Lord, how to please the Lord; ³³ but the married man is anxious about worldly affairs, how to please his wife, ³⁴ and his interests are divided. And the unmarried woman or girl is anxious about the affairs of the Lord, how to be holy in body and spirit; but the married woman is anxious about worldly affairs, how to please her husband. ³⁵ I say this for your own benefit, not to lay any restraint upon you, but to promote good order and to secure your undivided devotion to the Lord.

³⁶ If any one thinks that he is not behaving properly toward his betrothed, if his passions are strong, and it has to be, let him do as he wishes: let them marry—it is no sin. ³⁷ But whoever is firmly established in his heart, being under no necessity but having his desire under control, and has determined this in his heart, to keep her as his betrothed, he will do well. ³⁸ So that he who marries his betrothed does well; and he who refrains from marriage will do better.

³⁹ A wife is bound to her husband as long as he lives. If the husband dies, she is free to be married to whom she wishes, only in the Lord. ⁴⁰ But in my judgment she is happier if she remains as she is. And I think that I have the Spirit of God.[19]

With the fading of eschatology, these ethical and moral directives became necessary to guide the lives of Christians. As early as the letters of Paul, there existed lists of vices and virtues, common even in non-Christian circles, that defined sins and virtuous deeds. The list of sins, frequently encountered in the letters of Paul, was usually headed by the sins of impurity: adultery, fornication, homosexuality, concupiscence, and indecent language. Such were preeminently, in Paul's mind, the sins of the pagan Gentiles. The list of virtues, similarly, was not a product of Christianity, but was adopted from

---

[19] The Bible, I Cor. 6:9—7:16; 7:25–40.

the Jewish, Greco-Roman environment and might even be considered a fusion of two separate views of a "good work."

> There is a deep contrast between the ancient oriental and the classical conception of doing good; among oriental peoples . . . the object of this moral activity is always the poor and oppressed, while for the Greeks and Romans beneficence is not restricted to the poor but has a much wider extent, being given to the whole of society. This . . . is explained from the differences in social structure, and in political and religious attitude. . . .
>
> Let us first see what was the content of the idea [of doing good] among the Greeks and Romans. Though it is mentioned many times it is never connected with almsgiving; its objects are parents, friends, the state or nation; it is synonymous with "to be useful," "to do something agreeable to a person," "to assist" . . . either with material help, with good counsel or simple friendliness, even the poor can benefit the rich man. The motive may be the utilitarian principle *"do ut des"* [I give in order that you give] or the thirst for glory . . . . To summarize: it is a virtue of friendliness and willingness to help towards all men without distinction.
>
> Let us now turn to the Jewish side. In the rabbinical writings the expression "good works" is often found. . . . [Usually it is equated] with "works of charity" such as visitation of the sick, hospitality towards strangers, aid to poor brides, assistance in marriage and funeral ceremonies, care for the dead, comforting the distressed, etc. They are distinct from almsgiving (= righteousness!) because the latter can be done with money while the former demand personal participation, the latter can only benefit the poor and the living while the former have to do with the rich and the dead as well; therefore "works of charity" have more credit than almsgiving. . . .
>
> Was this duty extended to all men? . . . In view of the fact that the Jewish nation held a special place and that Jews ran great risks of uncleanness through contact with pagans (idolatry!), it is feasible that there were great restrictions. . . .
>
> [The early Christian ethic] is decidedly different from the Jewish type, since "good deeds" are not special works towards the poor [or] the dead. . . , have no special value for the acquirement of God's favour, but are extended to all without exception. . . . This "holiness" does not express itself in prayer, almsgiving and penitence, but in the right behavior towards the neighbor, be he Christian or not; they are not done for heaven's sake, but for neighbour's sake. . . .
>
> But the foundation is quite different from the Greek: God's calling and not human goodness; and its aim is different: not to earn glory for oneself, but to make the way free for the Gospel towards the disobedient.[20]

With each passing generation the ethical life of Christians increasingly depended on such "good works." Similarly, individual "sins," which Paul thought of as vices born of the "evil impulse" that should have no part in the life of the Christian, came to be considered moral failures for which the individual was volitionally responsible. While Paul's definition of sin as life-outside-the-Church remained alive, the Church tended to concentrate more on sins, conceived of as transgressions of Christ's law, the laws of the Church, or divine law.

One of the major reasons for this change—a change that affected the whole understanding of moral responsibility in the Judeo-Christian tradition—is that the new Gentile converts to Christianity did not share the Hebrew tradition that divided man into higher and lower natures, good and evil impulses. The common definition of sin (*peccata*) in the Roman world was a definite act, often one of sexual immorality, especially fornication, adultery, and marital infidelity. It was associated from an early date with *culpa*, the sense of responsibility and guilt for immoral action. Sin in the Roman sense (and

---

[20] W. C. Van Unnik, "The Teaching of Good Works in I Peter," *New Testament Studies,* I (1954), 95–97, 108–109.

in Hellenistic Greek) was always a definite act, a transgression of a higher law. Guilt, on the other hand, was the personal responsibility for such action, a burden "in the heart" which might be individual or collective. On the common level of Roman society, sin was inevitably associated with guilt and in many cases was defined as guilt.

Sin was considered a transgression of divine law, or of holy prescriptions, it was a burden, a stain, it could mean an actual sin, sin as guilt; there [one reads] of hereditary sin, original sin, sin of the world; sin resided in the heart; it was due to the ill will, or to error. These characteristics are still presented as living in the mind of the people of the early imperial age. It will make a great difference whether one interviews a sexton of a temple or a professor in rhetorics. The common man will have had more feeling of guilt than the educated intellectual who has reflected upon the injustice of heaven and become fatalistic and therefore had to find another cause of sin. The man in the country may have been still on a dynamistic level, while his friend in the city listened to the preachers of Stoic doctrine [which defined sin as "error"]. . . .

When we compare the [Roman] complex of sin (*confession, repentance, forgiveness, penance*) with the complex of sin in Judaism of about the same time, it can be said that there are some differences . . . . The main difference is the background of sin. To the Romans man alone was responsible for transgression, in Judaism the devil or demons were present as the deepest cause of sin, while man was responsible for the act of transgressing. Another difference is that in Rome sin was considered as guilt, in Judaism as guilt and "debt." [The term debt] was so strange to Greek readers that Luke substituted "sins" for "debts". . . . In Judaism obedience is required from man, sinning means being disobedient and therefore transgressing the divine [written] law. As in Rome there was no revealed law, there is no question of disobedience, but of transgressing the holy prescriptions or the divine law (the unwritten law). . . .

The early Roman Christian authors could not understand Paul because of their own background. . . . They twisted the doctrine of sin into their own complex of thoughts.[21]

Under the impact of the Greco-Roman conception of sin the Judeo-Christian concept of moral responsibility changed. By the fifth century of the Christian era the definition of sin as guilt had become common. Capital sins, such as the denial of the faith, murder, adultery, and

[21] A. E. Wilhelm-Hooijbergh, *Peccatum: Sin and Guilt in Ancient Rome* (Groningen, Netherlands: J. B. Wolters, 1954), pp. 113–114.

One of the earliest representations of the Last Judgment takes the form of the New Testament analogy of separating the sheep from the goats. Christ, the Good Shepherd, is seated in the middle of this scene from a fourth-century sarcophagus. (The Metropolitan Museum of Art, Rogers Fund, 1924)

The Face of Evil. The sense of the demonic is often personified in Hebrew thought, under the general influence of a Near Eastern tendency toward such characterization. This demonic mask from Mesopotamia dates back to the Old Babylonian period, 1800–1600 B.C. (Collection of Mr. and Mrs. Joseph Ternbach, New York)

fornication, were sufficient to exclude one if they were committed after baptism or after ecclesiastical penance, which normally could be administered only once. Such "excommunication" was inflicted on the sinner not so much because his actions showed him to be "not of the Spirit," but because he had broken the law of the Church, which was to be kept "holy and inviolate."

In like manner, by the fourth century "good works" were being defined not as an impersonal means of preparing the way for the Kingdom of God, but rather as the personal means of eradicating sins committed after baptism. Sins before baptism were "blotted out by the water of baptism and the cross of Christ . . . but much zeal is needed for what happens after baptism in order that it may be blotted out. For there is no second laver [or second penance by which sins are washed away], but what is needed is our tears, repentance, confession, almsgiving, prayer, and all other good works."[22] As the practice of penance grew in importance in the life of the Church, so did the concepts of sin and guilt.

This change in the concepts of sin and moral action was only one of the transformations experienced by the Christian Church in the first few centuries of its existence. The ethical change was accompanied by—and supported by—a shift in the composition of the Church. Christianity began to attract those who, not sharing the heritage of Jewish eschatology, were not seeking a shelter from the impending cataclysm, but who rather sought community in this world and salvation in the life beyond. As the motivation for becoming a Christian changed, so did the nature of the Christian life.

The change in the type of convert to Christianity facilitated the establishment of a more traditional kind of leadership in the Church. The vacancies left in Church leadership by the death of the last apostles were filled initially by leaders already present in the individual Christian congregations, which patterned their organization and much of their liturgy on the Jewish synagogue. By the second century leadership in many local congregations, each congregation usually comprising all the Christians in one urban area, had devolved upon one man who became known as a bishop. A vestige of charismatic power remained through the ceremony of the laying on of hands, a ceremony that ordained him into his office and symbolized the ongoing authority of apostolic leadership. The selection of such a man, however, began to reflect the considered judgment of the community according to its needs, so that leadership ability, wealth, social standing became primary considerations for holding office. This tendency toward episcopal control increased in the following centuries. With the recognition of Christianity at the beginning of the fourth century as first a permitted and then a favored religion, vast numbers were converted to Christianity. This influx of "fair weather" Christians quickened the process whereby the laity, that is, those Christians not holding office within the Church, ceased to function as a significant or necessary element within the life of the Church. The clergy slowly became the only group necessary for liturgy and administration, a career in itself which raised one above the rank-and-file Christians. These changes furthered the process of institutionalization. By the fifth century the Christian Church and Roman society had reached a general consensus that protected the ideologies of both institutions.

The religious experience exercises a call, and thereby mobilizes the inner dispositions of the person called to a voluntary adherence to religious leaders, beliefs, and movements. It involves that commitment of the individual which may be called the "act of faith." But faith as a commitment to the supraempirical involves the possibility of doubt. When the religious organization becomes institutionalized and accommodates itself to the society and its values, faith is supplemented by public opinion and current ideas of respectability. More precisely, faith is supplemented by consensual validation and by the approval and

---

[22] John Chrysostom, *Homiliae duae in Pentecosten*, I, 6 (PG 50, 463).

support of accepted authority. The result is that a specious obviousness tends to develop and render the content of faith commonplace. The content of faith tends to be accepted without examination, but is therefore vulnerable to questions when they do arise. Moreover, the compromise of religion with culture—with the "world" in Troeltsch's sense—tends to make religion the repository of the basic values of the society. Thus not only are religious beliefs made more vulnerable to questioning, but they are also functionally more significant to secular society. Faith and doubt remain closely related, and beneath the institutionalized "self-evidentness," the basic structure of religion and of society's legitimation remains vulnerable to questioning—questioning which dispels the consensually derived but only apparent obviousness of beliefs.

The ever present vulnerability of faith to doubt makes religious leaders tend to rely upon social consensus and even on legal authority to buttress and supplement voluntary adherence. Society's leaders, needing religion to sanctify society's values and support social control, tend to protect religion and religious institutions from threat. Thus there arises the possibility of an alignment of religious and secular authorities. This situation, as may be seen in the history of Christianity, draws religious and secular power together to enforce religious conformity. The heretic and the unbeliever weaken consensus and pose a social threat. Those weak in faith tend to project their own potential and half-conscious doubts onto the unbeliever, and then persecute him. Such "ritualistic" purgings of self have taken place both legally—that is, within the orderly and often careful procedures of courts of inquisition—and illegally, by mob action and other violent forms of attack. Thus intolerance and persecution come to perform two functions. For the society, they reinforce and protect a religion, and through the religion the society and its values, from the undermining of doubt. For individuals, they offer a way of externalizing their own doubts and striking at them in the persons of others. Yet it may be questioned whether indeed these functions are performed without quite negative unintended consequences. The consensus that is built upon or supported by threats of force is one to which genuine adherence is gradually weakened. The reliance upon power to supplement faith violates an important element of the religious experience upon which religious institutions ultimately rest: its spontaneous and voluntary character.[23]

This consensus preserved the transformation of the Christian ethic which had occurred with the entry of Judeo-Christian thought into the Roman world in the first few centuries of the Christian era. But the foundation of the Church's belief and moral code remained the Old and New Testaments which, in turn, preserved within Western culture a series of earlier, non-Roman traditions. Alongside the concept of sin as a feeling of guilt resulting from an infringement of God's law, there remained the concept of sin as a broken relationship which placed one temporarily outside the covenant with God. Alongside the concept of absolute rights and wrongs as determined by the laws revealed to man by nature and the Church, there remained the idea that ethical imperatives are determined by the situation in which ethical action takes place. Alongside the conceptions of individual moral responsibility and voluntary participation in the life of the Church, there remained the idea of corporate responsibility and the conception of the Church as the predetermined elect. The various and sometimes conflicting conceptions present within the Biblical sources, therefore, joined with those of ecclesiastical practice to keep alive these "oppositions" within the Western ethical conscience. If the tendency in Western religion toward renewal and reform has its foundation in the Hebrew prophets, the content of those reforms or changes in ethical perspective need seldom be sought outside the written sources of the Judeo-Christian heritage.

---

[23] Thomas O'Dea, *The Sociology of Religion*, p. 96.

STUDY QUESTIONS

1. What changes in the Christian ethic took place in the first two or three centuries of the Church's life and what are the reasons for those changes?

2. What shifts in emphasis, focus, and audience can you see between the teaching of Jesus and that of Paul?

3. Did Paul "Hellenize" the teaching of Jesus or is his approach basically Jewish?

4. What significance does Paul attach to the person and work of Jesus Christ?

5. What is the theological structure that Paul provides for the gospel message?

6. What areas of Paul's thought are affected by his concept of community?

7. How does Paul's theology relate to his ethical teaching?

8. What are the motivations and sanctions for ethical action in Paul?

9. What role does the conscience play in ethical action for Paul?

10. What does Paul conceive to be the Christian's proper relationship to secular culture?

11. What was Paul's attitude toward sex and marriage, and what effect has it had upon the development of a sexual ethic in Western culture?

12. What role did Paul play in adjusting the Christian communities to the delay in the Second Coming of Christ?

13. What happens to an eschatological ethic when eschatology fades?

14. Does the concept of a chosen, predestined elect grow out of the concept of communal responsibility, and if so, how?

15. Was the institutionalization of Christianity a regrettable corruption of the original vision or was it a necessary stage in the development of and preservation of the religious experience?

For those who have used The Contribution of Ancient Greece *edited by Jacqueline Strain:*

16. What aspects of the Hellenistic age created a need for the type of Christianity Paul preached?

17. Compare and contrast the Socratic view of the relation between knowing the good and doing the good with that of Paul.

SUGGESTIONS FOR FURTHER READING

The following select bibliography is intended for the student who wishes to investigate further the points raised by his reading. It does not include all of the works cited in the text. Therefore, students should also consult the footnotes. Much more comprehensive bibliographies are included in the general historical works cited below.

General Introductions
Albright, William F., "The Biblical Period," in L. Finkelstein, ed., *The Jews: Their History, Culture and Religion* (New York: Harper & Row, 1949).
———, *The Biblical Period from Abraham to Ezra* (Pittsburgh: Biblical Colloquium, 1950. Torchbooks; New York: Harper & Row, 1963).
———, *From the Stone Age to Christianity: Monotheism and the Historical Process* (Anchor Books; Garden City, N.Y.: Doubleday & Company, Inc., 1957).
Anderson, Bernhard W., *Understanding the Old Testament* (2d ed.; Englewood Cliffs, N.J.: Prentice-Hall, Inc., 1966).
Bright, John, *A History of Israel* (Philadelphia: The Westminster Press, 1959).
Wright, G. E., *God Who Acts* ("Studies in Biblical Theology," Vol. VIII; London: SCM Press, 1952).

Hebrew Origins, Society, and Psychology
Bright, John, *Early Israel in Recent History Writing* ("Studies in Biblical Theology," Vol. XIX; London: SCM Press, 1956).
Meek, T. J., *Hebrew Origins* (rev. ed.; New York: Harper & Row, 1950).
Nielson, Edward, *Oral Tradition* ("Studies in Biblical Theology," Vol. XI; London: SCM Press, 1954).
Pedersen, Johannes, *Israel: Its Life and Culture,* I–II (New York: Oxford University Press, 1926); III–IV (New York: Oxford University Press, 1940).
Robinson, H. Wheeler, *Corporate Personality in Ancient Israel* ("Biblical Series," Vol. 11; Philadelphia: Fortress Press, 1964).
———, "Hebrew Psychology," in A. S. Peake, ed., *The People and the Book* (New York: Oxford University Press, 1946).

———, *Inspiration and Revelation in the Old Testament* (New York: Oxford University Press, 1946).

Hebrew Law and Morality

Mendenhall, George, *Law and Covenant in Israel and the Ancient Near East* (Pittsburgh: Biblical Colloquium, 1955).

Noth, Martin, *The Laws in the Pentateuch and Other Essays* (New York: McGraw-Hill, Inc., 1966).

Stamm, J. J., and M. E. Andrew, *The Ten Commandments in Recent Research* ("Studies in Biblical Theology," 2d Ser., no. 2; London: SCM Press, 1967).

Conquest and Settlement of Palestine

Buber, Martin, *The Prophetic Faith*, trans. by C. Witton-Davies (New York: The Macmillan Co., 1949).

Driver, G. R., *Canaanite Myths and Legends* (Edinburgh: T. & T. Clark, 1956).

Eliade, Mircea, *Cosmos and History: The Myth of the Eternal Return* (Torchbooks; New York: Harper & Row, 1954).

Gray, John, *The Legacy of Canaan* (2d ed.: Leiden, Netherlands: E. J. Brill, N.V., 1965).

Israelite Prophecy

Anderson, B. W., and Walter Harrelson, eds., *Israel's Prophetic Heritage*, Essays in honor of James Muilenburg (New York: Harper & Row, 1962).

Clements, R. E., *Prophecy and Covenant* ("Studies in Biblical Theology," no. 43; London: SCM Press, 1965).

Johnson, Aubrey R., *The Cultic Prophet in Ancient Israel* (2d ed.; Cardiff: University of Wales Press, 1962).

Lindblom, Johannes, *Prophecy in Ancient Israel* (Philadelphia: Muhlenberg Press, 1963).

Mowinckel, Sigmund, *Prophecy and Tradition* (Oslo: Jacob Dybwad, 1946).

Post-Exilic Judaism and the Dead Sea Scrolls

Bultmann, Rudolf, *Primitive Christianity in Its Contemporary Setting* (New York: Meridian Books, Inc., 1956).

Burrows, Millar, *The Dead Sea Scrolls* (New York: The Viking Press, 1955).

———, *More Light on the Dead Sea Scrolls* (New York: The Viking Press, 1958).

Cross, Frank M., Jr., *The Ancient Library of Qumran and Modern Biblical Studies* (rev. ed.; New York: Doubleday & Company, Inc., 1961).

Enslin, M. S., *Christian Beginnings* (New York: Harper & Row, 1938).

Russell, D. S., *The Method and Message of Jewish Apocalyptic* (Philadelphia: The Westminster Press, 1964).

The Ministry and Teaching of Jesus
Bornkamm, Günther, *Jesus of Nazareth* (New York: Harper & Row, 1960).
Braaten, Carl E., and Roy A. Harrisville, *The Historical Jesus and the Kerygmatic Christ: Essays on the New Quest of the Historical Jesus* (New York: Abingdon Press, 1964).
Dibelius, Martin, *Jesus,* trans. by C. B. Hedrick and F. C. Grant (Philadelphia: The Westminster Press, 1949).
Jeremias, Joachim, *The Parables of Jesus* (London: SCM Press, 1954; rev. ed., 1963).
——, *The Problem of the Historical Jesus,* trans. by N. Perrin (Philadelphia: Fortress Press, 1964).
Kümmel, W. G., *Promise and Fulfilment* ("Studies in Biblical Theology," no. 23; London: SCM Press, 1957).
Manson, T. H., *The Servant-Messiah* (London: Cambridge University Press, 1953).
Robinson, James M., *A New Quest of the Historical Jesus* ("Studies in Biblical Theology," no. 25; London: SCM Press, 1959).
Schweitzer, Albert, *The Quest of the Historical Jesus* (3d ed.; London: A. & C. Black, Ltd., 1954).
Stauffer, Ethelbert, *Jesus and the Wilderness Community at Qumran* (Philadelphia: Fortress Press, 1964).

Paul and the Early Church
Bultmann, Rudolf, *Theology of the New Testament,* Vol. I (New York: Charles Scribner's Sons, 1951).
Cullmann, Oscar, *Early Christian Worship* ("Studies in Biblical Theology," no. 10; London: SCM Press, 1953).
——, *The Early Church* (London: SCM Press, 1956).
Davies, W.D., *Paul and Rabbinic Judaism* (London: S.P.C.K., 1948).
Dodd, C. H., *The Apostolic Preaching and Its Developments* (London: Hodder & Stoughton, Ltd., 1936).

STAFFORD LIBRARY
COLUMBIA COLLEGE
1001 ROGERS STREET
COLUMBIA, MO 65216